The Economic Implications of Aging Societies

The Costs of Living Happily Ever After

STEVEN A. NYCE
Watson Wyatt Worldwide

SYLVESTER J. SCHIEBER
Watson Wyatt Worldwide

CAMBRIDGE
UNIVERSITY PRESS

CAMBRIDGE UNIVERSITY PRESS
Cambridge, New York, Melbourne, Madrid, Cape Town, Singapore, São Paulo

Cambridge University Press
40 West 20th Street, New York, NY 10011-4211, USA

www.cambridge.org
Information on this title: www.cambridge.org/9780521851534

First published 2005
Reprinted 2005

Printed in the United States of America

A catalog record for this publication is available from the British Library.

Library of Congress Cataloging in Publication Data

ISBN-13 978-0-521-85153-4 hardback
ISBN-10 0-521-85153-X hardback

ISBN-13 978-0-521-61724-6 paperback
ISBN-10 0-521-61724-3 paperback

In memory of
Shannon J. Schieber

Contents

Figures and Tables

Figures

Tables

Figures and Tables

Preface

At the World Economic Forum's Annual Meeting in 2001, CEOs of our financial service industry member companies concluded there was a need for greater high-level, international attention to be paid to the economic and financial implications of the demographic challenges facing most industrialized countries. Increased life expectancy, the impending retirement of the baby boom generation, and lower fertility in many countries are creating unsustainable pressures on public and private pension systems. While this is a global problem, most of the policy debate has occurred in a national context with too little regard for the broader implications and opportunities for world economic growth and development. In addition, the discussion has largely overlooked the potentially significant distributional implications for living standards within national economies and how these are influenced by different policy choices.

During 2002 and 2003, the Forum's Pension Readiness Initiative, consisting of leaders from our financial services and employment industry member companies and other experts from labor unions, international organizations, senior citizen groups, and governments, decided to compile a comparative assessment of the retirement system readiness of OECD countries for the purpose of focusing high-level public and private attention on the need for greater action. The report was conceived in the belief that a tangible cross-country comparison of policy performance and conditions set in the context of a broader discussion about the stakes for the world economy could help to spur greater understanding and consensus for action.

The Forum entered into a partnership with Watson Wyatt Worldwide for the purpose of researching and drafting this assessment, which was released in summary form at the Forum's 2004 Annual Meeting. This book is based on that report. It is perhaps the most comprehensive analysis to date of the macroeconomic implications over the next few decades of current demographic trends in a wide range of countries. It also presents extensive cross-country data highlighting similarities and differences in the circumstances facing these countries as well as their approaches to policy reform.

The Forum is pleased to be associated with this important work and wishes to thank Watson Wyatt Worldwide, its President and CEO John Haley, as well as the authors for their commitment and scholarship. We also extend our appreciation to the representatives of the fifteen Forum member companies who participated in the process and the many academic, labor, international organization, and other experts who contributed their time and thoughts. And we wish to recognize with appreciation the Forum's own Nabi Niang, Project Manager of the Pension Readiness Initiative, and Fiona Paua, who provided valuable economic insight. Not all of the participants and organizations in the Initiative necessarily agree with all of the views expressed herein.

The Pension Readiness Initiative is an example of the World Economic Forum's portfolio of initiatives that engage business with other stakeholders in work processes on global, regional, or industry issues of common concern. These initiatives are developed and managed by our Global Institute for Partnership and Governance, which builds upon the "spirit of Davos" by serving as an informal, independent platform for multistakeholder partnership in three dimensions: stimulating action, improving governance, and expanding understanding through dialogue. In line with our mission, we hope that this book will help to stimulate greater public-private discussion on ways to turn the challenge posed by demographic change in industrialized countries into an opportunity for expanded economic growth and social progress the world over.

Klaus Schwab
Executive Chairman
World Economic Forum

Richard Samans
Managing Director
Global Institute for Partnership and
Governance World Economic Forum

Geneva, September 2004

Acknowledgments

An earlier version of this manuscript was prepared for the annual meeting of the World Economic Forum (WEF) held in Davos, Switzerland, during January 2004. The report was the culmination of the WEF Pension Readiness Initiative undertaken to develop a better understanding of the potential implications of population aging on the developed economies of the world and their retirement systems. The preface describes the project that led up to the development of the report. We have subsequently modified the content of discussion in response to a number of comments we received at the meeting in Davos and from various people who have reviewed the work.

The initial work was developed through our direct collaboration with Richard Samans, Nabi Niang, and Fiona Paua at the WEF. In addition to the authors of the report and the staff at the WEF, John Haley and Michael Orszag of Watson Wyatt Worldwide helped in conceptualizing the scope of the analysis. As we began to assemble various components of the report, we met with members of the WEF Pension Readiness Initiative and benefited from their comments and input. Much of the background work was developed with the assistance of Mirko Cardinale, Jonathan Gardner, Rachel Lakofka, and Michael Orszag from Watson Wyatt.

The Initiative's report and this book would not have been possible if the authors had not had access to substantial data and other information from various people and organizations. The Organization for Economic Cooperation and Development was particularly generous with time and resources. In particular, we wish to thank Andre Laboul and Mark Pearson, Romain Duval, David Lindeman, Howard Oxley, Monika Quiesser, Jean-Marc Salou, and Juan Yermo for the help and input they provided. We also thank Mandeep Bains and Kieran McMorrow of the European Commission for data support. Edward Whitehouse of Axia Consulting developed estimates of retirement program earnings replacement rates before and after taxation that are included in the report. The International Labour Organization's demographic projection model was used extensively in the analysis.

Throughout the book there are several brief analyses on a variety of subjects that have been written by technical experts that help to illuminate the points being made. We are particularly grateful to: Professor Monika Bütler, Ecole des Hautes Etudes Commerciales, University of Lausanne; Stefan Engström, Stockholm School of Economics, and Anna Westerberg, Ministry of Finance, Stockholm; Professor Tryggvi Thor Herbertsson, Institute of Economic Studies, University of Iceland, Reykjavik; Mr. Paul Hewitt, Deputy Secretary for Policy, Social Security Administration, Washington, DC; Dr. Estelle James, the Urban Institute in Washington, DC; Professor Alain Jousten, University of Liege, Liege; Professor Ronald Lee, University of California, Berkeley; Moshe Milevsky, York University and IFID Centre, Toronto; Professor Olivia Mitchell, Wharton School, University of Pennsylvania, Philadelphia; Todd Petersen, Help Age International, London; Professor John Piggott, The University of New South Wales, Sydney; Professor Timothy Smeeding, University of Syracuse and Luxemburg Income Study, Syracuse, New York; Professor Kent Smetters, Wharton School, University of Pennsylvania, Philadelphia; Dr. James Vaupel, Max Planck Institute, Saarburcken; Mr. David Willetts, MP and Shadow Secretary of Welfare and Social Security, London; Larry Willmore, consultant, New York; and Juan Yermo, OECD, Paris.

We are grateful for substantial comments we received from a number of reviewers. At the WEF annual meeting itself, we received substantial feedback regarding the report, especially from Peter Heller of the International Monetary Fund. John Laitner, Director, University of Michigan Retirement Research Center, organized a conference in Washington under the sponsorship of the Office of Policy, Social Security Administration, to discuss the report. At this conference, Edward Gramlich, a governor at the U.S. Federal Reserve Board, Alan Gustman from Dartmouth University, Richard Jackson from the Center for Strategic and International Studies, and John Shoven from Stanford University commented on the report. We also received comments in response to a presentation of our analysis at a conference at Oxford University organized by Professor Gordon Clark. Finally, we have received extremely helpful comments from five unidentified referees who reviewed the original draft of the study as it was being considered for publication.

This draft has also benefited tremendously from the help of Nancy Campbell, who has been our copy editor on both versions of the work. John Reynolds of Watson Wyatt helped us with the presentation of various figures and charts included throughout the document. The whole effort would never have come to fruition without the benefit of Susan Farris of Watson Wyatt who read the versions of the chapters as they evolved, offering helpful suggestions and proofing our work. She also managed the organization and assembly of the final document for submission to Cambridge University Press.

ONE

Introduction

All the world's a stage, and all the men and women merely players; they
have their exits and their entrances, and one man in his time plays many
parts, his acts being seven ages.

William Shakespeare
From "As You Like It"

Shakespeare's seven ages of life begin with youth and progress through
old age, which he describes as a period of second childhood when we
live in oblivion, our senses largely gone. In Shakespeare's day in the late
sixteenth and early seventeenth centuries, few people survived to an age
we would today consider the seventh stage of life, as life expectancy at
birth would have been between 25 and 30 years. Of those who made it to
old age, many had to continue working until shortly before their death
in order to meet their basic needs. Today, life expectancy is three times
that of Shakespeare's era in the developed world and is nearing that in
many of the developing countries. And when most people reach the final
stage of their lifetimes today, what we now call retirement, their senses
are still vitally intact and their lives are not all that different than those
they lived before crossing into old age. But as our life expectancies have
lengthened, our societies have grown older. As we look to the future, we
expect them to grow older still.

A great deal has been written in recent years about aging populations in the developed economies of the world, and how the phenomenon
will affect various facets of public and private life. Much of the discussion about population aging has focused on retirement systems. One
concern is that the number of retirees will soon overwhelm retirement

1

systems, which will then be unable to deliver on retirees' expectations. Another concern is that the working populations that support retirement systems will be so overtaxed that productivity will fall, bringing the history of steadily improving living standards since World War II to an abrupt halt.

This book explores the phenomenon of population aging, the issues it raises, and what our societies have been doing and might do about it. In telling the story, we look beyond the developed economies because populations are also aging in the developing economies, albeit more slowly than their richer counterparts. And some of the potential solutions to dealing with population aging would require more economic interaction between developed and developing economies.

We believe this analysis of population aging and its implications is different from many earlier studies, because it broadens the context of the discussion considerably beyond retirement system financing. This said, we devote three chapters to an analysis of pensions systems around the world, in recognition of their importance in the larger context of the aging issue. Beyond the discussion about pensions, the essence of this analysis is that population aging in the developed economies will present a relatively immediate problem for many of those macroeconomies. In many countries, policymakers will have to find ways to maintain or enlarge their workforces or otherwise increase productivity or, alternatively, face the dismal prospect of allocating a declining standard of living between the working-age and retiree segments of their societies.

Since the end of World War II, all of the developed economies have enjoyed steady economic growth and improvements in living standards. This remarkable economic success story has been helped along by improved health and education systems, new and better physical infrastructure, technology, and the relatively peaceful cross-national order that our governments have been able to establish and maintain. One cannot ignore, however, the role growing labor forces have played in this prosperity. In virtually every developed economy in the world today, the share of the total population now engaged in workforce activities is larger than it was in 1950, 1960, or over most of the last half century.

We believe that a half century of steadily improving standards of living has created an appetite in most of the developed world to continue the upward mobility. Indeed, any review of the five- to ten-year economic projections by currently sitting governments documents the expectation that these economies will continue to grow. The challenge for a number of governments is that their labor forces will start contracting during this decade and will continue doing so over much of the next quarter century and beyond. In most developed economies, even if the labor force holds steady in this decade, the contraction will likely occur during the next one. Policymakers in these societies may not be able to deliver on anticipated economic growth and improving living standards in the face of shrinking labor pools.

The issues related to population aging and its economic impact go beyond simply keeping the elderly out of poverty – that is affordable in the rich, developed world, despite the expected "graying" of the population. Instead, the issue is of stagnant or falling standards of living that could affect all segments of society in the developed world. If economic growth is brought to a halt by the changing demographic composition, pension policy is naturally one of the primary mechanisms for allocating the disappointing outcome across various segments of society. It is within this context that much of the angst over pension policy in the developed world is framed today.

The worry that our current retirement systems will demand taxes that are too high articulates a concern that workers' disposable income levels will fall or not keep appreciably abreast of improving worker productivity. If that happens, then workers will be producing more but receiving less, in that their productivity will not purchase the same increase in standards of living enjoyed by their parents. The worry that pension benefits will have to be reduced articulates the concern that retirees' disposable income levels will fall, potentially leaving future generations of our elderly more vulnerable to income insecurity.

Current labor force participation patterns in developed economies are the result of many changes over the last several decades. One of the most dramatic changes has been the retirement phenomenon itself. Fifty years ago in many of the developed economies, many more people worked well into their 60s than do today. Over this period, older people have become healthier and their life expectancies have increased dramatically. At the same time, the modernization of production techniques in manufacturing and the shift toward service-oriented work have reduced the strenuous nature of work for most people. If work is becoming less strenuous and people's ability to do it is improving, why are more workers retiring in their late 50s or early 60s?

The simple answer is that many of our societies have had a surplus of labor in recent decades. This was the result of two phenomena. The first was linked to a surge in fertility rates in many developed countries after World War II. Some 20 years or so later, these baby boomers began entering the workforces in their respective countries. The second phenomenon, which occurred about the same time in many countries, was that women entered the workforce in much larger numbers than ever before and often remained employed even after marrying and having children.

The duration of the baby booms varied from country to country, but by the mid 1960s the phenomenon had pretty much run its course across the developed economies of the world. The baby boom generations, which were larger than prior or subsequent generations, along with the different labor force patterns of women, swelled our workforces from around 1970 or so up until now. But those baby boom children are about to become the "elder boom" of the twenty-first century. In most countries, the lower fertility rates after the baby boom mean that there will soon be more workers exiting the workforce than entering it. The labor surplus of the last quarter of the twentieth-century is about to become history, one that we are not likely to repeat any time soon, at least not in any of the developed economies. A few countries have maintained combined fertility rates and immigration rates that suggest continued labor force growth over at least the next couple of decades, but even in these cases, the growth will be much slower than it was in the past.

Some people conclude we must radically change our retirement systems to cope with the new realities. The suggestions span a broad range and combination of options. In some cases, the debate focuses on whether our pensions should be organized as defined benefit or defined contribution arrangements. In others, it is about whether we should continue to support pay-as-you-go (pay-go) funding, where current workers' contributions are used to pay current retirees' benefits, or whether we should pre-fund plans by accumulating workers' contributions during their careers in order to diminish the burden on future workers' earnings. In yet other cases, the consideration is more about how we could modify the operating parameters of existing systems to bring them into financial balance without changing any of their basic structural characteristics.

We explore virtually all of these options in the analysis that follows but do not reach a specific conclusion about the best way for any particular country to deal with its demographic situation. We favor funding pensions to a much greater extent than they have generally been funded in the past, but we also explore systems in which pension funding has been more of an impression than a reality. We are largely neutral between the organization of plans along the defined benefit and defined contribution spectrums, although we explore the respective risks with the alternative systems. Our analysis supports a conclusion that to the extent policymakers are going to modify their retirement systems in ways that shift greater risks to individuals, these risks should fall more heavily on higher level earners.

In the final analysis, we believe that many societies will face a tradeoff between labor supply and standards of living. Societies that are determined to maintain or even improve their current standards of living will need to entice more people into the workforce and convince them to stay longer. This means looking at the incentives that now encourage people to retire at ages where they still are in good health and maintain the potential productive capacity to make a significant economic contribution to the national commonweal.

There are also other groups that should not be overlooked in attempts to increase workforce participation. We note that the rates at which various societies move their youth through their education systems and into the workforce vary widely. We do not advocate a return to the days of child labor, but there may be economic efficiency gains for some countries in streamlining their education systems, so young adults enter the workforce sooner rather than later. We also note that there are widespread variations in the labor force participation rates of women. We acknowledge the complexity of the situation and understand that expecting more women to join the labor force while also hoping to increase fertility rates may be impossible. The puzzle here is that countries like Italy and Spain have relatively low female labor force participation rates – and the lowest fertility rates in the developed world – while the United States, which has relatively high female labor force participation rates, has the highest fertility rate in the developed world. The answer to this puzzle is not simply that the United States has relatively more immigrants or minorities. Even among its native born white female population, the U.S. fertility rate is abnormally high by developed world standards.

The best option for policymakers may be to organize their pension systems so they continue to offer older people real income protection when they can no longer work, being particularly careful to protect the welfare of those most economically vulnerable – those people who have lived their whole lives with low incomes. Beyond this, our retirement systems should employ strong incentives to encourage workers to continue working throughout their productive older years rather than withdrawing from the workforce at the early ages they do now. There are a number of different ways to achieve this end, as we explore in the concluding chapter of the discussion.

There are clearly benefits from societies putting away more for the future, but the specific mechanisms for doing so must be considered carefully. Utilization of funding also should be a central concern. Added pension funding should increase savings if it is to have a real effect on the macroeconomic outcomes, and increased savings can provide the greatest benefit over time if those savings are directed to investment opportunities that provide market returns. In economies where labor forces are contracting, added investment in the local economy may not be optimal. Therefore, it is important for state pension sponsors to consider the world marketplace and invest wherever expected returns are higher. To this end, policymakers in many countries will need to eliminate current inherent or specific legislative biases against cross-national investment of pension assets. In a short-term perspective, adopting new investment policies that appear to export jobs to developing economies may not be politically popular. But if labor force contraction in the longer term is inevitable and it means that domestic labor forces cannot satisfy the appetite of consumers, then being able to realize returns on assets invested outside the economy may be the most effective long-term way to augment domestic economic production. Policymakers also need to be mindful of the risks involved in different funding strategies and seek to keep these under control.

If the developed economies of the world are to become the investment engine moving poorer countries up the development ladder, policymakers need to work through organizations like the World Bank and the United Nations to make sure their capital can be utilized efficiently. The challenge in achieving this goal may be best summed up by quoting from a recent cover story in *Business Week* magazine focusing on the potential high-technology workforce evolving in India. Besides extolling India's promise as a market with tremendous potential labor resources, the article noted:

For all its R&D labs, India remains visibly Third World. IT service exports employ less than 1% of the workforce. Per-capita income is just $460, and 300 million Indians subsist on $1 a day or less. Lethargic courts can take 20 years to resolve contract disputes. And what pass for highways in Bombay are choked, crumbling roads lined with slums, garbage heaps, and homeless migrants sleeping on bare pavement. More than a third of India's 1 billion citizens are illiterate, and just 60% of homes have electricity. Most bureaucracies are bloated, corrupt, and dysfunctional. The government's 10% budget deficit is alarming. Tensions between Hindus and Muslims always seem poised to explode, and the risk of war with nuclear-armed Pakistan is ever-present.[1]

---

[1] Manjeet Kripalani, Pete Engardio, and Steve Hamm, "The Rise of India," *Business Week* (December 8, 2003), p. 70.

If the developing countries can organize themselves to work with the developed economies of the world, there is a tremendous potential for mutual benefit. It is possible that dramatically improved standards of living and working conditions in India, China, elsewhere in developing Asia, across Africa, and in the Middle-East could simultaneously prove to be the real insurance against default by the retirement systems in the developed world.

TWO

Population Developments in a Global Context

There is a growing awareness around the world that national populations are aging. This phenomenon, which was not recognized until the later part of the twentieth century, is sweeping the world at different rates and for a variety of reasons. By itself, the fact that a particular country's population is aging would be of little consequence. In a world with increasing economic ties across borders, the aging phenomenon is likely to have significantly different implications from country to country, which will be heightened by differences in economic and governmental structures. Before we address these latter considerations, we first document the dynamics of population change across several countries.

A Brief Historical Perspective

The history of the human population is rife with uncertainty. National censuses taken at regular intervals are a relatively recent phenomenon. Sweden began the first census in 1750; the United States has conducted decennial censuses since 1790; and France and England have conducted them since around 1800.[1] Using qualitative data, however, statistical demographers have estimated the size of the world population using the observations of historians, archeologists, paleontologists, and anthropologists. Locations of cities and their estimated sizes are important clues. Historical descriptions of peoples and places are used in reconstructing estimates of areas. The ability of ecosystems to support humans in various

---

[1] Ansley J. Coale, "The History of the Human Population," *Scientific American* (September 1974), vol. 231, no. 3, p. 41.

Table 2-1. *World Population, Total Births, and Years Lived, 10,000 BC to AD 2000*

Demographic Index	10,000 BC	0	1750	1950	2000
Population (millions)	6	252	771	2,530	6,235
Annual growth (%)	0.0008	0.037	0.064	0.569	1.812
Doubling times (years)	8,369	1,854	1,083	116	38
Births (billions)	9.29	33.60	22.64	10.42	6.25
Life expectancy at birth	20	22	27	35	58

Source: Massimo Livi-Bacci, *A Concise History of World Population* (1989) (Malden, Mass.: Blackwell Publishers, Inc., second English edition, 1997), p. 31. For births, life expectancy, and years lived, the data refer to the interval between the date at the head of the column and that of the preceding column (for the first column, the interval runs from the hypothetical origin of the human species to 10,000 BC).

eras – e.g., pre-agricultural, agricultural, industrial – are important considerations. While historical population estimates are based on these sorts of non-quantitative clues, there appears to be order of magnitude comparability across demographers' estimates of world population at specific points in time. One such set of estimates is reflected in Table 2-1. Although other estimates of world population at the various early dates in the table vary, the trends are consistent. It was concerns over these trends that led Thomas Malthus to start a debate about how demographic growth affects economic development.

Malthus observed that the population increased at a geometric rate, while the resources available to sustain it grew at only an arithmetic rate.[2] His observation is borne out in the continually shortening period over which the population has been doubling. Joseph Schumpeter tells us that Malthus really borrowed this idea from Botero, who had developed it toward the end of the sixteenth century, more than 200 years before Malthus developed his mathematical specification of the theory.[3] The logic of the mathematical formulation is that mankind eventually would outstrip the resources needed to survive, with the proliferation of people leading to an ever increasing impoverishment of the masses. Pushed to its limit, the scarcity of resources, especially food, would constrain the population's natural instinct to expand. Massimo Livi-Bacci reports that from the sixteenth to the early eighteenth centuries, European countries experienced

---

[2] Thomas R. Malthus, *An Essay on the Principle of Population* (1798) (Norton, New York, 1976).

[3] Joseph A. Schumpeter, *History of Economic Analysis* (New York: Oxford University Press, 1954), p. 255.

repeated subsistence crises with subsequent adverse demographic consequences.[4]

The implications of the Botero-Malthusian concern can be appreciated
by as simple an exercise as multiplying the number two by itself six times
versus adding it to itself six times. The answer to the first problem is
64 but the answer to the second is 12. Princeton demographer Ansley
Coale illustrates the intuitively surprising implications of the geometric
compounding process. He tells of the "legend of the king who offered
his daughter in marriage to anyone who could supply a grain of wheat
for the first square of a chess-board, two grains for the second square
and so on. To comply with this request for all 64 squares would require
a mountain of grain many times larger than today's worldwide wheat
production."[5]

The alternative perspective on population also evolved during the seventeenth and eighteenth centuries. At that time, the perspective was of
countries that were poor in goods but rich in opportunity, and the concern was under-population. Schumpeter tells us that many economists
felt that a "numerous and increasing population was the most important *symptom* of wealth; it was the chief *cause* of wealth; it *was* wealth
itself – the greatest asset for any nation to have."[6] He names several early
English economists in the "populationist" camp. He suggests that German
and Spanish economists of the day held this view most strongly because
both countries had experienced depopulation for decades. The underlying theory is that humankind is ingenious in devising ever more efficient
ways to utilize the resources available to it.

While this debate dates back to the seventeenth century, it has never
been fully resolved. The potential compounding effect of the worldwide
birthrates during the second half of the twentieth century set off new
alarms about population explosions and their implications. During the
decade of the 1940s, the annual growth in the world's estimated population was 1 percent per year. During the 1950s, it jumped to 1.8 percent. During the 1960s, it was an estimated 2.03 percent per year.[7] By
the mid-1970s, the unprecedented population growth rates led Coale to
estimate that in "less than 700 years there would be one person for every

[4] Massimo Livi-Bacci, *A Concise History of World Population* (1989) (Malden, Mass.:
Blackwell Publishers, Inc., second English edition, 1997), p. 85.

[5] Ansley J. Coale, "The History of the Human Population," p. 43.

[6] Joseph A. Schumpeter, *History*, p. 251.

[7] United Nations, Population Division, *Demographic Indicators 1950–2050 and Sex and Age
Quinquennial 1950–2050* (1998 Revisions).

square foot on the surface of the earth; in less than 1,200 years the human population would outweigh the earth."[8] In the face of this prospect, Schumpeter observed that "the fact that a population *is physically capable* of multiplying until it lacks not only food but also ground to stand on is no cause for worry unless complemented by the additional proposition that *it actually will* tend to do this instead of merely responding to an expanding economic environment by growing along with it."[9] During the 1970s, the rate of expansion in the world population began to decline, falling to a growth rate of 1.85 percent per year. During the 1980s, the growth rate dropped to 1.72 percent, and during the 1990s, it was about 1.4 percent per year. These are still historically very high rates of growth, but they clearly indicate that the post-World War II phenomenon has abated.

The growth rate of the world's population is directly attributable to the relationships between life expectancy at birth and birth rates. The primary explanation for the increases in the population growth rate after the mid-eighteenth century was increasing life expectancy without an offsetting decrease in fertility rates. This relates in part to the higher standards of living that evolved from the industrial revolution. It also resulted from the evolution of science, improved hygiene, better sanitation, public health advances, and enhanced medical technology.

The improvements in standards of living, science, and medicine have swept across the world at varying rates and are still noticeably affecting life expectancy in some countries. The increases in life expectancy are expected to continue to drive up population levels for the foreseeable future. The declining rate of population growth over the last 30 years has been largely the result of declining fertility rates, which, once again, are changing at different rates in various countries. This suggests that age structures of populations across nations vary considerably and are likely to do so for many years. These variations have extremely important implications for individual national governments, their populations, and business enterprises.

Underlying Forces Driving Changing Population Structures

At the beginning of the twentieth century, the typical national population had an age structure essentially like that reflected in Figure 2-1. In

---

[8] Ansley J. Coale, "The History of the Human Population," p. 51.
[9] Joseph A. Schumpeter, *History*, p. 256.

Percent of total population

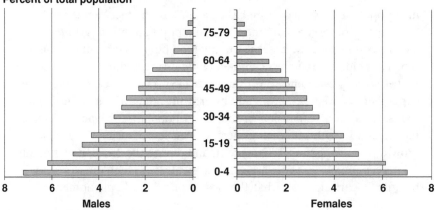

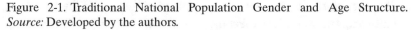

Figure 2-1. Traditional National Population Gender and Age Structure. *Source:* Developed by the authors.

this world, there were always more people at each successively younger age. The age structure reflected in the figure was consistent with the age structure that existed in most countries during the early decades of the twentieth century. While plagues, famines, and wars would take their tolls on populations of countries such as Germany and Spain, as mentioned earlier, even those countries expected that over the long term, the population structure shown in Figure 2-1 would be their natural evolutionary pattern. Toward the end of the nineteenth century, the combination of the industrialization of several economies in the world and scientific developments set off forces that would ultimately lead to a variety of new and different population structures. These forces matured at different rates in different parts of the world throughout the twentieth century.

Three primary forces affect the age structure of any country's population: life expectancy, fertility rates, and net immigration. Each of these is affected by a variety of economic, scientific, and social forces. The study of these forces and their effects on populations is the subject of many demographic theories and analyses. The purpose of this analysis is not to repeat those but to report on changes in life expectancy, birth rates, and immigration patterns in a variety of countries over the past half century and to look at further changes projected over the next three decades. Our analysis is limited to a subset of countries, but we believe that it reflects the patterns across the major nations of the world.

Changing Life Expectancy

How Quickly Will Life Expectancy Increase?

By Dr. James W. Vaupel, Director, Max Planck Institute for Demographic Research

Is life expectancy approaching its limit? Many – including individuals planning their retirement and officials responsible for health and social policy – believe it is. The evidence suggests otherwise.

Consider an astonishing fact. Female life expectancy in the record-holding country has risen for 160 years at a steady pace of three months per year. In 1840 the record was held by Swedish women, who lived on average a little more than 45 years. Among nations today, the longest expectation of life – just over 85 years – is enjoyed by Japanese women. There is no evidence of any slowing of this long-term rise in best-practice life expectancy.

In the 19th century and the first half of the 20th century, the increase in life expectancy was driven by progress in reducing infant, childhood and early adult mortality. Since 1950 and especially since 1970 the continued rise in the expectation of life has been fuelled by substantial declines in death rates at older ages. This progress has been accompanied by progress in extending the healthy, active period of life.

Given intelligent economic and social policy and continued investment in research, longevity and healthy longevity will continue to increase in coming decades. This is not a problem – it is a great achievement – but it will result in challenges for policymakers, especially concerning pensions and health care for the elderly.

For 160 years, best-practice life expectancy has increased steadily by three months per year. If this rise continues for another 60 years, then females in the record-holding country in 2060 will enjoy a life expectancy at birth of 100 years. Knowledge flows so freely across national boundaries that advanced countries will be clustered within five years or so of the record.

So my best guestimate of female life expectancy in 2060 in countries such as Germany, France, Japan and the United States is 95 to 100 years. Male life expectancy will probably be five years or so lower.

This forecast is much higher than most national forecasts. For instance, the U.S. Social Security Administration predicts that U.S. female life expectancy will gradually increase to a level of 83.9 in 2060 – compared with my prediction of 95 to 100. The Social Security forecast is, however, patently ludicrous because current female life expectancy in Japan is already 85.2 years. Is it plausible that U.S. females six decades from now will have a life expectancy that is less than current levels in Japan?

Progress in reducing mortality could accelerate as biomedical knowledge grows: instead of an increase of three months per year, an increase of four or even five months per year is possible. Economic and political instability and a failure to invest in research, on the other hand, could slow progress to perhaps one or two months per year. A reasonable, middle-of-the-road forecast is an increase of three months per year.

Mortality has been declining gradually across much of the world since the seventeenth or eighteenth century. The decline is partly the result of improved working and living conditions, especially for people at the lower end of the economic spectrum. Improvements in public health and sanitation have significantly reduced the incidence of infectious diseases that often led to premature death, and these improvements occurred earlier in the world's developed economies than in those less developed. Improvements in nutrition have also added years to many people's lives. Greater appreciation of the deleterious effects of smoking and other unhealthy habits has prompted campaigns that have reduced these behaviors in many societies. Evolving health technologies have devised successful treatments for illnesses that once were fatal. While most of the life expectancy news has been good over the past century, the gains have not been universal, due to the spread of AIDS in certain underdeveloped countries and the breakdown of the Russian socioeconomic system and its health system.

Table 2-2 shows the life expectancies at birth for a set of countries that we will consider throughout this discussion. The data cover two periods in the past, starting at mid-twentieth century and then 25 years later. It also covers the current time frame and then two sets of projections into the future, one 10 years from the beginning of the twenty-first century and the second 20 years further into the future from that. Life expectancies in the early 1950s ranged from a high of just over 72 years in the Netherlands to just under 41 years in China. The more developed countries consistently had higher life expectancies than the less developed ones.

From the middle to the end of the twentieth century, less developed countries generally made tremendous leaps forward in life expectancy. They gained substantially on the well-developed nations despite the fact that the latter continued to improve. The one country in the group that was in relatively poor shape at mid-century and barely advanced over the next 40 years was South Africa. The years of turmoil in that part of the world may have contributed to the lack of progress, but the high incidence of poverty and AIDS and related diseases certainly contributed as well.

Looking forward 30 years from the beginning of the twenty-first century, life expectancy is projected to continue improving across all countries. Generally, improvements in life expectancy in the less developed countries are expected to continue to outpace those in their highly developed counterparts. The one glaring exception to this trend is South Africa. Some estimates suggest that as many as one-third of its population

Table 2-2. *Improvements in Life Expectancy for Various Countries over Time*

	Life Expectancy at Birth at Various Times					Annual Improvement Rate	
	1950–1955	1975–1980	2000–2005	2010–2015	2030–2035	1950–2000	2000–2030
Argentina	62.5	68.5	73.8	75.6	78.4	0.33%	0.20%
Australia	69.6	73.5	79.2	80.1	81.8	0.26	0.11
Brazil	50.9	61.5	68.3	70.8	74.7	0.59	0.30
Canada	69.1	74.2	79.0	80.0	81.6	0.27	0.11
Chile	54.7	67.1	75.6	76.9	78.8	0.65	0.14
China	40.8	65.3	71.2	73.5	77.2	1.12	0.27
Egypt	42.4	54.1	68.3	71.4	75.6	0.96	0.34
France	66.5	73.7	79.0	80.3	82.5	0.34	0.14
Germany	67.5	72.5	78.2	79.7	81.9	0.29	0.16
Hungary	63.6	69.4	72.0	74.3	77.6	0.25	0.25
India	38.7	52.9	64.2	67.9	72.7	1.02	0.42
Ireland	66.9	72.0	77.0	78.3	80.3	0.28	0.14
Italy	66.0	73.6	78.7	79.7	81.3	0.35	0.11
Japan	63.9	75.5	81.5	83.3	86.3	0.49	0.19
Malaysia	48.5	65.3	73.0	75.0	78.2	0.82	0.23
Mexico	50.6	65.1	73.0	74.6	77.3	0.73	0.19
Netherlands	72.1	75.3	78.3	79.3	81.0	0.17	0.11
Pakistan	41.0	51.0	61.0	65.0	70.9	0.80	0.50
Poland	61.3	70.9	73.9	75.9	78.7	0.37	0.21
South Africa	45.0	55.1	47.4	42.0	53.8	0.11	0.42
Spain	63.9	74.3	78.8	79.7	81.4	0.42	0.11
Sweden	71.8	75.2	80.1	81.1	83.1	0.22	0.12
Switzerland	69.2	75.2	79.1	80.0	81.7	0.27	0.11
Turkey	43.6	60.3	70.5	72.9	76.6	0.97	0.28
U.K.	69.2	72.8	78.2	79.8	81.8	0.25	0.15
U.S.	68.9	73.3	77.5	79.2	81.5	0.24	0.17

Source: United Nations, Population Division, World Population Prospects (The 2000 Revision).

is infected with the AIDS virus. By the early 2030s, South Africa's life expectancy at birth is projected to be about where it was in the late 1970s. By contrast, all the other countries shown will have life expectancies of over 70 years at birth, and most of them will enjoy life expectancies of over 80 years.

The projections for further improvements in life expectancy were developed by the United Nations' Population Division. The two right columns in Table 2-2 show the annual rates of change in life expectancy in each country, with actual numbers for the period 1950 to 2000, and projections for the 2000 to 2030 period. In almost all cases, the projections suggest that the rate of improvements in life expectancy will slow somewhat from the rate in recent decades, though as we shall see below this is a controversial prediction.

One explanation for projected declining rates of improvement in life expectancy is that mortality improvements have varied quite substantially across age groups. Cutler and Meara investigated the causes for declining mortality rates in the United States over the last century. In general, increasing life expectancy is a function of two developments: (1) more infants and children reaching adulthood and (2) prolonging the life of the elderly. They show that the declines in the mortality rates in the early part of the century resulted primarily from advances that saved the lives of younger individuals. Improvements in public health and sanitation and increased consciousness about nutrition enhanced people's ability to fight off infectious disease, formerly a major cause of deaths among younger age groups. Improved working conditions reduced disease and accidental deaths among the working-age population. With advancements such as penicillin and sulfa drugs by the middle part of the twentieth century, mortality rates also began to decline for other age groups – in particular for older individuals. Ongoing major advances in medical technology will continue increasing life expectancy. However, as Cutler and Meara show, premature deaths caused by low birth weight, pneumonia, and other traditional killers of the young have already declined so significantly that further improvements will add very little to overall longevity. As a result, most of the additional years added to life expectancy over the last few decades of the twentieth century were among older age groups. And it is here that further improvements in life expectancy will largely be realized in the future.[10]

Although it seems reasonable that further improvements in life expectancy will slow, there are several arguments that suggest otherwise. In particular, we are living in a period of stunning breakthroughs in biomedicine and remarkable advancements in areas such as genetic research. Many demographers and health scientists expect that these developments will greatly increase overall longevity in the future. As shown in Schieber and Hewitt, estimates of the U.S. population over age 85 vary dramatically between those made by the Social Security Administration, U.S. Census Bureau, and three prominent demographers working for the National Institute on Aging. In fact, the three demographers on average expect that by 2050, there will be over twice as many individuals 85 years and older in the United States than currently projected by

[10] David M. Cutler and Ellen M. Meara, "Changes in the Age Distribution of Mortality Over the 20th Century" (Cambridge, MA: National Bureau of Economic Research, 2001), NBER Working Paper, no. 8556.

either government agency.[11] There are clearly good reasons to question whether the expected slowdown in increasing life expectancy may lead to a gross underestimation of population aging throughout many of the OECD countries.[12]

Changing Fertility Rates

Table 2-3 shows the changing total fertility rates across the set of countries in the analysis. The total fertility rate at a point in time is the expected number of children each woman would have if she were to bear children over her fertile period at the rate children are born to women at each age at that time. The total fertility rate and the actual numbers of children that might ultimately be born are not necessarily the same. For example, in the United States, the women in the early cohorts of the baby boom generation did not have their children until relatively later in their fertile period than prior cohorts of women had theirs. The relatively low rates of childbirth during the early years of the baby boomers' adulthood depressed the total fertility rate at that time. The decline in the fertility rate would have reduced the expected number of children that the early baby boomers would have over their lifetimes. But the early cohorts of baby boomers largely made up for their low birthing rates in their early fertile period by having their children later. The later cohorts of the baby boom tended to bear their children earlier in their fertile period, so when the late baby boom cohorts of women were having children, there were also many older women having children as well. In projecting the total fertility rate at that time, younger women would have been expected to have relatively high birthing rates across their whole fertile period. That generally has not happened.

The declines in the total fertility rates since the middle of the twentieth century have been remarkable. In most countries, the total fertility

---

[11] Sylvester J. Schieber and Paul S. Hewitt, "Demographic Risk in Industrial Societies," *World Economics* (October–December 2000), vol. 1, no. 4, pp. 27–72.

[12] Aside from advances in biomedicine serving as the source to additional gains in longevity, Lee and Carter (1992) used more advanced statistical methods to extrapolate life expectancy with no effort to incorporate knowledge about medical, behavioral, or social influences into their model. While the Actuary of the Social Security Administration forecasts life expectancy using combined age-specific trends with the views of medical experts on ultimate cause-specific rates of mortality decline, Lee and Carter allow each age-specific death rate to decline at its own historical rate. The advantage is that this is more consistent with historical trends than imposing that all age-specific rates ultimately decline at the same pace. The implications of this approach are that Lee and Carter forecast life expectancy to be 5.6 years greater by 2065 than the Actuary.

Table 2-3. *Changes in Total Fertility Rates for Various Countries over Time*

	Total Fertility Rates at Various Times					Annual Rate of Change	
	1950–1955	1975–1980	2000–2005	2010–2015	2030–2035	1950–2000	2000–2030
Argentina	3.15	3.44	2.44	2.19	2.10	−0.51%	−0.50%
Australia	3.18	2.09	1.75	1.78	1.92	−1.19	0.31
Brazil	6.15	4.31	2.15	2.10	2.10	−2.08	−0.08
Canada	3.73	1.74	1.58	1.64	1.84	−1.71	0.52
Chile	4.95	2.95	2.35	2.21	2.10	−1.48	−0.38
China	6.22	3.32	1.80	1.90	1.90	−2.45	0.18
Egypt	6.56	5.27	2.88	2.10	2.10	−1.63	−1.05
France	2.73	1.86	1.80	1.84	1.88	−0.82	0.13
Germany	2.16	1.52	1.29	1.31	1.49	−1.02	0.49
Hungary	2.73	2.12	1.20	1.26	1.70	−1.63	1.16
India	5.97	4.83	2.97	2.27	2.10	−1.39	−1.15
Ireland	3.38	3.48	2.02	2.07	2.09	−1.03	0.11
Italy	2.32	1.89	1.20	1.23	1.46	−1.31	0.67
Japan	2.75	1.81	1.33	1.43	1.63	−1.44	0.67
Malaysia	6.83	4.16	2.90	2.26	2.10	−1.70	−1.07
Mexico	6.87	5.30	2.49	2.22	2.10	−2.01	−0.57
Netherlands	3.06	1.60	1.50	1.52	1.70	−1.42	0.42
Pakistan	6.28	6.28	5.08	4.16	2.33	−0.42	−2.57
Poland	3.62	2.26	1.26	1.32	1.80	−2.09	1.20
South Africa	6.50	5.00	2.85	2.35	2.10	−1.63	−1.01
Spain	2.57	2.57	1.13	1.14	1.45	−1.64	0.84
Sweden	2.21	1.66	1.29	1.34	1.75	−1.07	1.02
Switzerland	2.28	1.53	1.38	1.37	1.58	−1.00	0.46
Turkey	6.90	4.65	2.30	2.10	2.10	−2.17	−0.30
U.K.	2.18	1.72	1.61	1.60	1.79	−0.60	0.35
U.S.	3.45	1.79	1.93	1.90	2.05	−1.15	0.20

Source: United Nations, Population Division, World Population Prospects (The 2000 Revision).

rate has declined at a rate of more than 1 percent per year over the last half century, and it has been falling even faster in some less developed countries than in the richer ones. The population replacement rate varies, depending on life expectancy, but for most countries today it would be somewhere around 2.1 births per woman who survives to adulthood. It takes more than 2.0 births per woman because the birth rates of males are slightly higher than of females, and all the females born in a given year do not survive to childbearing age.

The distribution of total fertility rates in the early 2000s is as remarkable as the changes during the prior 50 years. The less developed countries consistently have higher birth rates than those that are well developed. This turns the Malthusian contention discussed earlier somewhat on its head. Malthus believed that the scarcity of resources would drive down birth rates. In fact, the empirical evidence is that relative improvements in national wealth do so. Among highly developed countries, several have birth rates that are far below those required to support a stable population over time. Most specifically, Germany, Japan, Italy, and Spain stand out, with rates below 1.5. For the European countries combined, the rate is around 1.3 births per woman.

The projected total fertility rates suggest that those countries with extremely low rates now will make a recovery over the coming decades. Partly, this reflects the perception that all peoples want to perpetuate their lineage, but it also reflects an element of demographic projections that is extremely important. Virtually all population projections rely on a range of estimates about the future. Historically, these projections have been made on a deterministic basis, with certain assumptions made about how people will behave. Typically, a set of pessimistic and optimistic assumptions establishes a corridor around a "best guess" estimate. Projections based entirely on pessimistic assumptions often result in a gloomy outlook. For example, if the Japanese fertility rates of the early 1990s were to persist through the next millennium, the Japanese society would almost completely disappear. Some people argue that outcome is highly unlikely. Indeed, there is a long history of peoples perpetuating themselves, but there are also examples of peoples becoming extinct.

Will countries like Germany, Italy, Japan, and Spain reverse their declining birth rates, which bode ill for their long-term prospects of survival as a people? Maybe, but maybe not. Finding historical data on changes in fertility rates over long periods is difficult. We have gathered such information for white women in the United States back to 1800 and used it to plot Figure 2-2. The steady decline in U.S. fertility rates persisted for nearly a century and a half, until the baby boom phenomenon after World War II. But by the mid-1970s, birth rates were back down to levels more consistent with historical trends before the baby boom. Since the mid-1970s, the fertility rates of white women have risen slightly, but this relates more to the timing of births by baby boom women than to actual increases in the numbers of children these cohorts of women are expected to have. The U.S. Social Security actuaries believe that the long-term future total fertility rate for women will settle at a future equilibrium of around 1.9 births per woman. The point is that national trends in fertility rates have short-term anomalous variances and may actually reach plateaus beyond which the historic trend no longer persists. So far, however, there is no evidence that countries where historic trends have led to rates

Total fertility rate

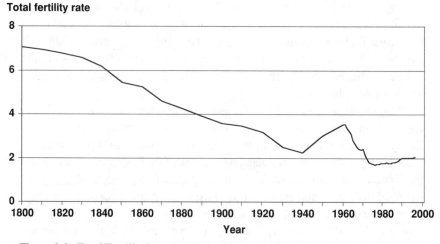

Figure 2-2. Total Fertility Rate for White Women in the United States for Selected Years. *Sources:* U.S. Bureau of the Census, *Historical Statistics of the United States* (Washington, D.C.: Government Printing Office, 1975), U.S. Bureau of the Census, *Statistical Abstract of the United States, 1992* (Washington, D.C.: Government Printing Office, 1992), U.S. Department of Health and Human Services, *Vital Statistics of the United States, 1996.*

below population maintenance levels will actually recover to maintenance levels.

Immigration Rates

Fertility rates that exceed replacement rates are not the only way to grow a nation's population. Immigration and emigration also affect a country's size and composition. The net immigration rates for the countries analyzed here are shown in Table 2-4. In the early 1950s, Ireland experienced a significant emigration, as did the Netherlands, Italy, Spain, the United Kingdom, Mexico, and Chile. At the other end, annual immigration rates for Canada and Australia were approaching 0.5 percent of their resident populations per year. Other substantial gainers were Sweden, the United States, Malaysia, Brazil, Argentina, and Switzerland. At the beginning of the twenty-first century, Mexico was still recording substantial emigration, and even less developed countries like Pakistan had become feeder nations to the more developed countries. The United Kingdom had shifted to being a significant importer of people along with Germany, Italy, the United States, Sweden, Australia, and Canada. From 1950 to 2000, Ireland

Table 2-4. *Annual Net Immigration Rates for Various Countries for Selected Years*

	Net Immigrants Per 1,000 People in the Resident Population				
	1950–1955	1975–1980	2000–2005	2010–2015	2030–2035
Argentina	1.8	−0.8	0.3	0.1	0.0
Australia	4.7	0.6	2.4	2.1	1.7
Brazil	1.0	0.0	0.0	0.0	0.0
Canada	4.3	1.7	2.4	2.5	2.3
Chile	−0.7	−0.8	−0.3	0.0	0.0
China	−0.1	0.0	−0.1	−0.1	−0.1
Egypt	0.0	−0.5	−0.2	−0.2	−0.2
France	0.4	0.3	0.3	0.3	0.3
Germany	0.4	0.4	1.1	1.1	1.2
Hungary	0.2	−0.1	−0.2	0.0	0.0
India	0.0	0.0	−0.1	−0.1	−0.1
Ireland	−6.0	1.3	1.3	1.2	0.0
Italy	−1.1	0.2	0.5	0.5	0.6
Japan	0.0	0.0	0.2	0.2	0.2
Malaysia	1.0	0.8	−0.2	0.0	0.0
Mexico	−0.7	−1.4	−1.5	−1.2	−0.9
Netherlands	−1.2	1.2	0.9	0.9	0.9
Pakistan	0.0	1.0	−0.7	−0.4	−0.3
Poland	−0.2	−0.6	−0.3	−0.3	−0.3
South Africa	0.2	0.3	0.1	0.1	0.1
Spain	−0.9	0.6	0.4	0.4	0.4
Sweden	0.6	1.0	0.6	0.6	0.6
Switzerland	2.4	−1.6	0.3	0.3	0.3
Turkey	0.0	−1.1	−0.4	−0.3	−0.3
U.K.	−1.0	−0.1	0.8	0.8	0.8
U.S.	0.7	1.4	2.1	1.8	1.5

Source: United Nations, Population Division, World Population Prospects (The 2000 Revision).

realized the largest reversal from being a significant net exporter of people to being an importer.

Looking to the future, the United Nations projections assume that the flow of populations across nations will decline slightly or remain roughly constant compared to very recent historical rates. Countries like Germany and Italy, with their extremely low fertility rates, might attempt to maintain high immigration rates because of their relatively high standards of living, but political reactions to large immigrant populations may prompt attempts to restrict legal immigration. Countries like Australia, Canada, and the United States, which generally have had relatively high immigration rates throughout the twentieth century, will also likely continue to attract workers from other parts of the world. But the increases in life expectancy and declining fertility rates might offer a clue as to why immigration rates could fall in the future.

In recent decades, less developed countries with high population growth were generating excess labor supply that could be put to better use in the highly developed countries. The workers themselves naturally migrated toward the better opportunities in the developed economies. But a number of the less developed economies are making considerable strides in their own economic development, and should potentially become far more attractive to their own workers as they move up the development ladder and begin realizing the effects of their own declining birth rates on their domestic labor supplies. As the incentives for workers to stay put in developing countries increase, there may be a simultaneous decline in the incentives to move to countries with populations that are rapidly aging. Rapid aging of a nation's population is likely to have adverse macroeconomic effects that we will investigate further as the story unfolds.

Evolving National Populations
The total population levels and the percentage changes in them over two intervals are shown in Table 2-5. The sizes of the countries are highly varied, ranging from three or four million in Ireland to more than a billion in China and India. Today these countries have combined populations of about 3.8 billion, approximately 60 percent of the total world population. The growth rates in these national populations over the period 1950 to 2000 were highly varied. Several of the western European populations grew by less than 25 percent over the period. In a number of the less developed countries, the population more than tripled over the same period. Overall, the total populations across these countries were 2.25 times the 1950 level by 2000. In the aggregate, these populations grew at an average compound rate of 1.6 percent per year between 1950 and 2000. This annual rate of growth is expected to shrink to half that between 2000 and 2030.

A number of the countries represented in Table 2-5 are expected to lose population between 1990 and 2030, with Hungary's population projected to contract by 14 percent and Italy's by 12 percent. Switzerland and Spain are expected to shrink by 9 percent, and Germany, Japan, Poland, and Sweden by 5 percent. If the assumptions about birth rates recovering from recent levels come up short, these populations could shrink by much more

Table 2-5. *Total Population Levels and Changes for Various Countries over Time*

	Total Population in the Millions					Annual Rate of Change	
	1950	1975	2000	2010	2030	1950–2000	2000–2030
Argentina	17.2	26.0	37.0	41.5	48.9	1.6%	0.9%
Australia	8.2	13.9	19.1	21.0	24.2	1.7	0.8
Brazil	54.0	108.1	170.4	191.4	226.5	2.3	1.0
Canada	13.7	23.1	30.8	33.2	37.7	1.6	0.7
Chile	6.1	10.3	15.2	17.0	20.2	1.9	1.0
China	554.8	927.8	1,275.1	1,366.2	1,484.6	1.7	0.5
Egypt	21.8	38.8	67.9	79.3	99.5	2.3	1.3
France	41.8	52.7	59.2	61.2	62.9	0.7	0.2
Germany	68.4	78.7	82.0	81.4	77.7	0.4	−0.2
Hungary	9.3	10.5	10.0	9.5	8.5	0.1	−0.5
India	357.6	620.7	1,008.9	1,164.0	1,408.9	2.1	1.1
Ireland	3.0	3.2	3.8	4.2	4.9	0.5	0.8
Italy	47.1	55.4	57.5	56.4	50.8	0.4	−0.4
Japan	83.6	111.5	127.1	128.2	121.3	0.8	−0.2
Malaysia	6.1	12.3	22.2	26.1	33.0	2.6	1.3
Mexico	27.7	59.1	98.9	112.9	134.9	2.6	1.0
Netherlands	10.1	13.7	15.9	16.3	16.6	0.9	0.1
Pakistan	39.7	70.3	141.3	181.4	272.7	2.6	2.2
Poland	24.8	34.0	38.6	38.3	36.6	0.9	−0.2
South Africa	13.7	25.8	43.3	45.1	43.9	2.3	0.0
Spain	28.0	35.6	39.9	39.6	36.4	0.7	−0.3
Sweden	7.0	8.2	8.8	8.7	8.4	0.5	−0.2
Switzerland	4.7	6.3	7.2	7.1	6.6	0.9	−0.3
Turkey	20.8	40.0	66.7	75.1	89.9	2.4	1.0
U.K.	50.6	56.2	59.4	60.3	61.3	0.3	0.1
U.S.	157.8	220.2	283.2	308.6	358.5	1.2	0.8

Source: United Nations, Population Division, World Population Prospects (The 2000 Revision).

than projected here. If the assumptions about the slowdown in rising life expectancy rates prove to be overly conservative, that would offset the projected population decline somewhat, but the additional population would be among the oldest segments of the populations. Most of the less developed countries are expected to continue to grow their populations significantly. Among the developed countries, Australia, Canada, and the United States are still expected to have growth of around 25 percent between 2000 and 2030.

One question that naturally arises is whether these projections are reasonable, given what is known about the various populations. In this presentation, we have relied on United Nations projections, in part because

Table 2-6. *Alternative Estimates of Population Age Distributions in 2000 and 2030*

	Source of Estimate	Percent of Populations at Ages Indicated					
		0–14	15–29	30–44	45–59	60–74	75+
Brazil							
2000	United Nations	28.8	28.5	22.1	12.8	6.2	1.6
	World Bank	28.8	28.6	22.2	12.8	6.1	1.5
	US Census	28.8	28.7	21.9	12.6	6.1	1.8
2030	United Nations	21.5	21.3	20.8	19.4	12.8	4.3
	World Bank	21.9	21.7	20.9	19.6	12.5	3.4
	US Census	18.4	20.0	22.0	20.9	13.7	5.0
Italy							
2000	United Nations	14.3	19.3	23.1	19.2	16.2	7.8
	World Bank	14.4	19.6	23.4	19.0	16.1	7.4
	US Census	14.1	19.5	23.5	18.9	16.0	7.9
2030	United Nations	11.0	13.3	16.5	21.8	23.6	13.8
	World Bank	13.1	13.5	16.1	21.3	23.0	14.6
	US Census	11.5	14.0	17.0	21.8	21.9	13.6

Sources: United Nations, Population Division, *World Population Prospects: The 2000 Revision*; The International Bank for Reconstruction and Development, World Bank, *World Development Indicators 1998*, CD-ROM; and the United States Bureau of the Census, *International Database* accessible at: http://www.census.gov/cgi-bin/ipc/agggen.

their historical population estimates are more complete than other sources. To evaluate the reasonableness of U.N. projections, we compared the population estimates with two other major databases of world populations: the World Bank, which has been studying the aging of the world's population for some time, and the U.S. Census Bureau. In Table 2-6 we show the population estimates for two countries, Brazil and Italy. The U.N. projections to 2030 show Brazil growing substantially and Italy contracting significantly. Given the diverse projected changes to these two populations between 1990 and 2030, one might expect their age distributions to be sensitive to the underlying assumptions about fertility rates, longevity increases, and immigration rates. There are differences in the three sets of projections, but they tend to be more at the ends of the age distributions than in the middle. Overall, however, we believe the United Nations estimates are reasonable, given the general distributions of the estimates by the other groups.

National Population Age Structures

The information in Table 2-6 suggests that the age structures in different countries vary, and they are evolving in dissimilar patterns. To show this, we have graphed the evolving population distributions in four countries: Pakistan, Canada, Mexico, and Italy. We chose these countries because they are each at different stages of demographic transition, and the four patterns generally reflect the evolution of population distributions across the world today.

Figure 2-3 shows the population age structure in Pakistan at three different points in time, 1950, 2000, and 2030. The first and second panels reflecting the populations in 1950 and 2000 are based on historical data. The bottom panel represents the U.N. projection for 2030. The bars in the left side of the panels represent the percentage of the population that was male and of a given age. The bottom bar in the left, top panel shows that in 1950, roughly 7.5 percent of the total Pakistani population was comprised of males between the age of zero and four. The right-hand side of the panel shows the percentage of the population that was female. The structure of the population in Pakistan in 1950 was the classic pyramid shape similar to most national populations around the beginning of the twentieth century.

In Table 2-3, we show that Pakistan's fertility rate fell by less between 1950 and 2000 than in the other three countries. Pakistan has relatively low per capita income, a phenomenon generally associated with relatively high fertility rates. It also has a predominantly Islamic population, another characteristic generally associated with high fertility rates. The striking similarity in the shapes of the Pakistani populations in 1950 and 2000 is largely due to this persistently high fertility rate.

A nation's fertility rate determines the additions being made to a population, leaving aside immigration for the moment. The mortality rates determine the deletions from a nation's population, again leaving aside emigration. Between the early 1950s and the beginning of the new century in Pakistan, life expectancy at birth increased by 20 years, from a base of 41 years.

It would seem that the longer life expectancy would begin to considerably increase the size of the elderly population in both absolute and relative terms, although such an increase does not show up in the middle panel of Figure 2-3. This is because much of the improvement in life expectancy was due to reductions in infant and child mortality.

Pakistan's Population Structure in 1950

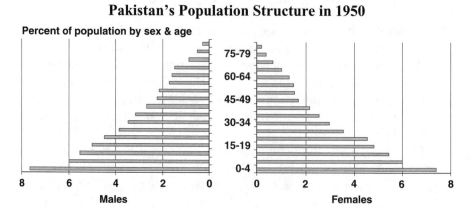

Pakistan's Population Structure in 2000

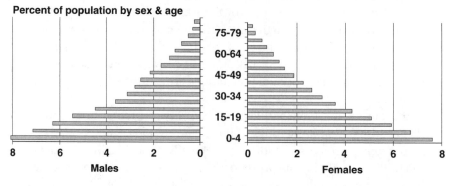

Pakistan's Population Structure in 2030

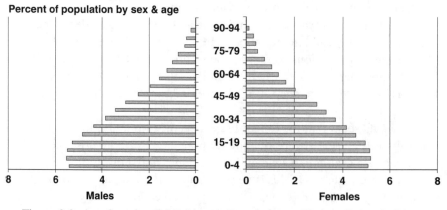

Figure 2-3. Age Structure of Pakistan's Population at Various Points in Time. *Source:* United Nations, Population Division, World Population Prospects (The 2000 Revision).

The population age structure in the third panel of Figure 2-3 is the projected Pakistani population for 2030. This projection suggests that the country is at the beginning of a population transformation. In part, this will be the result of a growing elderly population due to the historical improvements in life expectancy But to a greater extent, it will be driven by reduced fertility rates. Referring back to Table 2-3, Pakistan's fertility rate is expected to fall from 5.1 in 2000 to 2.3 by 2030. It is important to keep in mind that the projections are largely driven by the underlying assumptions, and if the expected patterns for variables like fertility do not play out, the projections will not be accurate. One of the hardest variables to predict in this sort of analysis is the fertility rate. The U.N. population projections predict significant fertility rate reductions for Pakistan and for a number of other similar countries. These predictions are based on what has occurred in several similar countries in recent decades. For example, the total fertility rate in Egypt fell from 5.1 in 1980 to 2.9 in 2000. Over the same time period, fertility rates declined from 4.5 to 2.8 in Iran; from 4.1 to 2.3 in Indonesia; from 4.2 to 2.3 in Turkey; and from 4.9 to 2.7 in Kuwait.[13]

In Figure 2-4, we show Mexico's evolving population age structure. In 1950, its age structure was very similar to that of Pakistan. But Mexico started with a higher life expectancy and made more rapid improvements between 1950 and 2000 than Pakistan. In addition, Mexican fertility rates began falling off fairly rapidly after the late 1970s. In Table 2-3, Mexico's total fertility rate fell from 6.87 in the early 1950s to 5.30 in the early 1970s, and to 2.49 early in the new century. Another factor affecting the changing population structure in Mexico was the improvement in life expectancy at birth. It rose from almost 51 years in the early 1950s to 73 years by the beginning of the 2000s. Mexico has consistently had a negative net immigration rate, largely due to its proximity to the United States and the different wage and income potential in the two countries. As a result of this combination of factors, the age structure of the Mexican population in 2000 was already at the point Pakistan is projected to reach by 2030.

The third panel in Figure 2-4 shows the projected distribution of the Mexican population in 2030. Here the effects of 30 years of essentially replacement-level total fertility rates and continued steady improvement in life expectancy become apparent. By 2030, the share of the population made up by each five-year birth cohort of people under age 55 is expected

---

[13] United Nations, Population Division, *World Population Prospects: The 2000 Revision.*

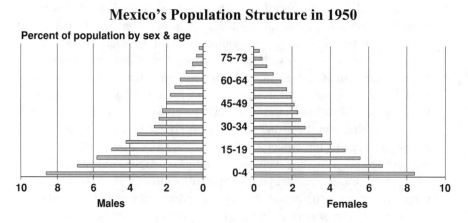

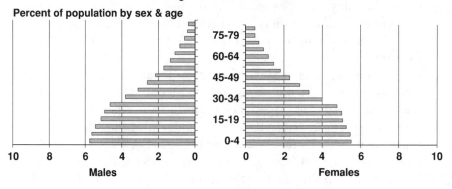

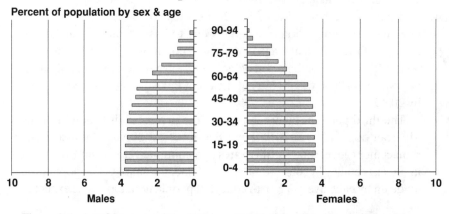

Figure 2-4. Age Structure of the Mexican Population at Various Points in Time. *Source:* United Nations, Population Division, World Population Prospects (The 2000 Revision).

to be relatively constant. The top part of the age distribution will still assume the pyramidal form that existed for the whole population in the early 1950s. The rest will be almost perfectly rectangular. The evolving population structures in Argentina, Brazil, Chile, India, Ireland, Malaysia, Mexico, and South Africa are all quite similar and tend to characterize the developing world.

In Figure 2-5, we show the evolving age structure of Canada. In 1950, its population age structure shared some similarities with Mexico and Pakistan but exhibited some significant differences as well. Drawing a line down the extremities of the bars would roughly trace the outline of the classical population pyramid. The substantial indentation for the age groups from roughly ages 10 to 25 reflected a significant drop in birth rates during the Great Depression and World War II. Like Australia, New Zealand, and the United States, Canada's birth rate increased substantially after World War II. The Canadian baby boom can be seen clearly in the middle panel in Figure 2-5 as the bulge in the center of the overall age profile.

In Canada, total fertility rates fell from roughly replacement rates of 2.1 in the early 1970s to 1.75 in the early 2000s. The fertility rate is now below population replacement levels, where it is expected to remain for most of the period up to 2030. Despite that, Canada has had extremely high immigration rates over the second half of the twentieth century, and its population growth rates since World War II exceed those in most developed countries. With the exception of the middle-age bulge in the total population structure in 2000, reflecting the baby boom birth cohorts, Canada's 2000 population structure closely resembles the structure Mexico is expected to have by 2030.

The bottom panel in Figure 2-5 shows the Canadian population structure in 2030. The squaring phenomenon in the age distribution that was becoming apparent by 2000 progresses much further up the age distribution. The pattern evolving in Canada is similar to the expected patterns in Australia and New Zealand. France and the United Kingdom, which have maintained relatively high fertility rates compared to most of the developed world, are also expected to evolve along these lines. Because these latter countries have not traditionally had the high rates of immigration experienced by Australia, Canada, New Zealand, and the United States, their patterns of evolution will be slightly different. In the United States, the combination of relatively high fertility rates and high immigration rates is expected to generate somewhat more robust general population growth than is expected in other developed countries.

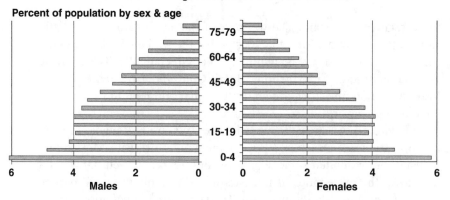

Canadian Population Structure in 1950

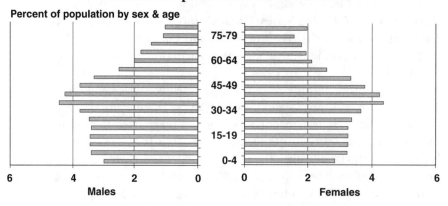

Canadian Population Structure in 2000

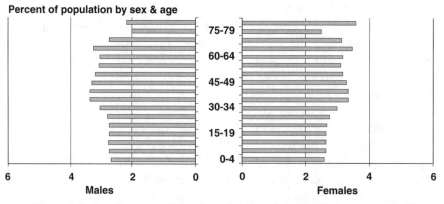

Canadian Population Structure in 2030

Figure 2-5. Age Structure of the Canadian Population at Various Points in Time. *Source:* United Nations, Population Division, World Population Prospects (The 2000 Revision).

Figure 2-6 shows Italy's evolving age distribution, the last of the evolving population styles. The top panel of the figure, representing the distribution in 1950, shows the squaring up of the population much earlier than in the other countries. With its fertility rate already falling off, Italy's 1950 age structure was probably 30 or so years ahead of the Canadian age structure. In 1950, each of the five-year birth cohorts younger than 30 already comprised a relatively comparable portion of the population. From the 1950s through the early 1970s, Italy's total fertility rate was around 2.8, but it dropped off precipitously to around 1.2 at the turn of the century. During the early part of the period under study here, Italy's net immigration rate was negative, but it has been marginally positive over most of the period since World War II.

The bottom panel in Figure 2-6 shows the projected effects of Italy's gradual improvements in life expectancy, fertility rates significantly below replacement levels, and relatively low immigration rates. The traditional population pyramid is projected to become inverted by 2030, based on the assumption that the Italian fertility rate will rebound to nearly 1.5 by 2030. If that does not occur, and there is reason to believe it might not, the inversion of the population pyramid will be even more pronounced than shown. If the Italian fertility rate does not increase, it portends the gradual elimination of the national population.

There are several countries whose population structures are similar to that evolving in Italy. Among countries being analyzed here, the list includes Germany, Hungary, Japan, and Spain. It also includes China, although the effects out to 2030 are not as extreme as those projected for Italy. But the projections for China assume that its total fertility rate will average 1.9 out to the early 2030s, which is not consistent with a government policy that allows most women to have only one child. If the Chinese persist in the one-child policy for an extended period of time, their population structure will evolve very quickly toward the pattern in Italy. The Netherlands, Sweden, and Switzerland also show signs of moving in this direction with their low birth rates and immigration levels, although their outlook is not quite as dire.

In 2000, 3.7 percent of Pakistan's population was age 65 or over. By 2030, 5.3 percent of the population will be over age 65. Comparable percentages are 4.7 and 10.9 percent in Mexico; 12.6 and 22.9 percent in Canada; and 18.1 and 28.6 percent in Italy, according to these projections. Population aging is relatively universal, but it is occurring at highly varied rates.

Italian Population Structure in 1950

Percent of population by sex & age

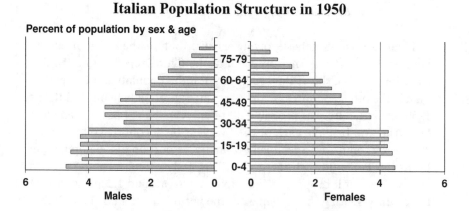

Italian Population Structure in 2000

Percent of population by sex & age

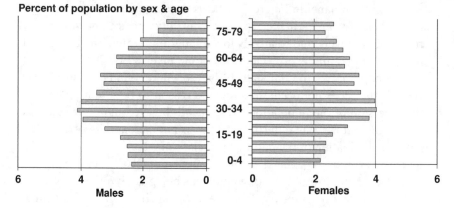

Italian Population Structure in 2030

Percent of population by sex & age

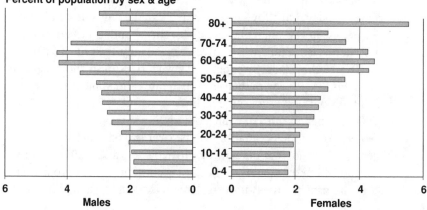

Figure 2-6. Age Structure of Italian Population at Various Points in Time. *Source:* United Nations, Population Division, World Population Prospects (The 2000 Revision).

The Prospects of Growing Age Dependency

The discussion thus far suggests that the aging of populations is occurring at differential rates across national landscapes. The phenomenon has raised fears that meeting the elderly's consumption needs will put significant stresses on economies with particularly old populations. Some analysts contend that, in part, the aging phenomenon simply means a shift in the dependency structure.[14] They argue that both the young and the old are dependent on the fruits of the productive efforts of the working-age population – the young because they have not yet embarked on their productive careers, the old because they have completed them. The argument here is that the declining birth rates in the more developed countries will free up resources that were previously spent on children to support the increasing numbers of elderly people. Later we will show that most societies finance the consumption of their youth and elderly populations through significantly different means that will have major macroeconomic implications for the countries affected. For now, however, we want to briefly look at how the two dependent populations are changing relative to each other.

Table 2-7 shows the evolving ratios of elderly to youth populations in our study countries. In developing these ratios, we included everyone under age 20 in the youth category and everyone age 60 and older in the elderly group. At the middle of the twentieth century in the study countries, there were between two and nine youths for each elderly person – more in the less developed countries and fewer in the highly developed countries. By the beginning of the twentieth century, Germany, Italy, Japan, and Spain had at least one elderly person for each youth. Of all the countries in the table, only Pakistan registered a decline in its ratio of elderly to youth between 1950 and 2000. In most of these countries, the shift toward elderly dependency and away from youth dependency is expected to accelerate between now and 2030.

By 2030, Germany, Italy, Japan, Spain, and Switzerland are all projected to have at least twice as many people over the age of 60 as under the age of 20. Most other European countries are projected to have at least 150 percent as many people over the age of 60 as they have under 20. By comparison, in the United States, there will be rough parity between the youth and elderly populations. In Mexico, there still will be roughly two

[14] For example, see Robert Ball, *Straight Talk about Social Security* (New York: The Century Foundation Press, 1998), p. 3.

Table 2-7. *Changing Ratios of Old to Young Persons in Various Countries over Time*

	Ratio of Elderly to the Youth in the Country					Annual Rate of Change	
	1950	1975	2000	2010	2030	1950–2000	2000–2030
Argentina	0.18	0.30	0.36	0.42	0.61	1.45%	1.72%
Australia	0.37	0.35	0.59	0.76	1.11	0.92	2.11
Brazil	0.09	0.12	0.20	0.29	0.59	1.52	3.69
Canada	0.30	0.34	0.65	0.88	1.36	1.54	2.50
Chile	0.15	0.16	0.28	0.37	0.70	1.25	3.14
China	0.17	0.14	0.31	0.44	0.99	1.17	3.95
Egypt	0.10	0.13	0.14	0.19	0.42	0.55	3.82
France	0.54	0.57	0.81	0.97	1.38	0.82	1.80
Germany	0.48	0.71	1.10	1.41	2.16	1.67	2.28
Hungary	0.34	0.66	0.84	1.10	1.60	1.84	2.15
India	0.11	0.12	0.18	0.22	0.47	0.86	3.34
Ireland	0.40	0.38	0.50	0.61	0.85	0.45	1.81
Italy	0.35	0.55	1.23	1.52	2.50	2.53	2.40
Japan	0.17	0.37	1.13	1.62	2.26	3.88	2.35
Malaysia	0.15	0.11	0.15	0.21	0.49	0.05	4.03
Mexico	0.14	0.10	0.16	0.23	0.54	0.31	4.12
Netherlands	0.31	0.45	0.76	0.99	1.63	1.83	2.58
Pakistan	0.17	0.11	0.11	0.12	0.19	−0.89	1.76
Poland	0.21	0.40	0.59	0.89	1.40	2.10	2.90
South Africa	0.12	0.10	0.13	0.17	0.32	0.06	3.15
Spain	0.30	0.40	1.03	1.34	2.35	2.50	2.79
Sweden	0.51	0.77	0.94	1.34	1.85	1.23	2.30
Switzerland	0.46	0.59	0.96	1.38	2.24	1.48	2.87
Turkey	0.12	0.13	0.21	0.27	0.55	1.13	3.24
U.K.	0.54	0.64	0.82	1.03	1.56	0.85	2.16
U.S.	0.37	0.42	0.56	0.69	1.05	0.86	2.11

Source: United Nations, Population Division, World Population Prospects (The 2000 Revision).

young people for every old person, and Pakistan is projected to have five people under the age of 20 for every person over the age of 60.

The mere fact that countries are aging really tells us very little. It is in the context of economic activities that the trends laid out in this chapter take on their relevance. Two aspects of these activities are important. One is how modern societies provide for the elderly. The other is the implication of aging populations on the economic capacity of the society and the business entities that comprise that capacity.

THREE

Pension Options, Motivations and Choices

In many regards, the aging of societies is overwhelmingly good news. Most people welcome the improvements in life expectancy realized in recent decades, especially because they are largely due to the elimination of diseases like smallpox and control of those like polio and malaria. For centuries, human beings have struggled to eliminate and control diseases and conditions that led to early death. The accelerated advances in hygiene and health sciences during the twentieth century and their effects on our lives are beyond the stretch of the wildest imagination of our forebears at the beginning of the last millennium, or even the last century. More recent progress in combating heart disease, cancer, and chronic conditions is both extending life and improving its quality. The advances leading to longer life spans in wealthy nations have generally spread to less wealthy societies, improving life for those citizens as well.

Another phenomenon, largely of twentieth century origins, that accompanied the aging of our societies was the evolution of organized retirement programs. Today, the prevalence and structure of these retirement programs, in conjunction with the aging of national populations, are raising concerns about the cost burdens ahead. Analysts believe the combination of an aging society and the promise of retirement benefits may cause economic difficulties in many countries.[1]

Like improvements in health and longevity, the evolution of retirement programs is very good news in most regards. The advent of formal retirement programs, whether employer- or government-based, enabled career employees to provide for their consumption needs when they could no

---

[1] Peter Peterson, *The Gray Dawn* (New York: Random House Times Books, 1999).

longer work. Today, these programs allow retirees to spend their old age in ways that would have been as unfathomable to their forebears as penicillin, inoculations against infectious diseases, and organ transplantation. Today's workers are much more likely to live to "retirement age" than their ancestors; they also have a much higher prospect of actually being able to retire when they get there. The elderly in developed societies now have a rightful claim on a decent level of living during their declining years. Not only have retirement programs significantly raised income levels and thus reduced poverty among the elderly, they have generally done so in a way that allows the vast majority of older people to maintain a sense of dignity and self-worth. But these advances have come at a cost.

Retirement Plans as a Consumption Allocation Mechanism

Retirement systems are essentially mechanisms that facilitate the distribution of goods and services produced by workers to the elderly, non-working members of a society. The utilization and productivity of labor and capital limit the total output in an economy, at a point in time. Workers receive their share of output in the form of wages. Owners of capital receive their share of output in the form of returns on their investments. Retirees can receive a share of output through their ownership rights of capital or from transfers from the wages paid to workers.

In the capital-based model, workers accumulate their ownership of capital during their working career by saving a portion of their earnings and letting their savings accumulate with interest until they retire. They can do this through personal savings vehicles or through formal retirement plans organized by government mandate, sponsored by their employer, or facilitated by some other cooperative entity. During retirement, retirees liquidate their assets to finance their consumption needs. In this regard, the retirement plan is a mechanism to transfer consumption rights across time periods. This intertemporal transfer of consumption is accomplished by the buying and selling of assets. In the parlance of retirement plan financing, formal programs that provide for the accumulation of assets during the working career to finance participants' consumption during their retirement period are referred to as being funded.

Financing retirees' consumption through intergenerational transfers can either take place on an informal basis or through more formal arrangements. The informal arrangements are typically worked out within families, where a younger generation commits to support its elders when they are no longer able to work. Governments generally sponsor formal arrangements, although some employers sponsor retirement plans that are intergenerational rather than intertemporal transfer mechanisms. These plans are known as pay-as-you-go (pay-go) plans, because they take money from current workers' production and transfer it to current retirees.

In both types of plans, workers finance retirees' consumption through a transfer of a share of their earnings. In funded retirement vehicles, workers do this by purchasing assets that earn returns while held and that are sold in retirement. In pay-go retirement systems, workers do it by surrendering a share of their earnings, which are then transferred to retirees. The popularity of pay-go systems in the face of aging populations has raised concerns about their viability. But aging societies will pose challenges to both types of retirement systems. Their relative ability to adapt to these challenges deserves careful exploration.

One problem with focusing on publicly sponsored retirement programs alone in cross-national comparisons of the economic implications of aging populations is that these programs vary widely from country to country. Traditionally, German and Italian retirees have relied primarily on government-sponsored retirement systems for most of their income support. In Canada and the United States, on the other hand, retirees receive income support from a mix of government and privately sponsored retirement programs. Retirement programs in Canada and the United States are not nearly as generous as those in much of Continental Europe. To help make up the difference, those countries have enacted a variety of tax incentives to encourage employers to sponsor supplemental plans and encourage individuals to save more themselves for retirement. The elderly in several Asian countries depend on provident funds, which legally require workers to save a portion of their income for retirement.

All the retirement systems briefly described here share some common characteristics. Workers accumulate their rights to an income stream or the assets to provide one during their working careers. Each system has rules, typically based on age, that govern when people can tap those assets or that income stream. In its simplest form, the concern about the economic burdens ahead is about the ever-growing number of people who will consume without contributing to the society's total output.

Approaches to Financing Pensions

Economists often employ a theoretical life-cycle model to explain saving and consumption patterns of individuals at varying ages and phases

Accumulated balance

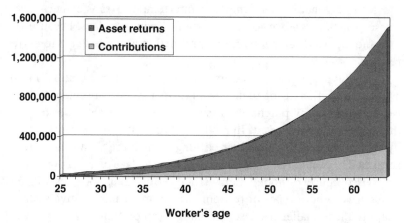

Worker's age

Figure 3-1. Accumulating Contributions and Income on Assets in a Funded Pension during a Worker's Career. *Source:* Developed by the authors.

of life.[2] In its simplest form, the life-cycle model suggests that workers borrow against the expected stream of future earnings during the early phases of their life, to start their families, buy their homes, and otherwise establish themselves. During the middle phase of their working life, workers pay off their early career debts and accumulate excess assets by regularly consuming less than they earn. The assets accumulate with interest, to be reclaimed and used later in life when the ability or inclination to "earn" a living wanes. The life-cycle model can be enhanced by allowing the family unit, as opposed to a single individual, to define the timelines for borrowing, saving, and retiring. It can also allow for the possibility of one generation bequeathing some share of its lifetime accumulation to subsequent generations.

The funding of an organized retirement program during the period that a worker earns his or her future benefit entitlements is consistent with the life-cycle model. How this works, at least in theory, is demonstrated in Figure 3-1. In this example, we assume that a young woman starts a career at age 25 and works continuously until she retires at age 65. We

[2] Franco Modigliani and Richard Brumberg, "Utility Analysis and the Consumption Function: An Interpretation of Cross-section Data," in Kenneth K. Kurihara, ed., *Post-Keynesian Economics* (Rutgers University Press, 1954); Albert Ando and Franco Modigliani, "The Life Cycle Hypothesis of Savings: Aggregate Implications and Tests," *American Economic Review*, vol. 53 (March 1963), pp. 55–84.

assume that she earns a beginning salary of €30,000 and receives annual pay increases of 5 percent per year over her career. We also assume that she contributes 8 percent of pay into an account and that the assets in the account earn returns of 8 percent per year.

This model has a number of features that many people who work with retirement plans find particularly appealing. First, the worker's retirement benefit is financed directly out of her own productivity. Second, if she invests her contributions wisely, the rate of return on assets can finance a significant portion of her retirement benefit. In fact, by the time this worker reaches age 65, the total accumulated balance should be slightly more than four times her accumulated contributions. When the worker retires, she could use the accumulated assets to purchase a life annuity or, alternatively, she could take partial distributions from the fund each year. While funded plans have a number of positive features, they also have some drawbacks that will be discussed later.

The financing of organized retirement plans through the pay-go method shares certain similarities with a funded retirement plan from an individual worker's life-cycle perspective, but it has significant differences as well. Probably the most significant difference is that there is no accumulation of real assets during the working life. In pay-go retirement systems, the total benefits paid to current retirees in a given year essentially equal the total revenues collected from active workers in that same year. Such systems generally utilize a small contingency trust fund as a leveling device to sustain operations over variations in benefits and revenues across economic cycles. Pay-go systems typically rely on taxes on workers' earnings – payroll taxes – as their primary means of revenue. The tax revenues available are equal to the payroll tax rate, including both the employer and employee portion of the tax, times the number of workers who pay the tax, times workers' average covered earnings level. The amount of benefits paid is equal to the total number of people receiving benefits times the average benefit paid. The underlying mathematics of such a system is shown in Equation (1) in Figure 3-2.

The "cost" of a pay-go retirement plan is generally considered in terms of the payroll tax rate required to sustain it. In many of these plans today, two very important ratios determine their cost. The tax rate required to support the system is the product of the number of beneficiaries relative to workers times the ratio of average benefits to average covered earnings. This is shown in Equation (2) in Figure 3-2. The ratio of beneficiaries to workers is called the dependency ratio – the number of retirees dependent on benefits relative to the number of workers supporting them. The ratio

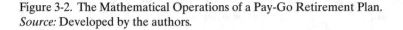

Revenues = Expenditures

$$(1) \quad t \cdot N_W \cdot W = N_B \cdot B$$

where:

t = payroll tax rate paid by employers and employees

N_W = number of covered workers employed in a year

W = average wages of covered workers during the year

N_B = number of retirees receiving benefits

B = average benefits paid to retirees

and such that:

$$(2) \quad t = (N_B/N_W) \cdot (B/W)$$

Figure 3-2. The Mathematical Operations of a Pay-Go Retirement Plan. *Source:* Developed by the authors.

of benefits to wages in a retirement plan is called the replacement rate – how much of an average worker's earnings are replaced by the retirement benefit.

The reason why population aging sets off alarms is clear from the dependency ratio measure in Equation (2) in Figure 3-2. As the ratio of pension beneficiaries to contributors rises under these plans, their cost rises proportionately. A simple proxy for the dependency ratio in Equation (2), the ratio of working-age to retirement-age people, demonstrates the underlying reason for the concern. Although this proxy does not precisely measure the implications of population aging on a pay-go plan for any one country, it provides a sufficiently reasonable approximation for our purposes. In Table 3-1, we show the ratio of people ages 60 and older as a proxy for the retiree population to the ratio of people ages 20 to 59 as a proxy for the working population. Over time, the trend in this proxy should approximate the trend in the actual dependency ratios.

In all but a handful of the countries shown in Table 3-1, the ratios increased between 1950 and 2000, in some cases substantially. With the exception of Argentina, the annual rate of increase is expected to be higher between 2000 and 2030 than it was between 1950 and 2000. This merely indicates the acceleration in population aging and potential aging dependency around the world. From this perspective, the elderly populations in countries like Malaysia, Mexico, and South Africa

Table 3-1. *Ratio of Retirement Age Populations to Working Age Populations*

	Ratio of People 60 and over to People Ages 20 to 59					Annual Growth Rate	
	1950	1975	2000	2010	2030	1950–2000	2000–2030
Argentina	0.13	0.23	0.27	0.27	0.33	1.41%	0.67%
Australia	0.23	0.25	0.29	0.35	0.51	0.48	1.91
Brazil	0.11	0.14	0.15	0.17	0.31	0.55	2.57
Canada	0.22	0.24	0.29	0.35	0.59	0.54	2.38
Chile	0.15	0.18	0.19	0.23	0.39	0.56	2.35
China	0.15	0.16	0.18	0.20	0.44	0.30	3.08
Egypt	0.11	0.15	0.13	0.14	0.23	0.31	1.79
France	0.30	0.37	0.38	0.43	0.63	0.45	1.71
Germany	0.27	0.40	0.42	0.46	0.77	0.91	2.04
Hungary	0.20	0.34	0.35	0.39	0.53	1.06	1.41
India	0.12	0.14	0.16	0.17	0.25	0.45	1.58
Ireland	0.31	0.35	0.28	0.31	0.43	−0.18	1.40
Italy	0.23	0.34	0.43	0.50	0.78	1.24	2.05
Japan	0.17	0.21	0.41	0.58	0.79	1.85	2.18
Malaysia	0.17	0.14	0.13	0.16	0.27	−0.51	2.34
Mexico	0.17	0.15	0.14	0.16	0.29	−0.42	2.44
Netherlands	0.22	0.30	0.32	0.40	0.65	0.70	2.44
Pakistan	0.19	0.13	0.14	0.14	0.16	−0.61	0.41
Poland	0.16	0.26	0.30	0.31	0.51	1.30	1.79
South Africa	0.13	0.12	0.11	0.14	0.22	−0.25	2.20
Spain	0.21	0.29	0.38	0.42	0.70	1.22	2.03
Sweden	0.27	0.41	0.42	0.51	0.72	0.88	1.86
Switzerland	0.25	0.33	0.38	0.49	0.84	0.80	2.73
Turkey	0.13	0.17	0.16	0.18	0.29	0.41	1.86
U.K.	0.28	0.40	0.38	0.43	0.66	0.62	1.86
U.S.	0.23	0.29	0.29	0.33	0.52	0.45	1.93

Source: United Nations, Population Division, *World Population Prospects* (2000 Revision).

are projected to grow as rapidly as those in many more highly developed countries. But since the less developed countries are starting out with younger populations, the effects of population aging should be less problematic for them over the coming 30 years than for more developed countries.

How Hard Is It to Predict Future Demography?

By Professor Ronald Lee, University of California, Berkeley

Turning points in population age distribution can be better predicted far in the future than can economic variables, because the future age distribution depends so strongly on the current age distribution. This is particularly true for the old age dependency ratio, a fundamental influence on the finances of pay-as-you-go pensions. Nonetheless, serious errors occur, as can be seen by comparing past projections to what actually happened. Analysis of United Nations projections for up to a 15-year horizon for Europe and North America combined shows impressive accuracy for ages 15 to 64, but a systematic downward bias at older ages. Above age 80, the 15-year projections were too low by 12 percent (National Research Council, 2000: 45–46). Similar results hold for official projections of most OECD nations.

These biases derive from a downward bias in projections of life expectancy by the United Nations and by official agencies in OECD nations (National Research Council, 2000). Official projections assumed, and still assume, that the rate of mortality decline would slow down in the future, and so far it has not. In fact, mortality declines at the older ages have accelerated in recent decades. Forecasts which simply extrapolate historical rates of decline in mortality by age since 1950 imply that life expectancy will rise by 7.5 years from 2000 to 2050 in the G7 countries, compared to only 4.5 years in official forecasts (Tuljapurkar, et al, 2000).

But a recent study shows that the highest national life expectancy observed in each year has been rising remarkably linearly at about 2.3 years per decade for 160 years, since 1840 (Oeppen and Vaupel, 2002). That pace suggests that life expectancy in the G7 could rise 11.5 years by 2050, two and a half times as much as in official projections. The implications for pensions are significant, but not staggering: a 7.5 year gain would raise pension costs by 1 percent more of GDP than in official projections, and the 11.5 year gain would raise them by 2.3 percent more of GDP.

Some biologists suggest that life expectancy might reach 150 years in this century, while other scientists raise the possibility that new diseases, drug-resistant strains of old diseases, and obesity could cause a reversal of life expectancy gains as has happened in Eastern Europe, Russia, and sub-Saharan Africa.

There is evidently a great deal of uncertainty about the future of mortality, and therefore about the future numbers of elderly. Fertility is even more difficult to project than mortality, because it has changed more rapidly in the past, both upwards in the baby booms and downwards in the baby busts, and has descended to new lows in many countries. Postponement of childbearing in many countries may be artificially depressing the Total Fertility Rate, the most commonly used measure. Immigration is largely determined by policy, and demographers have no particular insights on how to forecast that.

Literature Cited

Oeppen, J. and J. W. Vaupel. 2002. *Broken limits to life expectancy. Science* 296: 1029–31.

National Research Council (2000) *Beyond Six Billion: Forecasting the World's Population. Panel on Population Projections. John Bongaarts and Rodolfo A. Bulatao, eds. Committee on Population, Commission on Behavioral and Social Sciences and Education. Washington, D.C.: National Academy Press.*

Tuljapurkar, S., N. Li and C. Boe, 2000. *A Universal Pattern of Mortality Change in the G7 Countries. Nature* 405: 789–92.

China is projected to have the largest increase in its older population compared to its working-age population between 2000 and 2030. Although rising life expectancies play a role, China's increasing older population largely reflects the maturing of its national one-child policy. Despite this anticipated rapid aging in China over the next quarter century or so, the ratio of elderly to working-age people, by the definition used here, is not expected to be appreciably higher in 2030 than it already is in Germany, Italy, and Japan.

Keeping in mind Equation 2 in Figure 3-2, the implication of Table 3-1 is that in countries with pay-go retirement systems, increasing aged dependency ratios will drive up their pension costs significantly, unless something is done to reduce the second ratio on the right-hand side of the equation. The overall economic burden that these retirement systems will impose depends on the interaction of these two crucial ratios. Just as the dependency ratio varies across countries, the generosity of benefits also varies considerably from one country to the next.

Factors behind National Retirement Choices

The first national retirement program, set up in Germany by Otto von Bismarck in 1889, was a funded retirement system. To build up sufficient funding to pay meaningful benefits took some time. The original system provided benefits based on contributions that were tied to a worker's wage level during his working career. Originally the system was compulsory for about 40 percent of the workforce. By 1895, this percentage had risen to roughly 55 percent. The system was an invalidity – that is, disability – and retirement system and did not provide dependent or survivor benefits. Workers became eligible for benefits upon reaching age 70, an age achieved by only about 20 percent of German workers at that time. The first disability benefits were paid in 1891; the first old-age pensions were not paid until 1899. The system provided modest benefits, less than those provided through the poor relief system at the time.[3]

In Britain, the Old Age Pension Act of 1908 created a means-tested, non-contributory entitlement, which was available only to the "respectable" poor. As in the German social insurance scheme, pensioners could begin collecting benefits at age 70, and the benefits were set too low to serve as a disincentive to work. The pension act was supported

[3] John B. Williamson and Fred C. Pampel, *Old-Age Security in Comparative Perspective* (New York: Oxford University Press, 1993), pp. 26–27.

by many influential politicians, business, and civic leaders, partly due to the need to respond to the social challenges created by growing levels of "visible poverty" in major British cities.

In 1925 the Widows, Orphans and Old Age Contributory Pensions Act was passed, committing the United Kingdom to a system of social insurance. In addition to integrating the old-age pension scheme with the newly forming national insurance approach, this legislation provided an allowance to the wife of an insured worker and benefits for widows and orphans. It enacted a flat-rate for pension contributions, rather than tying contribution amounts to wages. Further, the 1925 legislation made male employees aged 65 to 70 eligible for a flat-rate contributory pension that would not be means tested.

In the early 1940s, pension policy in the United Kingdom shifted dramatically when Sir William Beveridge, a leading economist, established a government committee with himself as its head. The 1942 Beveridge Report argued for a comprehensive scheme of social insurance, without income limits, and formed the basis of much legislation passed later. The National Insurance Act of 1946 was based on that report, implementing most of the report's policy proposals by 1948.[4]

When the United States adopted its social security program in 1935, the system was designed to be funded, like the German system, with the first benefit payouts scheduled for 1942. The government planned to subsidize benefits somewhat for early beneficiaries, but benefits were supposed to grow over time along with accumulated contributions. Britain's National Insurance Act of 1946 took a different approach, granting full benefits to newly covered retirees without any transition period. This is not to say that there were no restrictions on who received benefits – for example, marrying an alien disqualified a worker from receiving a pension in the early days – but generally benefits were granted on a more nearly universal basis than in the United States.[5] The reason that Britain could pay full benefits from the outset was that it financed its system on a pay-go basis – the contributions coming in from current workers were immediately transferred to retirees.

In order to show how the pay-go financed system could provide higher benefits to initial beneficiaries at lower cost, consider a simple example. First, assume that birth rates are constant over time so that all age cohorts

[4] Ibid, pp. 45–47.
[5] P. Thane, *Old Age in English History: Past Experiences, Present Issues* (Oxford: Oxford University Press, 2000), p. 19.

are exactly the same size. Second, assume that everyone begins working at age 22 and works steadily until their 65th birthday, at which time they retire. Third, assume that all retirees receive a pension for 17 years and die on their 82nd birthday. Fourth, assume that all workers earn the same wages, which remain constant over their careers. Fifth, assume that in all funded systems, pensions are financed through contributions along with interest earnings on the assets. Finally, assume in this base case that assets in funded retirement accounts earn an annual return of zero percent per year.[6]

Given these conditions, suppose that a country implements a pay-go retirement plan that pays immediate benefits to all existing retirees at a level equivalent to 50 percent of the wages earned by workers. If there are 1,000 people in each birth cohort, there will be exactly 43,000 workers and 17,000 retirees, establishing a dependency ratio of approximately 0.3953 – i.e., 17,000 ÷ 43,000. The payroll tax required to finance these benefits would be approximately 19.77 percent of wages, which is the product of the dependency ratio multiplied by the ratio of benefits to wages – i.e., 0.5 by stipulation of the plan design. The day the program starts, it would begin paying benefits to current retirees, which in this case would include everyone over age 65. Under the prescribed assumptions, the system could continue paying those benefits indefinitely.

But if this same country were to establish a funded pension system that paid each birth cohort the actuarial value of its lifetime contributions plus interest, the outcome would be different. The problem is that at initiation, some birth cohorts are already at retirement age and have made no contributions. In addition, among the birth cohorts working at that time, only workers aged 22 and in their first year of employment will have a full career of 43 years over which to accumulate assets. All the earlier birth cohorts will have less time to accumulate assets and thus will end up with less than full benefits. Assume that the funded system is initiated under the assumptions stipulated above, and each worker must contribute approximately 19.77 percent of pay into the system. This funded system is structured to pay each birth cohort the equivalent of its lifetime contributions plus interest. As stipulated earlier, assume a zero percent annual interest accrual on retirement savings under the plan.

---

[6] These assumptions are essentially equivalent to those stipulated in Lawrence Thompson, *Older & Wiser: The Economics of Public Pensions* (Washington, D.C.: The Urban Institute, 1998), p. 98. We use his baseline assumptions here because we will follow his comparison of the financing of pay-go versus funded retirement systems later and want this example to be compatible with that analysis.

Percentage of preretirement earnings replaced

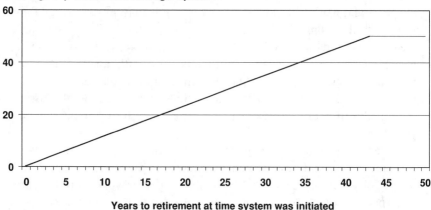

Figure 3-3. Replacement of Preretirement Earnings by a Hypothetical Funded Retirement Plan by Workers' Years to Retirement at the Time the System Was Initiated. *Source:* Derived by the authors.

Earnings replacement rates under the funded system for selected birth cohorts are shown in Figure 3-3. For each birth cohort, the figure shows the number of working years left until retirement at the time the system is implemented. Workers with a full career under the funded system receive benefits equivalent to those paid under the pay-go system. All older birth cohorts receive less than 50 percent of the benefits they would receive under the pay-go system, and the oldest cohorts receive significantly less. Indeed, for the birth cohort turning age 65 when the system is implemented and for earlier birth cohorts, there will be no benefits. Despite this difference in benefits paid to older generations in funded versus pay-go systems, the long-term costs for both systems in the example are the same.

There is an important wrinkle to add to this story because of modern-day deliberations about moving from pay-go pension systems to funded ones. Even in a funded system, governments can pay benefits to the first generations of retirees by funding accrued obligations when the plan is implemented. The government would issue bonds and deposit the proceeds into the pension accounts of the generations to receive augmented benefits. No one did this when they set up their original plans, probably because they were unwilling to issue such explicit debt to fund the pension system. Yet in practical terms, they achieved almost exactly the same result: creating a substantial implicit tax obligation to pay out full benefits to people who had not contributed or not contributed enough to the system. At least historically, one difference between funded and unfunded pension programs is that governments have been willing to issue implicit debt for their unfunded pensions, but unwilling to issue comparable explicit debt to fund their plans. This difference in willingness to create implict debt while refusing to take on a similar level of explicit debt likely reflects political realities in many countries, which could continue to complicate attempts to address many of the issues related to population aging that are explored here.

While the assumptions used in the above comparisons of funded and pay-go systems may not be realistic, they illustrate the issues that policy-makers faced in creating early retirement systems. In the United States, the debate over whether to finance the social security retirement system under a funded or a pay-go basis was explicit. President Franklin D. Roosevelt strongly believed that the U.S. system should be funded. Almost from the outset, however, members of Roosevelt's staff and many members of the U.S. Congress disagreed. One major reason for the opposition to a funded system was the desire to pay relatively full benefits without having to wait for a funded system to mature.[7] Immediately after the funded social security system was adopted in 1935, political pressure mounted to move toward pay-go financing. The initial legislation called for payroll tax collections to begin in 1937 and the first benefits to be paid to people reaching age 65 in 1942. In 1939, the U.S. Congress first amended the original law, significantly shifting operations in the direction of pay-go financing. By the mid-1950s, the benefit levels and tax rates were roughly at the pay-go rate needed to balance the system.

The implementation of social security in the United States was more gradual than in many other countries. In the first year the payroll tax was collected, slightly less than 60 percent of all U.S. workers were employed in a covered job some time during the year. This number grew gradually during the program's early years, as shown in Figure 3-4, partly because of the growth in the private industrial workforce during World War II. Coverage rates fell after the war as industrial activity declined. In 1950, Congress expanded social security coverage to farm and domestic workers. Further expansions in 1954 covered self-employed farmers and

---

[7] For a full discussion of the shift from a funded social security system in the United States to one financed on a pay-go basis, see Sylvester J. Schieber and John B. Shoven, *The Real Deal: The History and Future of Social Security* (New Haven: Yale University Press, 1999).

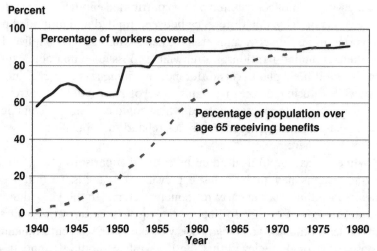

Figure 3-4. Percent of Workers Covered by Social Security and Percent of Persons over Age 65 Receiving Benefits. *Sources:* The coverage data for 1940 to 1970 are from the U.S. Bureau of Census, *Historical Statistics of the United States* (Washington, D.C.: Government Printing Office, 1975), p. 348; for 1971 to 1979, from the U.S. Bureau of Census, *Statistical Abstract of the United States 1979* (Washington, D.C.: Government Printing Office, 1980), p. 331; for 1980, from the U.S. Bureau of Census, *Statistical Abstract of the United States 1981* (Washington, D.C.: Government Printing Office, 1982), p. 326. Beneficiary data for 1940 to 1969 are from the U.S. Bureau of Census, *Historical Statistics of the United States* (Washington, D.C.: Government Printing Office, 1975), p. 357; for 1970 from the *Social Security Bulletin* (March 1981), p. 73; for 1971 to 1974 from the *Social Security Bulletin* (December 1978), p. 75; for 1975 to 1979, from the *Social Security Bulletin* (March 1982), p. 66.

allowed state and local governments, even those with their own pension plans, to cover their employees.

By the mid-1950s, almost 90 percent of the workforce was covered under the U.S. Social Security program. Those still outside the system were federal civilian employees, employees of state and local governments that chose not to participate, and some employees of nonprofit organizations. These latter groups would all remain outside the system until the 1983 Social Security Amendments brought in employees of nonprofit organizations and federal civilians hired after 1983. State and local government employees who were outside the system at that time and covered by their own retirement plans still remain outside it today.

As Figure 3-4 shows, the government expanded coverage very slowly. In 1940, the retirement program paid benefits to 112,000 retired workers – only about 1 percent of the population over age 65. Most of the elderly who had quit work before the first payroll tax collections in 1937 would never receive benefits. Even as the United States moved from a funded approach to pay-go financing, it retained the original funded system requirement that people must contribute in order to receive benefits, although early beneficiaries received tremendous windfall benefits. The U.S. approach was just the opposite of the path Britain had followed in adopting the National Insurance Act of 1946, which may account for some of the divergent histories of the social security retirement programs in the two countries.

By limiting participation, the U.S. national retirement system held costs abnormally low over the program's first four decades. Looking back to Equation (2) in Figure 3-2, it is clear that the initial implementation method kept the ratio of beneficiaries to payroll taxpayers low during the program's early decades. This low dependency ratio enabled the system to pay relatively higher benefits to beneficiaries at lower cost to taxpayers than would have been possible in a system more like Britain's. The U.S. program's architects used the start-up period to significantly expand the scope and level of benefits provided under the social security umbrella. The legislators who voted for the expansions may not have fully appreciated the long-term liabilities that they were creating when they did so. It is noteworthy that once the percentage of the population receiving benefits caught up with the percentage of the workforce paying taxes, there were no further program expansions. Indeed, since the early 1970s, there have been several benefit reductions.

The options open to retirement program policymakers at the end of World War II are summarized in Figure 3-5. The figure shows the percentage of benefits that would be paid under different approaches as the systems matured. Full maturity is defined as the level of benefits that would be paid to a birth cohort of workers who had worked their full careers under the system. The top line in the figure reflects the approach that Britain took in its National Insurance Act of 1946. The U.S. approach is a reasonable approximation of its program and is based on the pro rata share of people over age 65 receiving benefits compared to the share of workers subject to the payroll tax. The funded approach is derived from the same underlying simple model and assumptions used for Figure 3-3. The actual path of maturation for the funded system may vary somewhat from that shown in the figure due to the simplifying assumptions. For example, the estimates presented here assume that all beneficiaries die at age 82 – clearly an unrealistic assumption. The longer life expectancy

Percent of benefits paid relative to a mature system

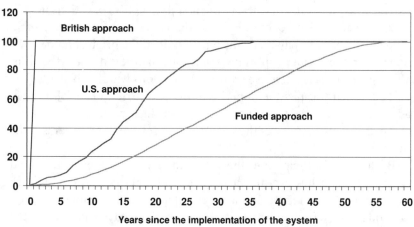

Figure 3-5. Payment of Retirement Benefits during the Start-up of National Retirement Systems under Alternative Funding Arrangements and Benefit Approaches. *Source:* Developed by the authors as described in the text.

of some people would extend the maturation period for the funded option. Despite these limitations, Figure 3-5 gives a good idea of the choices faced by national legislators as they considered their nations' retirement policies at the end of World War II.

After World War II, several countries adopted new contributory plans or added tiers to their existing systems. In addition to Britain, Switzerland (1949), the Netherlands (1957), Sweden (1960), Norway (1966), and Canada (1966) added new pay-go elements to their retirement systems. The remainder of Europe, Japan, and the United States all significantly expanded their pay-go programs.[8] The opportunity to provide full and very generous retirement benefits to early beneficiaries without any obvious disadvantage to workers seemed too good to pass up. The major flaw in the thinking of the time was the failure to consider whether the conditions that made pay-go programs so attractive would last.

Why Pay-Go Pensions Became So Popular

For many workers who were covered by the early pay-go pensions. the plans turned out to be a particularly good deal. In the United Kingdom,

[8] Estelle James, et al, *Averting the Old Age Crisis: Policies to Protect the Old and Promote Growth* (New York: Oxford University Press, 1994), p. 105.

Table 3-2. *Present Value of Payroll Taxes Paid and Present Value of Expected Lifetime Benefits for Workers Retiring at Age 65 in 1965 under the U.S. Social Security Retirement Pension*

		Lifetime Earnings	Taxes Paid	Expected Benefits	Net Transfer
Single Male	Low wage	$5.7	$38.5	$32.8
	Average wage	12.6	59.6	47.0
	High wage	14.7	65.2	50.5
Single Female	Low wage	6.2	59.1	52.9
	Average wage	13.8	91.4	77.6
	High wage	16.1	100.2	84.1

Source: Derived by the authors.

even the elderly who had never paid any payroll taxes during their working lives were eligible for benefits. In the United States, anyone who paid taxes for three years qualified for a full benefit, as though the worker had been contributing throughout his or her entire career. Table 3-2 shows the lifetime taxes paid and expected lifetime benefits for U.S. workers who qualified for a Social Security pension upon reaching age 65 in 1965. The value of lifetime taxes was calculated by accumulating both the employer and employee taxes paid at the interest rates at which assets in the plan were being credited – essentially a long-term government bond rate. Women's lifetime payroll tax contributions are higher than men's because the calculations take into account men's higher probability of dying before reaching retirement age. The value of expected lifetime benefits was based on the benefits paid to these individuals over their life expectancies at the time they retired, with future benefits discounted by the rate of interest accruing to the trust funds.

To the extent that expected benefits exceeded taxes paid, the system was a good economic deal for its participants. The U.S. program was a tremendous bargain – net transfers exceeded lifetime taxes by 3.4 to 8.5 times. It was a somewhat better deal for low-wage workers than for high-wage workers, because the system was redistributive. Women fared somewhat better under the system than men, because of the formers' longer life expectancy and the extra benefits that would accrue accordingly. While lower earners might have done better in relative terms than high earners, the latter could not complain because their absolute transfers were higher than those provided to their lower-earning counterparts. Although this does not appear in the table, the situation was even more advantageous for single-earner couples, because the U.S. system provides a dependent's benefit equal to 50 percent of the worker's benefit to spouses of retired workers, without requiring any extra payroll tax contributions. The questions no one was asking were: What would happen if current conditions, which were very favorable for a pay-go system, changed? What would happen if the system stopped being such a good deal for workers?

In 1958, Nobel Laureate Paul Samuelson characterized pay-go financing for retirement programs in the context of what he called the "consumption loan model."[9] Under this model, when workers pay taxes to finance the benefits for current retirees, they surrender current income they could be using to finance their own retirement. Under the life-cycle model, the money would go into an account to finance consumption after retirement. Samuelson explained that in the pay-go model, the consumption foregone by current workers is, in essence, "loaned" to current retirees. Workers are willing to extend such a loan on the condition that future workers will pay them back when it is their turn to retire.

Samuelson worked through the calculus of a national pay-go retirement system to assess how these systems compared to the traditional savings model, from the perspective of how workers fared under both systems. He calculated the return that workers received on their contributions by adding the rate of growth of real wages to the rate of growth in the covered workforce. He demonstrated that, in some cases, national pay-go retirement systems might actually be more economically efficient over the long term than funded alternatives.

A characterization of Samuelson's model is depicted in Figure 3-6.[10] In this model, each generation of workers contributes resources to retirees – i.e., loaning them some of their own current potential consumption and expecting to be repaid in kind later. In the figure, each row of X's represents a generation of adults in a hypothetical society. Those above the solid line are retirees while those below it are workers. At the end of each generation – moving from time period 1 to time period 2 in the figure – the retired population dies, the generation just below the retirement bar ages and retires, and a new generation enters the workforce. The contributions

---

[9] Paul Samuelson, "An Exact Consumption-Loan Model of Interest with or without the Social Contrivance of Money," *Journal of Political Economy* (December 1958), vol. 66, pp. 467–482.

[10] The next few paragraphs describing Samuelson's model draw directly from Sylvester J. Schieber and John B. Shoven, *The Real Deal*, pp. 109–110.

(Time period 1)

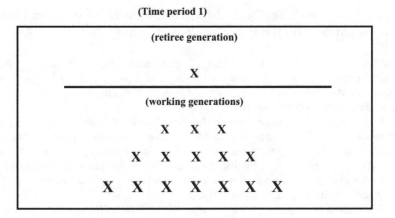

(Time period 2)

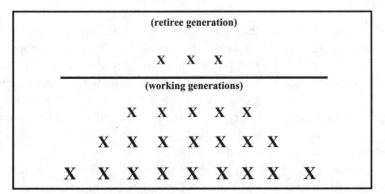

Figure 3-6. Hypothetical Population and the Operation of a Pay-Go Retirement System. *Source:* Developed by the authors.

from the working generations are mandatory and are a fixed fraction of earnings.

In this model, the population has two crucial characteristics: Each succeeding generation is larger and more productive than the last – represented in the figure by ever larger X's. Increasing productivity means that each generation of workers earns a higher wage than prior generations. With time, the aggregate size of contributions grows, because there are more workers and they earn higher taxable wages. Each generation of retirees receives more benefits from following generations than it transferred to prior generations.

In February 1967, Paul Samuelson wrote an article for *Newsweek* magazine describing how this system worked. He wrote:

The beauty of social insurance is that it is actuarially unsound. Everyone who reaches retirement age is given benefit privileges that far exceed anything he has paid in. And exceed his payments by more than ten times as much (or five times, counting in employer payments)!

How is it possible? It stems from the fact that the national product is growing at compound interest and can be expected to do so for as far ahead as the eye cannot see. Always there are more youths than old folks in a growing population. More important, with real incomes going up at some 3 percent per year, the taxable base on which benefits rest in any period are much greater than the taxes paid historically by the generation now retired.

Social security is squarely based on what has been called the eighth wonder of the world – compound interest. A growing nation is the greatest Ponzi game ever contrived.[11]

In the late 1950s and the 1960s, when Paul Samuelson developed his consumption loan model and wrote the article in *Newsweek*, the population structure in Figure 3-6 was still common in many countries around the world. In a few highly developed countries, such as Italy, Germany, and Japan, the population structures were beginning to assume a more rectangular than pyramidal shape, but it was too early in the process to seem significant from a retirement perspective. Looking 25 to 50 years ahead, however, the age structure of national populations will vary considerably from that suggested by Figure 3-6. As we discussed in Chapter 2, different countries will deviate from the general model by varying degrees.

It turns out that Samuleson's conclusion that the rate of return on pay-go pensions is the sum of labor force growth plus productivity is incorrect. Ole Settergren and Boguslaw D. Mikula of the National Social Insurance Board of Sweden use simple examples to show why. One example relates to changing wage patterns within a society. The other pertains to an unexpected change in life expectancy.

First, in the case of the wage patterns, Settergren and Mikula assume a society has two generations of workers, and each generation works two periods and then is retired for one period. They assume that there is no population growth or productivity improvement. Workers pay 25 percent of their wages to support retirees in the pay- go pension, and retirement benefits are 50 percent of average wages. In the beginning period, they assume workers in each generation are paid equal amounts: 1 unit of pay.

[11] Paul A. Samuelson, "Social Security," *Newsweek* (February 12, 1967), vol. 69, no. 7, p. 88.

So a worker pays 0.25 units in the first period of work and 0.25 units in the second period, and receives a benefit of 0.5 in retirement.

But then the wage structure changes, and now workers are paid 0.5 units of pay in their first period of work and 1.5 units in their second period. During this wage shift, a worker would pay taxes of 0.25 during the first period, because he was earning 1 unit of pay per period, and 0.375 during the second period, because he was earning 1.5 units of pay. Yet his benefit at retirement would still be only 0.5, or 50 percent of average wages. Clearly the rates of return for retirees in these two cases are different, although labor force growth and productivity growth remain the same over the two periods. Settergren and Mikula conclude that Samuelson's conclusion does not hold if wage structures are changing, assuming everything else is constant.[12] There is strong empirical evidence that wage structures do change over time, especially in response to significant demographic swings such as the post-World War II baby boom generations in a number of developed economies.[13]

In their second example, Settergren and Mikula revert to the original assumptions about wage structure in the society but assume that life expectancy suddenly increases from one period to two. The first cohort affected by this will receive a pension benefit of 0.5 during their first period of retirement and a pension of 0.25 during the second period. This latter adjustment has to be made so the benefits paid out by the retirement system still match the contributions paid into the system. The generation prior to the shift receives a lifetime benefit of 0.5 units of pay on lifetime contributions of 0.5 units of pay. The shift generation receives a benefit of 0.75 units of pay on contributions of 0.5, and the generation after the shift reverts to benefits of 0.5 units of pay. Once again, the returns for the various cohorts have to vary.[14]

New Realities Spur New Considerations on Pension Choices

Despite these later criticisms of Samuleson's work, his conclusions were widely embraced and he demonstrated that the relative efficiency of funded versus pay-go retirement systems depends on a host of demographic and economic variables. It is our changing demographic outlook

[12] Ole Settergren and Boguslaw D. Mikula, "The Rate of Return of Pay As You Go Pension Systems," mimeo, The National Social Insurance Board of Sweden, September 2003.

[13] Diane J. Macunovich, *Birth Quake: The Baby Boom and Its Aftershocks* (Chicago: University of Chicago Press, 2002).

[14] Op. cit., Settergren and Mikula.

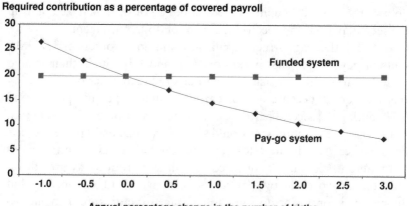

Required contribution as a percentage of covered payroll

Annual percentage change in the number of births

Figure 3-7. Contribution Rates Required to Finance Hypothetical Retirement Systems under Alternative Assumptions about the Rate of Change in Births. *Source:* Derived by the authors based on Lawrence Thompson, *The Economics of Public Pensions* (Washington, D.C.: The Urban Institute, 1998).

that has prompted concerns about the pay-go approach for national retirement system financing. We can use the simple model described earlier in this chapter to show the sensitivity of retirement program costs to various demographic and economic variables under alternative approaches to system financing.

Demographics and the Efficiency of Alternative Pension Systems
Our earlier discussion showed that, under certain assumptions, a mature pension system paying benefits equal to 50 percent of preretirement wages could be financed by either a funded or pay-go approach at an equivalent cost – in our example it was 19.77 percent of payroll. Figure 3-7 shows how the costs of the two systems vary under alternative assumptions about birth rates. Given the other assumptions used here, the funded system will be cheaper over time in a society whose population is contracting. The pay-go system will be cheaper when the population is growing. These assumptions, however, ignore changes in the rate of return on contributions that might arise because of variations in population growth rates. We will return to these issues later.

In Chapter 2, we identified a number of countries facing the prospect of declining populations over the coming decades, including Hungary, Italy, Japan, and Spain. In two-thirds of the countries around the world, fertility rates were below population replacement levels at the end of the twentieth century. Over the next quarter century, population growth

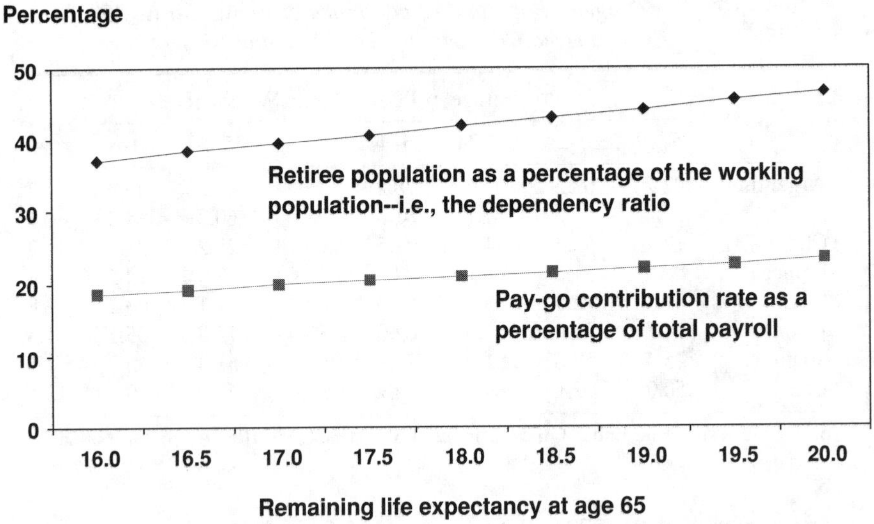

Percentage

Figure 3-8. Dependency Ratios and Contribution Rates Required to Finance a Hypothetical Pay-go Retirement System for Varying Life Expectancies. *Source:* Derived by the authors based on Lawrence Thompson, *The Economics of Public Pensions* (Washington, D.C.: The Urban Institute, 1998).

in most developed countries will result from immigration and longer life expectancies. The factor that directly links the costs of a pay-go retirement plan to birth rates is the dependency ratio. Funded systems are not affected by variations in the birth rate in this simplified model, but they are affected by other factors driving the dependency ratio. For example, in Figure 3-8, we plot dependency ratios and contribution rate requirements under our hypothetical pay-go retirement system as outlined earlier, except that we vary life expectancy during retirement.

Increasing life expectancy drives up dependency rates and directly affects the costs of pay-go retirement systems, and in this case, has an identical effect on funded systems. For a funded plan, it is not the dependency ratio itself that drives up costs, but rather the need to accumulate a larger fund to pay out benefits over a longer period. Even though the linkage is different in the two types of plans, the outcome is identical under our baseline assumptions.

Labor Supply Patterns and the Efficiency of Alternative Pension Systems

Labor force participation rates are another factor driving dependency ratios and pay- go pension costs. Our baseline model assumed that everyone

Table 3-3. *Percentage of Population Economically Active during 2001 for Selected Countries by Age of People*

	Percentage of People in the Workforce							
	15–19	20–24	25–34	35–44	45–54	55–59	60–64	65+
Argentina	22.7	63.2	77.6	78.2	73.8	63.2	46.9	22.7
Australia	59.4	81.8	81.1	81.6	79.0	60.7	34.3	6.1
Chile	12.7	53.2	71.7	71.5	69.1	28.2	43.3	14.3
France	8.7	51.2	86.1	87.8	84.6	58.9	14.5	1.3
Germany	31.5	72.5	83.9	88.0	84.4	67.1	23.2	2.8
Japan	17.7	71.9	81.0	82.0	83.4	75.8	55.1	21.8
Spain	25.4	59.7	81.0	77.9	68.5	51.3	30.9	1.6
U.S.	50.0	77.1	84.0	84.7	82.3	69.1	49.1	13.1

Source: International Labor Office, Bureau of Statistics, LABORSTA database on labor statistics.

begins working at age 22 and retires at age 65. This simplifying assumption helps to sort out how changing birth rates affect retirement plan costs under alternative approaches, but the extent to which actual behavior varies from the assumption may make cross-national comparisons of alternative retirement plan structures difficult to interpret. For example, Table 3-3 shows labor force participation rates during 2001, broken out by age group in several countries at various stages of economic development. If these percentages remain relatively constant over time, variations in birth rates would be a good long-term indicator of dependency ratios. However, the labor force behavior of particular groups within a population can change markedly over time. Certainly the labor force participation rates of older people have declined significantly in recent decades, and there is no reason they could not return to previous levels in the future. The changing labor force patterns of women in the United States over the last 50 years are a good example of a group that has significantly increased its workforce participation.

In 1950, 34 percent of the women in the United States between the ages of 25 and 34 were in the workforce, compared to 96 percent of the men in that age group. The difference in male and female labor force participation rates at that time is shown by the distance between the top and bottom lines in the left panel of Figure 3-9. In 2000, 93.4 percent of males between the ages of 25 and 34 were in the labor force, as were 76.3 percent of their female counterparts. The differences in the labor force participation rates of men and women, which had been 60 percentage points across the prime working ages in the United States at mid-century, had shrunk to roughly

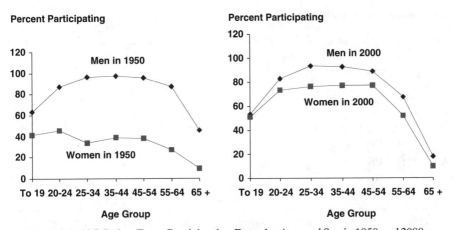

Figure 3-9. U.S. Labor Force Participation Rates by Age and Sex in 1950 and 2000. *Sources:* U.S. Department of Labor, Bureau of Labor Statistics, *Handbook of Labor Statistics* (Washington, D.C.: Department of Labor, August 1989), Bulletin 2340, pp. 13, 14, 19, and 20, and *Employment and Earnings* (January 2001), p. 168.

17 percentage points at its end. In labor supply terms, women had become similar to men over their life cycles. Comparable changes in the labor force participation of women have occurred elsewhere around the world.

When a group increases its labor force activity over time, it has a depressing effect on retirement system dependency ratios. Such changes tend to reduce the cost of pay-go retirement systems during the transition from relatively low participation rates to higher rates. Eventually, however, workers become retirees and most contributory retirement systems pay somewhat higher benefits to workers than to their non-working dependents. In the United States, non-working spouses receive 50 percent of their working spouse's benefit, if both are taken at normal retirement age. In the future, most retired women in the United States will receive higher social security benefits than they have in the past, because they will be receiving retired workers' benefits rather than dependent spouses' benefits. This will drive up the second of the ratios in Equation (2) in Figure 3-2, the ratio of average benefits to average wages on which the payroll tax is based.

The declining labor force participation rates of older people, especially men, across a broad range of countries has been dramatic in recent decades. For several of the highly developed nations, Figure 3-10 shows the labor force participation rates of men ages 60 to 64 from the 1960s through the mid-1990s. In France and Italy today, more than half of

Percentage in the labor force

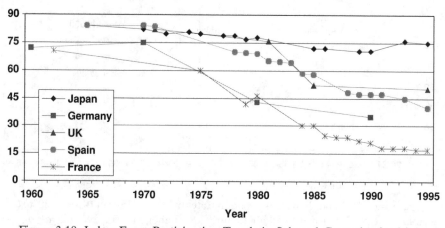

Figure 3-10. Labor Force Participation Trends in Selected Countries for Men Aged 60 to 64. *Source:* Jonathan Gruber and David A. Wise, "Introduction and Summary," in Jonathan Gruber and David A. Wise, eds., *Social Security and Retirement around the World* (Chicago: University of Chicago Press, 1999).

59-year-old men are retired; it is nearly half in the Netherlands. In the United Kingdom, Germany, Spain, and Canada, more than one-third of 59-year-old men are retired. In Sweden and the United States, 25 percent of men this age have left the workforce.[15] Early retirement patterns increase dependency ratios in two ways: They reduce the denominator and increase the numerator.

In many countries, the labor force participation rates of women in their late 50s and early 60s have been rising in recent decades. But this is a temporary phenomenon, which relates to the increasing labor force participation rates of women generally. There is no reason to believe that women will not eventually follow the same retirement patterns as men, since they increasingly follow the same traditional career patterns. Combined with the other demographic variables at play, Figure 3-9 portends a slowdown in future workforce growth.

In many developed countries, the birth cohorts entering the workforce in recent years have not assumed the pyramidal shape that is one of Samuelson's conditions for pay-go social security systems to provide

---

[15] Jonathan Gruber and David A. Wise, "Introduction and Summary," in Jonathan Gruber and David A. Wise, eds., *Social Security and Retirement around the World* (Chicago: University of Chicago Press, 1999).

Table 3-4. *Historical Labor Force Growth Rates and the Growth Rate of Populations between Ages 20 and 59 Projected from 2000 to 2030 in Various Countries*

	1970s	1980s	1990s	2000–2030
	(Compound annual growth rate during period in percents)			
Argentina	1.38	1.32	2.94	1.18
Australia	2.21	2.34	1.39	0.41
Brazil	4.26	3.21	3.21	0.97
Canada	3.46	1.89	1.29	0.14
Chile	2.55	2.7	2.13	0.86
China	2.47	2.24	1.74	0.16
Egypt	4.36	2.47	2.05	1.94
France	0.98	0.35	0.65	−0.26
Germany	0.56	0.63	0.34	−0.75
Hungary	−0.69	−0.78	−0.63	−0.76
India	2.99	1.89	2.33	1.62
Ireland	1.14	0.41	3.15	0.64
Italy	0.67	0.77	0.19	−1.12
Japan	0.72	1.14	0.49	−0.77
Malaysia	3.55	2.85	2.95	1.66
Mexico	4.18	3.51	5.33	1.35
Netherlands	1.62	2.03	1.59	−0.47
Poland	0.72	0.11	0.31	−0.39
South Africa	2.31	2.56	2.62	0.23
Spain	1.56	1.26	1.70	−0.87
Sweden	1.18	0.97	−0.25	−0.56
Switzerland	0.42	1.54	1.42	−1.13
United Kingdom	0.52	0.62	−0.63	−0.37
United States	2.31	1.35	1.41	0.42

Sources: Data for the 1970s and 1980s are from *World Development Indicators* 1998 CD-ROM, World Bank; for the 1990s they are from the International Labor Office, Bureau of Statistics, LABORSTA database on labor statistics; projections are from the United Nations, Population Division, *World Population Prospect* (2000 Revision).

decent rates of return for current and future workers. As we showed in Chapter 2, in many countries, younger cohorts are no larger than older ones. In countries like Germany, Italy, Japan, and Spain, birth cohorts born over the past 20 years are considerably smaller than those born earlier. The stabilization or declines in birth levels portend a stabilization or decline in workforces.

This has already begun happening in many countries, as shown in Table 3-4. The first three columns in the table show the labor force growth in our study countries during the 1970s, 1980s, and 1990s. In most of those countries, labor force growth rates have been significantly lower than they were just two decades ago. The right-hand column in the table shows the projected growth rates in these countries for people ages 20 through 59, the age group that makes up most of the workforce. Several of the highly developed countries are actually projecting a decline in their working-age population, suggesting that pay-go retirement systems will become much more expensive. The most rapid growth in the global workforce over the next 25 years will be in the developing nations.

Until now, the steadily increasing labor force participation rates of women have helped to offset the effects of the slowdown in birth rates in some countries. But looking toward 2030, continuing birth rates below population-replacement level will further shrink national workforces. Growing labor force participation rates of women may continue to offset that for a while, but in countries like the United States, there is little room for further increases. Participation rates for women today are approaching those of their male counterparts at various ages, and there are likely to always be some number of people, such as homemakers, who are never formally employed.

As the above discussion makes clear, a number of variables will determine future dependency ratios under national social insurance systems. We have sorted out the implications of population aging by holding all other variables constant, and present the results in Table 3-5. Our estimates assume that economically inactive people over age 60 in 2000 were retired. The dependency percentage for 2000 is this estimated number of retirees divided by the number of workers. In developing our projections, we assumed that the percentage of each age group that was economically active in 2000 would remain economically active, and that the percentage of the population over age 60 who were economically inactive in 2000 would remain economically inactive. We applied all relevant age-group labor force participation and retirement rates to future estimates of population compositions derived from the same U.N. population projections used in previous chapters. The results suggest that dependency ratios will increase universally. More women joining the workforce and more older workers delaying retirement could help to ameliorate this development in some cases, but will not change the overall outlook. For countries running pay-go retirement systems today, evolving demographics strongly predict much higher costs tomorrow.

Dependency ratio increases of similar magnitudes will not necessarily impose the same pressures on all economies. For example, the projected increases in retiree dependency for Germany and China are quite similar.

Table 3-5. *Estimated Retiree Populations as a Percentage of Workers Historically and Projected for Selected Years*

	Retiree to Worker Dependency Ratios			Percentage Increase from
	2000	2010	2030	2000–2030
Argentina	24.6	25.2	30.5	24.0
Australia	28.0	32.6	49.2	75.6
Brazil	10.5	12.5	22.3	113.6
Canada	27.3	32.4	54.7	99.9
Chile	20.2	24.0	39.2	94.0
China	12.3	14.2	29.5	140.5
Egypt	15.6	16.0	26.4	69.6
France	44.1	50.1	73.9	67.6
Germany	43.4	49.1	79.5	83.3
Hungary	46.1	51.5	71.7	55.4
India	11.6	12.6	18.8	61.7
Ireland	28.1	30.3	42.9	52.9
Italy	53.9	62.7	100.4	86.4
Japan	30.0	41.2	58.3	94.5
Malaysia	13.8	16.5	29.4	112.7
Mexico	10.6	12.5	21.7	105.0
Netherlands	32.9	40.5	67.5	104.9
Poland	32.2	34.5	55.7	73.2
South Africa	11.3	14.2	22.1	95.7
Spain	44.7	49.6	82.3	84.0
Sweden	39.9	46.2	67.4	69.1
Switzerland	23.7	30.8	47.5	100.2
United Kingdom	25.8	28.9	41.3	60.0
United States	24.5	26.6	42.0	71.4

Sources: Projections are computations by the authors based on data from the International Labor Office, Bureau of Statistics, LABORSTA database on labor statistics, projections are from the United Nations, Population Division, *World Population Prospect* (2000 Revision).

But it will take China until 2030 to reach the dependency ratio in Germany today. Indeed, most of the developing countries in our study group will not catch up to most developed European economies until well after 2030. By then, the aged dependency rates projected for Italy and Spain could require each worker to finance retirement benefits for at least one retiree and possibly more. Germany and Canada are projected to be close behind. Undoubtedly, other factors will influence labor force behavior and retiree dependency. But demographics in the developed countries have decidedly turned against pay-go retirement financing.

The demographic outlook for the less developed countries is not nearly as alarming as it is for the developed economies. But in 25 years or so, countries like Mexico will have demographic profiles similar to those in the developed economies today, and it would make sense for these countries to get ahead of the pension funding curve while demographics are still on their side. This is especially true given the time required to fund a pension system to the point where it can provide sufficient benefits.

Interest Rates and Wage Growth and the Efficiency of Alternative Pension Systems

Two important economic variables affect the relative costs of pay-go versus funded retirement plans: returns to capital and the rate of growth of wages. Each rate is important in its own right, but it is their interaction that ultimately determines the relative cost of pay-go versus funded systems over time.

The return on capital or interest rate is immaterial for a pay-go system, because there are essentially no funds to earn returns. A small contingency fund could be affected by the interest rate, but the typical contingency fund is so small that the interest rate effects are minimal. For funded plans, the higher the returns, the greater the economic horsepower provided by funding, and the lower the contributions required from workers.

Observers of national retirement systems often fail to realize that many of the plans were originally intended to be funded, usually by some form of government bonds. Table 3-6 shows the bond rates in a number of our study countries during the 1950s, 1960s, and the 1990s. Leaving out India, Malaysia, and South Africa, seven of the 13 remaining countries had negative real rates of return over the 1960s. In these same 13 countries, real bond returns were positive during the 1990s, and in 12 of them, real returns exceeded 5 percent per year.

Using the model described earlier, the funded retirement plan we described in our baseline example would cost 19.77 percent of pay at a zero real interest rate. While we generally think of interest earnings on assets in positive terms, many countries were facing negative real rates of return on national retirement plan assets during the 1950s and 1960s. Under our simple model, dropping the rate of return on assets from 0.0 to −1.0, holding everything else constant, would require a contribution rate of 26.55 percent of covered earnings for the funded retirement plan, up from 19.77 percent. The negative rates of return on the assets typically held by most national retirement systems during the first couple of decades after World War II help to explain the appeal of pay-go financing. But the same plan

Table 3-6. *Nominal and Real Bond Returns for Selected Countries and Selected Periods (Amounts in table reported as percent per year)*

	1951–1960			1961–1970			1990–2000		
	Nominal Bond Returns	Price Index	Real Bond Returns	Nominal Bond Returns	Price Index	Real Bond Returns	Nominal Bond Returns	Price Index	Real Bond Returns
Australia	3.10	5.59	-2.49	4.51	2.63	1.88	13.18	2.16	11.02
Canada	2.14	1.96	0.18	3.62	2.61	1.01	11.69	1.93	9.76
France	5.80	5.20	0.60	4.29	4.10	0.19	11.27	1.67	9.61
Germany	5.30	2.61	2.69	5.60	2.68	2.92	9.56	2.19	7.36
India	2.06	1.36	0.70	4.20	24.74	-20.55	10.66	8.40	2.26
Ireland	3.34	3.78	-0.44	0.04	5.01	-4.97	11.19	2.68	8.51
Italy	3.34	2.66	0.68	0.04	3.89	-3.85	11.19	3.56	7.63
Japan	4.21	3.32	0.89	12.04	5.96	6.08	7.40	0.83	6.56
Malaysia				5.81	0.96	4.85	9.21	3.62	5.59
Netherlands	3.64	2.88	0.76	3.34	4.47	-1.13	8.39	2.41	5.97
South Africa	3.28	3.10	0.18	4.90	2.87	2.04	17.83	8.52	9.30
Spain	5.40	4.68	0.72	4.78	6.40	-1.62	11.33	3.78	7.55
Sweden	2.50	4.51	-2.00	3.76	4.27	-0.51	11.31	2.07	9.24
Switzerland	2.99	1.40	1.60	2.94	3.59	-0.65	6.08	1.75	4.32
U.K.	3.30	3.93	-0.62	5.02	4.27	0.75	10.10	2.86	7.24
U.S.	1.86	3.93	-2.06	2.35	4.27	-1.92	8.93	2.86	6.08

Source: Global Financial Data, *Stocks, Bills, Bonds and Inflation: Total International Investment Returns, 1994–1995 [in paper we had 1995–2003]*, at http://www.globalfindata.com/march1/htm.

that would cost 26.55 percent of pay at a −1.0 percent return would cost only 10.64 percent of pay at a real interest rate of 2.0 percent per year, and only 5.53 percent of pay at a real interest rate of 4.0 percent per year. The relatively high rates of return on financial assets toward the end of the twentieth century help to explain the new interest in funded systems around the world today.

Pay-go retirement systems tend to be insensitive to changing wage rates because they are generally structured to directly link wages and benefits across time, so the ratio of benefits to wages remains relatively constant, assuming stable labor force participation patterns. One notable exception in recent years has been Great Britain, whose national basic pension benefits are expected to fall over time relative to workers' wage levels and GDP. But even in this case, the "State Second Pension/State Earning-Related Pension" and the pension credits for those contracted out of the second level system are rising, so total expenditures are expected to grow from 5.0 percent of GDP today to 5.7 percent of GDP 40 years from now.[16] Funded retirement plans are much more sensitive to wage growth rates than pay-go plans. Higher real wage growth means higher final pay, which raises replacement pay levels and thus requires greater funding.

Under the baseline simulation from above, a funded plan that costs 19.77 percent of pay at zero percent real wage growth will cost 26.21 percent of pay with 1.0 percent real wage growth per year, assuming that other variables affecting cost remain constant. The same plan would cost 34.23 percent with 2.0 percent real wage growth. Within this context, it is important to consider the structure of national retirement systems in light of workers' wages over time. Although we could not locate reliable data on actual wage growth rates dating back over the past half century, we did find estimates of the growth in labor productivity dating back to the 1960s across most of the countries we have been tracking. These labor productivity growth estimates are a good proxy for wage growth rates in these countries, especially in the market-based economies. The overall pattern of changes in productivity over the last half of the twentieth century among the developed countries is probably best summarized by the median rates of increase in productivity shown at the bottom of Table 3-7. Since the 1960s, productivity growth rates have been mixed. In several of the most rapidly aging countries, such as Italy, Japan, Spain, and Switzerland, they have declined steadily over the period. The medians in

---

[16] See http://www.dwp.gov.uk/asd/asd4/Table3_Long_Term_Projections.xls.

Table 3-7. *Historical Compound Annual Growth Rates in Real Gross Domestic Product per Worker for Selected Periods in Various Countries*

	1960s	1970s	1980s	1990s
	(Compound annual growth rate during period in percents)			
Argentina	2.43	1.57	−2.81	2.41
Australia	2.65	0.89	0.68	2.11
Brazil	2.91	4.86	−1.63	0.71
Canada		0.77	0.86	1.63
Chile	2.58	0.28	1.04	4.20
China	1.70	3.65	6.89	8.81
Egypt	3.03	4.39	2.91	1.38
France	4.61	2.31	2.11	1.07
Germany			1.55	1.43
Hungary	5.18	5.40	1.93	0.53
India	2.08	0.72	3.85	3.16
Ireland	4.15	3.54	3.21	5.07
Italy	5.54	2.92	1.48	1.02
Japan	8.54	3.71	2.92	0.78
Malaysia	3.51	4.13	2.87	3.90
Mexico	3.60	2.60	−1.50	0.66
Netherlands	3.58	1.28	0.22	2.18
Poland				3.04
South Africa	3.82	1.16	−1.45	−0.49
Spain	6.56	2.69	1.65	1.39
Sweden	3.24	0.78	1.19	1.41
Switzerland	3.04	0.84	0.50	0.04
United Kingdom	2.27	1.41	2.07	2.01
United States	2.10	0.88	1.82	1.79
Median for the developed countries*	3.41	1.41	1.34	1.40

* The medians do not include Argentina, Brazil, Chile, China, Egypt, Hungary, India, Malaysia, Mexico, Poland, or South Africa.

Source: World Bank, *World Development Indicators.*

the developed countries dropped after the 1960s and have hovered fairly steadily around the 1.35 to 1.40 level since then.

Since rising interest returns drive down the cost of funded retirement plans, and rising wages drive up their cost, it is the interaction of the two that ultimately determines cost. Using the simplified model described earlier, the relationship between pay-go and funded plan costs are shown across a range of differences in interest rates and wage growth rates in Figure 3-11, assuming a zero interest rate throughout. In this formulation, when wage growth exceeds interest rates, the pay-go system is cheaper.

Required contribution as a percentage of covered payroll

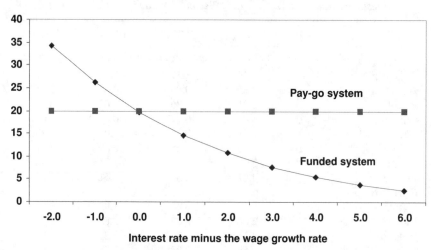

Figure 3-11. Contribution Rates Required to Finance Hypothetical Retirement Systems under Alternative Assumptions about the Excess of Interest Rates Over Wage Growth. *Source:* Derived by the authors based on Lawrence Thompson, *The Economics of Public Pensions* (Washington, D.C.: The Urban Institute, 1998).

Where interest rates exceed wage growth rates, the funded system is more economical. The cost of the funded system is slightly sensitive to variations in the interest rate assumptions, but the difference is minimal over a significant range of interest rate assumptions.

The median real rate of return on bonds for the 1960s for the developed economies in Table 3-5 was −0.51 percent per year. The median rate of increase in productivity – a proxy for wage growth – for the decade was 3.41 percent per year. Subtracting the wage-growth indicator from the real interest rate yields a net difference of −4.04 percent. Repeating the same exercise for the 1990s results in a net difference of approximately +6.15 percent. The pendulum has swung from an economic environment strongly favoring pay-go financing at mid-century to one strongly favoring funded retirement options today.

Aging Populations in the Context of Total Economic Dependency

Some analysts argue that growing aged dependency may be offset to a considerable degree by declining dependency by the young. This may be true to a limited extent, but the economic implications are very different for aged dependency versus youth dependency. Ignoring for now differences in how various age groups' consumption is financed, the economic burden for a worker supporting a young dependent is not qualitatively different than that of supporting an elderly one. In this context, the concept of dependency goes beyond looking at the young or the old, but rather looks at the working population producing the goods and services in comparison to the total consuming population. We go into more detail later, but here we explore the concept of total dependency versus aged dependency, and the timing differences that countries with alterative age structures will face in dealing with it.

Table 3-8 shows crude aged and total dependency ratios for 2000 and projected ratios for 2030. In this case, the youth dependency ratio, which is not shown in the table, was derived by dividing the population under age 20 by the total population ages 20 to 64 in each country. The aged dependency ratio is the ratio of the population age 65 and over divided by the total population ages 20 to 64. The total dependency ratio is the sum of the youth and aged dependency ratios. The two right-hand columns in Table 3-7 show the projected percentage change in both ratios over the period. In every case, the expected increase in the aged dependency ratio is significantly larger than the expected change in the total dependency ratio. In several of the less developed countries, total dependency is expected to fall over the next two or three decades, assuming fertility rates continue to decline as expected. The scenario conveyed by the right-hand column of Table 3-8 would be significantly different from that conveyed by the changes expected in the aged dependency ratios.

There is considerable evidence that in most developed societies, the average retired elderly person has somewhat higher levels of consumption than the average child. Thai Than Dang, Pablo Antolin, and Howard Oxley analyzed the implications of population aging on a number of the OECD economies and, in doing so, estimated the public expenditures on programs for the elderly and youth.[17] They had complete data for 10 countries on expenditures for publicly financed pensions, health care, and long-term care for the elderly, and child-family benefits including education. The relative level of public expenditures for the elderly and youth in these countries can be derived by comparing the separate estimates. But to understand the context of that spending, one must compare the relative spending levels to the relative size of the elderly and youth populations

---

[17] Thai Than Dang, Pablo Antolin, and Howard Oxley, *Fiscal Implications of Ageing: Projections of Age-Related Spending* (Paris: OECD, update of September 2001 report, forthcoming).

Table 3-8. *Crude Aged and Total Dependency Ratios for Selected Countries and Percent Change in Them from 2000 to 2030*

	2000 Dependency Ratios		2030 Dependency Ratios		Percent Change 2000–2030	
	Aged	Total	Aged	Total	Aged	Total
Australia	0.204	0.663	0.357	0.773	75.2	16.6
Austria	0.251	0.616	0.497	0.779	97.6	26.4
Brazil	0.092	0.790	0.204	0.688	121.2	−12.9
Canada	0.205	0.624	0.411	0.796	100.9	27.7
Chile	0.128	0.787	0.256	0.757	100.0	−3.8
China	0.114	0.656	0.260	0.649	128.7	−1.0
Egypt	0.084	1.024	0.144	0.651	71.8	−36.4
France	0.272	0.704	0.439	0.842	61.4	19.6
Germany	0.263	0.601	0.498	0.799	89.7	32.9
Hungary	0.236	0.614	0.359	0.653	51.8	6.3
Iceland	0.203	0.740	0.355	0.786	75.2	6.2
India	0.096	0.940	0.157	0.648	62.9	−31.1
Ireland	0.195	0.719	0.295	0.747	51.5	3.9
Italy	0.290	0.604	0.506	0.771	74.6	27.6
Japan	0.276	0.607	0.560	0.864	102.8	42.3
Korea	0.111	0.564	0.341	0.704	208.5	25.0
Malaysia	0.080	0.936	0.176	0.686	119.6	−26.7
Mexico	0.091	0.927	0.182	0.674	99.9	−27.3
Netherlands	0.219	0.605	0.430	0.776	96.1	28.1
Poland	0.202	0.667	0.362	0.690	79.1	3.4
South Africa	0.069	0.939	0.145	0.790	110.3	−15.8
Spain	0.274	0.616	0.452	0.706	65.0	14.6
Sweden	0.297	0.704	0.496	0.835	67.0	18.6
Switzerland	0.259	0.616	0.571	0.891	120.9	44.6
Turkey	0.107	0.851	0.185	0.666	72.8	−21.7
United Kingdom	0.267	0.693	0.440	0.809	65.1	16.7
United States	0.208	0.695	0.365	0.808	75.0	16.3

Source: United Nations, Population Division, *World Population Prospects* (2000 Revision).

in the respective countries. In developing this comparison, we considered youth to include everyone younger than age 20 and the elderly to include everyone age 65 and older.

Table 3-9 shows the relative spending on the elderly and youth as a percentage of GDP during 2000 in the 10 countries. It also shows the relative size of the two populations in each country in 2000, based on the United Nations' demographic profiles. The third column from the right is the ratio of public expenditures on benefits for the elderly to

Table 3-9. *Relative Public Expenditures as a Percentage of GDP for the Elderly and Youth Populations, Relative Size of the Respective Populations, and Relative per Capita Public Expenditures during 2000 for Selected Countries*

	Expenditures as Percentage of GDP for:		Millions of People Ages:		Ratio of Elderly to Youth Estimates for:		Ratio of per Capita Expenditures for Elderly to Youth
	Elderly	Youth	65 & Up	0 to 19	Expenditures	People	
Australia	16.7	6.1	2,346	5,283	2.738	0.444	6.17
Belgium	22.1	6.0	1,744	2,381	3.683	0.732	5.03
Canada	17.9	6.4	3,875	7,939	2.797	0.488	5.73
Czech	23.1	6.0	1,421	2,379	3.850	0.597	6.45
Denmark	29.3	6.3	798	1,246	4.651	0.640	7.27
Netherlands	19.1	5.4	2,165	3,818	3.537	0.567	6.24
New Zealand	18.7	7.2	441	1,136	2.597	0.388	6.69
Norway	17.9	5.5	687	1,146	3.255	0.600	5.43
Sweden	29.0	9.8	1,541	2,111	2.959	0.730	4.05
United Kingdom	15.6	5.7	9,359	14,963	2.737	0.625	4.38
United States	11.2	3.9	34,831	81,294	2.872	0.428	6.70

Sources: Thai Than Dang, Pablo Antolin, and Howard Oxley, *Fiscal Implications of Aging: Projections of Age-Related Spending* (Paris: OECD, 2003), p. 27, United Nations Population Division, *World Population Prospect* (2000 Revision), and calculations by the authors.

those for the youth. The second column from the right is the ratio of the number of people age 65 and older to the number under age 20. The right-hand column is the ratio of these two ratios and should approximate the relative public expenditures per elderly person compared to those for youth. Public expenditures are clearly much larger for the elderly than for the youth in these countries.

Public expenditures are only part of the picture. Much of the elderly's consumption is financed through retirement plans, whereas the consumption for youth is financed, to a much greater extent, through private transfers from parents. If people are having fewer children than in the past, then the level of support needed to provide for children's consumption should decline, too, potentially freeing up resources that could support the elderly without penalizing those in the workforce.

Edward Lazear and Robert Michael developed an empirically based equivalence scale, so that nominal income in one consumer unit can be converted to its equivalent in another consumer unit of different composition. The underlying assumption is that it does not take twice the income for a couple to achieve the same standard of living as a single person. One furnace or refrigerator will suffice for the two-person unit, for example, and the lamp in a common living area sheds as much light on two people as it does on one.[18] Lazear and Michael's empirical estimates differentiated between adults and minors, the latter being those younger than age 18. They assumed that the non-medical consumption needs of all adults were equivalent after having controlled for living arrangements. They estimated that the needs of a couple living with a minor child were 22 percent greater than those of a couple living by themselves, or 44 percent greater than the needs of each adult in the couple.[19]

David Cutler, James Poterba, Louise Sheiner, and Lawrence Summers extended the Lazear and Michael results by considering public expenditures on education and health care. They derived a total consumption equivalence measure for youth, non-elderly adults, and the elderly. They considered youth to be under age 20, non-elderly adults to be ages 20 to 64, and the elderly to be age 65 and older. Setting the consumption needs of the non-elderly adults at 1.00, the equivalence for the youth was 0.72 and for the elderly was 1.27. The youth factor was higher than Lazear's and Michael's because of the concentration of education

---

[18] Edward P. Lazear and Robert T. Michael, "Family Size and the Distribution of Real per Capita Income," *American Economic Review* (March 1980), vol. 70, pp. 91–107.

[19] Ibid, p. 102.

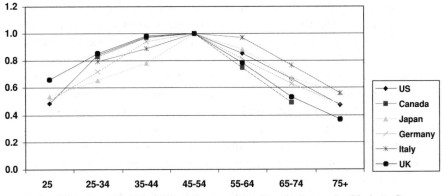

Figure 3-12. Age Profile of Total Consumption Expenditures for Various Countries (Indexed to 45–54 Age Cohort). *Source:* U.S.: Bureau of Labor Statistics, http://stats.bls.gov/cex/2000/Standard/age.pdf; Japan: Kitamura et al. (2000), Table 3, pp. 5; Italy: Brugiavini et al. (2000), Table 7, pp. 27; U.K.: Banks et al. (March 2000), pp. 63–4; Germany: Borsch-Supan et al. (2000), Table E1; Burbidge et al. (1994), Figure 1.9, pp. 39–41.

spending on youth. The elderly share was larger than the non-elderly share due to the concentration of health expenditures on the older segment of the population.[20]

The consumption equivalence measures derived by Lazear and Michael and Cutler and his colleagues were based on analysis of consumption patterns in the United States. We have been unable to find comparable measures of income equivalence for other countries. In fact, there is relatively limited consumption behavior data of any sort for most countries. The few studies that have analyzed consumption behavior across the age spectrum in the largest developed countries have found similar patterns of consumption when controlling for age. The basis of our conclusion is shown in Figure 3-12. To simplify the cross-national comparison of consumption patterns, we measured average consumption within each age group against the average consumption of people in the 45- to 54-year-old age group in their respective countries. The match across countries is not perfect, but the patterns are very similar across the major developed economies. Some major components of consumption among both the elderly and the youth groups are not reflected in Figure 3-12. Specifically,

[20] David M. Cutler, James M. Poterba, Louise M. Sheiner, and Lawrence H. Summers, "An Aging Society: Opportunity or Challenge?" in William C. Brainard and George L. Perry, eds., Brookings Papers on Economic Activity (Washington, D.C.: The Brookings Institution, 1990), p. 9.

consumption surveys of the sort that the pattern in the figure is based on would not capture public provision of education services to children or much of the publicly financed health services provided to the elderly. On the basis of the similar patterns of consumption across the countries reflected in Figure 3-12 and the comparability of retiree income to pre-retiree income explored earlier, we used the income equivalence scale developed by David Cutler and his colleagues to explore the changing level of dependency. We picked a range of countries along the spectrum of population aging, to facilitate the explanation of timing considerations that countries with varying demographic compositions will face in dealing with their aging populations.

In analyzing the combined youth and elderly dependency for the select set of countries, we took into account the difference in consumption rates for the elderly dependent population and the young dependent population in accordance with the estimates developed by Cutler and his colleagues. In developing our estimates, we considered historically reported labor force participation rates for various age groups. In some cases, we had such data back to 1960, but in others the earliest labor force participation statistics we could find were much later. In each case, we applied the earliest rates we could find back to 1950 to the population composition estimates developed by the United Nations Population Division. We treated individuals between the ages of 15 and 20 reported to be in the workforce as workers rather than as youth dependents. At the upper end of the age distribution, we assumed that people age 55 and older classified as economically inactive were actually retired. Thus some youth were considered to be workers, some working-age people were considered to be retired, and some retirement-age people were considered to be workers. We applied the labor force participation rates for the latest year we had data, 2000 in most cases, to the evolving population age structures projected by the United Nations. We calculated the total dependency ratios by adding up the consumer-adjusted, non-working youth and non-working elderly, and dividing that total by the estimated workforce in each year. We did not consider working-age individuals who were not in the workforce to be dependent. Many working-age people who are not in the formal labor force make significant economic contributions to their households that do not appear in national income accounts.

Figure 3-13 shows the dependency ratios just described for Italy, Poland, and China from 1950 through 2050. The evolving patterns in the three countries will be significantly more diverse in the coming half century than they have been over the past half century. Italy, one of the most

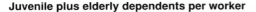

Juvenile plus elderly dependents per worker

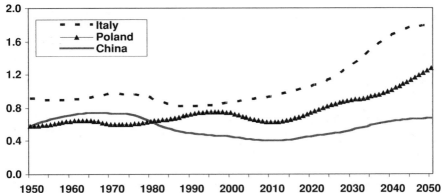

Figure 3-13. Ratio of Juvenile and Elderly Dependency Relative to Active Workers in Italy, Poland, and China for Selected Years. *Sources:* International Labor Office, Bureau of Statistics, LABORSTA database on labor statistics, United Nations Population Division, *World Population Prospect* (2000 Revision), and calculations by the authors.

rapidly aging countries in the world, will experience one of the most momentous increases in economic dependency on workers. The growth in dependency started slowly around 1990, will accelerate slightly during this decade, and is expected to accelerate significantly around 2025. By 2030, the combined youth and aged dependency in Italy will be more than 50 percent higher than it was in 2000. The U.N. demographic projections suggest that Italy's fertility rate, which was 1.2 at the end of the twentieth century, will increase moderately over the period, but most of the anticipated increase in dependency will be due to the growing elderly population. If the fertility rate does not increase as expected, the dependency path might moderate slightly from that depicted in Figure 3-13, but lower than projected birth rates could be more than offset by increased life expectancy among the elderly. While their paths might not be exactly the same as Italy's, Germany, Japan, and Spain appear to be moving down a similar trajectory.

The story in Poland is somewhat different. Poland is currently in the middle of a 20-year period of declining dependency. This occurs after a significant decline in the fertility rate but before the increase in aged dependency takes hold. In Poland, this decline in dependency is relatively moderate, with total dependency expected to decline about 12 percent between 1995 and 2015. After that, dependency will increase sharply, largely driven by increasing aged dependency, although the U.N. projections

Juvenile and elderly dependents per worker

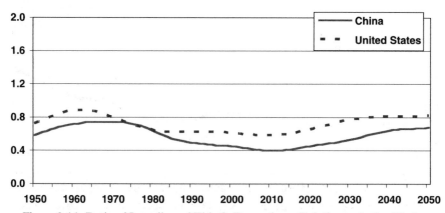

Figure 3-14. Ratio of Juvenile and Elderly Dependency Relative to Active Workers in China and the United States for Selected Years. *Sources:* International Labor Office, Bureau of Statistics, LABORSTA database on labor statistics, United Nations Population Division, *World Population Prospect* (2000 Revision), and calculations by the authors.

assume that Poland's total fertility rate will increase from 1.2 in 2010 to 2.0 by 2050. By 2030 in Poland, total dependency is expected to be 20 percent higher than it was in 2015, and to continue increasing steeply thereafter. Most of the Eastern European countries that were formerly part of the Soviet bloc are expected to follow somewhat similar patterns. Whatever else the prospect of these countries joining the EU might bring, it will do nothing to dampen the increasing levels of dependency anticipated within the Union.

China is evolving a somewhat unique pattern of total dependency for the variety of reasons laid out earlier. Its birth policy moderated dependency levels from the mid- to late 1970s. The ameliorative effects of this policy on total dependency will end over the current decade. All else holding steady, declining birth rates dampen labor force growth rates some 20 to 30 years later. In relative terms, compared to Italy and Poland in Figure 3-13, China is not expected to have the severe swings in total dependency or to experience the high rates of total dependency that many of the more developed countries will face over the coming half century. However, it would be a mistake to conclude that these significant differences between China and the developed countries of the world are universal.

Figure 3-14 compares the situation evolving in China to that in the United States. The two patterns of evolving demographic dependency are

Juvenile and elderly dependents per worker

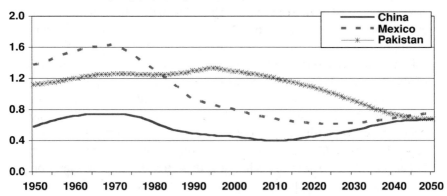

Figure 3-15. Ratio of Juvenile and Elderly Dependency Relative to Active Workers in China, Mexico, and Pakistan for Selected Years. *Sources:* International Labor Office, Bureau of Statistics, LABORSTA database on labor statistics, United Nations Population Division, *World Population Prospect* (2000 Revision), and calculations by the authors.

remarkably similar. Both countries have recently had periods of declining dependency, with the trend in the United States evolving somewhat earlier and for different reasons. Total dependency in both countries is expected to start increasing moderately around 2010 and to steadily increase over the next 30 years or so. From this perspective, it appears that China and the United States are more like each other than like many of the world's other developed countries.

In terms of evolving demographic patterns over the next 30 years, the outlook for the United States is similar to that for Canada, Australia, and New Zealand, although the relative mix of youth and elderly dependency in the four countries will be somewhat different as the U.S. fertility rate has remained higher than those in the other three countries. One significant difference between the United States and China is the relative economic position from which they will face increasing economic dependency. The United States has much higher standards of living, wealth, and worker productivity. China, on the other hand, may be able to significantly increase worker productivity as a mechanism to finance the economic burdens associated with a growing retiree population.

The last countries analyzed in this discussion are Mexico and Pakistan, whose evolving dependency patterns are shown in Figure 3-15. Once again, China is included in the figure to provide a frame of reference to the earlier country comparisons. Mexico is in the midst of a lengthy period of declining dependency, largely attributable to its reduced fertility rates over the last couple of decades. The aging of the Mexican population is not expected to reverse this trend until about 2030 or so, thus providing an opportunity for the economy to reap a demographic dividend in its pursuit of higher living standards. By 2030, however, Mexico and a number of similarly situated countries will follow the path of aging dependency that many of their more developed counterparts will begin much sooner. These countries include many of those in Latin America and some Asian countries where fertility rates have fallen significantly during the last couple of decades. In Cuba and Puerto Rico, total fertility rates have already fallen below 2.0 and are still declining. If these trends continue, their population structures over the next 30 years or so may become similar to those in much of Europe today. Like China, these countries face the challenge of increasing productivity and living standards before significant population aging sets in, so they can deal with increasing dependency from a position of greater economic strength. One possible means to this end, as explored later, is for the developed economies to supply capital to help these countries grow their economies.

In Pakistan, dependency is projected to decline steadily over the next half century or so, largely driven by declining fertility rates. There are signs that fertility rates have begun to decline in several countries in this group, including many of the nations of Africa, and South-Central and South-Eastern Asia. Most of these countries are on the lowest rung of the development ladder today and could potentially supply labor to ameliorate the economic problems many developed countries will face for the next several decades, either through capital investment from the more developed countries or through emigration to the more developed countries. Both of these possibilities pose a number of challenges.

New Realities Raise Concerns for Policy Analysts

The conditions that Paul Samuelson laid down some 45 years ago as being more favorable for pay-go than for funded pension systems have changed or are changing. Long-term demographic trends suggest that even countries whose current conditions still favor pay-go systems will soon be in the same boat as the developed economies, although it may take some of these countries 25 or 30 years to get there.

The early phase-in of these pension systems generated tremendous economic windfalls for early participants, as shown in Table 3-2. No one

Table 3-10. *Present Value of Payroll Taxes Paid and Present Value of Expected Lifetime Benefits for Workers Retiring at Age 65 in 2005 and 2045 under the U.S. Social Security Retirement Pension*

		Lifetime Earnings	Value of Taxes	Expected Benefits	Net Transfer
Retiree age 65 in 2005					
Single male	Low wage	$75.9	$91.4	$15.5
	Average wage	168.7	153.7	−15.0
	High wage	327.1	226.7	−100.3
Single female	Low wage	78.5	124.7	46.1
	Average wage	174.5	209.7	35.2
	High wage	340.5	309.2	−31.2
Retiree age 65 in 2045 with benefit as defined by current law					
Single male	Low wage	144.0	160.4	16.4
	Average wage	308.8	269.3	−39.5
	High wage	785.6	425.5	−360.1
Single female	Low wage	147.5	198.3	50.8
	Average wage	315.0	345.8	30.8
	High wage	804.6	526.3	−278.3
Retiree age 65 in 2045 with benefit as funded under current law					
Single male	Low wage	144.0	104.9	−39.1
	Average wage	308.8	176.2	−132.6
	High wage	785.6	278.3	−507.3
Single female	Low wage	147.5	129.7	−17.8
	Average wage	315.0	226.2	−88.8
	High wage	804.6	344.2	−460.4

Source: Derived by the authors.

could expect that situation to last forever. The problem is that the pendulum is now swinging in a completely different direction.

Table 3-10 shows similar calculations to those in Table 3-2, except that the retirees are age 65 in 2005 and 2045. In the latter case, two sets of calculations have to be presented because the U.S. Social Security system is significantly underfunded for the baby boomers retirement period. The first set of calculations for 2045 simply determine benefits and contributions under current law, which will have to be amended. The second set of calculations for 2045 assume that the system has been brought back into balance by reducing benefits.

In 2005, contemporary retirees are roughly breaking even as a group. Those who earn less or live longer than average still receive slightly more than the value of their contributions. Higher earners can expect to receive less in retirement benefits than the value of what they pay into the system. For married couples, not shown in Table 3-10, both single and dual earners are still receiving a subsidy from the program.

By 2045, the prospects for workers and retirees turn decidedly negative under a realistic funding scenario. In Table 3-10, virtually all single workers would be realising smaller lifetime pension benefits than the value of their accumulated contributions. The same would be true for two-earner couples. Policymakers will eventually have to face the fact that workers and voters may not continue to support these programs when they realize what a bad bargain they have become.

In 1994, the World Bank published a landmark report, *Averting the Old Age Crisis*, which sounded alarms about the cost of population aging and drew attention to the precarious condition of many public retirement systems.[21] The study highlighted such problems as over-reliance on pay-go funding in national retirement systems, significant gaps in pension coverage, benefit structures that encouraged inefficient economic behavior, and inefficient utilization of assets in many funded plans. All these problems were examined within the context of population aging.

There were several reasons that the authors of the World Bank 1994 study were concerned about pension systems. One had to do with the growing economic "dependency" in aging societies, and the worry that swelling retiree populations could potentially swamp the pension systems in many countries. While demographics were the underlying factor that raised the alarm, another related issue was the funding structure of the pension systems and how the generosity of benefits promised could be at odds with new demographic realities. The pension systems of the mid-twentieth century had reached maturity and the outlook for their future operations was decidedly different than it had been a half century earlier.

---

[21] Estelle James et al, *Averting the Old Age Crisis: Policies to Protect the Old and Promote Growth* (New York: Oxford University Press, 1994).

FOUR

Pension Structures and the Implications of Aging

In much of the discussion about aging populations to date, the problem has been framed as being about retirement systems and the relative merits of one type of retirement system or the other. Policy analysts have focused mostly on whether our retirement systems should be funded or financed on a pay-go basis, or whether they should be run through the central government or "privatized" to some extent. Deciding whether a retirement system should be operated on a funded or pay-go basis depends on a variety of economic and demographic factors as we explored in Chapter 3.

In comparing the retirement systems from around the world today, especially the developed countries, it becomes very clear that although there are many similarities among systems, there are remarkable variations in how different countries provide income security for the elderly. It is important to understand these similarities and differences in order to appreciate why some countries seem to be better positioned to deal with their aging populations than others.

Contemporary Approaches to Providing Income Security for the Elderly

To some extent, the plans established in the early days of the social insurance movement in the late eighteenth and early nineteenth century are still operating today. But dynamic political and social environments have led to many changes in their structures. Around the world today, the government pillar tends to be made up of one or two tiers. The first tier encompasses floor benefit plans, in which a basic benefit is paid regardless of a beneficiary's lifetime earnings or contributions. The second tier is government-mandated contributory programs in which the benefit is based on retirees' earnings or contributions while working. Some countries have both tiers; others have only one or the other. Many countries also have a third tier, which consists of employer-sponsored retirement plans that are often encouraged through tax incentives or even mandated. Finally, in some countries, retirement security also depends on private savings, the importance of which largely depends on the generosity of the other tiers.

Public First Tiers in the Retirement System

A common approach to providing first-tier benefits today is through a universal retirement payment, with entitlement based on meeting citizenship or residency criterion or paying taxes for some period. Such payments were initially intended to provide a minimum income and thus offset poverty. Payments are usually determined on a flat rate basis, with the amount adjusted according to the consumer price index or other measurements of price changes. A few governments determine the annual amount of benefit payments on a discretionary basis through announcements and enabling legislation. For example, Australia has attempted to preserve the value of its old age pension by adopting measures to pay a benefit of 25 percent of male total average weekly earnings to everyone who retires after a relatively full career. Universal pensions are usually funded from consolidated national revenue sources. Although some governments are still funding this benefit as outlined above, most have started imposing income and asset tests to curtail expenditures.

In Australia, the benefit is means tested.[1] In the early 1990s, anticipating the costs to the national system that the retirement of the baby boom

---

[1] The income test is applied separately from the asset test with the rate of pension being determined by the lower benefit resulting from the application of the two separate tests. A single person under age 70 can earn up to A$112 every two weeks without having the pension reduced. For married pensioners, the two-week limit is A$200. These amounts are increased by $25 for the two-week consideration for each child in a pensioner's care. The single person's pension is reduced by A$1 for every A$2 of income earned in excess of the threshold. For married pensioners, the ratio is A$1 reduction in the pension for every A$4 of earnings over the income limit. Where the pensioner or couple own assets in excess of the limits specified under the program, the payable pension is reduced by A$3 for every A$1,000 in excess of the asset tests. For single homeowners, the asset test is A$141,000 and for couples it is A$200,500. For non-homeowners, the respective limits are A$242,000 and A$301,500.

generation would impose, Australian policymakers adopted a mandatory retirement savings program. One goal of mandating personal savings was to increase the number of people who fail the assets and income tests embedded in the basic pension provisions.

Canada has a basic pension system along with a supplementary second tier of benefits provided through the government. The Canadian Pension Plan (CPP) is financed by a payroll tax and benefits are based on a worker's lifetime of covered earnings. As in Australia, higher-income retirees are subjected to a means test on their basic pension, but for Canadian retirees, the basic benefit is reduced via an assessment through the income taxation system as other retirement income increases.

Some countries continue providing their first-tier benefit in the form of universal demogrants with no means testing. These are simply fixed benefit payments to individuals who reach a predefined retirement age. Rather than being subject to an explicit income or assets test, retirees must satisfy certain contribution conditions in order to receive a full pension. In the United Kingdom, all workers who have made National Insurance Contributions (NICs) for approximately nine-tenths of a full working life will receive a full pension. For the typical British worker, a flat-rate contributory benefit is paid once a man reaches the state pension age of 65. For women, the pension age is 60. Like Canada, Great Britain has a government-provided, second tier pension system, although its workers can "contract out" of the public program if they participate in a private alternative. Most workers have taken advantage of this opportunity and gain their second tier of coverage through employer-sponsored retirement plans or individual pensions.

Another type of first-tier benefit is the sort of welfare safety net that the United States provides through its Supplemental Security Income (SSI) program. In 1974, SSI merged programs for the aged, blind, and disabled that had been previously run at the state level with some federal funding. This program is supported by general tax revenues. Today, the Social Security Administration manages the program. Monthly checks are paid to people who are 65 or older, blind or have a disability, and whose asset and income levels demonstrate a need for government assistance. Further assistance is often provided to SSI recipients on a state and county level via food stamps, health programs, or other social services. The number of people served by the program has increased significantly since its inception, with most of this growth in disability claims. This type of benefit program simply provides a means-tested, guaranteed minimum income to those who meet the program's eligibility criteria. Unlike other first-tier benefits, the purpose of these programs is to help people avoid destitution rather than to support a particular lifestyle in retirement.

Public Second Tiers in the Retirement System

The second tiers or pillars of government pensions provide benefits tied to workers' careers in terms of contributions or covered earnings. Our study identified a wide divergence of approaches in these second-tier benefit programs. Many countries currently sponsor defined benefit programs mostly financed on a pay-go basis. Most Western European nations operate defined benefit, second-tier retirement programs of this sort. The U.S. program operates largely this way, although the 1983 amendments to the system have led to some very modest prefunding. These programs are increasingly plagued by growing pension costs and liabilities as national populations age.

Contributions linked with the pay-go defined benefit programs are usually levied on both employers and employees. Since World War II, contribution rates under these plans have steadily increased. During the early years, the cost increases were largely due to benefit enhancements. Recent cost increases have been driven more by the relative change in the number of covered workers and the number of people receiving benefits. In most cases, pay-go defined benefit programs will have to either increase contributions or reduce benefits to maintain their long-term viability. This process is already underway in Germany and Japan. Italy and Sweden have also modified their benefit structures so as to automatically reduce benefits if their programs become financially unbalanced.

Some countries have shifted their retirement programs to a more fully funded basis. That is, they retain the overall benefit and contribution structures that supported pay-go systems but have adopted at least partial prefunding measures to reduce or contain costs. For example, Canada has recently increased its contribution rates to the Canadian Pension Plan (CPP) and created a separate, non-government entity, the CPP Investment Board, to invest the resulting assets in productive capital. The Investment Board aims to generate higher returns on contributions via investments in equities, both domestically and internationally, than it could realize from investing solely in government bonds. The hope is that the extra funding and relatively high returns from investing in capital will reduce long-term program costs to a sustainable level.

In recent decades, Germany has sponsored one of the more generous state pension systems. Traditionally, the program has automatically indexed benefits to increase with the rate of wage growth. As initial benefit levels have grown along with wages over time, the percentage of wages replaced by the national pension has remained relatively constant from one generation of workers to the next. During retirement, benefits continued to be indexed to wages, keeping retirees' pension income abreast of workers' increasing productivity. In addition to keeping up with improvements in workers' standards of living over the years, the German social security system has traditionally been relatively generous, linking benefits to covered wages or contributions over the working career. At the end of the twentieth century in Germany, the state-provided pension provided about 80 percent of income for a typical retiree household. The pension replaced roughly 72 percent of net preretirement income for a full-career worker and offered very generous early retirement benefits. The demographic issues that this discussion is about have recently motivated German policymakers to adopt new pension provisions that will automatically adjust benefits for retirees as the relationship between the number of workers and retirees varies. In this regard, it has adopted provisions for its defined benefit plan that are akin to what Sweden and Italy have adopted for their national pensions although the latter two countries have also restructured their systems more completely.

Australian Mandatory Superannuation: Strengths and Weaknesses

By Professor John Piggott, University of New South Wales

Although occupational pensions have been well established in the public sector for several decades in Australia, private-sector coverage has historically been patchy – in the mid-80s only about a quarter of private-sector employees enjoyed superannuation coverage. Over the last 15 years, private superannuation has become mandatory for most employees. From its origins as a requirement in negotiated wage settlements, mandatory superannuation now enjoys full legislative status. Under the "Superannuation Guarantee" (SG), employers must pay 9 percent of wages into a superannuation fund on behalf of most employees. Coverage has leapt to more than 90 percent in both the public and private sectors.

The SG conforms to a paradigm which has received favourable comment from many quarters. It is broadly consistent with the World Bank's advocacy of compulsory funded retirement provision, and with the Chilean pension model which has been used as the gold standard for Latin American pension reform. Furthermore, no transition from an unfunded system has been necessary, because no prior employment-linked social security program existed.

Viewed from the standpoint of intergenerational equity, or (equivalently) in terms of its implications for future public liability, the SG has much to recommend it. Australians have become more aware of financial markets and saving strategies, and some of this is likely due to the SG. And evidence suggests that private saving has been improved by the SG. So the advantages claimed for a privately administered funded arrangement appear to be present. But important problems remain. Many of these stem from the voluntary superannuation structure which the SG took as its starting point.

Perhaps the most important concerns decumulation. Before mandatory superannuation, lump sums were pervasive, encouraged by highly favourable tax treatment. Although various measures have been adopted to alter this "lump sum mentality," most SG accumulations are still taken in this way. This predilection is reinforced by a lack of integration between the age pension and superannuation regulations. The superannuation preservation age is 55 to 60, but age pension eligibility is set at 65. It is therefore possible to use a lump sum withdrawal to finance an early retirement, and avoid losing any age pension through the means test by depleting financial wealth before reaching 65.

Taxation of superannuation, almost entirely tax-free before the mid-80s, needed to be modified as the SG came into force. But rather than move to a simple benefits tax model, a complex superannuation tax system was introduced. Taxes are levied on contributions, earnings, and benefits, but at concessional rates which vary with the type of benefit taken and the timing of contributions.

Finally, administration costs are high. A contributing factor is the complexity of taxation and compliance. A second reason may be that the SG requires that the employer pay 9 percent, not that 9 percent be deposited into an individual account. Since the financial services contract negotiations frequently do not include employees, incentives to minimise administration charges are blunted. After contributions, taxes, and administration charges are taken out, the 9 percent contribution can easily shrink to 5 or 6 percent, not really enough for adequate retirement income replacement.

Further Reading

Hazel Bateman, Geoffrey Kingston, and John Piggott. 2001. Forced Saving: Mandating Private Retirement Incomes. Cambridge University Press.
Hazel Bateman and John Piggott. 2002. Australia's Mandatory Retirement Saving Policy: A View from the New Millennium. World Bank Pension Primer, www.worldbank.org/pensions.

Since the 1980s, a number of countries have adopted defined contribution plan structures as the primary element of their second tier. One approach that has become common in places as diverse as Australia, Chile, and Sweden is implementing individual account plans. Australia's and Chile's plans are funded and Sweden's are partially funded. These plans require contributions by employers, workers, or both, which are invested through privately managed, individual accounts. There are a range of portfolio choices, which are decided either by firms or individuals. In these plans, workers essentially fund their own retirement during their working careers. In some countries, employers select the defined contribution plan provider. In others, individuals choose from a series of authorized private fund managers. The investment risk is largely borne by the individual account holder, although some systems provide a minimum guarantee or return on funds. Upon retirement, these types of defined contribution plans often offer participants the option of withdrawing their individual account balance in the form of an annuity, lump sum, or "draw down" (allocated pension) retirement vehicle.

National provident funds (NPFs) are another defined contribution approach, which is common in Asia and parts of Africa. These plans have long operated individual accounts on a defined contribution basis. Although NPFs are somewhat similar in structure to individual account plans like those in Australia and Chile, a major difference is that a government-appointed entity manages all contributions and accumulating assets. Participants become eligible for benefits, which are usually paid in the form of a lump sum, upon reaching a specified age or becoming disabled. If a worker dies before receiving his benefit, it is typically paid to survivors. Provident funds are not always strictly reserved for retirement; in many cases funds may be used for other purposes such as buying a home. In fact, David McCarthy, Olivia Mitchell, and John Piggott find that individuals in Singapore often do not have much money left in their provident fund accounts at retirement, because so much money was used for housing.[2]

Another problem with provident funds is that rates of return are determined by the government-appointed entity. There may be a conflict of interest between maximizing returns for account holders and satisfying the government's social protection and public savings goals. These plans are often plagued by lack of transparency about fund investments.

Finally, defined contribution plans have been established on a notional defined contribution pay-go basis using "virtual" accounts. These accounts are credited with annual contributions by wage earners, based on a "defined contribution" rate. The balance in the account is credited with an interest return each year, based on growth in wages, average income, or some similar measure. While workers' notional accounts grow steadily under these systems, their actual contributions are used in the present to pay benefits to current retirees. The advantage of a notional basis over a traditional pay-go defined benefit plan is that the benefit payout terms do not have to be stipulated until the worker is at or close to retirement age, and thus can reflect current demographics and the life expectancies

---

[2] David McCarthy, Olivia S. Mitchell, and John Piggott, "Asset Rich and Cash Poor: Retirement Provision and Housing Policy in Singapore," *Journal of Pension Economics and Finance*, 1(3), 2002.

of retirees. Sweden and Italy are transitioning into these sorts of systems. For Sweden, this part of its national retirement system is much larger than the funded individual account portion mentioned above.

Employer-Sponsored Third Tiers in the Retirement System

In addition to first- and second-tier programs, most retirees also depend on employer-based or occupational pensions, personal savings, and private transfers from family or organizations with which they are affiliated. Generally, the importance of these sources of income largely depends on the nature and amount of benefits provided by the government-mandated retirement system. Even within the developed world, these systems range from extremely generous to minimalist.

At the latter end, Germany's state pension has been so generous historically there has been little interest in supplemental pension systems, which is why such a large share of retiree income comes from the state pension. In many other countries, there are a variety of reasons that employer-provided pensions exist at relatively robust levels. Since most national systems rely on payroll taxes, the workplace is an ideal place to capture contributions. Beyond that, however, employers have created retirement savings mechanisms where the national system has not fully met the needs of retirees.

In contrast to Germany, the vast majority of employees in the Netherlands are covered by an employer-sponsored pension. While providing a pension is not required under law, most employers provide such benefits. The plans are funded under regulatory standards set by the government. Book reserve arrangements, where pension liabilities are "covered" by the net worth of the sponsoring organization are not allowed. Plans are organized and funded at the company level, through industry-wide funds or through an insurance company. Larger employers generally create and operate their own plans. Smaller employers take advantage of the alternative arrangements. The primary purpose of these plans is to pay pension annuities to the disabled, survivors, and retirees and lump-sum payments in lieu of a pension are virtually precluded.[3]

Switzerland has arrived at much the same place as the Netherlands but has done it by legally requiring employers to provide pensions as part of their three-tier retirement structure. The first tier is a basic, government-provided pension. The second is the employer tier. The third is a voluntary

---

[3] Watson Wyatt Data Services, *Western Europe Benefits Report, 2004* (Brussels: Watson Wyatt Data Services, 2004), pp. 295–319.

tier for personal saving. The mandatory occupational plans must register with the government and must provide minimum benefits specified by law. Employers must either set up their own plan or join a multi-employer arrangement. The benefits may be either defined benefit or defined contribution. Annual contributions are made on earnings between CHF 25,320 and CHF 79,560, referred to as the "coordinated salary." If the coordinated salary falls below CHF 3,165, contributions are required on this base. Contribution rates vary from a low of 7 percent up to 18 percent, depending on the age and gender of the worker – male and female schedules vary slightly. The employee pays up to one-half the contribution, and contribution rates increase as workers age. Each year, the accumulating benefit is credited with new contributions and an interest credit specified by the government. Benefits are paid as annuities unless they are less than a certain percentage of the minimum social security old-age pensions – 10 percent for retirement and disability, 6 percent for a widow's benefit, and 2 percent for an orphan's benefit. There are portability requirements, so that workers can transfer benefits from one employer to the next when they change jobs. Plans must be valued at least every three years by a recognized actuary, who verifies that the employee benefit institution has sufficient security to cover its obligations and that the actuarial provisions and actual financing of benefits meet all legal requirements. There is a guarantee fund to ensure benefits for plans with mature populations or that have become insolvent.[4]

In the United Kingdom, employer pensions are voluntary but play a significant role in the retirement system from both a public and private-tier perspective. The combination of benefits provided by the Basic Pension and the State Earnings Related Pension Scheme, which was the second tier of the U.K. system until March 2002, when it was replaced by the State Second Pension, provide only a basic level of retirement income. As a result, employer-sponsored pensions provide substantial benefits in the combined tiers of the total retirement system. Today about half of full-time workers in the United Kingdom are eligible to participate in an employer-sponsored plan. Private plans now shoulder a substantial portion of the burden mandated under the second government tier of the system, because since the late 1970s, occupational pensions have been able to "contract out" of the second government tier of the retirement system. Today, most workers participating in employer-sponsored schemes are in arrangements that have contracted out of the government

---

[4] Ibid, pp. 403–421.

plan. Most medium-size and large employers sponsor their own retirement plans. Benefits accrue on a tax-favored basis subject to some legal limits. Since October 2001, employers have been required to offer access to a "stakeholder pension scheme" on a payroll deduction basis. These are individual money purchase plans offered by financial services companies, trade unions, and the like. In these plans, annual charges are capped at 1 percent of the funds in the worker's personal account. Annual contributions are limited to £3,600 or an age-related percentage of earnings. These are primarily intended for workers whose employers do not already offer an occupational plan to most of their workers.[5]

Japan also has two tiers in its public system. The first tier, known as the National Pension, provides a flat benefit to everyone who contributes to the system. The second tier is called the Employees' Pension Insurance (EPI) program, which pays a benefit based on average indexed earnings under the system. Japan has adopted a number of reforms to both systems in recent years, recognizing the implications of its rapidly aging population. As with a number of other developed countries, the public tiers in the Japanese system leave room for an employer tier, and around 60 percent of Japanese workers are covered by an employer plan. As in the United Kingdom, employers can partially contract out of the system and provide benefits through their Employee Pension Fund (EPF), as long as they provide benefits that are at least 30 percent more valuable than the EPI benefit. Employers can also set up Tax Qualified Pension Plans (TQPPs), which tend to be concentrated among smaller employers. EPFs receive somewhat more favorable tax treatment on investment income than TQPPs. In 1999, there were about 1,850 EPFs covering some 12 million workers and 91,000 TQPPs covering over 10 million workers. The contracted-out portion of EPF benefits are paid in the form of a life annuity while supplemental benefits may be paid as lump sums. Roughly 40 percent of beneficiaries in 1997 took lump sums. Under the TQPPs, workers can take a 10-year certain payout, but most choose to take a lump sum. In Japan, most workers receive a severance benefit when they terminate employment from a plan that is financed on a pay-go basis by employers. Both the EPF and TQPP plans appear to be significantly underfunded – one study found that among 24 companies listed on the New York Stock Exchange, pension assets were worth only 40 percent of liabilities. Another study found that half of the EPF plans had less than 90 percent of the assets needed to cover liabilities. In 2001, lawmakers

[5] Ibid, pp. 423–450.

adopted new legislation offering employers the opportunity to establish defined contribution plans and allowing pre-tax employer contributions, and changing the operations of existing defined benefit plans. The benefits in the defined contribution plans vest in three years and are portable when workers change jobs. If employers do not want to contribute, they can establish a defined contribution plan that accepts contributions from workers. These plans allow workers with no other pension to contribute on a pre-tax basis. Retirees can take their benefits as lump sums or annuities. Under this reform bill, TQPPs are required to terminate by 2011. Employers offering an EPF are permitted to transfer back the liabilities they have assumed for the EPI benefits by transferring assets to the government. Participants in these modified plans will no longer be exempt from the assets tax that TQPP participants were always required to pay.[6] Through early 2004, few companies had converted to the new defined contribution plans.[7]

The United States also has a relatively robust, voluntary employer-based pension system. In contrast to the Netherlands and Switzerland, only about half of workers are covered under employer plans at any point in time. Because of job mobility, however, roughly two-thirds of retiring workers will receive a benefit from at least one employer plan. Employers can provide benefits through plans they organize themselves, participate in multi-employer arrangements, or purchase benefits through regulated insurance companies. Although establishing these plans is voluntary, the government encourages companies to sponsor plans by federal, and, in most cases, by state tax preferences. These preferences allow employers to deduct contributions to a qualified retirement plan as a business expense. Contributions to the plan and returns on assets are not taxable to plan participants until they start receiving benefits. In order to qualify for these tax preferences, plans must operate within strictly regulated federal laws. Anti-discrimination requirements are a major feature of the regulations, which require employers to provide proportionately comparable benefits to workers at all income levels. The regulatory structure also requires employers to fund benefits as they are accrued. Most state and local government entities also fund their benefits as accrued, although they are

---

[6] Robert L. Clark and Olivia S. Mitchell, "Strengthening Employment-Based Pensions in Japan," (Cambridge, Massachusetts: National Bureau of Economic Research, 2002) Working Paper 8891.

[7] Sarah (Ingmanson) McLellan, "Corporate Pension Reform in Japan: Big Bang or Big Bust" (Philadelphia: University of Pennsylvania, Wharton School, Pension Research Council, 2004), working paper.

not required to do so under federal law. For a variety of reasons, defined benefit plans can become underfunded – falling asset values, unexpected increases in liabilities, business difficulties, and so forth. The Pension Benefit Guarantee Corporation (PBGC), a government-mandated insurance entity, insures benefits, so that if an insufficiently funded plan terminates due to business failure, the plan participant receives benefits from the PBGC. The PBGC is supported by a variable rate premium structure, which bases premiums on a plan's funded status, although all trustee plans, including those that are over-funded, must make annual contributions. Beginning in the early 1980s, employers began to sponsor a new sort of defined contribution plan under section 401(k) of the Internal Revenue Code. For the first time, workers could make pre-tax contributions into tax-qualified plans. Over the last 20 years, there has been a marked shift toward 401(k) plans. The typical 401(k) plan today allows workers to contribute up to 6 percent of pay on a pre-tax basis. Most employers match employee contributions on some basis, typically 50 percent, to encourage participation. Defined benefit plans are required to offer an annuity to plan participants when they become eligible for retirement. Most defined benefit plans today also offer a lump-sum benefit option. Defined contribution plans are not required to offer annuity benefits. In the United States, the vast majority of benefits provided under the employer tier of benefits are paid out as lump sums.

Retirement Ages, Retirement Patterns, and Retiree Populations

All retirement systems, regardless of their structure, affect workforce behavior. Absent formal retirement systems, we would see very different patterns of work and retirement behavior. It is also very likely that, as a group, older people who could no longer work would have much lower standards of living.

The goal of retirement pensions originally was to provide a steady income stream to older people who could no longer support themselves by working. Policymakers had to establish a retirement eligibility age, and they generally tried to select the age at which employers considered the worker too old to be productive. When Otto von Bismarck set up the first national retirement system in Germany in the late nineteenth century, he established age 70 as the retirement eligibility age.

Across much of the world, the evolution of retirement systems during the twentieth century assumed that people who reached "retirement age" should be able to stop working and yet maintain a "standard of living" comparable to that they enjoyed while working. Perceptions of appropriate retirement age and standard of living have varied somewhat over time. During the twentieth century, virtually all the formal retirement systems around the world adopted younger retirement ages. In many countries today, the "normal retirement age" is age 65, although that is far from universal. But the normal retirement age is often the age at which full retirement benefits are paid – people may qualify to receive "early" retirement benefits at younger ages. Indeed, in many cases, far more people retire early than at the normal retirement age – thus creating a situation where "normal" is really abnormal.

Early Retirement in Belgium

By Alain Jousten, Université de Liège, IZA and CEPR

Over the past 30 years, the Belgian retirement landscape has changed dramatically. The predominant route into retirement used to be one of a simultaneous exit from the labor market and a transition into benefit claiming in one of the three main public pay-as-you-go retirement programs, with separate systems for civil servants, private-sector wage earners and the self-employed. Nowadays, the pattern is a different one, with two-thirds of private-sector wage earners transiting through some temporary "arrangement" bridging the gap between the time people leave the labor force and the moment they claim retirement benefits in the public retirement programs. While the trend for civil servants is not unlike the one just mentioned, the same is not true for the much less generous and restrictive system of the self-employed.

The change in routing is a symptom of another more general phenomenon, with even wider implications, namely the tendency towards earlier retirement, and this at a time of demographic aging and the resulting problems for the pay-as-you-go systems. It has lead Belgium to one of the top spots in the list of countries with the lowest activity rates for people aged 50 and above. While the blame for this low activity rate is often exclusively put on the architecture of the social insurance system (e.g., early retirement, unemployment, disability or sickness pay) and the use thereof for smoothing industrial restructuring, companies are also more than just bystanders in this early retirement bonanza.

Because of the highly progressive link of wages with age and/or job-tenure, companies tend to be more than eager to discharge their older workers once their wages grow larger than their productivity and to replace them with younger workers. In addition, company incentives play an important and increasing role in the decisions of individuals. Examples are extended periods of (partly) paid leaves-of-absence or more prominently lump-sum or annuity payments inducing people to accept being put on the unemployment rolls by compensating some (or all) of the shortfall of the public benefit as compared to previous earnings.

I use the term bonanza to describe this situation, as it truly resembles one – at least at first sight. Companies are not unhappy to have the flexibility to manage the size and composition of their workforce using these early retirement routes, and this at reasonable cost to them. Most individuals too are not unhappy with early retirement as the various arrangements allow them to enjoy high replacement rates of pension income relative to the last wage. The big losers are however not to be forgotten: Among them the government, and hence present and future taxpayers who ultimately foot the bill, but also those who would like to work, but would be financially unwise to do so in the face of prohibitive implicit tax rates. The routes for reform are thus clearly set.

In addition to early retirement provisions in their national pensions, many countries have also adopted other measures that allow workers to stop working and receive some income even before they qualify for the formal retirement pensions. Most countries provide some sort of disability insurance. In virtually all of these programs, the prevalence of disability increases as workers approach the age of retirement eligibility, and some countries explicitly allow older people to qualify more easily for disability pensions than their younger counterparts. In other countries, unemployment insurance programs provide extended periods of earnings replacement for older workers who lose their job before qualifying for a retirement pension. These bridge benefits, often characterized as unemployment insurance, are essentially early retirement programs.

The important point here is that there is no absolute standard for setting retirement eligibility ages in different countries' retirement systems. To a significant degree, the availability of benefits at varying ages accounts for disparities in labor force participation at various ages as reported in Table 4-1. Part of the concern about population aging relates to the retirement phenomenon itself. The undeniable fact is that many people, especially in the world's developed economies, are retiring at ages when they could still be highly productive.

Support for the argument that potentially productive workers have withdrawn from the workforce appears in Table 4-1, which shows the percent of the population that remains economically active across a range of countries at various ages. In interpreting the data, it is important to keep a couple of factors in mind. First, the relatively low labor force participation rates in less developed countries, such as Egypt and Mexico, reflect the relatively low labor force participation rates of women. Some developed countries, however, such as Italy and Spain, still have relatively low female labor force participation rates among older women. The second factor – and the one of greater immediate relevance in the current context – is the drop-off in labor force participation rates at successively higher ages. For example, the decline in labor force participation between

Table 4-1. *Labor Force Participation Rates of Selected Age Groups within National Populations in 2000*

	Percent of Age Group in Labor Force			
	50–54	55–59	60–64	65+
Argentina	70.6%	63.2%	46.9%	14.0%
Australia	75.8	60.7	34.7	5.8
Brazil	65.1	65.1	32.3	32.3
Canada	78.8	63.0	36.5	5.8
Chile	66.4	57.3	42.3	14.1
China	78.5	65.2	45.8	19.3
Egypt	58.4	58.4	34.8	18.0
France	82.2	58.8	14.5	1.3
Germany	81.1	66.0	21.7	2.6
Hungary	68.7	34.7	8.0	2.6
India	65.7	65.7	46.9	35.2
Iceland	93.7	88.6	81.3	20.9
Ireland	67.0	54.7	36.5	8.0
Italy	61.9	38.7	19.2	3.3
Japan	82.3	76.1	55.5	22.7
Malaysia	67.6	52.2	42.2	–
Mexico	63.6	58.5	47.6	31.7
Netherlands	74.6	56.5	19.5	3.0
Poland	66.5	41.0	22.4	7.9
South Africa	74.9	48.4	48.4	11.8
Spain	63.9	51.5	28.9	1.6
Sweden	87.8	81.5	52.3	–
Switzerland	87.2	65.1	65.1	9.5
Turkey	45.1	38.9	31.6	19.8
United Kingdom	79.5	66.1	37.8	5.1
United States	80.3	68.8	47.1	12.6

Sources: International Labor Office, Bureau of Statistics, LABORSTA database on labor statistics, current through 2001, United Nations Population Division, *World Population Prospect* (2000 Revision), and OECD, *Corporate Environment Database.*

the ages of 50 to 54 and 55 to 59 in Italy far exceeds that in most other developed countries. It is nearly twice the decline in United States and Switzerland, nearly three times the decline in the Netherlands, and four times the decline in Sweden. This differences in labor force participation rates largely reflect the characteristics of the retirement system in place in the various countries.

Further up the age distribution in Table 4-1, similar variations in labor force participation rates are apparent. In Iceland, 81 percent of the

Table 4-2. *Average Retirement Ages for Men and Women in Selected OECD Countries*

	Males		Females	
	1980	2000	1980	2000
Australia	62.4	62.0	58.2	59.1
Austria	60.1	59.2	59.3	57.0
Belgium	61.1	58.1	57.5	55.5
Canada	63.8	61.7	60.5	59.3
Denmark	64.5	61.6	61.0	59.8
Finland	60.1	59.9	59.6	59.6
France	61.3	58.8	60.9	58.4
Germany	62.2	61.0	60.7	59.3
Iceland	69.3	67.2	65.8	65.2
Ireland	66.2	62.9	66.0	58.5
Italy	61.6	59.7	59.5	57.0
Japan	67.2	66.6	63.9	64.6
Luxembourg	59.0	58.2	60.8	56.3
Netherlands	61.4	59.9	58.4	56.8
New Zealand	62.9	63.8	58.7	60.7
Norway	66.0	64.4	61.5	63.1
Portugal	64.7	64.7	62.9	62.7
Spain	63.4	61.0	63.6	57.0
Sweden	64.6	64.4	62.0	63.1
Switzerland	65.5	64.5	62.4	–
Turkey	64.9	61.4	67.6	65.1
United Kingdom	64.6	62.9	62.0	60.1
United States	64.2	63.6	62.8	62.5

Sources: The 1980 estimates are from Sveinbjorn Blondal and Stefano Scarpetta, "The Retirement Decision in OECD Countries," Organization for Economic Co-Operation and Development, Economics Department Working Papers, No. 202, February, 1999; the 2000 estimates were developed by authors off of Blondal and Scarpetta's 1995 estimates applied to the population age structures in the respective countries in 2000.

population between the ages of 60 and 64 is still in the labor force, and in Switzerland, 65 percent of the population is still economically active in the labor market. These relatively high rates are very different from the 14.5 percent of the same age group remaining in the labor force in France, 19 percent in Italy, and 22 percent in Germany.

Labor force participation rates for older people are directly related to average retirement ages. Table 4-2 shows estimated average retirement ages for men and women in a selected set of countries for 1980 and

2000.[8] A couple of important points are clear from the table. First, over the 20 years leading up to 2000, the average retirement age in most countries has declined somewhat, although it has held steady in a few cases. Second, women tend to retire at younger ages than men. Both are potentially important considerations in evaluating policy options for the future.

In Chapter 2 we considered another phenomenon, increasing life expectancies, that figures largely in a discussion about retirement burdens and one that interacts with earlier retirement ages in growing retiree populations. Chapter 2 discussed increasing life expectancy at birth, noting that in most developed countries, life expectancy has increased by as much as five or six years since the late 1970s, mostly due to increasing life expectancy among the older population. Although improvements in infant mortality undoubtedly helped, most of these gains had already been achieved in the world's developed countries by the early 1970s. With life expectancy among the elderly rising at the same time that average retirement ages were falling, the duration of retirement was increasing in two directions.

Table 4-3 reflects the implications of further increases in life expectancy at the retirement ages now prevalent in most OECD countries. The estimates shown in the table assume that recent retirement age patterns will continue and project the duration of retirement based on life expectancy at the average retirement age for each country. Taken together, Tables 4-1, 4-2, and 4-3 illustrate the major pension funding challenges many countries face.

In Switzerland, the typical male works until nearly age 65. In Belgium, the average male retires by age 58. In the United Kingdom, the comparable age is 62, in France it is 59. In Iceland, the average man works until age 69. These variations help to explain and identify the range of costs associated with different retirement systems. In Belgium, the average

---

[8] The calculation of the average retirement age is based on aggregate data on active and total population by gender by quinquennial age groups. The mathematical derivation of retirement ages follows D. Latulippe, *Effective Retirement Age and Duration of Retirement in the Industrial Countries between 1950–1990* (Geneva: International Labor Organization, 1996). There are a number of assumptions concerning the distributions of the population within each age group: first, minimum age of retirement is set at 45; second, within each age group the population is assumed to be normally distributed; and third, retirement within each age group is assumed to be linear with age. The retirement distribution of the whole population is estimated on the basis of the retirement distribution within an age group. This requires information on the expected age of retirement for each age group and the proportion of the population that is expected to retire over the next five years.

Table 4-3. *Current and Projected Average Retirement Period in Selected OECD Countries*

	Males			Females		
	2000	2010	2030	2000	2010	2030
Australia	19.0	19.7	21.0	27.1	27.8	29.1
Austria	21.1	22.1	23.8	27.3	28.6	30.2
Belgium	22.0	23.1	24.8	29.8	30.9	32.5
Canada	18.5	19.2	20.5	25.5	26.2	27.5
Denmark	17.3	18.0	19.3	22.9	24.1	25.7
Finland	20.3	20.9	22.3	25.2	26.0	27.2
France	20.5	21.4	23.2	26.7	27.5	29.0
Germany	19.4	20.2	22.1	25.3	26.6	28.2
Iceland	13.7	14.2	15.1	19.2	19.9	21.0
Ireland	16.9	17.4	18.7	22.7	23.6	25.2
Italy	19.5	20.1	21.4	27.0	27.8	29.1
Japan	16.3	17.3	18.9	23.5	24.7	26.8
Luxembourg	20.9	21.8	23.8	27.9	29.2	30.8
Netherlands	21.0	21.6	23.0	28.0	28.8	30.2
New Zealand	18.3	18.8	20.2	24.8	25.5	26.9
Norway	17.3	18.3	19.6	22.7	23.7	25.2
Portugal	16.1	16.7	17.7	22.1	23.0	24.6
Spain	18.8	19.3	20.7	25.7	26.4	27.7
Sweden	18.7	19.4	20.6	23.2	23.9	25.4
Switzerland	16.6	17.2	18.4	24.3	24.9	26.2
Turkey	14.8	15.4	16.7	15.3	15.9	17.0
United Kingdom	18.0	18.9	20.5	23.8	25.0	26.8
United States	16.8	17.6	19.4	22.0	23.2	24.9

Sources: Estimated by the authors based on average retirement age estimates for 1995 from Sveinbjorn Blondal and Stefano Scarpetta, "The Retirement Decision in OECD Countries," Organization for Economic Co-Operation and Development, Economics Department Working Papers, No. 202, February, 1999 and the United Nations life expectancy projections from *World Population Prospects* (2000 Revision).

male retiree has a remaining life expectancy of 22 years when he retires. In France, the average life expectancy at the typical retirement age is 20.5 years. It is 13.7 years in Iceland, 16.6 years in Switzerland, and 18.0 years in the United Kingdom. All else being equal, a male retiree in Belgium will cost about 60 percent more in retirement benefits than one in Iceland simply because of the different duration of retirement in the two countries. The most significant influence on when most people retire is the structure of the retirement system.

The current level and anticipated growth in retirement costs have attracted the attention of many analysts of the aging phenomenon. In proposals to bring retirement system costs under control, some have focused on reducing benefits. But focusing on benefit amounts rather than the duration of the retirement period may be missing a crucial part of the problem – and thus an effective solution. Not only do the shorter work lives of males in Belgium compared to Iceland cost much more in retirement benefits, longer retirements also reduce economic output, which affects a society's standard of living. This is true for both funded and pay-go pensions. If a growing consuming elderly population that does not contribute to national output is part of the problem, it may make little difference whether the vehicle is a national pay-go retirement system in Germany that encourages a productive worker to retire at age 59, or an employer-sponsored, funded retirement plan in the United States that encourages his American counterpart to do exactly the same thing.

Earlier we looked at increasing numbers of aging people around the world, but it is actually the combination of retirement and aging patterns that will determine levels of aged dependency. In a place like Iceland, the mere fact that the population is aging will have significantly different implications than in a place like Belgium. In Table 4-4, we show estimates of the retiree population in 2000 and projections to 2030 for the study countries. The 2000 estimates were developed by assuming the reported "economically inactive" population over the age of 55 to be retired. The projections for subsequent years were derived by assuming that future populations would have the same labor force participation rates by age and gender as people did in 2000. The column that is second from the right in Table 4-4 shows the percentage increase in the projected share of the total populations that will be retired due to population aging between 2000 and 2030 – i.e., if retirees grow from 10 to 15 percent of the total population, that is a 50 percent increase in the percentage of the population that is retired. The right-hand column shows the absolute difference in the shares of the populations retired betwee 2000 and 2030 given the assumptions – i.e., 15 percent minus 10 percent equals a growth of 5 percent of the population in retirement.

The underlying assumption that the labor force participation rates of older people will not change can be challenged. The reader should think of this as a baseline projection that reflects the state of affairs at the beginning of the twenty-first century, which is then applied to evolving population dynamics that will unfold over the next 25 years or so. The estimates reflect the potential aging burden various societies will face if retirement behaviors generally remain constant. We are intentionally imprecise in saying that it is "behaviors" that will have to change to lighten the potential

Table 4-4. *Estimated and Projected Retiree Populations as a Percentage of the Total Population for Selected Years*

	Inactive Population 55+ as Percent of Total Population				Percentage Increase 2000–2030	Percentage Difference 2000–2030
	2000	2010	2020	2030		
Argentina	11.8%	12.6%	14.0%	15.7%	32.6%	3.8%
Australia	16.2	18.9	22.4	25.3	56.4	9.1
Brazil	6.4	8.1	10.8	13.5	111.1	7.1
Canada	16.4	19.6	24.4	27.8	69.8	11.4
Chile	9.6	11.7	14.9	18.0	87.7	8.4
China	8.6	10.9	14.4	19.4	126.7	10.9
Egypt	5.9	7.1	9.5	11.8	100.6	5.9
France	21.6	24.6	28.4	31.7	46.6	10.1
Germany	23.5	26.3	30.7	35.8	52.4	12.3
Hungary	23.0	26.5	29.5	32.9	43.5	10.0
India	5.7	6.6	8.3	10.4	82.6	4.7
Iceland	10.5	11.7	14.4	17.8	69.4	7.3
Ireland	15.0	16.7	19.2	21.7	44.2	6.6
Italy	25.9	29.3	33.9	40.1	54.7	14.2
Japan	17.6	22.6	26.4	29.6	67.9	12.0
Malaysia	6.9	8.9	12.2	15.3	121.3	8.4
Mexico	5.5	7.0	9.3	12.6	126.8	7.0
Netherlands	19.4	23.3	28.2	32.7	68.3	13.3
Poland	17.1	20.9	25.5	28.3	65.7	11.2
South Africa	5.7	7.1	9.1	10.8	89.6	5.1
Spain	22.6	25.3	29.7	36.4	60.7	13.8
Sweden	20.5	23.8	27.7	31.0	51.2	10.5
Switzerland	19.7	23.9	29.5	34.3	74.5	14.7
Turkey	8.3	9.9	12.6	15.8	90.7	7.5
United Kingdom	19.8	22.1	25.8	29.9	50.5	10.0
United States	14.3	16.1	19.6	22.3	55.8	8.0

Sources: International Labor Office, Bureau of Statistics, LABORSTA database on labor statistics, current through 2001, United Nations Population Division, *World Population Prospect* (2000 Revision), and OECD, *Corporate Environment Database.*

retirement burdens that aging populations will impose. Changing retiree behavior is only one option among many. Countries could adopt policies that affect overall income growth in the economy or, alternatively, they could adopt policies that change the relative consumption levels of retirees or other members of the population. The range of options will be discussed later.

The second column from the right in Table 4-4 shows that the most rapid growth in retiree populations is projected for the less developed countries over the next quarter century. The right-hand column, on the other hand, shows that the most rapid absolute growth in the retiree population will occur across much of the developed world. The one notable exception among the less developed countries is China, whose percentage increase in the total share of the population that will be retired is comparable to those in several highly developed countries, and exceeds those projected for Australia, the United Kingdom, and the United States. Once again, China's relatively unique pattern relates to the maturing effects of the government's controlled birth policy. The important point in Table 4-4 is that large increases in the retiree population are looming, both for societies already at a relatively advanced stage of population aging and for those much less far along. Alternatively, the same point can be made about both the developed and the less developed societies. Population aging will be significant across most of the world, although prescriptions for dealing with it for the present, short-term and long-term future may vary, depending on a country's evolutionary stage and outlook.

Retiree Income Levels

Just as there is no absolute standard for when retirement benefits should become available to workers, there is no absolute standard for how much a retirement system should provide them. But the level of benefits and the rules under which they are provided play an important role in determining who receives benefits and when. In one form or another, many developed countries have designed their retirement systems so retirees can achieve a standard of living commensurate with what they achieved during their working lives or comparable to that achieved by people still working. But measuring standards of living before and after retirement is imprecise, so developing a retirement income level to allow retirees to maintain such a standard is somewhat subjective.

Part of the challenge in comparing standards of living before and after retirement results from our inability to precisely measure the economic value of leisure or to determine the reasonable substitutability between leisure and material consumption goods. Workers surrender their leisure in order to earn the wages with which to purchase their consumption goods. Retirement income gives retirees access to consumption goods without their having to sacrifice leisure to pay for them. Another problem in comparing standards of living for workers versus retirees is that the latter have considerably more free time and do many things for themselves – what economist call home production – that workers simply do not have the time to do.

In practical terms, the major consideration in designing retirement income systems is giving retirees an income stream that enables them to maintain consumption levels comparable to those achieved by workers. In doing so, the special expenses incurred by workers are taken into consideration. These would include the cost of commuting to and from work, a professional wardrobe, taxes assessed against wages but not against retirement income, and so forth. While there is no precise scale of how much retirement income is required to maintain the equivalent of a preretirement standard of living, there is considerable agreement that it is 75 to 85 percent of workers' incomes.

There is also some variation in perception about what is meant by workers' incomes. Should an individual retiree's income measure up to his or her own earnings shortly before retirement, or should it be compared with some broad distribution of workers' earnings over a longer span of the career? Since earnings generally rise over workers' careers and standards of living tend to rise along with them, the base used for comparing the adequacy of retirement income is important. Should retirees' income be measured against the earnings they and their contemporaries achieved before their own retirement, or should it be compared with the earnings of workers still employed? Variations in retirement systems reflect the different answers to these and other questions.

The measurement device typically used to assess comparability between preretirement and postretirement income levels is referred to as the "replacement rate," the quotient of retirement income divided by working income. Several recent studies have done cross-national comparisons of retiree income levels to those of various aggregations of people. Richard Disney and Edward Whitehouse summarize a number of these in a major 2001 report developed for the Department of Social Security in the United Kingdom.[9] At about the same time, the OECD published a similar analysis of income of the elderly in nine member countries.[10] Table 4-5 presents a summary of their results. They characterize their measure of comparison as "quasi-retirement income replacement rates" because of the way they were derived, which was to compare the income levels of people ages 65 to 74 to people ages 41 to 64. These are not precise

---

[9] Richard Disney and Edward Whitehouse, *Cross-Country Comparisons of Pensioners' Income* (London: Department of Social Security, 2001), pp. 20–28.

[10] OECD, *Ageing and Income* (Paris: OECD Publication Service, 2001).

Table 4-5. *Quasi-Retirement Income Replacement Rates for Selected Countries*

| | Percentage of Mean Disposable Income of People Ages 65 to 74 Compared to: | | | |
| | People Aged 51 to 64 | | People Aged 41 to 50 | |
	Mid 1980s	Mid 1990s	Mid 1980s	Mid 1990s
Canada	82.4	86.9	78.2	86.6
Finland	77.6	75.5	69.2	71.6
Germany	78.1	84.4	75.5	78.2
Italy	76.4	78.7	77.8	78.1
Japan	82.3	79.6	84.8	81.8
Netherlands	83.1	80.7	85.2	78.9
Sweden	76.1	76.1	73.6	80.3
United Kingdom	70.4	74.1	59.9	65.0
United States	82.2	79.9	84.3	83.6

Source: OECD, *Ageing and Income* (Paris: OECD Publication Service, 2001), p. 22.

comparisons of retiree income rates to those of working people, because some of the older population would still be working and some of the younger group would already be retired. The mixing of the two groups should have a relatively minor effect on the measures reflected in the table. In any event, the OECD's results show a remarkable consistency across countries.

Because many people in their 50s and early 60s in the developed economies are already retired, the OECD also compared the 65- to 74-year-old group with people ages 41 to 50, who are much less likely to have already completed their working careers. With the exception of the United Kingdom, and Finland to a lesser degree, the results shown in the right two columns of Table 4-5 are still remarkably comparable across the nations considered. These results are generally consistent with those in the studies summarized by Disney and Whitehouse.

Sources of Retiree Income

The comparability of retirement income across the developed countries reflected in Table 4-5 masks significant variation in the sources of that income. Table 4-6 shows the major sources of income for the retirement-age populations for the same set of countries included in Table 4-5, from the same OECD study cited earlier. To the extent people over

Table 4-6. *Disposable Income by Source of Income for People Ages 65 and Over for Selected Countries and Periods*

	Mid-1980s			Mid-1990s		
	Working	Capital	Social Transfers	Working	Capital	Social Transfers
Canada	22.9%	41.1%	36.0%	20.7%	44.1%	35.2%
Finland	22.4	11.4	66.2	13.7	6.8	79.6
Germany	18.2	11.5	70.4	10.3	16.7	73.0
Italy	45.8	2.3	51.8	33.0	1.8	65.2
Japan	85.3	5.0	9.8	63.9	6.3	29.7
Netherlands	18.0	41.1	40.9	12.7	47.0	40.3
Sweden	10.3	12.2	77.6	8.1	10.1	81.7
United Kingdom	19.1	34.9	46.1	14.1	43.0	42.9
United States	27.0	44.8	28.1	29.6	39.8	30.6

Source: OECD, *Ageing and Income* (Paris: OECD Publication Service, 2001), p. 28.

age 65 continue to work, they clearly do not pose the same sort of "aging burden" on society as those who are retired. Presumably, they are being paid for their marginal contribution to the output of the economy and their wages give them a prorated share of the claim on that output. This suggests that the effects of an aging population would be very different for a country like Japan than for a country like Germany, even if their age structures were identical. In many cases, however, the work-related income attributed to the elderly in Table 4-6 is not necessarily earned by the elderly themselves. The income sources listed here are based on household income distributions. In the late 1980s and early 1990s, nearly two-thirds of Japanese people over the age of 65 lived with their children, compared to 39 percent in Italy, 25 percent in France, around 15 percent in the United Kingdom, the United States and Germany, and 5 percent or less in Sweden and Denmark.[11] If one excludes the elderly who live with their children, the share of total income from work-related activities drops considerably below the levels shown in Table 4-6. In the mid-1990s, for Japanese men ages 65 to 74 living only with their spouse, the share of income from work was only 40 percent. In the United States, the percentage was about 25 percent, and it was 10 percent or less elsewhere.[12] For those living alone or older couples, it would have been even lower.

[11] Disney and Whitehouse, p. 13.
[12] OECD, *Ageing and Income*, p. 32.

Table 4-7. *Relative Role of Private and Public Pensions for Men Retired at Early and Normal Retirement Ages*

	Percent of Men Who Are:		Benefits as Percentage of Average Disposable Income of the Working-Age Population for:	
	Beneficiaries of Public Pensions	Beneficiaries of Private Pensions	Beneficiaries of Public Pensions	Beneficiaries of Private Pensions
Men ages 60–64				
Canada	85.6	63.2	19.2	46.3
Finland	100.0	4.1	89.0	0.0
Germany	99.3	19.2	66.8	2.1
Italy	98.6	4.2	86.3	2.1
Japan	99.4	15.1	56.8	4.1
Netherlands	7.6	95.2	7.3	na
Sweden	78.6	73.3	63.3	51.6
United Kingdom	41.9	80.1	0.2	47.8
United States	77.0	60.9	27.2	40.9
Men ages 65+				
Canada	99.8	60.7	41.0	30.6
Finland	100.0	3.3	95.2	0.0
Germany	100.0	16.4	79.3	4.6
Italy	97.5	5.2	75.0	4.2
Japan	99.3	12.8	65.2	2.5
Netherlands	95.0	82.7	50.2	52.5
Sweden	100.0	88.2	87.8	25.8
United Kingdom	99.0	80.7	27.2	36.6
United States	96.8	54.4	39.6	27.8

Source: OECD, *Ageing and Income* (Paris: OECD Publication Service, 2001), p. 172.

The reliance on capital income versus social transfers shown in Table 4-6 reflects the extent to which various countries rely on government-mandated retirement systems versus employer-sponsored plans. Table 4-7 shows the relative reliance on public versus private pensions for male retirees in the late 1990s. The conclusion is that, generally, where public pensions are rich, private pensions are spare, and where public plans are not so rich, private pensions tend to be more substantial.

One reason for the complementary sizing of public and private pensions relates to the adequacy discussion above. In the past, it made little sense for an employer to provide a rich pension in Germany, since the public pension benefits provided to Germans enabled them to maintain standards of living similar to preretirement levels or commensurate with contemporary standards of living. Providing a pension generally comes at a cost of either reduced wages for workers or reduced profits for the employer. And adding an employer pension on top of a very generous public pension could result in workers enjoying a somewhat higher standard of living during retirement than during their working careers.

All pension plans will have to deal with the pressures imposed by evolving demographics in their country, whether the plans are operated by the state or sponsored by employers. But the nature of those pressures will vary, depending on how the pension is organized and financed. In the next chapter, we turn to a discussion of how funding arrangements affect retirement costs.

FIVE

Retirement Systems and the Economic Costs of Aging

The discussion thus far has suggested that the way pension systems are structured might affect the costs associated with aged dependency. Lawrence Thompson of the Urban Institute cautions that analyses of this sort can often be misleading. He suggests that pensions are financed by a combination of contributions from labor income and returns on capital. He says that if a "lower charge to labor is offset by a higher charge to capital income, the total cost to the economy is the same even though it may be distributed differently."[1]

Thompson argues that the economic cost or burden of supporting a retired population is simply the total consumption of retirees divided by the total production in an economy. He expresses this relation as the product of three ratios. The first ratio is simply the consumption rate for all consumers in the economy relative to total output – i.e., the share of total output consumed rather than saved. The second ratio is the percentage of the total population that is retired. The third is the consumption rate of the elderly compared to people generally.[2] The mathematical derivation of the retiree burden rate as equivalent to the consumption rate of the retiree population relative to total output is shown in Figure 5-1.

The economic burden that retiree populations impose on their national economies is driven by the variables in these ratios. Anything that affects any one of the ratios will affect the interaction among the three. Despite this, Thompson argues that a retirement system's organization may not

---

[1] Lawrence Thompson, *Older & Wiser: The Economics of Public Pensions* (Washington, D.C.: The Urban Institute Press, 1998), p. 6.

[2] Ibid, p. 40.

The economic cost of supporting the retired portion of a population can be stated algebraically:

Equation IV-1: $RB = (C/Y) \bullet (R/P) \bullet (ACR/ACP)$

where RB is the retiree burden rate, C is the total consumption in the economy, Y is the total product produced in the economy, R is the total number of retirees in the population, P is the total population of the society, ACR is the average consumption per retiree, and ACP is the average consumption of the total population. The ACR is equal to CR/R, where CR is the consumption level of the retiree population, and the average consumption per person in the total population is C/P. The ratio of average consumption per retiree to that of the total population is the relative living standards ratio of the elderly. Mathematically it is:

$$ACR/ACP = (CR/R) / (C/P), \text{ or}$$
$$= (CR/R) \bullet (P/C).$$

Thus if,

Equation IV-1: $RB = (C/Y) \bullet (R/P) \bullet (ACR/ACP)$

and substituting for ACR and ACP,

Equation IV-2: $RB = (C/Y) \bullet (R/P) \bullet (CR/R) \bullet (P/C).$

Since C, R, and P appear in both the numerator and denominator of the equation, they cancel out leaving:

Equation IV-3: $RB = CR/Y.$

Figure 5-1. A Model Describing the Economic Cost of Aging Populations.

affect aging costs unless the differences in the systems result in changes to aged dependency ratios or to retirees' relative standards of living.[3] We have no quarrel with Thompson's algebra, but we believe that the way a retirement system is organized is likely to either accentuate or ameliorate the effects of aging on the ratios that determine pension costs.

Consumption and Savings Rates under Alternative Retirement Systems

The first of the ratios in Thompson's model is the relationship between consumption and income. An economy's savings is the residual of income left after expenditures for personal and government consumption expenses. Government consumption is generally financed by taxing income, although governments may borrow from credit markets to a limited extent. The role retirement systems play in determining the relationship between income and consumption levels is through their operation as

---

[3] Ibid, p. 7.

savings devices. In a macroeconomic context, higher savings can potentially increase the incomes and welfare of future workers and retirees by increasing capital formation and economic growth. If a pension system adds to savings, it facilitates economic growth. It increases savings by reducing the level of consumption.

Retirement Saving Versus Consumption Loans
To show how alternative pension structures operate within a national economy, consider an example of a worker who begins a career at age 25 earning €35,000 per year. Assume this individual has perfect foresight and knows that his pay will increase 4 percent per year until he reaches age 65, when he will retire and receive a pension that is 70 percent of his disposable income. His disposable income is his total wage minus what he has to contribute to a pension in order to finance his retirement income. To simplify determining how much the worker should save, assume he knows that he will live to be 81.5 years of age. Our worker anticipates receiving an annual rate of return on his assets of 5 percent per year.

If everything goes according to plan, this worker will earn roughly €161,600 in his last year of employment. After his retirement savings are put aside, his disposable income will be approximately €135,700 that year. As it turns out, this worker will need to save 16 percent of his annual earnings each year in order to fulfill his work and retirement plans. If he does that, he should be able to receive an annuity of €113,100 per year for each year of retirement, 70 percent of his final year's earnings or about 83 percent of disposable income in his final year of work.

This pattern of asset accumulation is reflected in Figure 5-2. Over the working period, the worker's steady saving plus interest accruing on accumulated assets gradually accelerates the growth in total assets. After retirement, the assets are steadily depleted over the worker's remaining lifetime and run out when he dies. Net savings over the worker's lifetime, in this example, are zero. Had he wished to leave a bequest to heirs, the worker would have had to save more during his working life or spend less during retirement.

If this same worker is covered by a pay-go retirement plan, the dynamics of his accumulating retirement rights are considerably different. First, his annual contributions to the retirement system are paid out to current retirees. Second, rather than becoming part of an accumulation of capital that can be invested in the economy, in most cases his contributions

Euros

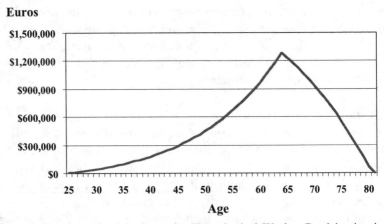

Figure 5-2. Accumulated Savings of a Hypothetical Worker Participating in a Funded Pension Plan. *Source:* Calculated by the authors.

merely purchase an entitlement to a benefit at retirement age. In other words, it results in an unfunded obligation – a "consumer loan" in Paul Samuelson's terms – that future participants in the system are obligated to pay when the current worker retires. The pattern of this transaction is reflected in Figure 5-3, which turns out to be a mirror image of Figure 5-2. In this case, the "accumulated savings" is the sum of the obligations owed to the worker. It grows on a gradually accelerating basis until the worker reaches age 65, and then is paid off over the remainder of his lifetime as annual retirement benefits.

Euros

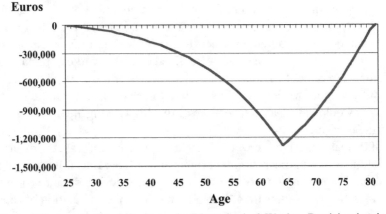

Figure 5-3. Accumulated Savings of a Hypothetical Worker Participating in a Pay-As-You-Go Pension Plan. *Source:* Calculated by the authors.

From the perspective of the worker, the accumulation of pension rights through a pay-go social security system is no different than accumulating wealth through personal savings or a funded pension. In the life-cycle context, the primary motivation for workers to save is to provide for their consumption after they retire. If a significant share of their retirement consumption needs will be met by a mechanism that does not require savings, and indeed actually creates substantial liabilities, it has the potential to lower national savings rates.

In the initial discussion about the differences between funded and pay-go retirement plans, we indicated that the latter are intergenerational transfer programs. The actual implications of these programs for national savings rates depends on what economists call the "marginal propensity to save" and how it differs across the age spectrum. This is simply the marginal rate at which individuals save part of their income. Conceptually, it is possible that our national retirement systems tax money away from people who would not save otherwise and give it to people who do save. If this were the case, then pay-go retirement systems might actually increase savings rates. If this sort of behavior were widespread, however, we would expect that most of the elderly would be leaving significantly larger estates than they actually do.

Over the years, there has been a considerable body of economic research developed regarding the implications of pay-go pensions for national savings rates, most of it developed by U.S. economists in the context of the U.S. Social Security program. For that reason, this part of the story focuses mostly on the United States, but the analysis is relevant to pay-go retirement systems around the world. The results generally suggest that pay-go pension programs reduce other savings, although the reductions are generally less than the social security benefits – i.e., the reduction in savings is not dollar for dollar.

For example, in 1974, Martin Feldstein estimated that for each $100 increase in social security wealth in the United States, private saving was reduced by $2.10.[4] Shortly after his study was released, Dean Leimer and Selig Lesnoy, two analysts working for the U.S. Social Security Administration, discovered a computation mistake in Feldstein's paper, which they corrected, and extended the computation period. Their estimate halved the effect that Feldstein had estimated and they

[4] Martin Feldstein, "Social Security, Induced Retirement, and Aggregate Capital Accumulation," *Journal of Political Economy* (September/October 1974), vol. 82, no. 4, pp. 905–926.

estimated that this reduced rate was statistically equivalent to zero.[5] According to Feldstein, the difference in results was because Leimer and Lesnoy extended the data series to 1974, without taking into consideration the program changes adopted in 1972.[6] In 1996, Feldstein updated the model and estimated that a $1 increase in Social Security wealth reduced savings by two to three cents. While two or three cents may seem trivial, Feltstein estimated that the U.S. Social Security system reduced personal saving by $416 billion in 1992, compared to $248 billion of actual savings – a reduction of 63 percent of potential personal saving.[7]

To date, the studies of the effects of pension saving in funded pensions on personal savings rates are no more conclusive than those examining the savings issue from the pay-go perspective. In both cases, there is a general consensus that these plans do reduce other personal savings. Since the pay-go systems do not compensate for the reductions in personal savings with the accumulation of real assets, these plans lead to an absolute reduction of savings within the total economy. In the case of funded plans, plan participation should raise savings rates, since a unit of pension accrual is matched by a unit of actual savings, and there is only a partial reduction in personal savings. If the pension program reduces national saving, it increases consumption. If it raises savings, it reduces consumption.

Another View of Consumption and Savings Rates under Retirement Systems

In 1983, the U.S. Congress adopted amendments to the Social Security Act that have been widely regarded as "prefunding" a portion of the baby boomers' retirement benefits. Since that time, the Social Security trust fund assets have grown from $31 billion in 1984 to $1,531 billion at the end of 2003, although 45 percent of that growth has been government-credited interest on the accumulating assets, which are held in long-term federal government bonds. There has been a considerable debate in the United States over whether this accumulating trust fund has added to the level of national savings. This debate centers on how holding the accumulating

---

[5] Dean R. Leimer and Selig D. Lesnoy, "Social Security and Private Savings: New Time Series Evidence," *Journal of Political Economy* (June 1982), vol. 90, no. 3, pp. 606–629.

[6] Martin Feldstein, "Social Security and Private Savings: Reply," *Journal of Political Economy* (June 1982), vol. 90, no. 3, pp. 630–642.

[7] Martin Feldstein, "Social Security and Private Savings: New Time Series Evidence," *National Tax Journal* (June 1996), vol. 49, no. 2, pp. 151–164.

trust fund entirely in government bonds affects the government's other fiscal operations.

The U.S. experience and debate is broadly relevant for many other OECD countries. Japan and Korea have national pension funds largely invested in government bonds. Belgium's Silver Fund is a government bond fund, as is largely the case with the Swedish AP funds. Much public discussion in Europe focuses on setting up trust funds to prefund social security as an alternative to setting up individual accounts or other forms of private pensions. In some cases, such as in Ireland and Norway, there is significant equity investment. In most countries, however, implicit or explicit investment in government bonds is the norm, making the U.S. experience directly relevant to them. It is somewhat unfortunate that other countries' experiences with public pension funds have not been analysed or studied as thoroughly as the U.S. case.

The analysts who argue that the U.S. accumulating trust fund has not added to national savings contend that the U.S. government has run larger deficits in its other fiscal operations due to the accumulating trust fund. That is, having the surplus annual revenue available to Social Security relieves policymakers from having to raise funds elsewhere to finance other government operations. A special commission established by President George W. Bush to make recommendations on Social Security reform fell into this camp. They acknowledged the theoretical possibility that the trust fund accumulation could add to national savings, but concluded that the reality since the passage of the 1983 funding legislation had taught the "nation a clear lesson about how unlikely this is as a practice. The availability of Social Security surpluses provided the government with an opportunity to use these surpluses to finance other government spending, rather than saving and investing for the future."[8]

Peter Diamond and Peter Orszag, two economists and noted participants in the debate over U.S. Social Security reform, reach the opposite conclusion. They looked at congressional attempts to reduce federal budget deficits throughout the 1980s and early 1990s that ultimately resulted in surpluses toward the end of the century. On the basis of the efforts to reduce the unified budget deficits, Diamond and Orszag conclude that it is plausible that U.S. policymakers were not raiding the

[8] President's Commission to Strengthen Social Security, *Strengthening Social Security and Creating Personal Wealth for All Americans: Final Report of the President's Commission to Strengthen Social Security* (Washington, D.C.: U.S. Government Printing Office, 2001), p. 38.

Social Security surpluses to finance other government operations. In addition, they note that if policmakers were pursuing such a policy, financing general government operations with payroll taxes would have imposed a greater burden on lower-wage workers than financing such operations out of the more progressive U.S. federal income tax. Given that people with lower incomes generally have higher marginal propensities to consume, such a policy would have reduced disposable income for people with high marginal propensities to consume and raised it for people with high marginal propensities to save. The net result would have been to increase the national saving level and reduce consumption levels accordingly.[9]

To some extent, it is impossible to know whether the U.S. Social Security trust fund balance represents wealth that will benefit future generations, since the answer partly depends on unobservable or counterfactual behavior. Kent Smetters argues, however, that by comparing variations in the financing of other government functions to the accumulation in the retirement system over time, we can tell whether the systematic growth in the pension trust funds has been paralleled by changes to the other balances. He devises an empirical test to see what happened in the United States. The logic of his model is that if the accumulating trust fund has not added to national savings, each dollar of growth in the trust fund should be offset by a dollar increase in the deficit. If the growing pension balances are being saved, then there should be no change in other government net deficits as the pension surplus grows. In his favored specification of the model utilizing data from 1949 through 2002, Smetters finds that for every dollar the pension trust funds increase, the other government net deficits increase by $2.76. He concludes that not only are the accumulating pension surpluses spent elsewhere in government, but that they act as some sort of accelerator to deficit financing of other government operations.[10]

The U.S. Social Security Trust Fund: Does It Represent Extra Savings?

By Professor Kent Smetters, the Wharton School, University of Pennsylvania

With over $1 trillion in assets, the U.S. Social Security trust fund is the largest pension reserve in the world, and potentially a model for other developed countries facing future financing problems.

[9] Peter A. Diamond and Peter R. Orszag, *Saving Social Security: A Balanced Approach* (Washington, D.C.: Brookings Institution, 2004), pp. 200–204.

[10] Kent Smetters, "Is the Social Security Trust Fund Worth Anything?" unpublished memo, The University of Pennsylvania, June, 2003.

But are those assets actually worth anything? This question has generated a heated debate in the United States among policymakers and academics. In "Is the Social Security Trust Fund Worth Anything?" (NBER Working Paper #9845, 2003), I provide a conceptual framework for thinking rigorously about the assets accumulated in the trust fund.

Multiple perspectives of the trust fund are identified and are summarized under two categories: (1) storage technology arguments, and (2) ownership arguments. Storage technology arguments focus on whether previous trust fund surpluses have actually reduced the level of debt held by the public or, alternatively, have been indirectly spent elsewhere in the government budget. Ownership arguments focus on property rights, i.e., how trust fund credits should be allocated regardless of whether they reduced the debt held by the public.

But only the storage argument can be empirically tested, as I do in this paper. Using a series of empirical tests and different econometric specifications, I find evidence that, not only have past trust fund surpluses failed to reduce the debt held by the public, those surpluses might have actually increased the debt level. I show how this counterintuitive result can be explained by a simple "split the dollar game" where competition between two political parties produces this overspending within the government's "unified budget" framework.

Consistently, I find that the adoption of the unified budget framework in the late 1960s appears to play a statistically significant role in this result. To be sure, this evidence is based on a limited annual time series (1949 to 2002) and so the results should be interpreted with caution. But as the paper explains, the empirical tests are, if anything, biased toward finding a reduction in the level of debt held by the public, and not the increase found. These findings suggest that to effectively pre-fund some of the projected shortfalls facing the nation's largest entitlement programs, an even stronger division in the federal budget might be needed between entitlement programs and the rest of the government's operations. Alternatively, a concerned Congress could augment existing entitlement programs with a personal account system as a way of taking the trust fund surplus money "off the table" in Washington, D.C., so that no political party can spend it.

Sita Nataraj and John Shoven have modified and updated Smetters' analysis. They note that Smetters only looked at the implications of U.S. Social Security trust fund accumulations on other federal fiscal operations. They expanded the analysis to include all U.S. government trust funds, because the Social Security trusts represent only about half of all government trust funds, and there was considerable correlation between their accumulations over time. In their preferred estimate, Nataraj and Shoven found that a dollar increase in the total federal trust funds increased federal deficits in other operations by $1.73, a result that was not statistically different from one. Carrying the analysis further, they broke their analytical period into two periods, 1949 to 1969 and 1970 to 2003. This split was important because in 1970, the U.S. government modified its budgeting procedures to explicitly combine the trust fund and other government operations into budget considerations on a unified basis. Before then, each had been considered seperately. For the period before the budgets were unified, Nataraj and Shoven found that the accumulating trust funds were not statistically associated with the deficits run in other government operations. After 1970, the accumulating trust funds did lead to added deficits in other government operations, once again statistically on a dollar-for-dollar basis.[11]

Barry Bosworth and Gary Burtless extended this sort of analysis in another way with two different groups of government entities. First they considered the pension systems sponsored by state governments in the United States for their own employees. At the end of 2000, these state pensions held approximately $2.3 trillion in assets, about half the amount held by private employer plans at that time. In this case, they found that as the pension funds increased their holdings by $100, the deficits in the states' non-pension accounts increased by about $8, an amount statistically equivalent to zero. These state systems are significantly different from the federal Social Security system in that they are not considered in the unified budget context of the federal program. In addition, many of these systems have funding requirements, with contributions held in strictly segregated trusteed accounts and invested in broadly diversified real assets. Finally, many U.S. state governments have strict balanced budgeting provisions embedded in their constitutions. State-level pension systems in the United States operate much like ordinary funded pensions offered by private-sector employers operating their plans under U.S. legal funding requirements.[12]

In the second part of their analysis, Bosworth and Burtless studied the pension funding in national pension systems and the government deficits associated with other government operations. They had data on 13 OECD countries from the period 1970 through 2000. They found that a 1 billion currency unit increase in social insurance trust funds increased the government deficit in other operations by 1.26 billion currency units. After adjustments for autocorrelation in their data series, this dropped to 0.57 billion currency units. When they limited the analysis to the five

[11] Sita Nataraj and John B. Shoven, "Has the Unified Budget Destroyed the Federal Government Trust Funds?" a paper presented at a conference sponsored by the Office of Policy, Social Security Administration and Michigan Retirement Research Consortium, Washington, D.C., 12–13 August 2004.

[12] Barry Bosworth and Gary Burtless, "Pension Reform and Saving," a paper presented at a conference of the International Forum of the Collaboration Projects, Tokyo, Japan, 17–19 February, 2004.

countries whose policies require them to fund a portion of their national pensions – Canada, Denmark, Finland, Japan, and Sweden – they estimated the offset at 0.64 billion currency units after adjusting for autocorrelation. In any event, the authors concluded that a unit increase in national pension funding significantly increased net deficits in other government operations.[13]

What is interesting about the debate over whether funding in national pension programs contributes to national savings is that both sides are looking at the same data, yet drawing opposite conclusions. In the United States,we have already mentioned that Peter Diamond and Peter Orszag concluded that the Social Security surpluses reflected in Table 5-1 reduced the unified budget deficit also shown in the table. A number of other prominent U.S. economists have come to similar conclusions,[14] despite the empirical evidence from Smetters, Nataraj and Shoven, and Bosworth and Burtless suggesting that national pensions' accumulations create deficits in other government operations.

What would the U.S. government have spent, and, for that matter, what would tax collections have been, without access to Social Security's cash-flow surplus over the last 20 years or so? No one knows for sure, but those who suggest that these accumulations have not contributed to national savings have, in our view, presented more compelling empirical evidence to support their conclusions. Part of the problem may be that the analysis is focused too narrowly on the subject at hand. In a broader context, the implications of operating a funded versus pay-go pension system are relatively clear. Once again, the U.S. example is a good one, because the United States has a relatively large funded pension system that runs parallel to its Social Security system, and there is reasonably good data on both systems that can be compared over time.

A pension system's contribution to national savings is not the net of the annual contributions into its trust fund minus the payout of benefits and expenses. It is the extent to which the annual inflow of funds into the plan covers the annual accrual of benefits that must be paid out to participants. The actuaries responsible for valuing the U.S. Social Security program

---

[13] Ibid.

[14] Henry J. Aaron, Alan S. Blinder, Alicia H. Munnell, and Peter Orszag, "Perspectives on the Draft Interim Report of the President's Commission to Strengthen Social Security," (Washington, D.C.: Center on Budget and Policy Priorities and the Century Foundation, 2001); Paul Krugman, "2016 and All That," *New York Times* (July 22, 2001) p. 13; Alicia H. Munnell and R. Kent Weaver, "Social Security's False Alarm," *The Christian Science Monitor* (July 19, 2001), p. 11.

Table 5-1. *U.S. Social Security Cash Flows and Federal Government Unified Budget Operations for Selected Years*

	U.S. Social Security Trust Fund Operations			U.S. Government Unified Budget Operations		
	Tax Revenues	Current Expenditures	Net Surplus	Current Receipts	Current Expenditures	Surplus or (−) Deficit
1984	$183.1	$180.4	$2.7	$1,112.5	$1,256.6	−$144.1
1985	197.5	190.6	6.9	1,213.5	1,366.1	−152.6
1986	212.8	201.5	11.3	1,289.3	1,459.1	−169.8
1987	225.6	209.1	16.5	1,403.2	1,535.8	−132.6
1988	255.2	222.5	32.7	1,502.2	1,618.7	−116.5
1989	276.7	236.2	40.5	1,626.3	1,735.6	−109.3
1990	301.1	253.1	48.0	1,707.8	1,872.6	−164.8
1991	307.8	274.2	33.6	1,758.8	1,976.7	−217.9
1992	317.2	291.9	25.3	1,843.7	2,140.4	−296.7
1993	327.7	308.8	18.9	1,945.8	2,218.4	−272.6
1994	350.0	323.0	27.0	2,089.0	2,290.8	−201.8
1995	364.8	339.8	25.0	2,212.6	2,397.6	−185.0
1996	385.7	353.6	32.1	2,376.1	2,492.1	−116.0
1997	413.9	369.1	44.8	2,551.9	2,568.6	−16.7
1998	439.9	382.3	57.6	2,724.2	2,633.4	90.8
1999	471.2	392.9	78.3	2,895.0	2,741.0	154.0
2000	504.8	415.1	89.7	3,125.9	2,886.5	239.4
2001	529.1	438.9	90.2	3,124.2	3,056.4	67.8
2002	546.3	461.7	84.6	2,980.7	3,224.0	−243.3
2003	546.9	479.1	67.8	3,012.8	3,426.4	−413.6

Sources: 2004 Annual Reports of the Board of Trustees of the Federal Old-Age and Survivors Insurance and Disability Insurance Trust Funds (Washington, D.C.: U.S. Government Printing Office, 2004), and U.S. Department of Commerce, *National Income and Product Accounts.*

each year estimate the obligations accrued under the system. They do this by assuming that there will be no future contributions, and that benefits will be paid out on a pro-rata basis to everyone currently over the age of 15 when they become eligible for retirement. From this amount, they net the value of the trust fund as of the valuation date, and the resulting difference is the estimated level of unfunded obligations accrued as of that date. The results of these estimates dating back over the past couple of decades are shown in the second through fourth columns of Table 5-2.

To put the results in perspective, consider a household that begins a year with a bank account balance of zero, runs up a $20,000 debt over the year, and, at year-end, has $5,000 in its bank account and a note for the $20,000 loan. No one would say that this household has saved $5,000.

Table 5-2. *Relative Role of Private and Public Pensions for Men Retired at Early and Normal Retirement Ages*

	Social Security			Private Pensions		
	Closed Group Obligations (Billions)	Trust Fund Assets (Billions)	System Overfunding (Billions)	Plan Obligations (Billions)	Trust Fund Assets (Billions)	System Overfunding (Billions)
1984	$4,293.1	$31.1	−$4,262.0			
1985	5,018.2	42.2	−4,976.0	$1,056.5	$1,260.8	$204.3
1986	5,238.5	46.9	−5,191.6	1,296.6	1,523.7	227.2
1987	5,423.9	68.8	−5,355.1	1,526.8	1,717.6	190.8
1988	5,787.6	109.8	−5,677.8	1,620.7	1,827.7	207.0
1989	6,853.3	163.0	−6,690.3	1,893.0	2,085.7	192.7
1990	6,399.1	225.3	−6,173.8	2,124.1	2,367.4	243.3
1991	7,207.2	280.7	−6,926.5	2,501.3	2,667.0	165.7
1992	7,506.5	331.5	−7,175.0	2,788.4	2,929.5	141.1
1993	8,312.3	378.3	−7,934.0	3,127.9	3,230.3	102.5
1994	8,105.0	436.4	−7,668.6	3,376.6	3,421.7	45.1
1995	8,877.8	496.1	−8,381.7	3,822.5	3,958.8	136.3
1996	8,058.4	567.0	−7,491.4	4,508.4	4,540.5	32.0
1997	8,662.1	655.5	−8,006.6	5,150.3	5,307.2	156.9
1998	9,056.2	762.5	−8,293.7	5,985.1	6,165.0	179.9
1999	9,739.6	896.1	−8,843.5	6,957.1	7,164.1	207.0
2000	10,654.3	1,049.4	−9,604.9	6,704.9	7,286.6	581.8
2001	11,353.6	1,212.5	−10,141.1	6,634.4	6,954.3	319.8
2002	11,888.5	1,378.0	−10,510.5	7,658.0	5,958.3	−1,699.7
2003	12,690.6	1,530.8	−11,159.8	7,454.1	7,154.8	−299.3

Sources: Social Security trust fund balances are drawn from *2004 Annual Reports of the Board of Trustees of the Federal Old-Age and Survivors Insurance and Disability Insurance Trust Funds* (Washington, D.C.: U.S. Government Printing Office, 2004); the estimated underfunding is unpublished data from the Office of the Actuary, U.S. Social Security Administration; private pension plan assets are derived U.S. Pension Benefit Guaranty Board's *Pension Insurance Data Book* for various years found at http://www.pbgc.gov/publications/default.htm for private defined benefit plans and from the Federal Reserve Bank's *Flow of Funds* data for various years for defined contribution assets and individual retirement account balances; private pension plan obligations for defined benefit plans also are taken from the PBGC *Data Book*, and defined contribution plan and individual retirement account obligations were calculated as the equivalent of assets.

Yet that is exactly the logic behind the claim that the U.S. Social Security program's trust fund accumulation is adding to national savings. In the household described above, it is clear that their net financial position has deteriorated by $15,000 over the year. One could claim that the household would have been $5,000 deeper in debt if it had spent the money rather than putting it in the bank, but it makes no sense to consider the $5,000 as savings in the face of the much larger debt.

The U.S. Social Security system has had a steadily growing balance in its trust fund accounts over the past two decades, but its underfunding has grown steadily as well. The accumulated funding can be considered saving only to the extent that had the assets not grown, the level of dissaving would have been even higher.

In contrast to Social Security, the private pension system in the United States is largely funded. The private system is comprised of three elements: employer-sponsored defined benefit plans, employer-sponsored defined contribution plans, and individual retirement accounts. In 1974, the U.S. Congress adopted legislation meant to secure private pensions for workers. For defined benefit plans, these requirements mean that benefits must be funded at roughly the same rate that benefits are earned by participants, and that unfunded liabilities must be amortized over a specified schedule. Defined contribution plans and individual retirement accounts are fully funded by the nature of the plans – i.e., the obligation of the plan equals its value.

The three right-hand columns of Table 5-2 reflect the growing obligations and assets in the U.S. private pension system and correspond with the three columns to their left for Social Security. In this case, private pension obligations in the United States were fully funded on an aggregate basis over most of the period. This does not mean that all defined benefit plans were fully funded; indeed some were underfunded, but the overfunding in some plans more than offset the underfunding in others. In a national savings context, it is the aggregate balances that are important. In 2002, the system slipped into an underfunded status, generally due to declining asset values in the financial markets. In addition, the value of liabilities also increased in defined benefit plans, because the interest rates used to calculate full funding requirements fell to historic lows. But by the end of 2003, much of the aggregate underfunding had been made up by a rebound in the financial markets and higher contributions from plan sponsors. Legal funding requirements ensure that the plans will soon be back in balance.

From 1984 to 2003, aggregate pension saving in Social Security fell from minus $4 trillion to minus $11 trillion, while private pension savings rose from $1 trillion to $7 trillion. Although all economists may not agree on the rate at which pension saving is offset by personal saving, most of them agree there is some offset and many of them believe it is substantial. Given the disparate paths of these two pension systems, it is hard to fathom that the U.S. Social Security system is not considerably reducing savings levels relative to what would happen if it operated like the funded pension system. If it is reducing savings, it is increasing consumption accordingly.

Retirement Patterns under Alternative Retirement Systems

According to Lawrence Thompson, the second ratio that determines the retiree burden rates is the percentage of the total population that is retired. In some regards, the structure of a plan – funded or pay-go – has little effect on when people retire. Both national pensions and employer-sponsored pensions often offer early retirement incentives. But some of the factors underlying the demographic challenges we face will operate quite differently under funded versus pay-go plans.

If people retire at the same age but live longer, that lengthens the period of retirement, thus driving up retirement dependency. As we noted in Chapter 3, increasing aging dependency ratios create higher pension costs in pay-go pension systems. In funded plans, the situation is theoretically similar, although the outcomes might be quite different.

First, consider what happens with a funded pension system. In the earlier example, we assumed that workers retire at age 65 and live until age 81.5. We also assumed that pension assets earned 5 percent per year. Under these assumptions, it would take an accumulated fund of just under €340,000 to pay a retiree €30,000 per year during each year of his retirement. If a worker's life expectancy rises from 81.5 years to 83.5 years, it throws the system out of balance. If the worker still retires at age 65 and draws a pension of €30,000 per year, the pension reserves will be empty when the worker reaches 81.5 years of age. If the retiree continues drawing an annuity after that, the net balance in the plan will be nearly a minus €65,000 by the time the retiree dies.

There are a number of different ways a worker might react to this situation. But for his retirement plans to work out, the worker must react quickly, either by saving more, working longer or living on less during retirement. In theory, the pay-go system could react the same way, adjusting plan features as necessary to bring the system back into balance. In the United States, the Social Security actuaries pronounce the system as being in "close actuarial balance" if existing trust funds plus the present discounted value of future income are within 5 percent of the projected present discounted value of future benefit obligations. The resources and liabilities are estimated over a 75-year time frame. Since the mid- to late-1980s, the actuaries have estimated the system to be out of "close actuarial balance" every year. By the beginning of 2004, the underfunding was approximately \$3.7 trillion.[15] While there has been considerable discussion among policy analysts and policymakers about how to close this gap, including raising the retirement age, nothing has been done. When phantom savings are being generated because of the demographic structure, the underlying financing imbalances remain largely invisible until the cash flows turn negative. At that point, policymakers have to act, although by then, there are far fewer options.

Retirement Living Standards under Alternative Retirement Systems

The third ratio in Thompson's formula for determining the retirement burden level is the standard of living that the elderly achieve relative to that achieved by the population as a whole. Harking back once more to our example of a worker who, out of the blue, discovers that she will live a few more years, if the worker still plans to retire at age 65 and still wants to receive €30,000 per year, she will need to accumulate nearly €365,000 instead of €340,000 – nearly 7.5 percent more than before. This means that something has got to give: she must either save more, retire later, or settle for a smaller annual annuity. If this worker saves more, she must scale back her standard of living while working. If she lives with a smaller pension, she must accept a lower standard of living in retirement. If she works longer, she must exchange leisure for a higher material standard of living over both her working and retirement years. In a funded plan, tradeoffs like these are inescapable.

In a pay-as-you-go plan these same set of options can be deferred and possibly shifted from one generation to the next. The pay-as-you go pension systems could operate the same way as a funded plan. As soon as policymakers realized that increasing longevity would increase pension costs, they could adjust one or more of the three pension parameters accordingly. Increasing taxes would create partial funding, the equivalent of saving more in the funded plan; reducing future benefits would bring liabilities back in balance with expected income streams; and raising the retirement age would change the working-leisure tradeoff. Despite the fact that most policymakers have known for some time that their pension systems were out of balance, the record in the United States and elsewhere around the world shows that policymakers have generally not adjusted their pension parameters accordingly, at least not in a timely

---

[15] Unpublished data from the Office of the Actuary, U.S. Social Security Administration.

fashion. In both Germany and Japan, policymakers failed to act until the situation became so dire they had to cut benefits for current retirees. In cases like the United States, there has been considerable discussion and hand-wringing about what to do, but so far, nothing has been done. To a large extent, this inaction arises because policymakers can ignore the long-term implications of current policy as long as they are accounting for the current operations on a cash flow basis. The lack of funding in the system results in a lack of discipline in its operation. Despite widespread knowledge that, under current policies, a system will soon be running on empty, program participants are usually unpleasantly surprised when the predictable consequences hit home. Predictable surprises of this sort are unnecessary and undesirable.

In the final analysis, the pension systems throughout most of the developed world today are in no position to meet the demographic challenges they will face over the coming decades. In many cases, policymakers may try to sustain benefits as long as possible. But simply throwing more money at broken systems could act as a significant fiscal drag on the economy. Part of the equation in considering how to bring our retirement security systems back into balance has to be on the benefit side – this may mean lower benefits or requiring workers to stay in the labor force longer than they do now. To the extent that additional resources are part of the solution, we believe that it would be better for countries to introduce changes that provide real savings opportunities, rather than simply continuing down the pay-go path.

Pension Funding Realities

At the outset, we stated that we had certain biases toward funded pension systems over pay-go financed systems, and the analysis in the previous two chapters explains why. Despite having reached that conclusion, we are not blind to the very real challenges involved in shifting from a pay-go to a funded environment. Glossing over these challenges could put us at risk of adopting new policies that provide illusory benefits in the short run and no real long-term advantages over our existing systems.

What Appears to be Pension Funding Might not be Real Funding
This analysis suggests that funded pension systems are likely to be more dynamic in their response to demographic shifts than pay-go systems. Partly in recognition of this fact, a number of countries have begun to shift from pay-go to funded pension systems. Such efforts are laudable

and appear to be a move in the right direction, but appearances can be deceiving. One must be careful to look beneath the surface before pronouncing such transitions a success.

Mexico adopted a pension reform measure in 1997 that appears to be moving to a funded individual account retirement system along the lines of the Chilean system adopted nearly two decades earlier. There are a couple of serious problems with the Mexican reform, however, that suggest the changes may create as many or possibly more problems than they solved. As with most of the reforms following the Chilean model, Mexico established private investment management firms, Administradores de Fondos de Ahorro para el Retiro (AFORES), to handle the investment of private accounts accumulated under their reforms. The administrative charges, at least in the early years of operation, have been high. Contributions to the system are 6.5 percent of a worker's wage plus a government contribution, known as the Social Quota, which is 5.5 times the minimum wage – the equivalent of 2.2 percent of wages on average. In practical terms, contributions range between 7.5 and 12.0 percent of pay, depending on salary level, before fees and commission. The latter are running approximately 2 percent of salary.[16]

In pension funding, a 10 percent contribution realizing a 4 percent real return would generate a benefit that is roughly the equivalent of final salary for a full career worker with steady wage growth over a career. An 8 percent contribution drops the accumulation to a level roughly equivalent to the amount needed to maintain preretirement standards of living. If administration costs in the Mexican system are skimming 2 percent off the top of an average contribution of around 10 percent, those costs are eating up any flexibility to cover less than 4 percent real returns. Another problem is that more than 90 percent of the funds accumulated during the early years of the system's operation have been invested in government bonds. This phenomenon has two implications. The first is that over time, government bonds are likely to generate lower returns than assets more broadly invested in the total economy. The second is that as more workers participate in the system and more of them retire, converting their accumulated assets into streams of income, the new system will essentially operate like a pay-go defined benefit system.

Mexico's conversion to its new defined contribution system is further complicated by a "lifetime switch option," allowing anyone with credits

[16] Gloria Grandolini and Luis Cerda, "The 1997 Pension Reform in Mexico," World Bank Policy Research Working Paper no. 1933 (Washington, D.C., 1998).

under the old system at the point of conversion to switch back to the old system at retirement. The old system provided long-career workers with a benefit roughly equivalent to their final average salary in the five years leading up to retirement at age 65. Everyone was immediately converted to the new system when it got underway in 1997. For many years, however, the old guarantees are going to supercede the benefits that can be funded out of individual accounts in the new system. Even in the longer term, a guarantee like this is highly susceptible to future inflation that can drive up salaries quickly at the end of a career but might have little effect on lifetime accumulations in a defined contribution type system.

It would seem that Mexico has moved its private-sector working population into a system that is largely invested in government bonds, with much higher administration fees than the government itself would incur from investing in its own bonds or than the fees individuals would incur if they bought bonds directly from the government. In spite of the individual account character of the new system, the government's guarantee to pay out benefits under the old system will perpetuate the features of that system for many years. The simple act of declaring that a system is going to be funded and setting up an individual account mechanism to do so does not guarantee that it will actually be achieved. The characteristics of plan design and transition features are extremely important.

Funded Pensions Cannot Overcome All Demographic Challenges
Even though funded pensions almost certainly result in higher savings than pay-go systems, savings rates still will vary with changing demographic circumstances, possibly even becoming negative in cases where there is rapid population aging. The example at the beginning of this discussion featured a worker who started working at age 25 earning €35,000 per year. He realized 5 percent pay raises each year, retired at age 65, and lived to age 81.5. We calculated that this worker needed to save 16 percent of pay in order to fund a pension that would pay 70 percent of his final salary during retirement.

Instead of considering this example of a single individual, assume that the whole society is made up of people with identical working careers, earnings profiles, retirement patterns, and life expectancies. We can use this simple example to show how alternative evolving demographic patterns would affect savings rates. In the base case, we assume there are 100,000 people at the oldest age of 81 who are expected to die this year. If we assume there are 2 percent more people age 80 than age 81, and 2 percent more age 79 than age 80, and so forth, we would have a pyramidal population structure somewhat similar to those in less developed countries described in Chapter 2. If we define the savings rate in this case as the total amount workers contribute to their pensions – which would be 16 percent of their pay – plus the interest income on assets, with the sum divided by total income in the economy, the national savings rate in this population would be 13.4 percent. It is less than 16 percent because some of the funded pension assets are paid out to retirees each year, which represents dissaving from the funded pension system.

In this example, if the rate of population growth drops to 1 percent from one age cohort to the next, the national savings rate drops to 8.2 percent. If the population growth rate drops to 0 percent, assuming the rectangular population structure occurring in some of the developed countries today, the national savings rate would drop to 0.9 percent. If the population growth rates turn negative, like the inverted pyramid now developing in countries like Italy, the savings rate turns negative. At a negative 1 percent growth rate, the savings rate in this society drops to minus 12.1 percent. With each younger cohort being 2 percent smaller than its predecesssor, the savings rate drops to a negative 32.9 percent. While these savings rates would be even lower if the pensions were financed on a pay-go basis, the point is that even countries that are attempting to move toward funded pensions could still face negative savings rates as their retirement levels soar because of their demographic structures.

Pension Transitions are Costly and Raise Equity Issues
Simply wanting to shift toward a funded pension system does not mean that countries that have committed historically to pay-go systems can shift to a funded alternative smoothly and swiftly. Some countries may never be able to achieve a fully funded system. The problem is that in many countries, especially the developed countries, the existing pension plans have massive unfunded liabilities that will have to be satisfied.

To once again cite the United States, the U.S. Social Security system had an unfunded obligation of $11.2 trillion at the beginning of 2004. To replace this system with a funded one, this unfunded liability would have to be paid. Simultaneously, a trust fund would have to be amassed and properly invested so as not to create other liabilities at the same time, to cover the obligations already earned under the existing system. The whole transaction would require something in the order of $15 to $20 trillion, the equivalent of several years' GDP.

To gradually replace existing pay-go systems with funded plans, poli-cymakers would have to either pay off the current liability or reduce it through various program modifications. Most of the developed countries are not running fiscal surpluses, so paying off the liabilities in a relatively short period of time seems out of the question in most cases. Germany and Japan have recently undertaken pension reforms aimed at reducing the obligations in their systems. In Germany, the goal is to hold the line on a payroll tax rate that is already approaching 20 percent of covered payroll. In Japan, substantial benefit reductions have been introduced, but the cuts are not large enough to keep the payroll tax from rising substantially in coming years. As the legislation was being debated and voted in the lower house of the Japanese Diet, physical scuffles broke out among legislators.[17] In Germany, the push for pension reform has contributed to a sense of malaise on the part of citizens and has been at least partly repsonsible for Chancellor Gerhard Schroeder's declining political ratings.[18]

Creating funded plans that amass substantial assets relatively quickly can be a daunting challenge. In Australia, policymakers mandated employer contributions to workers' funded pensions, but they were operating in an environment where the basic pension was relatively modest. In Germany in 2002, policymakers introduced tax incentives for workers to participate in private savings plans known as "Riester Pensions," named after the legislative sponsor of the measure. These plans were intended, in part, to allow workers to make up for some of the benefit reductions to the state pension that were adopted at that time. There was extremely limited utilization of these plans in their initial roll-out, because of their administrative complexity and insufficient tax incentives.

Proper structuring of voluntary vehicles can be highly effective in encouraging workers to participate in funded retirement savings vehicles. Since the early 1980s, U.S. workers have been able to make voluntary pre-tax contributions into 401(k) retirement plans. Most employers who have etablished these plans subsidize employee contributions to the plans. In a typical plan today, a worker may contribute up to 6 percent of pay up to the annual maximum contribution, and the employer matches employee contributions on a 50 percent basis. The assets in the accounts accrue interest on a pre-tax basis. Distributions taken before retirement are subject to normal income taxes plus a 10 percent excise tax. Distributions taken

[17] BBC News "Japan Divided on Pension Reform," (June 7, 2004), found at: http://news.bbc.co.uk/2/hi/business/3783069.stm.

[18] *Economist*, "Wanted: A Cure for Weltschmerz," (June 25, 2004), found at: http://www.economist.com/agenda/displaystory.cfm?story_id=2804117.

after retirement are subject to normal income taxes. In the typical 401(k) plan today in the United States, voluntary participation rates range between 70 and 85 percent and total contributions average between 7 and 9 percent of pay.

James Poterba, Steven Venti and David Wise have estimated that by 2025, the 401(k) system in the United States will be generating retirement income comparable to that projected from the national Social Security pension system, assuming that current laws remain in place.[19] This system will never be considered a full substitute for the government-run pension, because it is voluntary and lower-income workers have much lower participation and contribution rates than other workers. But it is a completely voluntary system that will generate substantial levels of retirement income in the future and may give policymakers some flexibility in restructuring the social security pension.

The variation in retirement systems across the nations of the world mean that every case is unique in terms of what needs to be done to respond to the challenges that aging populations will pose. Delaying the needed changes will never simplify or moderate what ultimately has to be done. Failure to take up the challenges on a timely basis will exacerbate the negative implications of changes that ultimately are required.

---

[19] James M. Poterba, Steven F. Venti, and David A. Wise, "Implications of Rising Personal Retirement Savings," in David A. Wise, ed., *Frontiers in the Economics of Aging* (Chicago: University of Chicago Press, 1998), pp. 125–167.

SIX

Beyond Pensions to Health Care Considerations

The discussion about aging populations and pension costs is partly about how societies share the output of their economies between the working and retiree populations. We will explore this in greater depth in coming chapters. The consumption of health care goods and services, however, is unique in virtually all developed societies and so should be considered on its own for a variety of reasons. Health care is largely financed through separate insurance mechanisms than are used to finance health care consumption. In most countries, these insurance mechanisms are predominantly publicly financed and administered, and generally cover both the elderly and the non-elderly populations. The notable exception is the United States, where health insurance is largely privately financed for the non-poor, working-age people and their dependents, and is financed on a mixed public-private basis for the elderly population.

In the context of the current discussion, health care includes the goods and services delivered by health practitioners as acute care or long-term care. Acute care includes ambulatory care delivered by health providers outside of hospitals, care provided to patients who are hospitalized, pharmaceuticals, and so forth. Beyond acute care, long-term care is either institutional care or home services provided to the disabled and others unable to care for themselves. The intersection of aging populations and existing health financing arrangements will create financing challenges for all developed countries in the coming decades for a couple reasons. The first has to do with the utilization of health care at various ages. The second relates to consumption and expenditure patterns for health care goods and services.

Age and Health Consumption Patterns

One of the concerns about population aging and health care is that, on average, older people consume considerably more health care than younger ones. Figure 6-1 shows the pattern of age-related public per capita expenditures on health care in several European countries. The underlying data do not include private expenditures for health-related goods and services or for long-term care expenditures. Across this set of countries, about three-quarters of all health expenditures are publicly financed, so the figure should accurately convey overall health expenditure patterns. Our own analysis of the United States suggests a similar pattern of consumption to that represented in Figure 6-1. In a few cases, the expenditure rates are depicted as being flat beyond certain ages, which simply reflects the lack of detailed estimates at older ages. When you consider that older people consume the most health care and that populations in these countries are aging, health costs seem poised to explode over the coming decades.

But there is an alternative perspective on how aging populations will affect health care costs, based on the observation that lifetime health care costs tend to cluster disproportionately in a relatively brief period before death. James Lubitz and Gerald Riley analyzed Medicare expenditures in the United States from 1976 to 1988. They found that beneficiaries in the last year of life cost about seven times as much as other beneficiaries – about 27 to 28 percent of all Medicare payments were made to people in their last year of life.[1] Medicare in the United States covers people ages 65 and older and people of all ages who qualify for disability pensions. In a subsequent analysis, Alan Garber, Thomas MaCurdy, and Mark McClellan analyzed U.S. Medicare expenditures on elderly beneficiaries from 1988 through 1995. Their findings were similar to the earlier analysis of the total Medicare population.[2]

Even within the last year of life, expenditures tend to be very concentrated in the final months. Lubitz and Riley found that about 52 percent of all Medicare payments in the last year of life were for care in the last two months and about 60 percent were for care in the last quarter year of life. Garber and his colleagues found somewhat less concentration, with

---

[1] James D. Lubitz and Gerald F. Riley, "Trends in Medicare Payments in the Last Year of Life," *New England Journal of Medicine* (1993), vol. 328, pp. 1092–1096.

[2] Alan M. Garber Thomas E. MaCurdy, and Mark McClellan, "Medical Care at the End of Life: Diseases, Treatment Patterns, and Costs" (Cambridge, MA: National Bureau of Economic Research, 1998), NBER Working Paper, no. 6748.

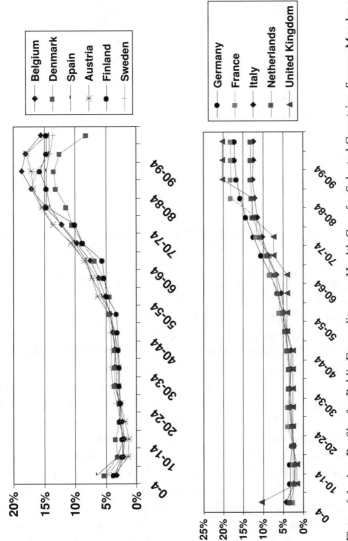

Figure 6-1. Age Profiles for Public Expenditure on Health Care for Selected Countries. *Source:* Mandeep Bains and Howard Oxley "Ageing-related Spending Projection for Health and Long-Term Care," *Towards Higher-Performing Health Systems: Policy Studies from the OECD Health Project* (Paris: Organization for Economic and Cooperative Development, 2004), p. 321.

Table 6-1. *Relative Size of the Elderly Population and Its Share of Health Care Spending*

	Source Year for Health Care Observation	Portion of Population Age 65 or Over	Percent of Total Health Spending on Persons Age 65 or Over	Ratio of Spending for Persons 65 or Older to Those Under Age 65
Australia	1994	11.9	35	4.0
Canada	1994	12.0	40	4.7
France	1993	15.1	35	3.0
Germany	1994	15.5	34	2.7
Japan	1995	14.6	47	4.8
New Zealand	1994	11.5	34	3.9
United Kingdom	1993	15.7	43	3.9
United States	1995	12.5	38	3.8

Sources: Population data from United Nations, Population Division, World Population Prospects (The 2000 Revision) and Gerard F. Anderson and Peter Sotir Hussey, "Population Aging: A Comparison Among Industrialized Countries," *Health Affairs* (May/June 2000), p. 195.

between 40 and 45 percent of payments in the last year of life concentrated in the last quarter. A similar study looking at the health costs of members aged 65 and older of a large Swiss sickness fund found results consistent with Garber et al. A rural sample of cases spanning 1983 to 1992 found that 49 percent of terminal year costs were concentrated in the last quarter. A more urban sample covering 1983 to 1994 found that 42 percent of terminal year costs were incurred in the last quarter.[3]

Peter Zweifel and his colleagues developed an econometric analysis to test whether health care expenditures were driven by advancing age or by remaining time until death. They found that in the last two years of life, age had no effect on health costs after controlling for remaining lifetime. Extending their analysis to cover the last five years of life produced the same result. They concluded, "per capita [health care expenditure] is not necessarily affected by the aging of the population due to an increase in life expectancy. Rather an increase in the elderly's share of population seems to shift the bulk of [health care expenditure] to a higher age, leaving per capita [health care expenditure] unchanged."[4]

Table 6-1 shows the implications of the patterns of health care expenditures reflected in Figure 6-1, with its concentration of health care

[3] Peter Zweifel, Stefan Felder, and Markus Meiers, "Aging of Population and Health Care Expenditure: A Red Herring?" *Health Economics* (1999), vol. 8, pp. 485–496.
[4] Ibid, p. 493.

expenditures on the elderly across a number of countries. The data simply highlight the importance of determining whether population aging implies a proportionate increase in health expenditures or merely a postponement of health costs until the end of life. Steven Lieberman and several colleagues have looked at the spending patterns of participants in the U.S. Medicare system in a way that may shed some light on the issue. They found that 5 percent of the covered population accounted for 47 percent of program expenditures between 1995 and 1999. In the most expensive 5 percent of cases, beneficiaries were five times more likely to die within a given year than the average beneficiary. However, only one-fifth of these very high-cost individuals died within a year. Among those enrolled in Medicare's fee-for-service program in 1995, which includes the vast majority of those eligible for Medicare, 27 percent accounted for 75 percent of the five-year cumulative spending for the whole group. Of the 27 percent, two-thirds were included in the top quartile of spenders in each year for at least two consecutive years. The high-cost cases accounted for 57 percent of cumulative expenditures for the group over the five-year period. Among the persistently high-cost cases, 60 percent of the beneficiaries were alive at the end of the five-year period, leading the authors to conclude that most of the spending was associated with costly beneficiaries who continue to live.[5]

The OECD and the European Commission (EC) recently projected the effects of population aging on health care costs in various developed nations. While they undertook this modeling as a joint project and their input assumptions are generally consistent, the reported results published by the two organizations contain a number of slight differences. The results published in 2001 by the OECD are shown in Table 6-2. More recently, Mandeep Bains from the EC and Howard Oxley from the OECD also presented results from this effort. Aside from some slight differences, their results are essentially the same as those in Table 6-2.[6] In Table 6-2, we have included the OECD projections of public expenditures for both health care and pensions for comparative purposes. We use the earlier OECD health cost projections here because they allow us to do a direct comparison to the pension projections and because they are so close to the later EC-OECD joint presentation. In most cases, the

[5] Steven Lieberman, Julie Lee, Todd Anderson, and Dan L. Crippen, "Reducing the Growth of Medicare Spending: Geographic versus Patient-Based Strategies," *Health Affairs* (December 2003), pp. 603–613.

[6] Organization for Economic Co-Operation and Development, OECD *Economic Outlook* (Paris: OECD, June 2001), no. 69, p. 154.

Table 6-2. *Total Public Expenditure on Health Care and Pensions*

	Health Expenditure as Share of GDP in 2000	Increase in Health Expenditure as Percent of GDP from 2000 and 2050		Pension Expenditure as Share of GDP in 2000	Increase in Pension Expenditure as Percent of GDP from 2000 to 2050
		per Capita	Per Worker		
Austria	5.7%	1.7%	2.0%	14.5	2.5
Belgium	5.3	1.3	1.5	10.0	3.3
Denmark	5.1	0.7	1.1	10.5	2.8
Finland	4.6	1.2	1.8	11.3	4.6
France	6.2	1.2	1.9	12.1	
Germany	5.7	1.4	2.1	11.8	5.0
Greece	4.8	1.7	1.6	12.6	12.2
Ireland	5.9		2.3	4.6	4.4
Italy	4.9	1.5	1.7	13.8	0.3
Luxembourg				7.4	1.9
Netherlands	4.7	1.0	1.3	7.9	5.7
Portugal	5.4	0.8	1.3	9.8	3.4
Spain	5.0	1.7	1.5	9.4	5.9
Sweden	6.0	1.0	1.2	9.0	1.7
United Kingdom	4.6	1.0	1.4	10.4	2.9

Source: Declan Costello and Mandeep Bains, *Budgetary Challenges Posed by Aging Populations,* (Brussels: Economic Policy Committee, European Economic Commission, October 2001), pp. 22 and 44.

projected increases in public expenditures on health are considerably less than projected increases in pension expenditures over the same period. But these health projections should be interpreted with caution.

Costello and Bains warn that the health care cost projections in the OECD and EC exercise "cannot be considered to be likely 'real' levels of future public expenditure on health and long-term care expenditures." They point out that the projections only measure the impact of anticipated demographic changes under two limited sets of assumptions about health costs growth rates. The projections ignore other factors, most notably technology, which might drive up future health expenditures. Assuming that per capita health costs simply grow along with a country's demographic profile indexed by increases in per capita GDP or productivity could either overestimate or underestimate future costs.

A primary reason there will be more old people in the future is because death rates at every age are declining. If future populations of the elderly do not die at the same rate as contemporary elderly populations, and health costs are largely tied to dying, projecting health costs on the basis of aging alone would tend to overestimate the cost increases. On the other hand, failing to model the evolution of medical technology, higher rates of medical price inflation than of general inflation, and the relative intensity of services provided to older people not immediately approaching death would tend to underestimate the cost increases.[7]

Factors Other than Aging Driving Up Health Costs

George Schieber and Jean-Pierre Poullier[8] and later Schieber, Poullier, and Leslie Greenwald[9] laid out the arithmetic for sorting out the components of growth in health costs across countries. Manfred Huber used their structure to evaluate health trends in OECD countries from 1970 to 1997.[10] We have adopted their approach to evaluate historical patterns of utilization, sometimes referred to as volume intensity, and to evaluate relative price inflation for medical services across the OECD countries. There are always problems with such cross-country comparisons because of differences in accounting for medical services from one nation to the next. But in recent years, the OECD has been working with its member countries to standardize definitions and procedures, so that these sorts of analyses yield more meaningful comparisons. While there may not be perfect consistency across all countries, the patterns are certainly illustrative of the implications of ignoring volume intensity and inflation when projecting long-term health costs.

One factor driving health cost increases in most developed countries is disproportionate price inflation in the health sector, as reflected in Table 6-3. Out of 19 countries, health price inflation lagged behind general price inflation only in Denmark, Korea, and France from the early 1970s through the end of the twentieth century. George Schieber has suggested that faulty health care price deflators might account for France's result.[11] To the extent some countries had decades in which they registered a

---

[7] Ibid, p. 40.

[8] George J. Schieber and Jean-Pierre Poullier, "International Health Spending and Utilization Trends," *Health Affairs* (Fall 1988), vol. 9, pp. 105–112.

[9] George J. Schieber, Jean-Pierre Poullier, and Leslie M. Greenwald, "U.S. Health Expenditure Performance: An International Comparison and Data Update," *Health Care Financing Review* (Summer 1992): pp. 1–87.

[10] Manfred Huber, "Health Expenditure Trends in OECD Countries, 1970–1997," *Health Care Financing Review* (Winter 1999), vol. 21, no. 2, pp. 99–117.

[11] George Schieber, "Health Expenditures in Major Industrialized Countries," *Health Care Financing Review* (Summer 1990), pp. 159–167.

Table 6-3. *Rate of Growth in Health Care Price Inflation over Economy-Wide Price Inflation for Selected Countries and Selected Periods*

	Annual Compound Rate of Growth in Percents			Last Year in Data Series
	1970–1980	1980–1990	1990–2000	
Australia	0.61	0.46	0.40	2000
Austria	3.10	1.51	2.97	1995
Belgium	0.28	0.59	2.30	1996
Canada	0.16	1.06	0.23	2000
Denmark	−0.16	−0.20	−0.16	2000
Finland	−0.51	1.40	1.09	2000
France	−1.14	−0.86	−0.16	2000
Germany	0.60	0.52	na	1990
Iceland	2.32	0.00	1.42	2000
Ireland	−3.82	2.50	1.48	2000
Italy	na	na	0.17	2000
Japan	na	0.14	0.88	1997
Korea	−0.17	−0.99	−0.37	1997
Luxembourg	0.42	1.20	4.39	1996
Netherlands	3.71	0.35	0.30	1996
Spain	1.07	−0.54	−0.13	1996
Switzerland	2.33	0.36	0.95	2000
United Kingdom	−0.54	1.07	1.36	1996
United States	0.83	3.07	1.47	2000

Source: OECD Health Data 2004.

negative rate in Table 6-3, their results overall were mixed. The trend in most countries has been for health price inflation to outpace general price inflation, often substantially.

As with any good, price is only one dimension of the cost of consumption. The demand for health care partly relates to a country's income level. Richer countries tend to consume more health care goods and services than less developed ones. If price inflation in the health sector tends to exceed that in the rest of the economy, and rising income levels tend to result in more health care consumption, there is a cross-compounding effect driving up total expenditures. The underlying factors that help to explain this are complex and vary somewhat from country to country, although the net result seems to be relatively consistent.

Table 6-4 shows that, in most developed countries, per capita health expenditures have grown faster than per capita GDP levels over most of the last three decades. The rates are calculated by subtracting the growth in

Table 6-4. *Growth in Real Health Expenditures per Capita and the Excess Over Real Growth in GDP per Capita for Selected Countries and Periods*

	Compound Annual Growth in Real Health Expenditures per Capita			Growth in Real Health Expenditures per Capita Minus Real GDP Growth per Capita		
	1970–1980	1980–1990	1990–2000	1970–1980	1980–1990	1990–2000
Australia	1.96%	2.59%	3.88%	0.59%	1.09%	1.50%
Austria	7.37	1.49	2.83	3.87	−0.72	0.88
Belgium	8.15	3.38	3.60	4.99	1.49	1.73
Canada	3.11	3.91	1.77	0.22	2.40	−0.08
Denmark	1.37	0.83	1.76	−0.16	−0.71	−0.18
Finland	4.65	4.75	−0.12	1.35	2.14	−1.61
France	5.61	3.85	2.35	2.91	1.90	0.87
Germany	6.19	1.82	2.47	3.57	−0.20	2.23
Greece	4.54	1.32	4.73	0.89	1.16	2.78
Iceland	8.32	4.19	3.07	3.01	2.58	1.42
Ireland	8.46	0.12	6.79	5.21	−3.20	0.41
Italy	na	na	1.55	na	na	0.14
Japan	7.08	2.44	3.67	3.78	−0.94	2.48
Korea	na	na	6.76	na	na	1.58
Luxembourg	7.23	4.75	3.01	5.36	0.30	−1.07
Mexico	na	na	3.23	na	na	1.44
Netherlands	3.14	2.31	2.45	1.06	0.64	0.19
New Zealand	2.06	2.87	2.72	1.40	1.68	1.28
Norway	9.17	3.31	3.04	4.92	1.09	−0.09
Portugal	11.54	4.22	6.56	8.03	1.10	4.13
Spain	6.89	4.72	3.36	4.34	2.17	1.14
Sweden	4.44	1.10	1.68	2.82	−0.79	0.06
Switzerland	4.12	2.68	2.72	3.10	1.24	2.35
United Kingdom	4.16	3.15	4.07	2.30	0.68	1.95
United States	4.49	5.50	2.98	2.32	3.27	1.01

Source: Derived by authors from *OECD Health Data 2004.*

per capita GDP from the rate of increase in per capita health expenditures. A positive number in the table means that per capita health expenditures were growing faster than the economy; a negative number means the opposite. In all 22 of the countries for which we could calculate values in the 1970s, the rate of per capita health expenditures outstripped per capita economic growth. The record was more mixed in the 1980s and 1990s, but few countries managed to keep a lid on health expenditures over both decades.

Another driver of increasing health costs in recent decades has been greater utilization of health goods and services. This derives partly from the evolution of health technologies – there are simply more things that medical providers can do to keep people alive and well than in the past. The appetite for an ever-expanding menu of goods and services derives partly from the overall growth in incomes and the observed positive relationship across countries between income level and health consumption. Insurance mechanisms also tend to increase utilization. When consumers are shielded from the market prices of goods or services, they tend to demand more than when they pay directly for their purchases themselves.

The growth in the intensity of health consumption is not directly measurable, but it can be derived by factoring out the increases in health care expenditures associated with price inflation and population growth. We have done this in Table 6-4. The growing intensity in the utilization of health goods and services is shown by two different measures. In the first set of columns, we focus on the compound growth in real spending per capita for health care. In the second set of columns, we look at the rate of increase in health care consumption per capita relative to the rate of growth in GDP per capita. The first set of growth rates focuses on the absolute growth in the consumption of health care, whereas the second looks at growth relative to overall economic capacity.

Focusing first on the growth in real spending on health care per capita, once again, the vast majority of the table entries are positive. France, where health price inflation seemed to be under control from the data in Table 6-3, has consistently sustained substantial growth in real per capita expenditures on health. In several of these countries, the rates of growth in real health expenditures per capita have slowed in recent years, reflecting the implementation of aggressive programs to bring their health care costs under control. In more countries, however, the rates of growth in real health expenditures were higher during the 1990s than they were during the 1980s.

Possibly a better indicator of the increasing utilization of health services is to compare the growth in health consumption on a per capita basis to the country's growing economic capacity as measured by GDP per capita. Among the larger economies, Germany and Japan stand out as recording significantly increasing utilization of health services over the past decade. In the majority of countries, the trends in recent years have been toward slower growth in utilization, once again reflecting the aggressive efforts undertaken to bring health care costs under control. Laureen Graig has used a variety of colorful terms to describe the systems and efforts to reform them in various countries. She characterizes the U.S. system as being in "constant flux;" "health care reform as a permanent state" in Germany; and the implementation of competition and free market principles in the United Kingdom's National Health Service as "mission impossible."[12]

The combination of Tables 6-3 and 6-4 bring to mind a characterization sometimes applied to health system financing, which is that of a bulging balloon that policymakers squeeze to control its overall expansion. The problem is that squeezing one side of a balloon simply causes another part to bulge. The cost of health care services in any country is the product of prices and the volume of services delivered. Pressures to bring prices under control often result in health providers simply providing a higher volume of services. Pressures to control the volume of services delivered throws pressure right back on prices.

In the 18 countries for which we have all the elements for computing excessive health inflation and increasing intensity in per capita utilization during the 1990s, six recorded positive growth in one of the two and negative growth in the other. Eleven of these countries recorded both excessive inflation and higher volume intensity during the 1990s. Only in Denmark did both decline. Thanks to the combination of health care cost inflation, higher utilization, and population growth, health consumption in most developed countries has outpaced the rest of the economy as shown in Table 6-5. We believe that it is unrealistic to assume that excessive price inflation will moderate in the future, or that we will not continue to experience further increases in per capita utilization of services in most developed countries.

Longer Lives and Health Care Consumption in Old Age

There are two important questions in evaluating whether the EC or OECD projections are reasonable. First, does assuming that health costs increase with age and ignoring the fact that costs tend to be concentrated at the end of life overestimate future health care costs? Second, does ignoring excessive price inflation and increasing utilization underestimate future health care costs? David Cutler and Louise Sheiner have developed an analysis for the United States that helps sort out this question in at least one country. Their analytical framework takes into account

---

[12] Laurene A. Graig, *Health of Nations: An International Perspective on U.S. Health Care Reform*, third edition (Washington, D.C.: *Congressional Quarterly*, 1999).

Table 6-5. *Health Care Expenditures as a Percent of GDP and the Rates of Growth in Health Care as a Percent of GDP for Selected Countries and Periods*

	Health Care as Percent of GDP in 1970	Annual Compound Growth Rate in Health Expenditures as Percent of GDP			Health Care as Percent of GDP in 2000
		1970–1980	1980–1990	1990–2000	
Australia	5.5[a]	2.72	1.09	1.44	9.0
Austria	5.3	3.67	−0.68	0.81	7.7
Belgium	4.0	4.81	1.46	1.75	8.8
Canada	7.0	0.14	2.40	−0.11	8.9
Denmark	8.0[a]	1.44	−0.68	−0.12	8.4
Finland	5.6	1.34	2.00	−1.51	6.7
France	5.4	2.77	1.94	0.79	9.3
Germany	6.2	3.45	−0.23	2.23	10.6
Greece	6.1	0.79	1.15	2.74	9.7
Iceland	4.7	2.81	2.58	1.41	9.2
Ireland	5.1	5.12	−3.15	0.48	6.4
Italy	na	na	na	0.12	8.1
Japan	4.5	3.75	−0.96	2.56	7.6
Luxembourg	3.6	5.06	0.33	−1.03	5.5
Mexico		na	na	1.55	5.6
Netherlands	6.9[b]	0.84	0.65	0.25	8.2
New Zealand	5.1	1.47	1.58	1.36	7.9
Norway	4.4	4.75	0.96	0.00	7.7
Portugal	2.6	7.97	1.02	4.03	9.2
Spain	3.6	4.14	2.18	1.13	7.5
Sweden	6.9	2.81	−0.80	0.00	8.4
Switzerland	5.4	3.06	1.29	2.28	10.4
United Kingdom	4.5	2.21	0.69	1.98	7.3
United States	6.9	2.35	3.18	0.97	13.1

[a] Original year for which there was data was 1971.
[b] Original year for which there was data was 1972.
Source: Derived by authors from *OECD Health Data 2004.*

the number of people in each age group, their average health status, and the average medical spending conditional on health status. Their analysis is limited to the Medicare program in the United States, so it is a narrower segment of the population than that covered by the national health insurance program in many countries.[13]

---

[13] David Cutler and Louise Sheiner, "Demographics and Medical Care Spending: Standard and Non-Standard Effects" (Cambridge, MA: National Bureau of Economic Research, 1998), NBER Working Paper, no. 6866.

Table 6-6. *Forecasts of Medicare Acute Care Expenditures Accounting for Changes in Age at Death and Disability among Survivors*

	1992	2010	2030	2050
Forecast holding constant age-specific spending	$3,232	$3,342	$3,272	$3,510
Estimate as ratio of 1992 baseline	1.00	1.03	1.01	1.09
Forecast accounting for change in age of death	3,232	3,261	3,121	3,287
Estimate as ratio of 1992 baseline	1.00	1.01	0.97	1.02
Forecast accounting for change in age of death and 1 percent annual reduction in disability	3,234	3,138	2,903	2,947
Estimate as ratio of 1992 baseline	1.00	0.97	0.90	0.91

Source: David Cutler and Louise Sheiner, "Demographics and Medical Care Spending: Standard and Non-Standard Effects," (Cambridge, MA: National Bureau of Economic Research, 1998), NBER Working Paper, no. 6866, Table 11.

Cutler and Sheiner assess the implications of accounting for changes in age of death on per capita medical costs under the U.S. Medicare program through a series of simulations. They also control for declining disability rates among the surviving elderly. They used historical evidence on reported limitations to daily activities and on days confined to bed for people at advanced ages to show that disabling limitations were declining across the surviving elderly population at any given age. They present evidence showing that these gains in the United States are also being made in other countries. They used their analysis of the U.S. population to develop a regression analysis of the relationship between disability and medical expenditures from which they concluded "that a large part of the relationship between health costs and age is better attributable to the relationship between disability and age. Once disability is accounted for, the relationship between health expenditures and age is much weaker."[14] They estimated that two-thirds of the difference in spending on medical care for those over 85 is attributable to disability rather than age. They used these results to simulate future health costs assuming disability continued to decline in line with the empirical evidence.

The results of Cutler's and Sheiner's simulations of future health costs for the elderly, taking into consideration improving life expectancy and the improving health status of survivors, are reflected in Table 6-6. In

[14] Ibid, p. 22.

Table 6-7. *Forecasts of U.S. Medicare Spending on the Aged as a Share of GDP*

	1992	2010	2030	2050
Medicare costs grow with GDP per capita				
Holding constant age-specific spending	1.7	1.8	2.7	3.1
Accounting for change in age of death and 1 percent annual reduction in disability	1.7	1.7	2.4	2.5
Medicare costs grow at historic rate of increase relative to GDP				
Holding constant age-specific spending	1.7	2.9	7.1	12.8
Accounting for change in age of death and 1 percent annual reduction in disability	1.7	2.7	6.1	10.4

Source: David Cutler and Louise Sheiner, "Demographics and Medical Care Spending: Standard and Non-Standard Effects," (Cambridge, MA: National Bureau of Economic Research, 1998), NBER Working Paper, no. 6866, Table 11.

their baseline projection, which essentially parallels the EC projections, average health costs in 2050 would be 9 percent higher in constant dollars than in 1992. By accounting for changes in the age of death, the 9 percent increase disappears. By accounting for further improvements in the health of survivors, they project that average health costs in 2050 will decline by 9 percent from the 1992 baseline.

Cutler and Sheiner also analyze the implications of changes in death and disability patterns in estimating future U.S. Medicare spending on the elderly in combination with assumptions that health care costs will continue rising more rapidly than GDP, as they have historically. The results of this analysis appear in Table 6-7. In this case, they presented the estimated Medicare spending on the elderly as a percentage of GDP. As in Table 6-6, the improvements in life expectancy and reduced disability among survivors reduce the projected costs of Medicare relative to assumptions that age-specific costs will be constant over time. In the simulation, where they assume that the cost of medical services will increase at the rate of growth in GDP per capita, the increased costs associated with the aging population are projected to rise from 1.7 percent of GDP in 1992 to 3.1 percent in 2050. In this case, the increase in Medicare costs from 1992 to 2050 for the elderly is projected to be about 40 percent less when improving health status is considered. It appears that disregarding the improving health status of the elderly does lead to significant overestimates of future health care costs attributable to the aging populations in developed countries.

However, while ignoring improvements in the health status of the elderly may overstate future health costs, Cutler's and Sheiner's analysis suggests that disregarding the relative increase in the cost of medical services might lead to a far more serious understatement of future costs. In the last two lines of Table 6-7, we show the results of simulations that projected the growth of Medicare costs at their historic rate relative to GDP growth. While taking into account the improving health status of the aged is still important, the effects of medical costs outpacing GDP growth swamp the health effects. Including the historical escalation in health costs relative to economic growth increases the estimates of Medicare costs for the elderly in 2050 by more than four times.

Some may claim that the United States is unique when it comes to health care costs because U.S. per capita health care expenditures are the highest in the world. But looking back at the earlier analysis, one-third of those countries had higher rates of excess health price inflation during the 1990s than the United States. And half of them recorded higher rates of growth in the real per capita utilization of services than the United States. Finally, almost every developed country in the world is facing more severe aging of its population over the coming decades than the United States. Even though controlling for increases in longevity and declines in disability among the elderly reduces the projected health costs, an older population will still consume more health care than a younger one. Any set of long-term health care projections that does not take into account the peculiar nature of the health care market is not accurately projecting the future costs. We believe the current method of valuing these long-term costs in most developed countries is substantially underestimating the challenges ahead.

Explaining the Intensity Spiral in Health Care Consumption

In the early 1970s, Lewis Thomas, in a widely renowned collection of essays entitled *The Lives of a Cell*, described a taxonomy for evaluating technological change in medicine. Thomas's classification system included three levels of health technology.

The first level is called "nontechnology," which includes treatment regimens that help patients cope with diseases that are poorly understood or have no known cures. Thomas characterized this type of medicine with such terms as "supportive therapy," "caring for," and "standing by." In the past, this type of treatment was prescribed for diseases such as diphtheria and meningitis; today it would treat patients with some types of cancer or multiple sclerosis. Care provided under this kind of regime is typically relatively inexpensive, although it may entail intensive nursing and palliative medication during the terminal stages of the disease.

Thomas called his second level "halfway technology," which includes treatments that do not cure the disease in question but do sustain life. These treatments include organ transplants, renal dialysis, and insulin maintenance for diabetics. Thomas also puts much of contemporary cancer treatment in this category, because surgery, radiation, and chemotherapy are directed at existing cancer cells, rather than at the mechanisms that caused the cancer in the first place. Treatments like this sustain life, sometimes for extended periods, but they often also reduce the quality of life.

The third level in Thomas's classification system is "high technology" treatments that are preventive or curative. These might include immunizations for diphtheria or polio or the medical capacity to treat syphilis and tuberculosis. High technologies evolve because the underlying disease mechanisms are well understood, the treatment regimens are well known, and, when available, they are relatively inexpensive, simple, and easy to deliver.[15]

Burton Weisbrod, an economist who has studied the evolution of health technology, observes the unprecedented changes in three areas related to the health sector of the economy since World War II.[16] First, new technologies have revolutionized the practice of medicine. Second, the role of health insurance has become far more important, as the level of coverage rose after the war. Finally, personal health expenditures have increased dramatically in inflation-adjusted dollars, as we documented in the earlier discussion.

Weisbrod's fundamental premise is that there is a two-way causal relationship between health technology and health insurance. He argues that some technologies increase the expected costs of health treatments while others reduce them. Furthermore, some technologies increase the variance in the cost of certain treatments while others reduce costs. If a given technology increases both the average costs of treatment and the unpredictability of its costs, it encourages the demand for insurance as consumers attempt to protect themselves against unexpected

---

[15] Lewis Thomas, The Lives of a Cell (New York: Bantam Books, 1975), pp. 31–36.

[16] Burton A. Weisbrod, "The Health Care Quadrilemma: An Essay on Technological Change, Insurance, Quality of Care, and Cost Containment," *Journal of Economic Literature* (June 1991), vol. 29, pp. 523–552.

and high-cost items. If a given technology decreases both, it discourages the demand for insurance. Using Lewis Thomas's classification system, "nontechnologies" and "high technologies" tend to be relatively inexpensive to deliver, while "halfway technologies" tend to be expensive. In the context of Weisbrod's argument, the development of nontechnologies or high technologies would discourage the demand for health insurance, while the development of halfway technologies would have the opposite effect.

Weisbrod also contends that the type of insurance available to consumers affects the kinds of technologies developed in the health sector. He notes that the historical pattern of insurance coverage for new products and procedures, once they move beyond the "experimental" stage, is particularly important in explaining the development of expensive technologies. If technology developers believe that the costs of delivering a future product or service will eventually be paid by insurance, even though it is not covered during the "experimental" stage, it is still in their best interests to invest in that product or service. An insurance system that pays for most treatments considered nonexperimental, as well as the costs incurred retroactively in the delivery of health treatments, encourages the development of halfway technologies that extend life, regardless of their cost.

According to Weisbrod, the retrospective payment structure for health consumption, which characterizes the operation of health purchasing mechanisms in most countries, has tended to encourage the development of halfway technologies. As a result, there are often few incentives for providers to avoid expensive technologies, even those that are only marginally effective, unless a separate regulatory framework is put in place to limit their use. At the same time, the development of expensive technologies encourages consumers to buy health insurance to avoid the high or unpredictable cost of the resulting medical treatment.

Policy Concerns over the Evolution of Health Technology

In the earlier discussion of the projections of health care expenditure growth in a number of EC and OECD countries, we noted that the projections assumed that, beyond aging, health costs would grow at the rate of growth in per capita GDP or wages. David Cutler has developed a similar set of projections for a larger set of the OECD countries. On the basis of demographic changes alone, he estimates that, by 2030, the OECD countries will be spending 2.2 percent more of their GDP on health care than in 2000. Factoring in continued technological innovation in medicine at historical rates, however, raises the projected increase to 5.7 percent of GDP by 2003.[17] If Cutler's estimate pans out – and we believe it is a more reasonable estimate than those that ignore technology changes – then population aging will increase health care costs as much as it will increase retirement costs.

One of the major lifelines into new health technologies is the health care financing system in the United States. What makes the United States so important in a global context is that it spends so much more on health care than other developed countries. In 2000, at U.S. dollar exchange rates, the United States spent slightly more on health care than the other 29 countries in the OECD combined.[18] Earlier we discussed how health insurance stimulates health technology development and that is particularly true for the U.S. health financing system. There are several factors at play here.

In recent years, a number of governments in the developed world have increased their research and development budgets for health care because of the high social priority on health.

In 2001, OECD governments spent more than USD 25 billion for health-related R&D. Between 1995 and 2001, health R&D appropriations increased on average by 9% every year in the OECD area. The US government remains the major contributor, accounting for three-quarters of total health-related R&D expenditures. U.S. appropriations have continued to grow faster than those in many countries.[19]

In 1994, the U.S. government spent $10.6 billion on health research and development. Over the next decade, that R&D budget grew at an annual compound rate of 9.9 percent per year. By comparison, U.S. government expenditures on defense R&D grew by 5.2 percent per year over the same period. All R&D outside of defense and health shrunk at an annual compound rate of 8.9 percent per year.[20]

Of course, the federal investment in new health technology in the United States is only part of the picture. Peter Neumann and Eileen

---

[17] David M. Cutler, "An International Look at the Medical Care Financing Problem," at: http://post.economics.harvard.edu/faculty/dcutler/papers/cutler_japan_paper_7-03.pdf, (July 2003).

[18] Organization for Economic and Cooperative Development, *OECD Health Data 2004* (Paris: OECD, 2004).

[19] OECD, *Science and Innovation Policy: Key Challenges and Opportunities*, Meeting of the OECD Committee for Scientific and Technological Policy at Ministerial Level, 29–30 January 2004, p. 17.

[20] *Historical Tables, Budget of the United States Government, Fiscal Year 2004* (Washington, D.C.: U.S. Government Printing Office, 2003), pp. 177–178.

Sandberg estimate that total investment in R&D in the U.S. health sector has been outpacing both total health expenditures and R&D investment in other sectors of the economy. They show that health R&D was 12.0 percent of total R&D expenditures in 1985 – but climbed to 20.3 percent by 1995.[21] Part of the reason that private sector entities are also willing to make major investments in the health sector also relate to the unique role the United States plays in the world health care market.

Other developed countries tend to have more highly structured regulatory infrastructures than does the United States, which limits the distribution of new technologies in those countries or at least limits the pricing at which they are utilized. For example, Elias Mossialos and Monique Mrazek describe regulatory frameworks to limit entrepreneurial behavior in pharmaceutical markets around the world. Recognizing that the cost of any product consumed is the product of the quantity consumed and the price paid, there has been considerable focus on regulating the latter. Germany, New Zealand, Sweden, and British Columbia in Canada have all used reference pricing systems to limit reimbursement from health care systems for new pharmaceuticals. The reference is to prices charged for other drugs in a given category. Australia, the Netherlands, Portugal, and the United Kingdom require producers and vendors to provide economic justifications for the prices they charge for prescription drugs. The United Kingdom limits the rate of return pharmaceutical companies can realize on products provided through the National Health Service.[22]

The differences in regulatory approaches taken by the United States versus most of the remainder of the developed world have some profound effects on the delivery and pricing of the product resulting from the massive investment in health products. For example, Mark McClellan, who first headed the Food and Drug Administration and the Centers for Medicare and Medicaid Services in the George W. Bush Administration, has observed:

This year, Americans who account for a fraction of prescription drug use worldwide, will pay for about half of all pharmaceutical spending worldwide. By contrast, citizens of the world's third largest economy, Germany, paid less than

---

[21] Peter Neumann and Eileen Sandberg, "Trends in Health Care R&D and Technology Innovation," *Health Affairs* (November/December 1998), vol. 17, no. 6, pp. 111–119.

[22] Elias Mossialos and Monique Mrazek, "Entrepreneurial Behavior in Pharmaceutical Markets and the Effects of Regulation," in Richard B. Saltman, Reinhard Busse, and Elias Mossialos, eds., *Regulating Entrepreneurial Behavior in European Health Care Systems* (Buckingham, England: Open University Press, 2002), pp. 146–162.

5 percent. The same kind of disparity is true for many other developed nations who have about as much ability to pay as Americans do.[23]

This is a classic case of market segmentation where producers realize they can maximize profits by charging different prices in two markets where the consumers in each are willing to pay different prices for the goods offered. The high prices the U.S. market is willing to pay in this case warrant much of the investment that is being made in many of the new health technologies around the world. Once that investment is covered, further distribution of the products on a profitable basis simply requires that the producers be able to produce them at something above the marginal cost of actual production.

While the proliferation of new products may be cheaper for other economies than it is for the United States, the other countries still are being hit with the marginal cost of an ongoing stream of new products resulting from the massive investment in technology in this sector. A number of countries have taken measures to hold back the tide here as well. In addition to regulating prices, many governments also limit the availability of various sorts of medical goods or services that they will support. David Cutler compares cardiovascular care in the United States to that in Canada to make the point. In Ontario, the Canadian government has allowed fewer than 10 open-heart surgical units to operate. California, which has three times the population of Ontario, has 10 times the number of heart surgery units. As a result, physicians in Canada are forced to prioritize patients more carefully and far fewer patients end up getting bypass surgery or angioplasty operations. Yet the survival rates after a heart attack in the two countries are virtually identical.[24] Limiting the delivery of health services can be accomplished in various ways. To the extent the central financing mechanism controls the budgets that support service delivery, simply limiting total expenditures forces the health sector to restrict and prioritize the delivery of services. Alternatively, licensing and practice authorizations can be used to limit system capacity.

Despite regulatory efforts to curb utilization, the evidence shows that the proliferation of health technologies is leading to more and more intensive delivery of health care services throughout virtually all OECD

---

[23] Mark B. McClelland, "Remarks before the First International Colloquium on Generic Medicine," Cancun, Mexico, September 23, 2003, found at: www.fda.gov/oc/speeches/2003/genericdrug0925.html.

[24] David M. Cutler, *Your Money or Your Life* (Oxford: Oxford University Press, 2004), p. 58.

countries. Cutler's projections suggest that further proliferation of technology and the accompanying intensity of health service delivery will multiply the costs associated with population aging in the developed world. Indeed the major developed societies of the world recognize the pressures that are mounting here and have mounted a specific health project through the OECD. The first stated purpose for undertaking this cross-national effort was to respond to rising health care demand due to population aging and the diffusion of medical technology.[25]

Long-Term Care Provision in Changing Societies

Another health-related cost primarily associated with aging is long-term care delivered in a nursing home or through a home health arrangement. This is maintenance care provided outside the acute care environment to people who need assistance in meeting basic daily functions. Table 6-8 suggests somewhere between 4 and 7 percent of people aged 65 or over in the developed countries are in some form of institutional care arrangement. Another 5 to 25 percent of them are receiving some sort of aid at home.

In many countries, long-term care has not received the same sort of insurance coverage provided for acute health care services. One exception is the Netherlands, which has provided non-means tested benefits financed through a social insurance program dating back to the 1960s. More recently Austria (1993), Germany (1994), and Japan (2000) have instituted long-term health care programs.[26] Figure 6-2 shows the relationship between age and costs associated with the provision of long-term care in several countries. It suggests that long-term care is another area that may dramatically raise the overall health care price tag for aging populations in the developed societies of the world.

A number of countries – including France, Italy, and Greece – have enacted filial responsibility laws that obligate family members to care for their aging parents.[27] With fertility rates falling, however, older people will have fewer family members available to help them. Most health and aging analysts believe that older people will increasingly turn to long-term care facilities when they can no longer manage on their own. However,

---

[25] OECD Health Project, http://www.oecd.org/document/28/0,2340,en_2649_33929_2536540_1_1_1_1,00.html

[26] Mary Jo Gibson, Steven R. Gregory, and Sheel M. Pandya, "Long-Term Care in Developed Nations: A Brief Overview" (Washington, D.C.: AARP Public Policy Institute, 2003), Working Paper 2003–13.

[27] Ibid, p. 5.

Table 6-8. *Share of Population Age 65 and Older in Institutions or Receiving Home Care*

	Source Year	Share of Population Aged 65 and Over in Institutions (Percent of Total)[a]	Share of Population Aged 65 and Over Receiving Formal Help at Home (Percent of Total)[b]
Australia	2003	5.7	21.0
Austria	1998	4.9	24.0
Belgium	1998	6.4	4.5
Canada	1993	6.2	17.0
Denmark	2001	9.1	25.0
Finland	1997	5.3	14.0
France	1997	6.5	6.1
Germany	2000	3.5	7.0
Israel	2000	4.5	12.0
Japan	2003	2.9/6.0	8.0
Netherlands	2003	8.8	12.5/13.0
Norway	2001	11.8	15.6
Sweden	2001	8.2	7.9
United Kingdom	1996	5.1	5.5
United States	2000	4.2	8.7

[a] Estimates vary according to the definition of institutions. For example, 2.9 percent of Japanese 65 and over are in nursing homes; if individuals in long-stay hospitals are also included, the share rises to around 6 percent. The United States data do not include individuals in assisted living facilities, while those from the Nordic countries and the Netherlands include those in "service housing." For Denmark, "older persons" refers mostly to people over age 67.

[b] Proportion of older persons receiving formal help at home, including district nursing and help with activities of daily living. For Australia, data include those receiving services under both CACP and HACC.

Source: Mary Jo Gibson, Steven R. Gregory and Sheel M. Pandya, "Long-Term Care in Developed Nations: A Brief Overview," (Washington, D.C.: AARP Public Policy Institute, 2003), Working Paper 2003–13, p. 3.

long-term care is not exempt from the same cost pressures that affect acute health care services. Indeed, there is evidence that some countries are already shoring up home health services in an effort to shift care out of institutional environments, thus reducing the cost and maximizing the availability of these health services. Denmark, Sweden, and Australia have all undertaken such efforts in recent years.[28]

Table 6-9 shows public expenditures on long-term care in 2000 and projected to 2050 for a number of the OECD countries. If lower birth

[28] Ibid, p. 24.

Average expenditure per head as a share of GDP per capita

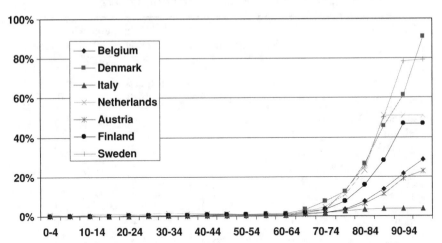

Figure 6-2. Per Capita Long-Term Care Costs by Age Group in Selected Countries. *Source:* Mandeep Bains and Howard Oxley "Ageing-related Spending Projection for Health and Long-Term Care," *Towards Higher-Performing Health Systems: Policy Studies from the OECD Health Project* (Paris: Organization for Economic and Cooperative Development, 2004), p. 322.

rates reduce the amount of care provided to the elderly by immediate family, then countries with extremely limited programs today will be under increased pressures to expand them. It is also likely that the current projections of the growth in costs associated with population aging could turn out to be conservative.

The Health Care Dilemma

The right two columns in Table 6-9 combine the estimated growth in public expenditures for both acute and long-term health care services for countries that were part of the EC/OECD projection project and for which there is complete data. If we add the 3 to 4 percent of GDP that David Cutler estimates new technologies will add to health expenditures to the right-hand column, then total health expenditures for the elderly will rise somewhere in the neighborhood of 6 or 7 percent over the level of GDP being spent on these services at the beginning of the century.

Given the other higher costs related to aging, significantly higher health costs will raise fundamental questions about what is affordable, even in richer societies. Analysts like David Cutler argue that we can afford to

Table 6-9. *Projections of Long-Term Care Costs Separately and Combined with Total Public Health Care Expenditures as a Percentage of GDP*

	Long-Term Care		Total Public Health and Long-Term Care	
	Expenditure in 2000	Change in Expenditure 2000–2050	Expenditure in 2000	Change in Expenditure 2000–2050
Austria	0.7%	1.1%	5.8%	3.1%
Belgium	0.8	0.8	6.1	2.4
Denmark	3.0	2.5	8.0	3.5
Finland	1.6	2.1	6.2	3.9
France	0.4	0.3	6.9	2.5
Ireland	0.7	0.2	6.6	2.5
Italy	0.6	0.2	5.5	2.1
Japan	0.1	0.5	5.4	5.0
Netherlands	2.5	2.5	7.2	3.8
New Zealand	1.4	2.0	5.7	3.8
Norway	3.9		8.6	
Sweden	2.8	2.1	8.8	3.3
United Kingdom	1.7	1.0	6.3	2.5

Source: Mandeep Bains and Howard Oxley "Ageing-related Spending Projections for Health and Long-Term Care," *Towards Higher-Performing Health Systems: Policy Studies from the OECD Health Project* (Paris: Organization for Economic and Cooperative Development, 2004), p. 323.

pay more for health care, and that the benefits are worth it. For example, Cutler analyzed the demand for air bags on automobiles in the United States before they were mandatory. In the early years of their availability, air bags cost roughly $300 per car, and many people were willing to pay that price. The data show that air bags save the life of roughly one driver in 10,000 who has them. So, Cutler concluded that consumers were collectively willing to spend $3 million to save one life. He cites other studies where similar estimated values range from $3 million to $7 million per life. To keep the example in round numbers, he uses $4 million as the value of a life and estimates that someone with a remaining life expectancy of 40 years would typically spread the value over those years. Thus he estimates that each additional year of life in U.S. terms would be worth $100,000, on average. He recognizes that this is a rough estimate, but uses it to compare the costs and benefits of alternative health technologies. One of the first ailments he considered was heart attacks. In the United States in the mid-1980s, it cost about $12,000 to treat a patient who had suffered a heart attack. By the late 1990s, it cost about $22,000 – $10,000 more. Over the decade and a half, life expectancy after a heart attack rose by about a year. For an additional $10,000 worth of treatment, the patient received a benefit worth $100,000 – clearly a bargain.[29]

Cutler does not claim that there is not considerable waste in health care systems in the developed world, especially in the U.S. system. But he argues that, in many cases, the new technologies are delivering benefits worth far more than they cost, even though the cost is high. In the context of a discussion about aging populations and their growing claims against economic capacity, however, this analysis raises fundamental questions. To the extent that health technologies are concentrated on the elderly, enabling them to live longer with fewer health and disability limitations, one has to wonder whether the benefits of these technologies are being equitably distributed. For a worker who is still contributing to society, extending life has the potential to benefit everyone. If expensive health advances accrue mostly to retirees, enabling them to draw a pension for a much longer period of time, then higher health costs would also lead to higher retirement costs. We are not urging developed societies to stop pursuing new technologies that enhance the health of their citizens. But investing heavily in technologies that extend the healthy lives of older individuals raises basic philosophical questions about asking more of retirement programs than they were ever meant to deliver. As retirement and health care systems siphon off an increasing portion of GDP, we run the risk of denying younger people opportunities that older generations were able to enjoy or a fair reward for their efforts.

[29] David Cutler, *Your Money or Your Life*, pp. 16–21.

SEVEN

Labor Supply and Living Standards

Much of the discussion in the last two chapters has focused on the prospect of aging populations in the world's developed economies claiming a disproportionate share of economic output and potentially slowing economic expansion. In this chapter, we begin to explore these prospects more directly.

A fundamental dynamic in every economy is the interplay between consumer demand for goods and services and society's ability to meet that demand. From the earliest systematic study of economic behavior, economists have sought to explain the production of output in terms of its inputs. While there is no universal agreement on the mathematical formulation of the model, it is well understood that the basic building blocks of economic prosperity are determined by the number of workers and the efficiency with which output is produced.

Although economists often employ complex terminology in their descriptions, at a fundamental level, economies operate in a very simple fashion, as shown in Figured 7-1. The rate at which an economy's output – what economists call gross domestic product (GDP) – grows essentially equals the sum of labor force growth plus worker productivity growth. Labor productivity is simply how much a worker can produce in a period of time – typically economists consider hourly output as the best measure.

Labor force and productivity growth are based on three basic inputs into the production of goods and services: human capital, physical capital, and innovation. The individuals that make up the labor supply and their work-related capabilities comprise the human capital. The capital stock is the physical plant and tools, both hardware and software, used by

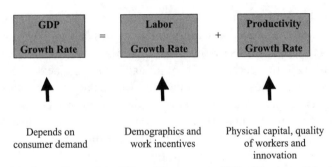

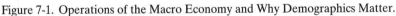

Figure 7-1. Operations of the Macro Economy and Why Demographics Matter.

workers to produce goods and services. Innovation comprises the level of knowledge and know-how that is embedded in production processes.

A basic premise of the relationship in Figure 7-1 is that human capital can be expanded in two dimensions. First, the number of workers or the hours worked can be increased. Increasing the supply of human capital in this way typically increases production. Second, workers can acquire new attributes or skills that make them more productive. In many developed countries, the supply of human capital has grown over time, and the characteristics of workers have changed in ways that have enhanced average productivity levels.

Another premise of the model is that more physical capital will make workers more productive, up to a point. But the substitution of capital for workers has limits, both in quantity and quality. Beyond some level, workers cannot use more tools or cannot fully utilize them. This limit to capital intensiveness, at least across a whole economy, is reached gradually.

Innovation evolves over time and may enhance the productivity of physical capital, human capital, or both. Technology can also change the extent to which capital and labor can be substituted for each other. The effects of innovation on economic activity are very seldom sweeping or fast. There are two important aspects to innovation in a developed economy. First, innovation evolves over time as a result of research and development activities. Once discovered, it can generally be widely adapted. But simple creation or discovery does not automatically translate into enhanced worker productivity; innovation must be adapted to be effective. Second, innovation evolves and is adapted unevenly across sectors of an economy and, thus, its effects on productivity tend to be uneven and gradual.

What is most constructive about the representation of economic output in Figure 7-1 is that it clearly shows the linkage between nations' demographics and the pace of economic expansion. As the discussion below will show, the aging populations in the world's developed economies are going to significantly slow the growth in the labor forces in those countries, starting in this decade and continuing through the next. This is not idle conjecture – most of the people who will make up our workforces over the next 20 years are already alive. We know a lot about their working patterns, when they usually retire, and how long they usually live. While some of these patterns may change slightly over time, they are not likely to change drastically over the near future.

For many developed nations, slower-growing labor supplies will become a significant drag on economic growth. Slower economic growth sounds an alarm because it has the potential to lower standards of living. The developed world has enjoyed steadily improving standards of living – which economists tend to measure as per capita GDP – for over at least six decades now. Discounting brief interruptions for war and some economic downturns, this prolonged period of growing prosperity actually dates back to the beginning of the industrial revolution.

If aging populations slow economic growth and bring improvements in standards of living to a halt, societies will need to look for ways to get back on track. They may try to attract more workers into the workforce, including groups whose workforce participation has traditionally been minimal. They may try to improve workers' skills and abilities or give them more tools to step up their productivity. Or, they may try to discover new ways of doing things – what economists call technological innovation. Any of these strategies has the potential to achieve greater economic prosperity and, to a certain extent, alleviate some of the burdens of that aging populations will impose.

Building Blocks for Producing National Output

The number of workers in the economy is a crude measure of the amount of human capital. It is crude because it does not account for variations in working hours or worker characteristics. But even this crude measure provides a rough sense of changes in worker productivity in recent decades. For example, Figure 7-2 shows the growth in the U.S. workforce since 1946 and how much the inflation-adjusted GDP has increased since then. The labor force and GPD for each year are defined by their change from the 1946 baseline.

In 2000, civilian employment levels in the United States were 2.4 times larger and real GDP was 6.2 times larger than they were in 1946. In other

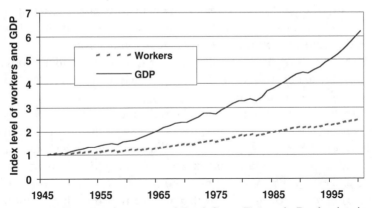

Figure 7-2. Civilian Employment and Real Gross Domestic Production in the United States for Selected Years Relative to Baseline Levels in 1946. *Sources:* Calculated by the authors from the *National Income and Product Accounts* published by the U.S. Department of Commerce at www.bea.doc.gov/bea/dn/gdplev.htm; and from civilian employment data from the U.S. Department of Labor, in *Economic Report of the President* (January 1969), Table B-23 and (January 2001), Table B-35.

words, on average, workers in 2000 produced approximately 2.5 times as much output as their forebears did in 1946. Some part of the increase in worker productivity was attributable to growth in capital. But much of it was attributable to the enhanced capabilities of workers, which were largely the result of more education and innovation.

Economists have not agreed on the precise model that best explains patterns of economic outputs over time. One commonly used model was derived in the 1920s and named after the two economists who developed it, C.W. Cobb and P.H. Douglas (1928). The Cobb/Douglas model, known as a production function, is stated in mathematical terms as:

$$P = AK^a L^{1-a}$$

where P represents economic production in an economy, A represents the state of technical knowledge used in production, K equals capital inputs, L represents labor inputs, and "a" and "$1 - a$" are proportional to the marginal product of capital and labor respectively.

Most economists agree that in a market economy, the factors of production are rewarded in accordance with the value of their marginal contribution to the production process. Thus, "a" and "$1 - a$" are fractions that represent relative shares of total national output that capital and labor receive as compensation. In a market economy, the total value of goods produced accrues to either workers or owners of capital, so these two fractions sum to one. Neither workers nor capital owners get to keep all of the fruits of their labor or investment, as the government skims off a share in the form of taxes, which are used to provide public goods and services and to redistribute income across a society. Of course, the process varies from one country to the next.

Since we are interested in population aging and its implications for national economies, we are also interested in how the factors relating to production change over time and how those changes affect total output. After all, a country's total output largely determines the standard of living of its citizens. It is possible to measure the effects of the growth in the factors of production on the growth of productivity over time. If output at a point in time is the product of labor inputs, capital inputs, and available technology, then changes in output over time are the product of changes in those same three factors.

Christopher Gust and Jaime Marquez (2000) at the Federal Reserve Board in Washington, D.C., have estimated rates of growth in GDP, labor hours, and capital stock for a number of developed countries over the past couple of decades. Their results are shown in Table 7-1. The GDP growth figures reflect the average annual growth rates for business-sector GDP. From 1981 to 1999, all of the countries recorded output growth, although a number of them surged ahead quite dramatically during the latter part of the 1990s. Several factors in play at that time help to explain why.

In all the countries shown in the table, capital stock has grown over the past couple of decades, although at varying rates within and across countries over time. In central and southern continental Europe and Japan, the rate of growth in capital stock slowed during the latter half of the 1990s. It accelerated in northern continental Europe and in the predominantly English-speaking countries.

In Table 7-1, there is considerably more variation in the labor supply trends than in the capital stock. In a number of countries, labor supplies contracted in some periods, but capital stock did not. The measure of labor supply used here is the number of hours worked in the total economies, including both government and private sectors. The GDP and capital stock numbers correspond to the figures for the private sectors only. Unless massive numbers of workers have shifted between governmental and private employers, the growth rates estimated here should still be reliable. In some countries, the labor force contraction may simply reflect a lengthy economic slump, although this would also show up in a lower or negative GDP growth rate. It may also reflect relatively soft labor demand for

Table 7-1. *Average Growth Rates for GDP, Labor Hours, and Capital Stock for Selected Countries and Selected Periods, 1981–1999*

	1981–1989	1990–1995	1996–1999	1981–1989	1990–1995	1996–1999
		Australia			*Italy*	
GDP	3.97	3.09	4.78	2.36	1.59	1.38
Labor hours	2.50	1.29	1.61	0.04	−1.09	0.71
Capital stock	3.96	3.02	4.44	2.78	2.87	2.73
		Belgium			*Japan*	
GDP	1.96	1.79	2.39	4.09	2.15	1.31
Labor hours	0.61	−0.37	1.33	0.95	−0.73	−0.76
Capital stock	2.84	3.26	2.93	5.84	4.88	3.31
		Canada			*Netherlands*	
GDP	3.25	1.51	3.53	2.00	2.66	3.65
Labor hours	1.81	0.17	2.59	−1.35	−0.24	3.31
Capital stock	5.74	3.86	4.85	1.66	2.08	2.78
		Denmark			*Norway*	
GDP	2.01	2.82	2.74	1.17	2.10	3.15
Labor hours	−0.06	−0.82	1.88	−0.26	−1.03	1.73
Capital stock	3.02	2.69	3.42	3.02	1.05	2.69
		Finland			*Spain*	
GDP	3.54	−0.46	5.51	2.70	1.67	3.69
Labor hours	−0.29	−4.18	2.34	−1.10	−0.86	3.34
Capital stock	n.a.	−0.14	0.85	5.63	4.47	4.00
		France			*Sweden*	
GDP	2.40	1.30	2.53	2.43	1.21	2.93
Labor hours	−0.95	−0.94	0.91	0.90	−0.88	1.19
Capital stock	2.57	2.58	2.17	2.93	2.10	n.a.
		Germany			*United Kingdom*	
GDP	n.a.	1.62	1.72	3.54	2.37	2.78
Labor hours	n.a.	−0.62	−0.41	0.22	0.60	1.29
Capital stock	n.a.	2.95	2.33	1.69	2.64	3.10
		Ireland			*United States*	
GDP	3.91	5.84	9.87	3.64	2.52	4.84
Labor hours	−0.10	1.67	5.79	2.06	1.04	2.30
Capital stock	2.58	2.28	4.74	4.36	3.16	5.59

Note: U.S. results are based on U.S. Bureau of Labor Statistics data and other countries results are based on OECD data.

Source: Christopher Gust and Jaime Marquez, "Productivity Developments Abroad," *Federal Reserve Bulletin* (October 2000), p. 669.

structural reasons that we will come back to in Chapter 12. At some juncture, however, the aging of populations may lead to sustained labor force contractions, which are likely to start affecting Germany, Italy, Japan, and Spain fairly soon.

The Story behind Changing Labor Productivity Levels

As described at the outset in Figure 7-1, an economy's total output can grow because of an increasing supply of workers or because existing workers become more productive. In the world's developed economies, a combination of these two factors has persisted for several decades. If labor productivity levels rise over time, the economy's output is growing faster than its labor supply. In virtually all of the world's developed economies, labor productivity has increased steadily since World War II. Higher labor productivity can be attributed to additional capital investment, more productive workers, and innovation.

It is possible to sort out how much a growing labor supply and capital stock contribute to output growth over time. As we noted earlier, in a market economy, the factors of production are rewarded according to the value of their respective contributions to production. Labor receives its share of output in the form of compensation. Table 7-2 shows the share of GDP that has been paid to workers in a number of countries over recent decades. Capital owners receive the residual in the form of returns on their investments.

In Table 7-3, we show the growth in worker productivity for the same set of developed economies included in the prior two tables. This measure

Table 7-2. *Labor's Share of GDP in Selected Countries for Selected Periods*

	1981–1989	1990–1998	1990–1995	1996–1999
Australia	0.65	0.62	0.62	0.62
Belgium	0.64	0.64	0.64	0.63
Canada	0.66	0.70	0.70	0.70
Denmark	0.69	0.63	0.63	0.63
Finland	0.71	0.69	0.71	0.64
France	0.67	0.61	0.62	0.61
Germany	n.a.	0.64	0.66	0.62
Ireland	0.76	0.68	0.70	0.63
Italy	0.68	0.64	0.65	0.62
Japan	0.77	0.72	0.72	0.72
Netherlands	0.61	0.60	0.61	0.60
Norway	0.72	0.68	0.67	0.69
Spain	0.67	0.61	0.62	0.60
Sweden	0.69	0.68	0.68	0.68
United Kingdom	0.69	0.69	0.70	0.69
United States	0.68	0.68	0.68	0.67

Source: Christopher Gust and Jaime Marquez, "Productivity Developments Abroad," *Federal Reserve Bulletin* (October 2000), p. 669.

Table 7-3. *Average Growth Rate of Productivity Estimates in Selected Developed Countries for Selected Periods, 1981–1999*

	1981–1989	1990–1995	1996–1999	1981–1989	1990–1995	1996–1999
		Australia			*Italy*	
Labor productivity	1.45	1.79	3.12	2.33	2.72	0.67
Capital deepening	0.45	0.64	1.06	0.87	1.36	0.82
MFP	1.01	1.15	2.11	1.45	1.32	−0.14
		Belgium			*Japan*	
Labor productivity	2.32	2.18	1.05	3.12	2.89	2.07
Capital deepening	0.82	1.28	0.60	1.15	1.56	1.23
MFP	1.51	0.87	0.46	2.00	1.31	0.85
		Canada			*Netherlands*	
Labor productivity	1.42	1.34	0.92	3.40	2.98	0.35
Capital deepening	1.31	1.08	0.67	n.a.	0.90	−0.21
MFP	0.14	0.26	0.27	n.a.	1.99	0.55
		Denmark			*Norway*	
Labor productivity	2.53	3.69	0.86	1.44	3.18	1.39
Capital deepening	n.a.	1.27	0.56	0.92	0.66	0.29
MFP	n.a.	2.37	0.31	0.50	2.48	1.13
		Finland			*Spain*	
Labor productivity	3.85	3.91	3.10	3.89	2.58	0.34
Capital deepening	n.a.	n.a.	−0.53	n.a.	2.01	0.26
MFP	n.a.	n.a.	3.70	n.a.	0.52	0.08
		France			*Sweden*	
Labor productivity	3.41	2.26	1.61	1.52	2.11	1.73
Capital deepening	1.10	1.35	0.50	0.61	0.89	n.a.
MFP	2.26	0.89	1.12	0.92	1.19	n.a.
		Germany			*United Kingdom*	
Labor productivity	n.a.	2.26	2.14	3.37	1.78	1.47
Capital deepening	n.a.	1.22	1.06	0.42	0.57	0.54
MFP	n.a.	1.03	1.07	2.90	1.21	0.95
		Ireland			*United States*	
Labor productivity	5.14	4.10	3.96	1.59	1.47	2.57
Capital deepening	n.a.	0.15	−0.39	0.73	0.68	1.11
MFP	n.a.	4.01	4.47	0.86	0.79	1.47

Note: U.S. results are based on U.S. Bureau of Labor Statistics data and other countries' results are based on OECD data.

Source: Christopher Gust and Jaime Marquez, "Productivity Developments Abroad," *Federal Reserve Bulletin* (October 2000), p. 671.

simply captures the average growth in output per hour of labor. It is the top line in the table for each country, and is approximately equal to the growth rate in GDP minus the growth rate in labor hours shown in Table 7-1. The second line for each country shows the added productivity that can be attributed to capital deepening – each worker's having more capital available to work with in the production process.

The last line in Table 7-3 for each country, labeled MFP (multifactor productivity), captures the added productivity attributable to the improved quality of workers and innovation. The MFP is essentially the difference in the increase in total labor productivity minus that attributable to capital deepening. There are some slight variations in the table due to statistical rounding errors in estimating the numbers.

Ireland was the outlier in terms of productivity growth during the 1980s and 1990s. But Ireland lagged behind virtually all of the other countries at the beginning of the period. On a purchasing power parity basis, in 1980, the average GDP per capita in the other 15 countries in Table 7-3 was just over 1.5 times that in Ireland. In 1990, the average in the other 15 countries was still 1.35 times that in Ireland. But by 2000, Ireland's GDP per capita was about 12 percent higher than the average of the other countries compared here.[1]

Beyond Ireland, there are some other important productivity patterns in the table. From the early to late 1990s, productivity improvement rates fell throughout the European continental countries, Canada, Japan, and the United Kingdom. In most of these countries, improvements in productivity attributable to both capital deepening and the MFP component were falling, although the latter rose slightly in Germany and somewhat more in France. In Australia and the United States, on the other hand, there was a substantial surge forward in labor productivity during the later 1990s. Their higher productivity was due to capital deepening and the MFP factors, innovation, and improving the quality of workers.

The reasons for the surge in productivity in the latter part of the 1990s in the United States have been the subject of considerable discussion in the economic literature. Robert Gordon concludes that about 40 percent of the acceleration in productivity in the United States during the late 1990s was due to an unsustainable cyclical effect – in other words, a blip. The remainder was due to increases in MFP growth in the durable manufacturing sector, specifically the manufacturing of computers, peripherals, telecommunications, and other types of durables.[2] A number of other prominent economists acknowledge that the information technology (IT) sector played an important part in boosting productivity growth during the late 1990s, but believe there's more to the full story. These economists are convinced that the spread of IT throughout the entire U.S. economy helped to accelerate productivity through capital deepening. They also

[1] OECD.

[2] Robert J. Gordon, "Has the 'New Economy' Rendered the Productivity Slowdown Obsolete?" (June 14, 1999) full copy can be found at the web site: http://faculty-web. at.northwestern.edu/economics/gordon/indexlayers.html under "Research, Topical Essays, and Web Links."

believe that organizational innovations and new methods of adapting technology boosted productivity.[3]

In cross-national comparisons, the United States has been investing more heavily in IT capital than other major developed countries and realizing a greater boost in productivity because of it.[4] Colecchia and Schreyer found that in the late 1990s, IT investment provided a bigger productivity boost to Australia, Finland, and the United States than it did to the major European countries and Japan.[5] In a follow-on to their earlier paper, Gust and Marquez looked at the role of IT and regulatory practices in explaining variations in productivity across OECD countries during the 1990s.[6] They found that countries hampered by restrictive regulatory environments were less likely to invest in IT, thus slowing their productivity growth.

The role that technology, capital deepening, improvements in the quality of workers, and other innovations will play in the coming decades will take on increasing importance as the labor pools in some economies grow more slowly or begin to shrink. In a number of developed economies, the demographic outlook suggests that their citizens may have to live with slower-growing or reduced standards of living unless enhancements to productivity are able to offset slower labor force growth.

Improving Productivity Leads to Improved Living Standards

One result of the increases in U.S. workforce size and productivity shown in Figure 7-2 is that the average standard of living in 2000 was much higher, on average, than it was in 1946. Over this period, inflation-adjusted GDP per capita increased roughly 3.2 times.[7] GDP per capita is the best measure

[3] Organization for Economic Co-Operation and Development, *OECD Economic Outlook* (Paris: OECD, June 2001), no. 69.

[4] Paul Schreyer, "The Contribution of Information and Communication Technology to Output Growth: A Study of the G-7 Countries," OECD Science, Technology, and Industry Working Paper, 2000/2 (OECD, 2000).

[5] A. Colecchia and P. Schreyer, "ICT Investment and Economic Growth in the 1990s: Is the United States a Unique Case? A Comparative Study of Nine OECD Countries," OECD Directorate for Science, Technology, and Industry, Working Paper No. 7 (Paris: Organization for Economic Cooperation and Development, 2001).

[6] Christopher Gust and Jaime Marquez, "International Comparisons of Productivity Growth: The Role of Information Technology and Regulatory Practices," International Finance Discussion Papers, no. 727 (Washington, D.C.: Board of Governors of the Federal Reserve System, May 2002).

[7] GDP is not a perfect measure of improved standards of living across this period, in part because of the changing labor force behavior of women. For example, in 1946, fewer than

Table 7-4. *Population and Output Measures in the United States for Selected Periods*

	Resident Population (in Millions)	GDP in 1996 Chain-Weighted Dollars (in Billions)	Annualized GDP Growth Rate from Prior Date (Percent)	GDP per Capita in 1996 Dollars	Annualized Growth Rate in per Capita GDP from Prior Date
1950	152.3	$1,686.6		$11,076.30	
1960	180.7	2,376.7	3.49	13,154.78	1.73%
1970	205.1	3,578.0	4.18	17,449.23	2.87
1980	227.8	4,900.9	3.20	21,518.11	2.12
1990	249.5	6,707.9	3.19	26,686.43	2.25
2000	275.3	9,318.6	3.34	33,854.69	2.33

Sources: U.S. Department of Commerce, Census Bureau, and U.S. Department of Commerce, Bureau of Economic Analysis.

for calibrating how general levels of economic well-being vary across time. Table 7-4 shows population estimates, GDP stated in 1996 dollars, and per capita GDP over the last half of the twentieth century in the United States. There was a fairly stable pattern of growth in per capita GDP over the decades, although it has varied considerably from year to year.

Without going into the detail we have presented for the U.S. economy, Table 7-5 presents summary evidence that economic expansion also took place in the world's other developed economies. The rates vary somewhat from decade to decade and from country to country, but in virtually every case, GDP per capita has consistently increased across the last four decades in all of these countries. Long-term patterns of this sort tend to create expectations within societies about what the future should look like.

Most people hope for continued improvements in their standards of living. Even those who are satisfied with their own achievements and rewards typically want an even better life for their children and grandchildren. And most younger people aspire to move up in the world. Improving the status of generations across time typically implies economic expansion.

half of working-age women in the United States were employed outside the home whereas nearly 80 percent were during 2000. As more women have entered the workforce, many tasks that were previously done by housewives and not measured in the government's calculation of GDP have been commercialized and are now included in measures of national output. GDP does not indicate changing life patterns and environmental factors that affect people's lives, nor does it reflect the distribution of output from an economy across society.

Table 7-5. *Compound Annual Growth in GDP per Capita for Various OECD Countries over Selected Decades*

	1960s	1970s	1980s	1990s
Austria	4.05	3.54	2.07	1.74
Belgium	4.34	3.15	1.92	1.84
Canada	3.07	3.04	1.56	1.64
Denmark	3.56	1.84	1.91	1.96
Finland	4.39	3.09	2.67	1.80
France	4.47	2.66	1.84	1.34
Germany	3.71	2.70	2.10	2.33
Ireland	3.76	3.27	3.28	6.24
Italy	4.97	3.10	2.16	1.44
Japan	9.01	3.25	3.51	1.07
Korea	–	5.70	7.61	5.19
Netherlands	3.74	2.08	1.62	2.31
New Zealand	1.55	0.56	1.76	1.39
Norway	3.36	4.19	2.01	2.80
Portugal	6.58	3.51	3.03	2.46
Spain	6.35	2.45	2.46	2.47
Sweden	3.91	1.60	1.87	1.39
Switzerland	3.23	1.19	1.54	0.18
United Kingdom	2.29	1.81	2.47	1.88
United States	2.92	2.25	2.16	2.25

Sources: UN Population Projections (2000 Revision); unpublished series of projections provided by the OECD; *OECD Economic Outlook*, OECD, June 2001.

In most developed economies, the populace will likely expect economic expansion and rising standards of living to continue their upward momentum. But these countries will need to find a way to overcome the effects of demographic shifts on labor force growth and economic expansion.

Demographics and Output Demand

Since World War II, the world's developed economies have leveraged growing labor forces into steadily improving levels of prosperity. Now we face the prospect of slowing labor force growth across the developed world, with some countries expecting labor force shrinkage within this decade and accelerated shrinkage after that.

For centuries, economists and demographers have debated the implications of a growing population for economic growth. But they have paid less attention to the prospects of declining populations and their consequences. One notable exception was John Maynard Keynes, who wrote in his seminal work, *The General Theory of Employment, Interest, and Money* (1937), "... an era of increasing population tends to promote optimism, since demand will in general tend to exceed, rather than fall short of, what was hoped for... But in an era of declining population the opposite is true." Keynes went so far as to say that a shift from an increasing to a declining population might be "disastrous."

The ultimate effects of population aging, shrinking workforces, and declining populations on developed economies are not yet known. We know there will be labor force implications, and that changes to the labor force will affect levels of output. But these developments will also affect the other side of the economic coin, namely the markets for goods and services. Older people consume different things and at different rates than younger ones, and smaller populations generally consume less than larger ones. This implies that consumer spending and saving behaviors may vary considerably among countries in the developed world, depending on the age of their populations. These consumer characteristics will likely have very real effects on their economies.

As we discussed in Chapter 3, economists generally analyze consumption patterns in the context of a theoretical "life-cycle" or "permanent income" model that explains typical consumption and savings patterns over a lifetime.[8] The life-cycle model presumes that younger workers borrow against their future earnings to establish themselves. Over their middle years, they pay off those early debts and begin accumulating rainy-day and retirement savings.

The life-cycle model has been widely used to study consumption and savings patterns by people at various ages. We have been able to gather a number of studies using household survey data from a variety of countries to analyze variations in consumption expenditures by age. The *International Savings Comparison Project*, performed under the auspices of the European Union-sponsored TMR (Training and Mobility of Researchers) *Project on Savings and Pensions*, set up a comparable database that allows analysis into the relationship between pension policies and saving behavior. One of the offshoots of the calculation of savings rates using the residual approach is that a consumption profile by the age of the household head is estimated for each of the countries. For this analysis, we use the consumption profiles for Japan, Germany, Italy, and the United

---

[8] Franco Modigliani and Richard Brumberg, "Utility Analysis and the Consumption Function: An Interpretation of Cross-section Data," in Kenneth K. Kurihara, ed., *Post-Keynesian Economics* (Rutgers University Press, 1954).

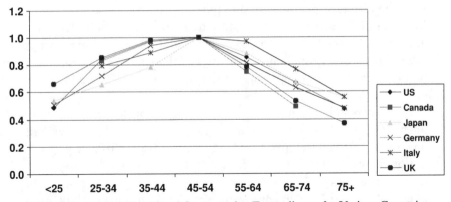

Figure 7-3. Age Profile of Total Consumption Expenditures for Various Countries (Indexed to 45–54 Age Cohort). *Source:* United States: Bureau of Labor Statistics, http://stats.bls.gov/cex/2000/Standard/age.pdf; Japan: Kitamura et al. (2000), Table 3, pp. 5; Italy: Brugiavini et al. (2000), Table 7, pp. 27; U.K.: Banks et al. (March 2000), pp. 63–4; Germany: Borsch – Supan et al. (2000), Table E1; Canada, Burbidge et al. (1994), Figure 1.9, pp. 39–41. *Notes:* Ages represent those of the household head/reference person and consumption expenditures in each age group are for all households in their respective samples. Total consumption expenditures are indexed to the 45 to 54 age cohort.

Kingdom. Consumption estimates for the United States are derived from the Consumer Expenditure Survey at the U.S. Bureau of Labor Statistics and estimates for Canada are derived from Burbidge et al.[9]

Figure 7-3 provides a compilation of consumption profiles for those six countries. The profiles are derived from the household surveys for the most recent year available, which for most countries is the mid-1990s. We index average consumption expenditures for each age cohort to the 45- to 54-year-old age group in order to make reasonable comparisons across countries – controlling for currency and price differences. All six countries exhibit a characteristic hump-shaped consumption profile, with household expenditures peaking at the 45- to 54-year-old age cohort. In general, both the younger and older cohorts' consumption levels are considerably below the peak, with the oldest cohort (age 75 and older) consuming the least.

The hump-shaped profile may seem inconsistent with the life cycle model, in which mid-career workers save more than other groups. But

---

[9] John B. Burbidge and James B. Davies. (1994) "Household Data on Saving Behavior in Canada," in J.M. Poterba, editor, *International Comparisons of Household Saving*, University of Chicago Press for the NBER, pp. 11–56.

while middle-aged people consume the most, they also earn the most. Banks et al.,[10] Borsch-Supan,[11] and Attanasio et al.[12] show that after accounting for the higher earnings levels of mid-career workers, savings rates in the United Kingdom, Germany, and the United States also take on the characteristic hump-shaped pattern consistent with the life-cycle model.

The potential implications of population aging on consumer demand might best be understood by considering Japan, which is aging faster than any country in the developed world. Between 2000 and 2010, the percentage of Japanese households headed by 45- to 54-year-olds is expected to decline from 19.4 to 15.0 percent. At the same time, the percentage of households headed by someone age 75 or older is expected to climb from 8.8 to 13.1 percent. Because of Japan's shrinking population, there will be an actual decline in the number of households that consume the most and an increase in the number of households that consume the least. This is only a partial picture of the future of consumer demand in Japan, because it only considers two age groups. To understand the full story, we have to look at all age groups.

The demographic transition now underway could significantly dampen economic expansion in the decades ahead. This is because, with the exception of health care, older individuals generally consume less than other segments of the population, and in most cases, the elderly population is growing, while the younger population is remaining stable or shrinking. Not only do older populations demand fewer goods and services; they tend to purchase a different basket of goods, with fewer consumer durables and more services, particularly health and living support services. In virtually all developed economies, the service sectors tend to have lower rates of productivity and productivity improvement than the goods-producing sectors. The shift in consumer demand toward services could further impede economic growth, possibly compounding the effect of falling aggregate demand related to aging.

---

[10] James Banks and Susann Rohwedder. (2000) "Life-cycle Saving Patterns and Pension Arrangements in the UK," *Training and Mobility of Researchers Project on Savings, Pensions and Portfolio Choice: International Savings Comparison Project*, Draft Paper, March.

[11] Axel Borsch-Supan, Anette Reil-Held, Ralf Rodepeter, Reinhold Schnabel and Joachim Winter. (2000) "Household Saving in Germany," *Training and Mobility of Researchers Project on Savings, Pensions and Portfolio Choice: International Savings Comparison Project*, Draft Paper, March.

[12] Orazio Attanasio and James Banks, "Trends in Household Savings: A Tale of Two Countries," The Institute for Fiscal Studies, Working Paper 98/15, (March 1998), p. 29.

To estimate how population aging will affect total consumption expenditures, we applied the average indexed consumption profile from the six countries in Figure 7-3 to the population age distributions for the OECD countries in our analysis. We use an average indexed profile approach largely because most countries in the OECD do not have consumer expenditure surveys readily available, so we could not apply country-specific consumption profiles to the changing population age structures in these countries.

Since our objective was to compare a cross-section of countries, we chose to employ this simplified approach despite the loss of variation in age-specific consumption behavior across the countries. Figure 7-3, however, shows a reasonable level of consistency across the countries, so that using an averaged consumption profile should not appreciably distort the estimates. We are not implying that there are no differences in consumption profiles across these economies. In fact, Figure 7-3 shows some pronounced differences in their trajectories across age cohorts. These differences result from many factors, including definitional differences, family size and composition, cultural attitudes, and social policies, especially toward health and retirement plans. To be thorough, we calculated estimates of the demographic effects, allowing for the average propensities to consume for each age cohort to change by each of the six country profiles. We found no significant differences in our estimates, leading us to report only the average profile results in Table 7-6.

One other issue we did not address is the possibility that aging populations could have some feedback effects that would reshape the consumption profiles in Figure 7-3. For example, if older segments of the populations become a strong enough political force, they might be able to extract sufficiently high transfers from the working-age group so that their consumption would rise relative to that of younger people. Haley, Nyce, and Schieber suggest that the political risks of such a development will rise along with the relative size of the elderly populations in the developed countries.[13] If older people increase their consumption relative to younger ones as populations age, it could accentuate the negative effects on productivity growth mentioned earlier – that consuming more services and fewer durable goods tends to lower rates of productivity improvements.

---

[13] Haley John J., Steven A. Nyce, and Sylvester J. Schieber. (2002) "Underfunding of National Retirement Systems: The Reality and the Risks of Current Policies," Watson Wyatt Working Paper.

Table 7-6. *Percentage Increase in Total Consumption over the Next Two Decades Attributable to Population Size and the Age Distribution for Selected Countries*

	Total Demographic Effect		Population Size Effect		Age Distribution Effect	
	2000–2010	2010–2020	2000–2010	2010–2020	2000–2010	2010–2020
Austria	−0.31	−3.10	−1.57	−2.74	1.28	−0.36
Belgium	1.07	−1.03	0.46	−0.51	0.61	−0.52
Canada	8.74	6.01	7.99	7.17	0.69	−1.08
Denmark	0.99	−1.13	1.01	−0.16	−0.02	−0.98
Finland	0.05	−1.78	0.30	−0.43	−0.25	−1.35
France	3.56	1.09	3.32	1.97	0.24	−0.87
Germany	−0.53	−2.61	−0.81	−1.83	0.28	−0.79
Ireland	12.25	9.34	10.47	9.35	1.61	−0.01
Italy	−1.14	−4.81	−1.98	−4.49	0.85	−0.34
Japan	−0.08	−2.98	0.88	−1.76	−0.96	−1.24
Korea	8.75	3.52	6.17	3.60	2.44	−0.07
Netherlands	3.31	0.22	2.83	1.19	0.47	−0.96
New Zealand	7.67	4.13	6.96	4.52	0.67	−0.37
Norway	4.04	2.05	3.24	2.59	0.77	−0.53
Portugal	2.14	−1.07	0.67	−1.41	1.47	0.35
Spain	1.42	−2.74	−0.86	−3.28	2.29	0.55
Sweden	−1.04	−1.62	−1.57	−1.52	0.55	−0.10
Switzerland	−1.40	−4.43	−1.36	−3.01	−0.04	−1.47
United Kingdom	2.22	0.70	1.43	1.13	0.78	−0.43
United States	9.50	7.37	8.94	8.31	0.51	−0.87

Notes: Growth rates represent the total change over the respective periods. Estimates are based on the age profiles of average indexed consumption expenditures for the country estimates in Figure 7-3. In order to include all individuals in the population, we assume individuals under age 20 consume at the same level as the 20- to 24-year-old cohort. Additionally, individuals 80 years of age and older in Italy were assumed to consume at the same level as those 80 to 84, and those older than 90 years of age in the U.K. were assumed to consume at the same level as those in the 85- to 89 year-old cohort. Estimates were also completed for the sub sample population between 20 and 74 years of age for the above countries. The results are qualitatively similar to those reported above.
Source: Derived by the authors.

The use of an indexed profile is important, since it enables us to isolate the impact of demographics on consumption expenditures by controlling for per capita income growth over the estimation periods. Table 7-6 reports our estimates of the demographic effect on total consumption expenditures over the coming two decades. The total demographic effect can be separated into two factors: the population size effect and the age distribution effect.

The population size effect measures the change in consumption that results from a change in population size. For example, as an economy's population grows, the number of people demanding goods and services grows along with it. As populations decline, the opposite is true. As Table 7-6 shows, the population size effect on consumption will vary widely across the developed economies. In most OECD countries, populations are likely to continue growing over the coming decade, albeit at a slower pace than in previous decades. However, between 2010 and 2020, populations will begin declining in over half of the countries in Table 7-6. OECD countries such as Italy, Spain, and Austria, which are expected to experience the largest population declines over the coming decades, could potentially face a considerable drag on total consumption growth in the future.

Of particular interest for this analysis, however, is how the growth in consumer demand will be affected by population aging, which we call the age distribution effect. As a population gets progressively older and a greater share of the population falls into age cohorts that have historically consumed less, total consumption demand is likely to drop. Columns six and seven in Table 7-6 show the age distribution effect across these economies. Overall, the shifting age distribution will have a relatively minor effect on consumer demand in most of these countries between 2000 and 2010. In fact, despite the aging transition, most economies will experience a positive consumer demand effect from changes in population in this decade.

Surprisingly enough, Spain – whose population is likely to begin declining in this decade – will experience one of the largest positive age distribution effects over both periods. This is because a higher concentration of individuals will be aging into the peak consumption profile. Unsurprisingly, however, Japan, with the oldest and most rapidly aging population among the developed nations, is likely to experience the largest drop in consumption expenditures over the coming decade.

As we look beyond the current decade, several more countries are likely to experience a similar negative effect on aggregate demand levels due to population aging. In fact, the age distribution effect is expected to become more pronounced across all countries by 2010. In the 2010-to-2020 period, all but two of the countries in Table 7-6, Spain and Portugal, will be experiencing a drag on aggregate demand because of their age composition. So while the age distribution effect is unlikely to slow the growth in consumer expenditures in this decade, it is likely to become a significant drag on consumer demand and economic growth after that. In the oldest countries, the negative age distribution effects will dominate consumption levels and patterns in the 2010s and will likely become even more pronounced during the 2020s.

The Linkages between Output Demand and Labor Demand

The demographics of all but a handful of the developed economies suggest an appetite for continuing economic growth over the coming decade. There are only two ways that an economy can increase the supply of goods and services at rates in excess of population growth: to import more or to produce more. Even though a number of OECD countries maintained a negative net import balance in 2000, their balances are currently and have historically been relatively small as a share of GDP. In fact, most of these countries maintain current account deficits of less than 5 percent of GDP. Unless the OECD economies are willing to significantly increase their balance of trade deficits for a sustained period, and other societies around the world are willing to provide the capital for them to do so, the potential to improve their standards of living is largely bound by what can be produced within their borders. How much these economies can produce, of course, depends on the availability of labor and capital. With a given supply of labor, the productivity of workers determines total output. Worker productivity is largely determined by the quality of workers and the capital and technology available to them.

To a certain extent, there is a "chicken and egg" element in a discussion about increasing labor productivity and the growth in output. The demand for goods and services is what propels most market economies to grow. During periods of high demand, economic growth tends to be relatively high as the producers of goods and services try to increase production to meet consumer demand. Low unemployment, overtime, and other vestiges of a high-performance economy generally characterize such periods. Workers have relatively high earnings at these times, further stimulating the demand for goods and services. There is evidence that worker productivity increases during such periods.

Labor productivity improvements slow or even fall during slack periods in the economy. Inventories build up as demand for goods and services slackens, often creating surplus capacity as employers slow production accordingly. At least initially, employers may hesitate to lay off surplus labor temporarily, not wanting to risk losing their substantial investments in their workers' expertise and experience. In addition, many countries have widely negotiated or mandated severance programs that impose substantial fixed costs on the termination of workers. It is often cheaper to carry surplus labor during these periods than to find and train new workers when the economy picks up.

Late Retirement in Iceland

By Professor Tryggvi Thor Herbertsson, IoES, University of Iceland

Labor force participation of older workers has been declining in the industrialized countries over the last decades even though life expectancy has risen sharply at the same time. This combination of earlier retirement and longer life expectancy has resulted in a much longer span of inactivity than before. Indeed, one of the more important current policy challenges is that early retirement has become commonplace in many countries. Although labor market participation rates of older workers all share a common trend, they do differ significantly across countries. More importantly, regardless of its causes, the withdrawal of older workers from the labor force leads to an increase in unused production capacity, a reduced tax base, and a heavier load on pension and fiscal systems.

Costs related to early retirement, measured in terms of foregone output, averaged 7.1 percent of potential gross domestic product in the OECD countries in 2000 and are forecasted to amount to 9.1 percent by 2010, (see Table 1). The costs, which vary greatly from country to country, were highest in Hungary, but by far the lowest in Iceland. The low cost in Iceland reflects very high participation rates of older workers and consequently low rates of inactivity – only 7.2 percent of males in the age group 55 to 64 had left the Icelandic labor market in 2001, compared with 38.8 percent on average in the OECD. Is there a lesson to be learned from the Icelanders? *(Continued on page 33.)*

The Icelandic pension system consists of three pillars: basic benefits and an income-tested supplement provided by pay-as-you-go financing; a fully funded, compulsory, occupational pension system; and newly introduced voluntary individual accounts with tax advantages. The official retirement age is 67 years although public-sector employees can retire at the age of 65 with reduced benefits – benefits are adjusted downwards for each month in retirement before the age of 67 and accordingly upwards if they postpone retirement beyond the official retirement age. Today, no formal vehicle exists for early retirement in the Icelandic pension system.

The single most important factor for low levels of early retirement in Iceland is low unemployment in the past, but the structure of labor markets and employment opportunities is particularly important when explaining the decision to retire. Many of the current early retirement programs in Europe were developed in response to high unemployment in the 1970s and 1980s. Iceland, on the other hand, never experienced a serious demand shock to the labor market, and consequently, there was never any pressure on developing early retirement schemes. Furthermore, favorable demographic conditions may have contributed to the high labor force participation rates of older workers in Iceland: First, the younger the population, the fewer the people leaving the labor market due to disability, since morbidity rates increase with age. Second, the larger the fraction of a given population at early retirement age, the greater the political pressure to implement early retirement programs paid for by the public. Third, the greater the pool of people at early retirement age, the higher the probability of

Table 1. *Cost of Early Retirement in the OECD Countries as a Share of Potential GDP*

	1980	1990	2000	2010		1980	1990	2000	2010
Hungary	–	–	16.5%	19.4%	Ireland	4.6%	6.9%	6.8%	8.9%
Belgium	–	15.2%	14.1%	17.9%	Australia	7.5%	7.5%	8.1%	11.1%
Luxemburg	–	12.5%	12.6%	15.1%	Canada	5.5%	6.7%	7.2%	10.5%
Austria	–	–	14.4%	15.9%	Sweden	5.9%	4.7%	5.2%	7.5%
Germany	7.8%	9.5%	13.2%	12.6%	USA	5.6%	5.4%	5.7%	8.1%
Greece	–	10.4%	10.7%	11.2%	New Zealand	–	7.9%	7.8%	11.6%
Czech Republic	–	–	11.1%	15.2%	Turkey	–	5.0%	4.0%	5.1%
France	6.2%	11.2%	10.3%	15.1%	Japan	2.8%	4.3%	5.4%	7.5%
Netherlands	8.1%	10.5%	11.2%	15.9%	Norway	5.0%	4.9%	5.2%	8.1%
Poland	–	–	7.7%	11.1%	Switzerland	–	2.9%	6.7%	9.3%
Finland	8.2%	9.6%	10.6%	15.8%	Korea	–	2.2%	3.7%	5.0%
Spain	4.8%	9.7%	9.3%	11.1%	Mexico	–	2.1%	2.8%	3.7%
Portugal	6.0%	9.1%	8.6%	9.4%	Iceland	–	0.5%	1.6%	2.2%
Denmark	–	6.9%	8.2%	11.3%					
U.K.	–	7.5%	7.2%	10.1%	OECD Average	5.3%	6.7%	7.1%	9.1%

Source: Tryggvi Thor Herbertsson and J. Michael Orszag (2003) "The Early Retirement Burden: Assessing the Costs of the Continued Prevalence of Early Retirement." Watson Wyatt technical report, No. 2003-LS04, also published as IZA Discussion Paper No. 816.

leaving the labor market in order to engage with other retirees in recreational activities.

Disability benefits also create disincentives to work and, as a consequence, misuse is common, especially for low-income workers who often use disability programs to secure early retirement. Disability programs have also been usesd as a substitute for early retirement pensions and as a youth-unemployment reduction mechanism in Europe. This, however, is not the case in Iceland, as unemployment has been low and disability benefits are only moderate, compared with neighboring countries in northern Europe. The number of disability pensioners varies greatly between the Nordic countries. The difference is only moderate in the 16 to 49 age group, but after that, the differences become striking. For example, there are 3.5 times as many people disabled in Finland as in Iceland in the 60 to 64 age group and 2.5 times as many as in Sweden. It is hard to believe that the differences reflect physical reality, since the population in the Nordic countries is relatively homogeneous; life expectancies are not that different, and economic conditions, aside from unemployment, similar. It therefore seems that people retire early through disability schemes in Finland, Norway, and Sweden but less so in Denmark and Iceland. This can possibly be explained by the relatively generous disability benefits in Finland, Norway, and Sweden, compared with Denmark and Iceland.

Although the current situation is favorable in Iceland, early retirement will most likely increase in the future, as the population grows older. In addition, the recent establishment of an individual accounts system in Iceland might encourage early retirement when the system has matured, as withdrawal is possible from the age of 60 until the official retirement age. However, the attitude of the Icelanders towards work seems to be different from that of workers in continental Europe. The Icelanders not only work until later in life, but they also work longer days. In this respect Icelanders bear more resemblance to North Americans than to their neighbors in Europe, which might be a reflection of the fact that Iceland is geographically situated closer to the American continent than the rest of Europe.

Further reading: Tryggvi Thor Herbertsson (2001), *Why Icelanders Do Not Retire Early*, Pensionsforum, Stockholm (*http://www.pensionsforum.nu/Why.pdf*).

Can We Make the Retirement Age More Flexible?
The Swiss Debate

By Monika Bütler (HEC)

In 2002, 53 percent of Swiss men and 44 percent of Swiss women retired before the statutory retirement age, although the Swiss first-pillar pension system AVS does not even offer any early retirement options. Most of those who leave the workforce early benefit from generous packages provided by their occupational pension plan. This route into early retirement, however, suffers from several problems, and may lead to potentially inefficient and inequitable outcomes. Firstly, financial imbalances of many pension providers make it unlikely that these packages will be offered in the future. Secondly, low-income workers do not have access to such plans, as the second pillar is only mandatory for middle and higher-income individuals. As a result, those with the shortest life expectancy work longest, while employees with high levels of human capital can afford to leave the workforce after a relatively short working spell. Indeed, the data show that even for beneficiaries of an occupational pension, richer men (but not women) tend to retire earlier than those with a lower average lifetime income. Not surprisingly, two recent popular initiatives asking for broader access to flexible retirement schemes within the first pillar (along with a general reduction in the retirement age) – though not approved of – enjoyed a large support.

As part of the ongoing reform of the first pillar, the need to accommodate the rising demand for early retirement was undisputed and, therefore, recently discussed by parliament. Due to unfavorable demographic trends and important financial problems of the first pillar, a general reduction in the retirement age did not find a majority – and would hardly be supported at the ballot as recent experience suggests. As part of the proposed reform, however, it will be possible to advance pension benefits by three years, as well as half of the benefits by an additional three years, both at an actuarially fair adjustment rate. It is feared that lower-income individuals might not be able to afford an earlier exit from the labor market, but propositions to reduce the adjustment rate for lower-income groups were abandoned for budgetary reasons. In the end, the combination of early retirement options with several other proposed changes to the first pillar, many of which negatively affect women, led to a somewhat peculiar political compromise in the final version of the reform bill: During a transition period of five years, only women will be granted a reduced adjustment rate if they opt for early retirement. The last word has not been spoken yet. A referendum has been announced, with a high chance to reach the required quorum of signatures. It is then up to the Swiss voters to decide.

A growing workforce at a given level of productivity means more output. If the workforce grows at the same rate as the population but productivity is constant, there will be no improvement in output per capita – a rough measure of the standard of living in a society. If the workforce grows faster than the population at a given level of productivity, standards of living will rise. Of course the opposite is true as well – if the population grows faster than the workforce at a given level of productivity, standards of living will fall. But worker productivity is not constant over time. Over the longer term, worker productivity in the developed economies of the world has been rising, and, in fact, has been central to improving standards of living in these countries.

Given the linkage between labor inputs and production, labor demand in the developed countries in the coming decades will largely depend on the appetite for continued improvements in standards of living, which have been rising since World War II. Table 7-7 shows the compound annual growth in GDP per capita for various countries in the OECD over the last four decades, along with the OECD and EC projections for the decade 2000 to 2010. While standards of living, as measured by GDP per capita, have grown appreciably over the past 40 years in all of the developed countries, the patterns of growth across decades and countries have varied considerably. For example, Germany, the Netherlands, Spain, Sweden, the United Kingdom, and the United States have realized relatively steady rates of improvement in GDP per capita, especially over the last three decades. However, in several other countries, including Austria, Finland, Italy, and Japan, the rates of improvement have steadily declined from decade to decade. Ireland is unique with its dramatic run-up in standards of living over the last decade.

OECD and EC projections of the growth of GDP per capita for the first decade of the twenty-first century are generally consistent with historical patterns of growth over the last 40 years. Their projections are based on underlying assumptions about demography, behavior, and economic performance. In many of the largest countries, such as Canada, Germany,

Table 7-7. *Compound Annual Growth in GDP per Capita for Various OECD Countries over Selected Decades*

	1960s	1970s	1980s	1990s	2000s
Austria	4.05	3.54	2.07	1.74	2.36
Belgium	4.34	3.15	1.92	1.84	2.38
Canada	3.07	3.04	1.56	1.64	1.46
Denmark	3.56	1.84	1.91	1.96	1.42
Finland	4.39	3.09	2.67	1.80	2.96
France	4.47	2.66	1.84	1.34	1.66
Germany	3.71	2.70	2.10	2.33	2.23
Ireland	3.76	3.27	3.28	6.24	3.56
Italy	4.97	3.10	2.16	1.44	2.49
Japan	9.01	3.25	3.51	1.07	1.12
Korea	–	5.70	7.61	5.19	5.21
Netherlands	3.74	2.08	1.62	2.31	1.82
New Zealand	1.55	0.56	1.76	1.39	1.99
Norway	3.36	4.19	2.01	2.80	0.98
Portugal	6.58	3.51	3.03	2.46	2.95
Spain	6.35	2.45	2.46	2.47	3.13
Sweden	3.91	1.60	1.87	1.39	2.54
United Kingdom	2.29	1.81	2.47	1.88	2.05
United States	2.92	2.25	2.16	2.25	2.19

Sources: *U.N. Population Projections* (2000 Revision); An unpublished series of projections provided by the OECD; The *OECD Economic Outlook*, OECD, June 2001.

the United Kingdom, and the United States, GDP per capita is projected to increase between 2000 and 2010, at rates consistent with prior periods. However, in several countries, such as Finland, Italy, and Sweden, standards of living are projected to rise slightly, while other countries, such as Denmark, the Netherlands, and Norway, are anticipating a slowdown.

Reflecting on the growth projected by the OECD and EC, or projections from other economic prognosticators, it is important to keep in mind how such projections are made. They are typically based on the solutions to a set of simultaneous equations reflecting the pattern of activity in various sectors of the economy. Beyond the immediate short term, the OECD and EC projections do not attempt to model cyclical variations in the demand for goods and services that pull the economy forward. Underlying assumptions about the rate of growth in the capital base and technology drive the projected rates of improvement in labor productivity. Applying a given pool of labor and assumptions about increasing productivity then results in the estimated level of growth over the projection period. As long as projected output is consistent with prior patterns of production, most of these models assume that the necessary demand to clear markets of the goods and services produced will persist. Certainly the fact that many of the OECD economies have balances of trade deficits or very small surpluses suggests that their consumers are capable of keeping up with increasing production capacity for the near future. The soft aggregate domestic demand in Japan's economy over the last decade, however, should be noted and may reflect the population size and age distribution effects discussed in relation to Table 7-6.

In the next chapter of this book, we investigate the challenges employers will face as they are called on to deliver the projected growth in output. We consider a number of alternative scenarios. One assumes that all the OECD countries will attain the levels of productivity improvement implicit in the development of the OECD and EC projections.[14] Other scenarios assume that the developed economies will realize levels of productivity improvement more in line with historical patterns.

If productivity improvement slows to the rates that have persisted over the last two decades, one potential outcome is that many of these countries will simply end up with less output. We believe, however, that there will

---

[14] The OECD and EC projections of GDP growth are consistent with their underlying assumptions about changes in the size of the labor force and productivity improvements over the coming decade. Elsewhere, we have criticized some of the underlying assumptions used in developing the OECD and EC aging cost projections (Nyce and Schieber, 2002), but the issues we raised are fundamentally different from our concerns about using the baseline inputs for the projections in our current analysis. Our criticisms of the assumptions used in projecting the costs associated with aging in developed countries in our earlier analysis focused on the demographic and behavioral assumptions that are important in projecting labor force participation rates over the next half century. But the implications of assumptions that might deviate from actual economic performance are fundamentally different for this analysis compared to the earlier one. For example, in our earlier analysis, we questioned the EC and OECD assumptions that there will be a substantial rebound in fertility rates, especially in countries currently reporting low rates. Such an assumption will have a major effect on the labor supply 30 or 40 years in the future but will have virtually no direct effect on the labor supply over the current decade. Our earlier analysis focused on aging costs in the developed economies over the next half century. This analysis focuses on the potential economic performance of these economies over this decade.

On the behavioral side of the projections developed by the OECD and the EC, we have been somewhat critical of assumptions that labor force participation rates of women or people in their late 50s or early 60s might increase substantially. In the current analysis, we begin with a baseline assumption that current labor force participation rates by age and gender will persist over the remainder of this decade. We then calculate how these rates would have to change under a number of scenarios to meet the GDP growth expectations set by the OECD and EC.

be significant consumer demand to increase production at rates consistent with the OECD and EC projections. This is based on our assumption that the citizens in these societies will want to continue improving their standards of living and will be willing to make fundamental changes to their lifestyles if necessary. Recent employment behavior supports this assumption, as evidenced by the remarkable increase in labor force participation of women over the last half of the twentieth century across nearly all developed economies.

Stagnating economies are also likely to give rise to political pressure on public policymakers to adopt policies to restart the growth process, to settle a restive citizenry. In large part this entails enacting policies that allow for market forces to function more freely – an issue we discuss in greater detail in Chapters 9 and 10. Yet, we believe public policy officials will be under tremendous pressures when their economies languish, because that is what has happened in the past when economies have stagnated or declined in democratic societies.

Take the case of the United States. Whenever the economy has slowed for any substantial period of time, the public has wielded extraordinary pressure on policymakers to restore economic growth. For example, the presidencies of Jimmy Carter and George H. Bush were limited to single terms, largely because the voting public was disenchanted with the state of the economy during their terms as president. Bill Clinton careened from one personal crisis to another throughout his eight years in office, but he consistently received high ratings as president because the economy marched ever upward.

Political upheaval from an economic slowdown is not only characteristic of the United States; it has occurred across many developed societies. The rapid drop-off in economic growth in Japan in the early 1990s spurred enough public discontent to break up nearly 40 years of uninterrupted rule by the Liberal Democratic Party (LDP).[15] This has been followed by years of political unrest with calls for early elections, as the people have become increasingly frustrated with the corruption and the suffocating blanket of bureaucratic controls. The inability of ensuing political leaders to live up to their campaign promises of social and economic reform that brought them to power has led to their rapid dismissal. Morihiro Hosokawa, for example, assumed power in August 1993 after promising major reform, only to resign the following April after quickly losing favor as the economy continued to deteriorate. In fact, Japan has seen seven

---

[15] *Economist*, "Murayama's Defeat," (July 29, 1995), p. 12.

different Prime Ministers since the unseating of Kiichi Miyazawa in August 1993.

Similar political pressures have been witnessed across a number of the largest European powers. For example, Helmut Kohl's demise after 16 years, arguably as Germany's most successful chancellor, was largely brought about by the growing frustration of the German people with the slow progress of unification.[16] There was growing disappointment and disillusionment in the East, with stubbornly high rates of unemployment of over 18 percent. This spilled over into the West as the economic boom of the post-unification years ran out of steam. Gerhard Schroder, the leader of the Social Democratic Party and the current chancellor, who unseated Mr. Kohl in 1998, came close to a similar fate as slower economic growth and rising unemployment threatened his reelection against the conservative Edmund Stoiber in 2003.[17]

A lackluster economy has also led to major political upheaval and an erosion in confidence for current French President, Jacques Chirac. Winning the presidency under a pledge to effect "profound change" and to reduce the country's high rates of unemployment, Jacques Chirac's inability to meet these campaign promises led in 1997 to the center-right suffering its worst political rout since the beginning of the Fifth Republic in 1958.[18] The two main center-right parties, the Gaullists' Rally for the Republic (RPR) and the more free-market Union for French Democracy (UDF), lost more than 200 of their 464 seats in the 577-member parliament in 1997, leaving Chirac little opportunity to restructure the current labor and tax structures, which have severely hindered France's economic competitiveness throughout the EU. Similar political reaction to high unemployment and slow economic growth occurred in Spain, where calls for early polls could be heard in 1995, when Felipe Gonzalez lost favor.[19]

Italy's self-made billionaire and media mogul, Silvio Berlusconi, regained power in 2001, after his previous reign failed in 1994 after only seven months. Prime Minister Berlusconi gained control in brash style with his five-point contract with Italians, which commits him to leave office if he does not deliver upon at least four points in his first five

[16] BBC News, "Kohl's Mark on History," World: Europe (October 3, 2000) at: http://news6.thdo.bbc.co.uk/hi/english/world/europe/newsid_543000/543955.stm.

[17] *Economist*, "Edmund Stoiber to lead Germany?," (January 19, 2002).

[18] *Economist*, "The Right Rejected in France," (January 7, 1997), p. 49.

[19] *Economist*, "Murayama's Defeat," (July 29, 1995), p. 12.

years of power. Since the new government is Italy's 59th in the post-war years, the challenges facing his conservative, pro-American administration seem like quite a tall order for a country whose economy is stifled by red tape and bureaucracy – in addition to the tight corset of the EU guidelines. In fact, only months into his term, the Italian prime minister faced strong opposition in the form of a 2 million-person protest to his promised liberalization of the labor markets, which is viewed by the country's poorest people as a direct assault on their established rights and material well-being. With such strong resistance to change, there is little hope for Berlusconi to stimulate economic growth in Italy through his revolutionized free-market ideology.

If there is demand pressure to increase output, but worker productivity improvement slows, there are a host of ways employers can try to attract more workers into the labor markets. We will explore the extent to which additional workers are needed in the labor market and how employers can get them there.

The Foundation for Growth in the Coming Decades

Output growth in an economy is driven by the combination of worker productivity and workforce size. Table 7-8 shows the historical patterns of labor productivity growth in various economies around the world. The pattern of productivity improvement is somewhat mixed from country to country. Among the largest countries, France, Germany, Italy, and Japan have shown consistently declining rates of productivity improvement over the last three decades. The United Kingdom and the United States have shown a mixed pattern, with declines in some decades and increases in others. Canada, however, shows a steady pattern of improvement. Most of the countries for which we could do the calculations have shown consistently declining rates of improvement in labor productivity growth.

As we saw in earlier sections of this analysis, the implications of demographic trends for the labor forces of the OECD economies are quite significant. Table 7-9 shows the decade-by-decade compound annual growth in labor supply for the last four decades and projections for the next two decades for many of the OECD countries.

For our baseline projection of labor supply, we assume that labor force patterns for men in terms of participation and average hours worked remain constant over the projection period. For example, assume that 87 percent of the men between the ages of 50 and 54 were in the labor force in 2000 in a particular country. In developing our baseline labor force

Table 7-8. *Compound Annual Growth in Labor Productivity for Various Countries in the OECD over Selected Decades*

	Compound Annual Growth in Labor Productivity				
	1960s	1970s	1980s	1990s	Late 1990s
Australia	2.66	1.59	0.96	2.05	2.27
Austria	–	2.97	2.20	1.99	2.10
Belgium	4.22	3.20	1.91	1.62	1.72
Canada	2.26	0.85	0.97	1.50	1.59
Denmark	3.37	1.81	1.04	2.07	1.70
Finland	4.67	2.52	2.60	3.00	2.83
France	–	2.72	2.08	1.23	1.15
Germany[a]	4.25	2.56	1.28	1.49	1.09
Greece	–	4.00	−0.34	1.76	2.99
Iceland	2.75	3.64	0.97	0.27	2.15
Ireland	4.21	3.76	3.57	3.30	3.95
Italy	6.21	2.57	1.65	1.54	1.02
Japan	8.63	3.57	2.84	1.12	1.46
Luxembourg	–	1.38	3.19	1.84	2.11
Mexico	–	–	0.13	0.69	1.71
Netherlands	3.85	2.69	1.60	1.27	0.96
New Zealand	–	0.60	1.42	0.89	1.36
Norway	3.46	3.16	1.77	2.24	1.28
Portugal	6.39	2.97	1.82	1.82	2.08
Korea	–	3.86	5.89	4.55	4.23
Spain	–	3.95	1.88	1.31	0.80
Sweden	3.95	1.13	1.44	2.49	2.11
Switzerland	3.21	1.24	0.29	0.65	1.23
Turkey	4.63	2.16	3.58	2.78	3.26
United Kingdom	2.94	1.75	1.95	1.93	1.52
United States	2.26	0.81	1.31	1.48	1.96

[a]For years 1991–2000 for Whole Germany.
Source: The OECD *Economic Outlook*, OECD.

projections for that country, we assumed that 87 percent of the men in this age group will be in the labor force each year of the projection period. In addition, we assumed that on average, workers within each age group will continue to work the same number of hours per year as they did in previous years.

For women, however, our baseline labor force projections assume the continuation of current trends in female labor force patterns. In many developed societies, female labor force participation rates are still rising. In Spain, for example, roughly 41 percent of women ages 40 to 45 were

Table 7-9. *Compound Annual Growth in Labor Supply for Various OECD Countries over Selected Decades*

	1960s	1970s	1980s	1990s	2000s	2010s
Australia	2.49	1.96	2.32	1.34	1.08	0.52
Austria	−0.82	0.64	0.51	0.64	−0.05	−0.78
Belgium	0.53	0.70	0.11	0.50	0.30	−0.32
Canada	2.66	3.60	1.75	1.17	0.94	0.21
Denmark	0.87	0.93	1.08	−0.02	−0.36	−0.34
Finland	0.18	1.21	0.57	0.02	−0.48	−0.80
France	0.94	0.93	0.57	0.57	0.21	−0.34
Germany	0.15	0.43	0.86	0.69	0.15	−0.54
Ireland	0.00	1.10	0.66	2.87	1.98	0.71
Italy	−0.52	0.84	0.52	0.10	−0.13	−0.85
Japan	1.34	0.92	1.23	0.58	−0.13	−0.42
Korea	2.82	3.67	2.54	1.70	0.37	−0.10
Netherlands	−	0.65	1.05	1.76	1.06	0.44
New Zealand	2.23	1.82	0.77	1.65	0.53	0.13
Norway	0.67	1.55	0.99	0.93	0.45	−0.09
Portugal	0.25	2.16	1.03	0.86	1.18	0.41
Spain	0.83	0.64	1.21	0.98	0.89	−0.01
Sweden	0.67	0.99	0.54	−0.45	−0.36	−0.43
Switzerland	1.47	0.13	1.93	0.36	−0.21	−0.75
United Kingdom	0.07	0.57	0.68	0.28	0.24	−0.10
United States	1.74	2.60	1.64	1.13	1.15	0.59

Notes: The labor force projections allow female labor force participation rates to rise by each cohort's growth rate averaged over the two five-year periods of 1990–95 and 1995–2000. For example, 55- to 59-year-old females between 2000 and 2005 are assumed to increase their rate of labor force participation based on the average of their participation changes between 1995 and 2000 when they were 50- to 54-years-old, and between 1990 and 1995 when they were 45- to 49-years-old. Participation rates for women were capped at males' labor force participation rates for countries where female labor force participation rates grew more rapidly.

Sources: Watson Wyatt's estimates of United Nations (2000); The OECD Labour Market Statistics Database at http://www1.oecd.org/scripts/cde/members/LFSDATA-Authenticate.asp

working in 1990. By 2000, the participation rate for women these ages was over 62 percent – a 50 percent increase over a decade. Much of this rise in female labor force participation reflects successively younger cohorts getting older, what is commonly referred to as a cohort effect. In many countries, each new generation of women has obtained higher levels of training and education at younger ages than previous cohorts, which has played a significant role in attracting more women into the workplace. Moreover, for younger cohorts, working careers are increasingly the norm. The result has been a steady transition of women into the labor force, which has lasted more than half a century in some countries. At some point, however, the transition will be complete. In the United Kingdom and the United States, for example, the growth in labor force participation rates for women has slowed considerably for many age groups and appears to have topped out for the others. In a number of other countries, however, female labor force participation continues to rise for all age groups.

To account for the continued rise in female labor force participation rates in many developed societies, we raise female labor force participation rates by each cohort's growth rate averaged over the two five-year periods of 1990 to 1995 and 1995 to 2000. For example, between 2000 and 2005, we assumed that 55- to 59-year-old females would increase their labor force participation based on the average of their participation rate increases between 1995 and 2000, when they were 50- to 54-years-old, and between 1990 and 1995, when they were 45- to 49-years-old. Participation rates for women were capped at male's labor force participation rates for countries where female labor force participation rates grew more rapidly.

The estimates of available labor for the current decade show that virtually none of the world's developed economies will see the labor force growth rates of the past four decades. In fact, in seven out of the 20 countries in the table, labor forces will shrink from 2000 to 2010. The labor force projections for 2010 to 2020 are even gloomier. In the 2010s, roughly two of every three countries will face shrinking labor supplies under our baseline projections.

Our baseline assumption that male labor force participation rates will persist into the future and female labor force participation rates will continue their 1990s trends, when controlling for age, is not our forecast of the future. We believe that labor force participation rates for older people are likely to rise. But these estimates demonstrate that population aging has the potential to significantly reduce economic growth rates. Unless current labor force patterns change – and in some cases the changes would have to be extreme – several developed countries almost certainly will find themselves with a shrinking pool of workers.

Contracting workforces in developed economies could leave employers struggling to find enough talented employees to run their operations. Depending on the severity of the contraction, the alternatives could be slower economic growth, prolonged economic stagnation, or even a decline.

Our earlier analysis of the aging phenomenon and its implications for the world's developed economies concluded that some of the country projections are based on overly optimistic assumptions about labor force and productivity growth.[20] In Table 7-10, we show the OECD estimates of GDP growth for the major economies of the world between 2000 and 2010. As noted above, the developed societies seem to have a strong appetite for continued rising standards of living. As a result, we estimate GDP growth rates for the 2010s that maintain the standards of living growth projected by the OECD/EC for the 2000s. We also developed an alternative set of projections that assume that worker productivity continues increasing at its 1990s growth rate, and that the labor force grows in accordance with our estimates presented earlier. In several cases, our projections of the growth rate for total output falls somewhat below the OECD's projections. In countries facing the most severe aging problems, such as Germany, Italy, and Japan, the slower growth in output we project could profoundly affect standards of living over the next couple of decades. If expected economic growth does not materialize and standards of living begin to erode, who will end up with the lower levels of consumption? The characteristics of the retirement systems in place are likely to play a large part in determining the answer.

Retirement Systems' Role in Determining Retirement Burden Levels

In many countries, retirement benefit levels are tied to growth in worker productivity levels through some form of wage indexing. Even where pension benefits are tied to general GDP growth or to inflation, the exploding cost of retiree health benefits tends to increase the cost of total benefits at rates approaching those of wages. If pensions grow along with worker productivity or wages, the pension systems may actually insulate retirees from an economic slowdown. This could divert a disproportionate share of the fruits of productivity to retirees, essentially asking workers and their dependents to settle for slower-growing

---

[20] Steven A. Nyce and Sylvester J. Schieber, "The Decade of the Employee: The Workforce Challenges Facing the Developed Economies of the World over the Next Ten Years," presented at Tenth Annual Colloquium of Superannuation Researchers, University of New South Wales, Sydney, Australia, July 2002.

Table 7-10. *Growth in Real GDP at Historical Productivity Growth Rates under Current Workforce Patterns*

	Real GDP Growth OECD Estimates		Productivity Growth	Estimated Growth in GDP at 1990s Productivity Growth	
	2000–2010	2010–2020	1990s	2000–2010	2010–2020
Australia	–	–	2.05	3.13	2.57
Austria	2.26	2.15	1.99	1.94	1.21
Belgium	2.47	2.37	1.62	1.93	1.30
Canada	2.22	2.17	1.50	2.44	1.71
Denmark	1.52	1.47	2.07	1.70	1.72
Finland	3.03	2.92	3.00	2.53	2.20
France	2.00	1.89	1.23	1.45	0.89
Germany	2.21	2.09	1.49	1.64	0.95
Greece	–	–	1.76	2.44	1.74
Iceland	–	–	0.27	1.42	0.75
Ireland	4.60	4.38	3.30	5.28	4.01
Italy	2.28	2.03	1.54	1.41	0.70
Japan	1.22	0.94	1.12	0.99	0.70
Luxembourg	–	–	1.84	3.49	2.95
Mexico	–	–	0.69	3.12	2.50
Netherlands	2.09	1.98	1.27	1.64	1.18
New Zealand	2.69	2.64	0.89	1.96	1.33
Norway	1.27	1.30	2.24	2.77	2.37
Poland	4.73	4.58	5.38	5.84	4.94
Portugal	3.12	2.86	1.82	2.27	1.74
Korea	5.84	5.63	4.55	5.73	4.95
Spain	3.05	2.79	1.31	2.20	1.30
Sweden	2.39	2.44	2.49	2.12	2.06
Switzerland	–	–	0.65	0.39	−0.05
United Kingdom	2.22	2.28	1.93	2.17	1.82
United States	3.10	3.11	1.48	2.63	2.07

Notes: See Table 7-9 for a description of labor force growth. GDP growth in the 2000s is based on OECD/EC projections. Future periods represent the GDP growth necessary to maintain standards of living growth consistent with the 2000s.

Sources: OECD *Economic Outlook,* Source OECD Database; an unpublished database from the OECD; an unpublished database from Eurostat; United Nations Population Division, *World Population Prospects* (2000 Revision); The OECD Labour Market Statistics Database http://www1.oecd.org/scripts/cde/members/LFSDATAAuthenticate.asp.

standards of living. The transfer mechanism would be higher tax burdens to support public retirement programs or reduced consumption allowed by higher saving rates as workers liquidate their assets in the funded pension system. Workers' standards of living would not only fail to keep up

Table 7-11. *Consumption as a Share of Output for Developed Nations*

	1960	1970	1980	1990	2000
Australia	0.618	0.591	0.616	0.609	0.595
Austria	0.552	0.527	0.545	0.556	0.561
Belgium	0.569	0.509	0.541	0.539	0.532
Canada	0.619	0.568	0.583	0.581	0.559
Denmark	0.568	0.577	0.529	0.496	0.477
Finland	0.510	0.528	0.506	0.524	0.487
France	0.586	0.574	0.580	0.563	0.541
Germany	0.483	0.515	0.546	0.536	0.566
Greece	0.661	0.581	0.616	0.712	0.710
Iceland	0.550	0.606	0.597	0.595	0.624
Ireland	0.787	0.730	0.689	0.584	0.496
Italy	0.525	0.556	0.574	0.600	0.607
Japan	0.607	0.546	0.561	0.533	0.541
Luxembourg	0.498	0.543	0.626	0.515	0.429
Mexico	0.759	0.751	0.713	0.712	0.691
Netherlands	0.448	0.500	0.523	0.490	0.498
New Zealand	0.603	0.629	0.627	0.599	0.592
Norway	0.608	0.581	0.524	0.491	0.479
Portugal	0.722	0.672	0.641	0.614	0.631
Korea	–	0.680	0.604	0.549	0.506
Spain	0.633	0.624	0.638	0.608	0.593
Sweden	0.622	0.569	0.549	0.523	0.501
Switzerland	0.566	0.564	0.597	0.566	0.579
Turkey	0.830	0.769	0.849	0.692	0.680
United Kingdom	0.611	0.583	0.601	0.649	0.681
United States	0.636	0.648	0.652	0.667	0.677

Source: OECD Economic Outlook, OECD Database.

with their own higher productivity, but in many cases, their standards of living would rise more slowly than those of retirees.

In order to project the effects of population aging on the elderly and non-elderly populations in developed economies, we estimated the growth in total consumption over the current and next decades. We began by estimating output, using the labor force projected for 2010 and 2020 in each country and productivity growth rates for the 1990s. To derive total consumption levels, we assumed that the average propensity to consume would remain constant for the populations over the coming decades. Aging populations may well change the ratio of consumption to income, but the evidence from Table 7-11 suggests that it may remain relatively flat over the next couple of decades. With projections of total consumption

for the developed economies, we distributed consumption between retirees and non-retirees and their young dependents. For simplification,
our baseline case assumed that the retired population was everyone over
age 60. We included everyone from age 0 to 59 in the working-age and
young dependent population.

In order to divide total consumption between the two groups, we again
used the estimates of consumption expenditures by age in Figure 7-3,
which are based on household survey data from a variety of countries
used to analyze variations in consumption expenditures by age. To dis-
tribute total consumption expenditures between preretirement individuals – people aged 0 to 59 – and retirees, we applied the average indexed
consumption profile to the population age distributions for the OECD
countries in our analysis. We then divided each of the age group's indexed
consumption expenditures by the indexed average for all individuals to
arrive at the relative consumption weighting of per capita consumption
expenditures for the pre- and post-retiree populations. We used an average indexed profile approach largely because most OECD countries do
not have consumer expenditure surveys readily available to estimate their
consumption profile. As a result, we were unable to apply country-specific
consumption profiles to the changing population age structures in these
countries.

To estimate the impact of population aging on each of the retired and
non-retired groups, we allowed the retiree group's income to grow at
the pace of workers' productivity improvement in our baseline estimates.
Since we assume the average propensity to consume to be constant, the
retirees' per capita consumption will also grow at the pace of productivity.
As the retiree population becomes a greater share of the population, it
will capture more productivity from the active workforce. As a result,
retiree consumption will grow at a faster clip than consumption for the
rest of the population. To show this, we subtracted the consumption of the
retiree population from total consumption. The residual consumption left
after taking out the retirees' share is then apportioned among the younger
segments of the populations.

Table 7-12 provides estimates of per capita consumption growth for
each of the two groups for the scenario that places the aging burden on
the active workforce and its dependents. A number of elements of this
table should be considered. First, it seems anomalous that per capita consumption rates for the elderly and non-elderly segments of the population
could both grow more rapidly than that of the total population. This occurs
because the elderly's share of the population is growing in virtually every

Table 7-12. *Annual Growth in per Capita Consumption over the Coming Decades Apportioned between the Elderly and Non-Elderly Population with the Non-Elderly Population Treated as a Residual*

	Total Consumption per Capita		Active Workers and Dependents per Capita		Eldery Population per Capita	
	2000–2010	2010–2020	2000–2010	2010–2020	2000–2010	2010–2020
Australia	2.03	1.64	2.08	1.61	2.05	2.05
Austria	1.93	1.34	2.00	1.23	1.99	1.99
Belgium	1.43	1.13	1.44	1.05	1.62	1.62
Canada	1.55	0.91	1.63	0.87	1.50	1.50
Denmark	1.80	1.73	1.83	1.70	2.07	2.07
Finland	2.69	2.41	2.73	2.29	3.00	3.00
France	1.07	0.71	1.08	0.63	1.23	1.23
Germany	1.47	1.02	1.53	0.95	1.49	1.49
Greece	1.87	1.47	1.96	1.45	1.76	1.76
Iceland	0.64	0.09	0.75	0.16	0.27	0.27
Ireland	3.39	2.89	3.44	2.86	3.30	3.30
Italy	1.37	1.09	1.40	1.00	1.54	1.54
Japan	0.79	0.81	0.84	0.76	1.12	1.12
Luxembourg	1.76	1.56	1.76	1.54	1.84	1.84
Mexico	1.34	1.07	1.41	1.17	0.69	0.69
Netherlands	1.02	0.71	1.05	0.63	1.27	1.27
New Zealand	1.10	0.52	1.19	0.53	0.89	0.89
Norway	2.38	1.93	2.48	1.95	2.24	2.24
Poland	5.81	4.99	5.95	5.05	5.38	5.38
Portugal	1.87	1.72	1.93	1.75	1.82	1.82
Korea	4.91	4.44	5.02	4.54	4.55	4.55
Spain	1.42	0.91	1.50	0.88	1.31	1.31
Sweden	2.67	2.22	2.85	2.24	2.49	2.49
Switzerland	0.61	0.16	0.73	0.12	0.65	0.65
Turkey	3.23	2.95	3.29	3.01	2.78	2.78
United Kingdom	1.98	1.52	2.05	1.48	1.93	1.93
United States	1.67	1.09	1.74	1.10	1.48	1.48

Notes: The growth in total consumption is based on the feasible rates of output growth from Table 7-10. This assumes historical productivity growth rates under our baseline projections of labor force growth. Per capita consumption for the elderly population (ages 60 and over) is assumed to grow at the 1990s productivity growth rate. Consumption for the non-elderly (ages 0 to 60) is treated as the residual.

Sources: OECD National Accounts – Source OECD Database; an unpublished database from the OECD; an unpublished database from Eurostat; United Nations Population Division, *World Population Prospects* (2000 Revision); also see Figure 7-3.

case, and this group's relative consumption is smaller than that of the younger population. In several cases, this phenomenon is accentuated by declining absolute numbers of people in the younger group.

A comparison of the right two columns of Table 7-10 with those of the middle columns in Table 7-12 clearly shows that workers' standards of living are going to grow much more slowly than the rates at which they grow their economies, which are also slowing in most cases. In what looks like another anomaly in the tables, per capita consumption in a country like Austria grows at the same rate or more rapidly than GDP growth over both decades and, at least during the current decade, the younger population appears to do quite well relative to overall economic growth. But much of this rise in standard of living comes at the expense of a shrinking younger population. During this decade, the number of people younger than 60 in Austria is expected to decline by 6 percent. During the following decade, the number of people younger than 60 is expected to decline another 9 percent.

Over the long term, developed economies will not be able to sustain improvements in their standards of living if productivity growth rates do not make up for the rates of decline in working-age people. Higher rates of labor force participation among people between the ages of 20 and 60 and smaller families may mask this deficit for a while, but as this scenario plays out, there simply will not be enough workers to bear the burden of an ever-growing, elderly dependent population. One way out of our baseline scenario in this analysis would be to constrain the resources that go to the elderly. A recent presidential commission for reforming social security pensions in the United States would do just that. Several other countries, including Germany, Italy, Japan, and Sweden, have already adopted alternative measures to restrict the growth of their retirement systems.

In Table 7-13, we show the results when the slowdown in economic growth caused by population aging is shifted to retirees. Here we assumed that the workers' standards of living would fully reflect their improving productivity and their increasing labor supply. The retiree population would get what is left. This would insulate workers from the slowdown, so their earnings would grow right along with the rate of productivity over the coming decades. The fundamental changes made to retirement systems to achieve this end would erode the benefits provided to retirees. The results shown in Table 7-13 suggest that, under this scenario, retirees might have to endure a significant slowdown in standards of living growth or even reductions in some cases.

Over the current decade, retirees in the Netherlands would see their benefits decline by roughly 1 percent per annum, while retiree benefits in

Table 7-13. *Annual Growth in per Capita Consumption over the Coming Decades Apportioned Between the Elderly and Non-Elderly Population with the Elderly Population Treated as a Residual*

	Total Consumption per Capita		Active Workers and Dependents per Capita		Eldery Population [per Capita	
	2000–2010	2010–2020	2000–2010	2010–2020	2000–2010	2010–2020
Australia	2.03	1.64	2.37	2.10	0.40	−0.12
Austria	1.93	1.34	2.41	1.97	0.31	−0.34
Belgium	1.43	1.13	1.75	1.70	0.40	−0.41
Canada	1.55	0.91	1.93	1.54	−0.15	−1.28
Denmark	1.80	1.73	2.32	2.17	−0.02	0.50
Finland	2.69	2.41	3.36	3.05	0.45	0.78
France	1.07	0.71	1.36	1.21	0.04	−0.82
Germany	1.47	1.02	1.84	1.57	0.38	−0.38
Greece	1.87	1.47	2.17	1.87	0.95	0.43
Iceland	0.64	0.09	0.95	0.66	−0.94	−2.17
Ireland	3.39	2.89	3.63	3.23	2.11	1.37
Italy	1.37	1.09	1.80	1.57	0.14	−0.05
Japan	0.79	0.81	1.74	1.35	−1.78	−0.30
Luxembourg	1.76	1.56	1.88	1.83	1.23	0.56
Mexico	1.34	1.07	1.54	1.42	−1.04	−2.10
Netherlands	1.02	0.71	1.54	1.33	−1.01	−1.16
New Zealand	1.10	0.52	1.43	1.03	−0.51	−1.46
Norway	2.38	1.93	2.73	2.41	1.03	0.45
Poland	5.81	4.99	6.16	5.85	4.29	2.22
Portugal	1.87	1.72	2.11	2.07	1.03	0.64
Korea	4.91	4.44	5.39	5.23	1.66	0.96
Spain	1.42	0.91	1.73	1.41	0.40	−0.50
Sweden	2.67	2.22	3.28	2.69	0.87	1.11
Switzerland	0.61	0.16	1.27	0.92	−1.47	−1.65
Turkey	3.23	2.95	3.43	3.29	1.21	0.18
United Kingdom	1.98	1.52	2.30	1.92	0.87	0.31
United States	1.67	1.09	1.90	1.63	0.51	−1.05

Notes: The growth in total consumption is based on the feasible rates of output growth from Table 7-10. This assumes historical productivity growth rates under our baseline projections of labor force growth. Consumption for the non-elderly population (ages 0 to 60) is assumed to grow at the rate of productivity growth plus the growth in the labor force. Consumption for the elderly (ages 60 and older) is treated as the residual.

Sources: OECD National Accounts – Source OECD Database; an unpublished database from the OECD; an unpublished database from Eurostat; United Nations Population Division, *World Population Prospects* (2000 Revision); also see Figure 7-3.

Japan would erode by 1.75 percent per year. In the second decade of this century, the picture would be even grimmer under this scenario, as income growth for retirees would continue to slow. In over half of the countries, per capita consumption growth for retirees would actually turn negative over the second decade of this century. Retirees in several countries, such as the Netherlands, the United States, and France, could see declines in per capita consumption of roughly a full percentage point per annum during the decade.

The two possible scenarios described above show the opposite ends of the spectrum in terms of how demographic aging could affect retirees and workers and their dependents. Although in each scenario, the outlook for one group or the other appears dire, policymakers have other, less depressing options. One way to mitigate a slowdown in standards of living growth over the coming decades would be to convince workers who could retire to continue working instead. This would have a beneficial effect on at least two of the three ratios defining the retiree burden rate. Keeping workers in the labor market further into their lives would reduce the number of retirees, thus ameliorating the effect of retiree dependency. The increased number of workers would also increase total output, giving policymakers more flexibility in redesigning retirement programs, so workers could realize the fruits of their improved productivity without having to drive the retiree population into poverty.

Over the past decade, a number of countries have begun raising the retirement eligibility age in their national programs. Countries such as Sweden, the United States, and Belgium have all taken measures to increase the normal retirement age under these programs, while other countries, such as Germany, have enacted policies that slowly increase the eligibility age for unreduced early retirement benefits. These reforms shift the incentives in the right direction – that of keeping workers in the workforce longer than they have been in recent decades. If workers follow the incentives, it would promote economic growth in many of the developed economies, by boosting labor force growth and reducing the number of retirees depending on improvements in worker productivity for their support. Reductions in the ratio of retirees to the total population are not limited to public policy solutions. Nyce and Schieber discuss a number of ways in which the private sector can build incentives into their benefits programs to entice older workers to remain in the workforce.[21]

The problem is that raising the labor force participation rates of older people may not provide enough horsepower to propel many of the countries out of the aging dilemma they face. For example, consider the United States, where labor force participation rates drop off fairly significantly starting around age 55. In 2000, about 80 percent of 50- to 54-year-olds were in the labor force, but the rate declined to 69 percent for 55- to

---

[21] Ibid.

Table 7-14. *Changes in Total Consumption Growth Due to Increased Labor Force Participation of Workers Near Retirement*

	Total Consumption Growth Under Current Workforce Conditions		Total Consumption Growth with Increased Workforce Participation of Older Aged Workers	
	2000–2010	2010–2020	2000–2010	2010–2020
Australia	2.91	2.57	3.07	2.77
Austria	1.94	1.08	2.16	1.46
Belgium	1.52	1.08	1.73	1.37
Canada	2.23	1.69	2.40	1.92
Denmark	1.99	1.91	2.18	2.10
Finland	2.71	2.60	2.97	2.84
France	1.20	1.07	1.47	1.35
Germany	1.56	0.83	1.76	1.16
Greece	1.89	1.30	2.05	1.50
Iceland	1.14	0.71	1.27	0.91
Ireland	4.35	3.97	4.49	4.14
Italy	1.21	0.67	1.42	0.96
Japan	1.05	0.89	1.39	1.30
Luxembourg	2.98	2.65	3.17	2.88
Mexico	2.72	2.20	2.85	2.40
Netherlands	1.31	0.93	1.52	1.19
New Zealand	1.68	1.25	1.83	1.46
Norway	2.51	2.39	2.64	2.54
Poland	5.64	4.97	5.86	5.24
Portugal	2.08	1.67	2.30	1.95
Korea	5.62	4.85	5.82	5.20
Spain	1.38	0.59	1.51	0.78
Sweden	2.53	2.30	2.70	2.47
Turkey	4.53	3.97	4.66	4.16
United Kingdom	2.10	1.76	2.27	1.98
United States	2.45	2.07	2.61	2.31

Notes: The growth in total consumption is determined by the sum of labor productivity growth and labor force growth. Labor force participation of an older age cohort is assumed to increase by half the difference between the average labor force participation of the preceding five-year age cohort. The changes in the labor force participation rates are based on those in 2000 and assumed to occur gradually between 2000 and 2020.

Sources: OECD National Accounts – Source OECD Database; an unpublished database from the OECD; an unpublished database from Eurostat; United Nations Population Division, *World Population Prospects* (2000 Revision); also see Figure 7-3.

59-year-olds. It dropped to 47 percent for those aged 60 to 64, 24 percent for those 65 to 69, and to 13.5 percent for those 70 to 74. If each of these differences could be halved by 2010 – that is, increase the rate to about 75 percent for the 55- to 59-year-olds, 58 percent for the 60- to 64-year-olds, 36 percent for the 65- to 69-year-olds, and 19 percent for the 70- to 74-year-olds – it would increase the labor force by about 3.5 percent. Although this is a meaningful increase, it is not enough to offset the effects of population aging. To show this, we assumed that countries would universally adopt changes that would increase their workforces by similar relative amounts between 2000 and 2020. The implications for production of extra output are shown in Table 7-14.

Table 7-14 estimates how delaying the retirement of older workers could improve future growth in standards of living. In the scenarios presented earlier, we estimated total output based on the growth in the labor force given population projections by age and gender, assuming current labor force patterns persist in the future. In the projections for this alternative, we assumed that labor force participation rates for five-year age cohorts for those 50 and older would increase by half the difference from those five years younger. The changes in labor force participation rates were gradually adjusted between 2000 and 2020. The additional output achieved by this change in labor force behavior would result in a commensurate increase in the growth rate in consumption over the coming decades. In terms of who benefits from the increased rate of economic growth, it is likely that the additional workers and their dependents would garner most of the benefits from their workforce participation. But given the nature of public retirement systems as a mechanism for transferring income between generations, at least some of the additional growth would likely accrue to the retiree population. While these improvements in consumption growth are relatively small for most countries, at only a 20 to 30 basis point increase per annum, the results show how certain measures could lessen the burden of population aging on the society as a whole.

As we noted above, a number of countries have taken measures to encourage workers to delay retirement. However, we do not see many changes of the magnitude required to prompt the sorts of labor supply responses that appear in Table 7-14. Unless policymakers begin changing their retirement systems now in order to keep people at work later into life, they will likely face the prospect of determining how to allocate disappointing rates of economic growth between workers and retirees. In some countries, the demographic transition to an aging society may be so far along that this fate is already cast in stone.

EIGHT

Too Many Wants or Too Few Workers?

We began the discussion in Chapter 7 with a simple model of an economy depicted in Figure 7-1. The model showed that the level of labor demand in an economy is ultimately determined by two factors: the efficiency with which workers are employed in producing output, and the level of output that employers produce. The amount of output produced by employers is driven by the level of demand for goods and services. Of course, government programs affect aggregate demand, and imports to and exports from other countries are also important. In estimating the amount of labor the OECD economies might need to meet future demand, we can simplify the macroeconomic discussion by focusing on the inputs used in producing GDP. Keeping Figure 7-1 in mind will help in understanding how the analysis unfolds.

In this chapter, we evaluate the probability of the developed economies not having enough workers to satisfy consumer demand for goods and services over the next couple of decades. There are two ways around the projected labor shortfalls. One is to boost productivity high enough to make up for labor shortages. Achieving such high rates of productivity improvement poses its own set of challenges to employers, which we will explore in Chapter 10. The other is to boost workforce participation, either by attracting more workers into the workforce, convincing existing workers to work more hours or delay retirement, or some combination of the two.

Countries that cannot boost productivity or workforce participation by enough to make up for slower labor force growth may simply have to accept stagnant or slower-growing rates of improvement in their standards of living. In countries where labor supplies contract, citizens may actually have to learn to live with declining standards of living. But before scaling back their aspirations, most countries will want to explore options that hold out the promise of an economic future that is at least as bright as the past.

Increasing workforce participation would require certain fundamental labor force behavior patterns to change. Employers would either have to attract more people into the workforce who are outside it today, or convince their current workers to work more hours. We have developed detailed estimates of the increases in labor force participation required to alleviate labor supply shortfalls. These estimates are based on GDP growth assumptions developed by the OECD and EC in conjunction with public policy officials from member countries, and they assume that productivity will continue to grow at 1990s rates.

In each scenario, we estimate market clearing rates of labor force participation as the equilibrium scenario, where labor supply equals labor demand. We focus on four sources of additional labor: all individuals, all women, retirement-age people, and young adults. Under each scenario, we assume that changes in workforce participation would be distributed on a pro rata basis across the age cohorts relative to their current participation rates. For example, if 40 percent of one group now works and 20 percent of another group does, and they both have to increase their participation rates by 10 percent, then the first group's new rate would increase to 44 percent and the second to 22 percent. For each scenario, we estimate the increases in labor force participation rates required to supply enough labor to attain 1990s productivity levels. Although any combination of these scenarios could entice additional labor supply, we separate them in order to isolate their potential for solving labor shortfalls.

Framework and Baseline for Viewing the Labor Market Options

This part of the story begins by revisiting the productivity of workers in the various OECD economies measured in amount of GDP produced with each unit of labor input. As we saw in Table 7-8 in the preceding chapter, historical patterns of productivity improvement are somewhat mixed from country to country. Several countries, such as Germany, France, and Italy, have fallen into a pattern of consistently declining rates of improvement in labor productivity growth. Other countries, such as the United States and the United Kingdom, have experienced mixed rates of productivity growth, while Canada's productivity has steadily improved over the last three decades. If the past is any indication of the future, it is important to keep these recent patterns in mind when considering the productivity growth rates projected for the upcoming decade.

There are different ways of estimating future output levels, but most of them begin with some estimate of the demand for goods and services, which is based on the size and composition of various sectors of the economy. For this discussion, we use the OECD and EC projections of economic growth that were used to study the effects of population aging on government budgets. These projections are largely consistent with the historical pattern of ever-improving standards of living across these societies.

In order to describe the magnitude of the challenge that many developed economies will face in meeting the OECD and EC projections over the coming decade, we look at the relationship between baseline labor supply and projections of labor demand. For our baseline labor supply projections, we assume that current labor force participation and average hours worked by males at each age remain at their current levels over the coming decade. We assume that female labor force participation will continue increasing at the average rate of increase for each cohort over the last decade. Also, we assume that unemployment rates remain at current levels, a point we will return to later.

We estimate labor demand by using the GDP projections by the OECD and EC discussed above, under the assumption that labor productivity growth rates will continue at the average rate achieved throughout the 1990s. This assumption about future patterns of productivity growth seems reasonable, given the conflicting evidence about how information technology has affected workplace efficiency and the mixed rates of productivity growth over the last three decades. In an alternative scenario, we assumed that output per hour would increase to a rate where labor demand equals labor supply, a market clearing solution.

Our labor supply and labor demand projections are presented in Table 8-1. Columns two and three provide the ratio of our baseline estimates of labor supply relative to our labor demand projections for 2010 and 2030. The most succinct description of these results is that unless a number of these countries can raise or at least sustain their 1990s growth in output per hour of work over the coming decade, they could face significant labor shortfalls under our baseline workforce patterns. These countries may have a difficult time meeting the output growth expectations set out by the OECD and EC, and, in some cases, their standards of living may stagnate or even decline.

Table 8-1. *Percentage of Labor Demand Met Under Recent Rates of Productivity Growth*

	Percentage of Labor Demand Met		Market Clearing Productivity Growth Rates		Productivity Growth Rates	
	2010	2030	2010	2030	1990s	1980s
Australia	0.99	0.89	2.13	2.45	2.05	0.96
Austria	0.97	0.76	2.31	2.95	1.99	2.20
Belgium	0.95	0.74	2.16	2.64	1.62	1.91
Canada	1.02	0.93	1.27	1.74	1.50	0.97
Denmark	1.02	1.04	1.89	1.92	2.07	1.04
Finland	0.95	0.83	3.53	3.63	3.00	2.60
France	0.95	0.78	1.78	2.09	1.23	2.08
Germany[a]	0.95	0.72	2.06	2.63	1.49	1.28
Greece	1.06	1.02	1.18	1.69	1.76	−0.34
Iceland	0.94	0.71	0.95	1.41	0.27	0.97
Ireland	1.07	1.02	2.57	3.24	3.30	3.57
Italy	0.92	0.67	2.41	2.92	1.54	1.65
Japan	0.98	0.94	1.35	1.33	1.12	2.84
Luxembourg	0.85	0.55	3.50	3.90	1.84	3.19
Mexico	1.01	0.93	0.56	0.94	0.69	0.13
Netherlands	0.96	0.78	1.72	2.13	1.27	1.60
New Zealand	0.93	0.71	1.61	2.04	0.89	1.42
Norway	1.16	1.38	0.74	1.15	2.24	1.77
Portugal	0.92	0.72	2.66	2.96	1.82	1.82
Republic of Korea	0.99	0.83	4.60	5.20	4.55	5.89
Spain	0.92	0.63	2.15	2.89	1.31	1.88
Sweden	0.97	0.86	2.76	3.02	2.49	1.44
Switzerland	0.97	0.81	0.99	1.35	0.65	0.29
United Kingdom	0.99	0.88	1.98	2.35	1.93	1.95
United States	0.96	0.78	1.93	2.33	1.48	1.31

[a] For years 1991 to 2000, the calculation is based on the combined Germany. In the prior periods, the calculation is based on West Germany only.

Sources: UN Population Projections (2000 Revision); *OECD Labour Market Statistics*; an unpublished series of projections provided by the OECD; The OECD Economic Outlook, Source OECD; an unpublished series of hours from the U.S. Social Security Administration; an unpublished series of hours from Statistics Canada; and an unpublished series of hours from Eurostat.

For example, under current workforce patterns, unless Germany can achieve labor productivity growth rates of 2.06 percent per annum over the coming decade – a rate it has not achieved since the 1970s – we estimate a potentially significant labor or output shortfall over the coming decade. If productivity in Germany improves at a rate of 1.49 percent per year – its rate of improvement during the 1990s – the shortfall will be over 5 percent of total labor demand by 2010, which is equivalent to over 2 million full-time equivalent (FTE) workers. We estimate similar labor shortfalls for other rapidly aging countries such as Italy and Spain. In fact, all of these countries will need to raise their respective productivity growth rates by nearly a full percentage point over the rates they achieved during the 1990s in order to meet the growth expectations set out by the OECD and EC.

In several countries, such as Canada, Ireland, Norway, and the United Kingdom, GDP growth expectations appear to be in line with their most recent productivity growth rates. However, as we saw in Table 7-7 in the preceding chapter, expectations of output growth are quite low for Canada and Norway in comparison to recent history. In Canada, GDP per capita grew at a rate of 1.64 percent per year during the 1990s, but the projection for this decade is only 1.46 percent per year. In Norway, the 1990s rate of growth was 2.8 percent per capita, but projections for this decade are much lower, at only 0.98 percent per year. In most countries, such a significant slowdown in the rate of improvement in the standard of living would likely cause considerable discord among the citizenry, possibly leading to political problems for the ruling parties.

Increasing Labor Force Participation Generally

The first scenario calculates the increase in overall labor force participation rates required to meet labor force demand. The changes could come from increasing the number of people working or increasing the hours they work. As shown in Table 8-2, a number of countries, including Germany, Italy, France, and Spain, would need rather sizable increases in participation rates to eliminate the labor shortfalls. Most dramatically, Spain and Italy would need to increase participation rates for all age groups by over 8 percent, and Germany and France by over 5 percent to meet their labor needs under the OECD and EC output growth projections. The United Kingdom, Australia, and Sweden face less daunting labor shortfalls over the coming decade, requiring only marginally higher participation rates. If Canada, Denmark, and Norway achieve productivity growth rates similar to those of the last decade, they will have all the labor they need under these output growth expectations.

Although increasing participation rates across all individuals may seem achievable, enticing additional hours from people at prime working ages who are already working full time may be difficult to manage without

Table 8-2. *Increases in Labor Force Participation Rates Needed to Offset Projected Labor Shortfalls over the Coming Decade*

	LFPR 15+ in 2000		Needed LFPR 15+ in 2010	
	Males	Females	Males	Females
Australia	68.5	48.0	69.1	47.5
Austria	72.1	54.8	74.4	56.5
Belgium	61.4	43.5	64.7	48.3
Canada	72.2	58.7	72.2	58.1
Czech Republic	69.8	51.6	78.0	55.1
Denmark	71.6	59.9	71.6	56.0
Finland	66.1	56.5	69.5	53.6
France	62.4	47.9	65.9	50.1
Germany	69.9	49.1	73.9	52.5
Greece	64.9	39.8	64.9	43.3
Hungary	58.9	41.7	66.8	42.8
Iceland	81.5	71.4	87.2	77.6
Ireland	70.8	46.9	70.8	57.5
Italy	62.1	35.6	67.6	38.1
Japan	76.5	49.3	78.2	48.6
Luxembourg	64.8	40.5	76.2	54.8
Mexico	83.9	39.3	83.9	42.9
Netherlands	72.2	51.9	75.5	57.7
New Zealand	73.6	57.0	79.0	62.6
Norway	71.9	60.1	71.9	61.5
Poland	63.7	49.4	63.7	47.6
Portugal	70.8	53.5	76.8	60.7
Republic of Korea	73.1	48.6	73.6	50.1
Spain	66.2	40.8	71.8	50.2
Sweden	67.0	58.2	68.9	54.3
Switzerland	77.5	58.7	80.1	60.3
United Kingdom	66.9	58.0	67.2	56.2
United States	74.6	59.5	78.0	62.8

Sources: UN Population Projections (2000 Revision); *OECD Labour Market Statistics*; an unpublished series of projections provided by the OECD; The OECD Economic Outlook, Source OECD; an unpublished series of hours from the U.S. Social Security Administration; an unpublished series of hours from Statistics Canada; and an unpublished series of hours from Eurostat.

triggering significant wage inflation. It would be more plausible to focus on enticing more people into the labor force. For example, female labor force participation rates have been increasing steadily in many societies over the past several decades but still lag somewhat below male rates at almost all ages.

Table 8-3. *Increases in Prime-Age Female Labor Force Participation Rates Necessary to Offset Projected Labor Shortfalls Over the Coming Decade*

	Male LFPR 25–54 in 2000	Female LFPR 25–54 in 2000	Needed Female LFPR 25–54 in 2010
Australia	93.3	75.6	79.4
Austria	90.3	70.7	79.1
Belgium	92.1	73.1	92.6
Canada	91.1	78.6	79.5
Czech Republic	94.9	81.8	111.7
Denmark	91.5	84.4	81.2
Finland	90.8	85.0	93.2
France	94.1	78.4	92.1
Germany	95.9	77.0	95.0
Greece	94.5	62.2	69.5
Hungary	84.5	70.3	91.7
Iceland	96.1	88.1	116.0
Ireland	92.0	64.9	79.3
Italy	90.6	57.9	77.4
Japan	97.1	66.5	75.3
Luxembourg	94.1	64.5	116.1
Mexico	96.3	45.7	51.1
Netherlands	93.4	71.4	94.8
New Zealand	91.3	73.8	97.2
Norway	91.4	83.5	86.7
Poland	88.5	76.6	75.0
Portugal	92.7	77.2	99.5
Republic of Korea	91.9	57.5	62.7
Spain	92.9	63.1	92.9
Sweden	90.6	85.6	86.6
Switzerland	96.7	78.0	92.2
United Kingdom	91.8	76.1	79.2
United States	91.6	76.8	89.3

Sources: UN Population Projections (2000 Revision); *OECD Labour Market Statistics*; an unpublished series of projections provided by the OECD; The OECD Economic Outlook, Source OECD; an unpublished series of hours from the U.S. Social Security Administration; an unpublished series of hours from Statistics Canada; and an unpublished series of hours from Eurostat.

Increasing Female Labor Force Participation Rates

In one set of scenarios, we estimated how much female labor force participation rates would have to grow under each productivity scenario in order to achieve the total output growth set out by the OECD and EC. Table 8-3 shows the estimates of how much participation rates for women between ages 25 and 54 would have to rise to offset labor shortages. In a number of countries, female labor force participation rates would need to rise by a third or more over current rates. In Spain, Germany, the Netherlands, and the United States, the labor force participation of working-age women would need to rise to levels equivalent to those of their male counterparts. In Belgium and Italy, female participation rates would have to increase 27 percent and 34 percent, respectively, for annual productivity growth rates to equal those of the last decade. Can these countries entice that many more women into the workforce? Maybe, but evidence suggests that, in some countries, female labor force participation rates may be peaking.

One possible complication of looking to women to make up labor shortfalls is that, to a considerable extent, the demographic dilemma we face results from low fertility rates. Policies aimed at enticing more women into the workforce could be counterproductive if higher female labor force participation leads to yet further declines in fertility. Comparisons between Italy or Spain and the United States clearly show that high female labor force participation is not necessarily the root of low fertility rates, but more research is required to understand all the relationships in this area.

Increasing Labor Force Participation of Older People
Another alternative is enticing more older people into the workforce. Stories abound in the general and scientific press about today's longer life expectancy and better health at advanced ages. If people are living longer, staying robust and healthy into their older years, they should be able to remain in the workforce longer, helping to expand output and general standards of living. Our estimates of the increases in the labor force participation rates of people ages 55 and above that would be required under the alternative productivity scenarios are shown in Table 8-4.

If the labor force participation rates increase proportionately across all ages in this group, old age labor force participation would need to rise quite dramatically over the coming decade in many of the developed countries. For example, for Italy to achieve output growth rates over the coming decade comparable to those it managed during the 1990s, labor force participation rates for older men and women would need to nearly double by 2010 in order to meet the OECD and EC growth projections. Spain would have to increase its workforce participation rates by over 60 percent among its older population and Germany by almost 45 percent. Even with recent policy changes to old-age retirement programs in several

Table 8-4. *Increases in Old Age Labor Force Participation Rates Necessary to Offset Projected Labor Shortfalls over the Coming Decade*

	LFPR 55+ in 2000		Needed LFPR 55+ in 2010	
	Males	Females	Males	Females
Australia	22.6	7.6	24.0	8.0
Austria	33.7	16.1	45.2	28.0
Belgium	16.6	6.2	25.5	15.3
Canada	33.1	18.4	33.1	22.7
Czech Republic	30.0	10.8	60.5	23.2
Denmark	32.8	20.3	32.8	20.7
Finland	25.5	17.6	34.7	26.2
France	18.2	11.5	27.7	24.2
Germany	29.6	14.0	42.7	21.4
Greece	29.2	11.4	29.2	12.8
Hungary	17.5	6.0	44.7	16.9
Iceland	57.1	36.7	76.9	53.9
Ireland	38.3	12.9	38.3	23.7
Italy	21.8	6.8	37.1	15.6
Japan	57.5	28.4	62.4	30.0
Luxembourg	19.3	7.0	58.7	33.9
Mexico	66.6	21.7	66.6	26.7
Netherlands	25.9	10.0	36.3	20.0
New Zealand	39.5	21.9	58.1	38.5
Norway	36.3	23.9	36.3	29.0
Poland	25.3	12.3	25.3	13.4
Portugal	42.7	24.5	62.5	46.1
Republic of Korea	58.4	35.2	60.3	34.2
Spain	26.0	8.5	41.7	20.9
Sweden	36.3	25.7	41.6	28.8
Switzerland	45.1	29.2	54.1	36.7
United Kingdom	28.0	20.7	29.1	21.1
United States	40.0	25.7	51.9	39.8

Sources: UN Population Projections (2000 Revision); *OECD Labour Market Statistics*; an unpublished series of projections provided by the OECD; The OECD Economic Outlook, Source OECD; an unpublished series of hours from the U.S. Social Security Administration; an unpublished series of hours from Statistics Canada; and an unpublished series of hours from Eurostat.

of these countries, this would be a radical deviation from current labor force participation and retirement patterns.

Increasing Labor Force Participation of Young Adults
Young people are another possible source of additional workers. Several factors may account for young people not being in the workforce. Some

young adults are enrolled in undergraduate or graduate programs at universities. In some cases, young people may enter the labor force for a while but then return to a university or a graduate program. Young parents may choose to have one parent stay at home to raise the children during their formative years. In some countries, young people must complete military service requirements before entering the workforce.

For these reasons and likely for others as well, societies report varied rates of labor force participation for individuals age 20- to 29-years-old as reflected in Table 8-5. Labor force participation rates for young adults are highest in the United States, Denmark, the United Kingdom, and Austria. They are considerably lower in France, Italy, Spain, and Sweden. In fact, young adult labor participation rates for both men and women in France and Italy are over 10 percentage points lower than those of countries with the highest rates.

The delayed entrance of young adults into the workforce has a potentially immediate effect on total economic productivity but may influence other important variables as well. In many societies, young people must become economically independent before they can establish their own domicile, marry, and have children. As with other elements of this puzzle, a balance must be sought. There is a fine line between giving young people enough time to prepare themselves for careers that provide maximum productive capacity for our societies, and creating barriers that unnecessarily delay their productive contributions to themselves and society.

To help explain the variations in labor force participation among young adults, Table 8-6 shows estimates of the percentage of young adults not in the labor force by education grouping. A major reason why such high percentages of young people in France, Italy, and Spain are not in the labor force is because many of them are still in school. In France, over 40 percent of young adults ages 20 to 24 are pursuing their educations rather than working, while in Italy and Spain, nearly 35 percent of this age group is still in school. This is nearly three times the percentages reported in the United Kingdom, the Netherlands, and the United States.

We are not implying that students should leave school to enter the labor market as early as possible. Education makes workers more productive. However, the data indicate that some developed nations move their youth through school and into the labor force more swiftly than others. Additionally, some countries have high percentages of young people who are neither working nor in school. Generally, the highest rates occur in the less developed countries. However, from the last two columns of the table, it appears that this is mostly due to a higher percentage of

Table 8-5. *Increases in Younger Workers Labor Force Participation Rates Necessary to Offset Projected Labor Shortfalls over the Coming Decade*

	LFPR 20–29 in 2000		Needed LFPR 20–29 in 2010	
	Males	Females	Males	Females
Australia	82.4	74.6	85.6	76.9
Austria	88.2	74.9	102.8	87.4
Belgium	80.9	71.2	102.9	90.0
Canada	85.3	76.9	85.3	77.0
Czech Republic	87.1	63.3	141.0	102.7
Denmark	87.5	77.7	87.5	77.3
Finland	79.8	70.4	101.9	90.4
France	74.5	64.1	96.7	82.3
Germany	84.4	72.5	111.6	95.5
Greece	80.7	64.4	80.7	65.0
Hungary	78.2	55.2	129.2	91.8
Iceland	87.7	80.5	120.5	110.7
Ireland	85.4	74.6	85.4	75.7
Italy	73.2	56.6	118.5	91.1
Japan	85.1	71.2	97.4	81.6
Luxembourg	75.7	65.7	138.9	121.3
Mexico	89.4	44.7	89.4	44.7
Netherlands	88.9	81.5	108.9	99.6
New Zealand	84.9	68.7	115.4	93.2
Norway	84.3	75.3	84.3	74.6
Poland	80.1	66.0	80.1	67.1
Portugal	81.1	70.8	120.0	105.9
Republic of Korea	68.6	58.2	70.9	60.0
Spain	78.4	67.6	120.4	105.1
Sweden	78.2	70.8	89.9	80.2
Switzerland	84.3	72.7	99.6	85.3
United Kingdom	87.9	72.7	90.1	74.1
United States	87.5	75.2	105.4	90.6

Sources: UN Population Projections (2000 Revision); *OECD Labour Market Statistics*; an unpublished series of projections provided by the OECD; The OECD Economic Outlook, Source OECD; an unpublished series of hours from the U.S. Social Security Administration; an unpublished series of hours from Statistics Canada; and an unpublished series of hours from Eurostat.

women not in the workforce. In a macroeconomic context, the ability to get young people into productive roles has a potentially positive effect on standards of living. This will become increasingly important as aged dependency rates increase.

Table 8-6. *Percentage of Young Adults Not in the Labor Force by Education*

	In School and Not in the Labor Force		Not in School and Not in the Labor Force			
	All		All		Women	
	20–24	25–29	20–24	25–29	20–24	25–29
Australia	10.2	3.6	7.0	12.7	10.5	21.2
Austria	22.1	6.4	9.4	9.8	8.5	14.7
Belgium	36.9	3.5	6.1	8.1	8.8	13.3
Canada	18.7	5.4	8.0	9.7	10.2	14.3
Czech Republic	22.2	2.6	8.7	17.7	15.6	34.1
Denmark	16.8	10.5	3.6	5.7	6.0	8.7
Finland	28.9	8.9	8.3	9.4	7.9	15.1
France	41.3	5.0	4.9	9.2	7.1	15.5
Germany	16.7	6.8	10.8	12.2	14.6	20.0
Greece	32.8	5.0	9.3	13.2	12.4	23.9
Hungary	29.5	3.7	14.7	22.1	20.8	34.8
Iceland	14.6	8.9	2.1	3.4	3.3	6.4
Ireland	22.4	2.7	6.0	10.7	9.0	17.1
Italy	33.6	13.5	13.8	15.3	15.4	23.8
Luxembourg	38.9	5.9	5.5	10.7	8.1	18.0
Mexico	14.1	2.5	25.1	29.4	44.5	53.0
Netherlands	12.9	2.3	6.6	9.8	9.5	15.7
Norway	21.1	8.2	5.5	7.0	6.9	10.3
Poland	29.2	2.9	8.2	13.0	11.2	22.0
Portugal	28.5	4.4	5.6	7.8	7.1	11.5
Slovakia	18.5	2.2	12.1	15.7	16.9	26.9
Spain	34.9	8.2	5.6	11.2	7.9	17.9
Sweden	28.0	11.8	5.1	3.8	5.8	6.1
Switzerland	13.7	4.8	5.6	9.5	0.0	16.1
Turkey	0.9	0.3	36.7	35.0	59.0	67.5
United Kingdom	15.3	3.2	9.7	12.5	15.2	19.9
United States	13.1	2.9	10.2	13.5	14.4	20.9

Source: OECD, *Education at a Glance 2003*, Table C4.1, http://www.oecd.org/dataoecd/47/35/14923829.xls; statistics from 2001.

In all likelihood, raising the labor force participation rates of younger adults would only marginally reduce the labor shortages anticipated over the coming decade. Roughly half of the countries would need to raise labor force participation rates for these cohorts to over 100 percent in order to eliminate the projected labor shortfalls. This is an improbable solution, but at the margin it is worth considering as part of a broad set of policies to increase economic efficiency.

Matching Labor Force Participation Rates of High-Rate Countries

So far, we have discussed the extent to which labor force participation rates for women, the elderly, and young adults would need to rise in each country to offset the potential shortfalls in workers over the coming decade. As we have seen, several countries already have achieved high rates of labor force participation. This suggests that an alternative way to look at this macroeconomic puzzle is to project the future for aging societies under the assumption that they could raise their labor force participation rates to those in the countries with the highest rates.

Table 8-7 provides estimates of the percentage of labor demand that would be met in 2010 if all these countries brought their labor force activity rates up to the median rates achieved by the Top-5 countries for each age and gender group. As shown in the second column of the table, if male labor force participation increases to nearly 78 percent and that of females to about 60 percent for all age groups, many countries would have an ample supply of labor to achieve the OECD and EC growth expectations over the coming decade. Simply keeping older workers in the labor force longer would help considerably in ameliorating the potential labor force shortfalls. This is true even in several of the most rapidly aging societies. In many countries, increasing the labor force participation rates for 25- to 54-year-old women to 85 percent would meet their workforce needs over the coming decade. However, Spain, France, and Germany would still face shortfalls and would need to look elsewhere to expand their workforce. Finally, as the last column shows, raising the labor force participation rates of younger workers would have only a limited impact on increasing labor supply over the coming decade.

Attracting more women, older people, and young adults into the workforce could go a long way toward reducing labor shortages in aging economies. However, our analysis suggests that some countries may have considerable difficulty attracting the number of workers they need to meet the growth projected by the OECD and EC. Alternatively, another way of increasing the number of employed individuals would be to reduce unemployment rates, especially in countries where unemployment has been chronically high.

Table 8-8 reports unemployment rates in a number of OECD countries at selected points during the last 30 years and the unemployment rates assumed in the estimation of future output growth by the OECD and EC for the coming decade. The most noticeable trend since the 1970s is that, in many of the OECD countries, unemployment rates have risen substantially. For example, Germany's unemployment rate in 2000 was

Table 8-7. *Percentage of Labor Demand Met in 2010 at Median of the Top-5 Labor Force Participation Rates*

	All – 15 and Over	All – 55 and Over	Women 25 to 54	All – 20 to 29
Australia	1.18	1.26	1.02	1.00
Austria	1.05	1.02	1.02	0.97
Belgium	1.21	1.17	0.97	0.97
Canada	1.08	1.10	1.04	1.03
Czech Republic	1.03	1.01	0.90	0.91
Denmark	1.10	1.11	1.03	1.02
Finland	1.12	1.07	0.97	0.97
France	1.18	1.11	0.97	0.98
Germany	1.08	1.06	0.97	0.96
Greece	1.34	1.24	1.13	1.08
Hungary	1.26	1.07	0.97	0.92
Iceland	0.94	0.94	0.94	0.94
Ireland	1.15	1.13	1.10	1.08
Italy	1.29	1.13	1.03	0.95
Japan	1.08	0.98	1.03	0.99
Luxembourg	1.04	0.99	0.89	0.88
Mexico	1.08	1.01	1.16	1.07
Netherlands	1.03	1.08	0.97	0.96
New Zealand	0.97	0.98	0.96	0.95
Norway	1.20	1.23	1.16	1.17
Poland	1.37	1.27	1.16	1.14
Portugal	1.00	0.95	0.95	0.94
Republic of Korea	1.10	0.99	1.09	1.05
Spain	1.12	1.08	0.97	0.94
Sweden	1.12	1.05	0.99	1.00
Switzerland	0.98	1.00	0.98	0.98
United Kingdom	1.12	1.11	1.02	1.00
United States	0.98	0.99	0.98	0.96
Median Top 5 LFPR				
Males	77.5	57.5	–	88.2
Females	59.9	29.2	85.0	77.7

Sources: UN Population Projections (2000 Revision); *OECD Labour Market Statistics*; an unpublished series of projections provided by the OECD; The OECD Economic Outlook, Source OECD; an unpublished series of hours from the U.S. Social Security Administration; an unpublished series of hours from Statistics Canada; and an unpublished series of hours from Eurostat.

Table 8-8. *Unemployment Rates for Selected Years*

	Percent of Total Labor Force Unemployed			
	1970	1990	2000	2010
Austria	1.4%	3.3%	5.9%	4.7%
Belgium	1.9	6.9	10.2	7.9
Canada	5.7	8.4	6.7	6.5
Denmark	0.7	8.6	6.3	5.8
Finland	2.0	3.1	9.8	7.0
France	1.7	9.3	9.8	8.8
Germany	0.6	4.8	7.9	6.3
Ireland	5.8	13.1	5.0	5.0
Italy	2.9	10.5	10.7	9.7
Japan	1.1	2.0	4.7	4.0
Korea	–	2.4	4.1	3.5
Netherlands	1.0	7.4	3.2	4.0
New Zealand	0.2	7.7	6.1	6.0
Norway	0.7	5.1	3.6	3.8
Portugal	–	4.7	4.5	4.5
Spain	2.6	15.7	14.2	6.9
Sweden	1.5	1.8	6.0	5.2
United Kingdom	2.2	6.8	5.3	5.6
United States	4.9	5.6	4.1	5.1

Source: For the period 1970–2000, OECD Health Data 2001: *A Comparative Analysis of 30 Countries*; and for the period 2000–2050, data based on an unpublished series provided by the OECD.

10 times what it was in 1970. Some of the increase undoubtedly related to the reunification between East and West Germany, but unemployment rates have risen similarly in France, Italy, and Spain. The trend in rising unemployment is not consistent, as a number of countries have posted declining rates during the 1990s.

The assumptions used by the OECD and EC to project the growth in output across these countries suggest that unemployment rates will fall in the countries that have recently experienced high rates, and will rise, albeit moderately, in countries whose recent rates have been low. In fact, significant declines in unemployment are projected over the coming decade for a number of economies, including Spain, Finland, and Germany.

There are several possible explanations for differences in the economic performances of Europe and the United States over the most recent decade. One common explanation is that U.S. labor markets are more flexible than those in Europe. In Europe, unemployment protection, fixed-term contracts, minimum wages, and so forth have created market inefficiencies and disincentives for employers providing jobs. An alternative explanation is that the European economies are governed by more restrictive macroeconomic policies, which impede capital investment and therefore restrain economic growth. Yet another explanation is that employers perceive the relatively high social insurance costs they must pay as a fixed cost of hiring workers, thus making potential workers who would make relatively low marginal contributions to the enterprise seem like a bad economic deal.

Whichever theory is correct, there is widespread agreement that some fundamental changes are in order to reduce labor market rigidities and promote capital investment. This will not be easy for policymakers. It is unlikely that any policy changes could make enough of a difference in the near term to eliminate projected labor supply shortfalls. However, even if these economies could reduce their unemployment rates to the OECD and EC targets, many of them would still face significant labor shortfalls over the coming decade. Even Spain, whose unemployment rate is projected to drop more than 7 percentage points over the coming decade, could still confront a labor shortfall if productivity growth persists at the rate of the prior decade under current labor market patterns.

Immigration as a Potential Source of Added Workers

In the earlier discussion about immigration, we noted that Germany has recently debated attracting more foreign technical workers to make up for labor shortfalls. Targeted immigration policies certainly have the potential to help ameliorate some worker shortages. But immigration alone cannot make up for the low fertility rates in many of the developed countries, and a look at the arithmetic explains why.

The Perils of Low Immigration in an Era of Global Aging

By Paul S. Hewitt, Associate Commissioner for Policy, U.S. Social Security Administration

Pity poor Japan, a shrinking society whose intense tribalism makes its culture among the world's least hospitable to immigrants, and whose geographic isolation enables it to act out this prejudice to the detriment of its economy, welfare state, and international standing. Japan's bleak prospects provide a case study of the perils of low immigration in the era of global aging and depopulation.

Despite the recent introduction of government-sponsored dating services, fertility in Japan continues to plunge. In 2000, the Ministry of Health and Welfare issued the startling estimate that, unless birthrates rose, by the year 3000 there would be only

500 Japanese left. But that was back when fertility still hovered above 1.4 children per woman. Since then it has fallen to just above 1.3 – moving forward by a century or so Japan's projected date with cultural and racial extinction.

Of course, Japan's birthrate is hardly the lowest in the G7. That honor goes to Italy, whose fertility rate recently plumped to 1.26, according to Eurostat, after falling below 1.2 in 1999. But, unlike Japan, Italy faces a wave of illegal immigration that, like it or not, almost certainly will replenish its working-age population.

Consider the forces at play: During the first three decades of this century, Italy projects that its labor pool (the population aged 20 to 65) will shrink by some 7 million – a decline of 20 percent. Yet during this same period, labor pools in the Arab world will swell by 149 million, while sub-Saharan Africa's will balloon by 402 million. In the countries experiencing them, population explosions invariably lead to falling per capita incomes, deteriorating public services, and civil conflict. These forces already are creating intense pressures to migrate. And Italy looms as a prime destination.

During the election of 2000, George W. Bush became the first American presidential candidate to attempt a campaign speech in Spanish. By 2030, it is quite possible – and indeed desirable – that European politicians will be honing their Arabic language skills with similar zeal.

But much will have to change in the meantime. While national identity in "immigration countries" like the United States is essentially a legal concept, it is a matter of blood in much of the rest of the world. The European Union is waging a determined campaign, in the name of social tolerance and economic revival, to shed its once-rampant tribalism. Yet, even here, multiculturalism remains the exception rather than the rule.

This was brought home recently when a provincial German politician named Juergen Ruettgers coined the surprisingly popular rallying cry, "Inder statt kinder" (children instead of Indians) in protest to Chancellor Gerhard Schröder's plan to provide work permits to third world computer experts. A 2000 study found that 24 percent of employees in America's famed Silicon Valley were either Indian or Chinese immigrants. It only stands to reason that a globally competitive Germany would want to tap into the same deep reservoir of human capital.

Among the G7, however, only the United States appears to be succeeding in this quest. The OECD estimates that, during 1995–1998, 40.9 percent of U.S. immigrants had some college-level education, compared to 14.6 percent in Germany and just 13.8 percent in France. Yet it remains that even low-skilled foreign workers can add to the pool of technical talent in developed societies with flexible labor markets. Witness the extent to which affordable child care has freed college-educated American mothers to stay active in the workforce.

In 1998, only 1.2 percent of Japanese were foreign born, compared to 5.2 percent of Western Europeans and 9.8 percent of Americans. Japanese officials talk quietly of importing large numbers of Filipinos to help care for the nation's exploding elder population – where life expectancy for women recently topped 85 years. But popular resistance to such plans remains broad and deep-seated.

At a conference I organized in Tokyo in the summer of 2001, an international panel – including one of the principal authors of this report – expounded at length on the potential value of immigration for aging and depopulating societies like

Japan. Imagine our dismay when an academic in the audience rose to declare that immigrants were not acceptable. Instead, he explained, Japan's future workforce needs would be met by retraining elderly Japanese ladies.

Table 8-9. *Increase in Immigration Required to Offset the Extent Fertility Falls below Population Replacement Levels*

	Average Total Fertility Rate 1995–2000[a]	Average Births 1995–2000 (000s)	Additional Births at TFR = 2.1[a] (000s)	Average Net Immigration 1995–2000 (000s)	Multiple of Current Immigration to Offset Low Fertility
Australia	1.8	1250	42	95	0.4
Austria	1.4	408	41	5	8.2
Belgium	1.5	553	44	13	3.4
Canada	1.6	1782	111	144	0.8
Denmark	1.7	328	15	14	1.1
Finland	1.7	290	14	4	3.4
France	1.7	3649	172	39	4.4
Germany	1.3	3815	470	185	2.5
Greece	1.3	500	62	35	1.8
Iceland	2.0	21	0	6	0.0
Ireland	1.9	263	6	18	0.3
Italy	1.2	2623	393	118	3.3
Japan	1.4	6160	616	56	11.0
Korea	2.1	2034	0	−9	0.0
Luxembourg	1.7	27	1	4	0.3
Netherlands	1.5	935	75	32	2.3
New Zealand	2.0	276	3	8	0.3
Norway	1.8	289	10	9	1.1
Poland	1.5	2018	161	−20	−8.1
Portugal	1.5	563	45	13	3.5
Spain	1.2	1823	273	37	7.4
Sweden	1.5	441	35	9	3.9
Switzerland	1.4	367	38	4	9.6
United Kingdom	1.7	3530	166	95	1.7
United States	2.0	19983	200	1250	0.2

[a] The fertility rate reported here is rounded from the actual rates reported by the United Nations. The additional births that would have occurred if the total fertility rate was 2.1 were derived using the actual rates reported by the United Nations.

Source: Derived by the authors from 1955–2000 based United Nations Population Division, *World Population Prospects* (2000 Revision).

In Table 8-9, we show net immigration in the developed countries during the late 1990s, juxtaposed against the shortfalls in fertility. The table illustrates the increase in immigration required to make up for low fertility rates. The right-hand column in Table 8-9 shows the multiple of actual immigration during the last half of the 1990s that would have been required to hold the population steady. For example, Austria would have to increase its immigration rate by 8.2 times its current rate to offset its low fertility rates. For Germany, the multiple is 2.5, for Italy it is 3.3, and for Japan it is 11.0. More immigration can help some of these countries but probably not enough to put an end to their labor shortages.

In most countries with low fertility rates, the citizenry would probably protest the massive infusions of foreigners required to offset their low birthrates. Japan's immigration rate is significantly higher now than it used to be. But it is still miniscule when compared with those in most other developed countries, and Japan is unlikely to embrace immigration more enthusiastically in the future. There have already been signs of growing resentment of "foreigners" in several European countries. Far-right political parties running on anti-immigration themes have recorded gains at the polls in Austria, Italy, Norway, and Switzerland. In Germany, anti-immigrant factions are reportedly gaining strength. Policymakers may recognize the need for more immigration, but political considerations will likely limit its use as a means of shoring up labor supplies. In spring 2002, Denmark's refugee minister, Bertel Haarder, said, "We want more [immigrants] with special qualifications to come and help us." But other forces were at work as well. While Denmark's refugee minister was professing the need for more immigrants, the Danish parliament was considering legislation to limit immigration in one of Europe's most welcoming countries for foreigners.[1]

---

[1] Peter Finn, "A Turn from Tolerance," *Washington Post* (March 28, 2002), p. A1.

NINE

Alternatives to Finding More Workers

Enticing more people into the workforce could help alleviate the burdens of population aging throughout the world's developed economies, but it may not be enough to keep pace with the growing demand for goods and services. Once again referring back to the model of economic operations that we laid out in Figure 7-1, if labor growth rates remain too low to meet rising levels of consumer demand, the other variable that has possibilities is productivity.

Our analysis of the OECD and EC projections suggest that, in many developed nations, the higher labor force participation rates that would be required to meet consumer demand for goods and services are probably not attainable. So, in addition to realizing all the gains they can in labor force participation rates, policymakers and capital owners will need to set their sights on enhancing productivity as well. We explore two options here. One is simply providing workers with more physical capital. The other is figuring out how to get more output from existing workers through productivity-enhancing human resource policies and processes.

Capital Deepening as a Possible Alternative to Additional Labor Supply

One way to enhance labor productivity is through increased capital investment. To some degree, capital complements the existing pool of workers by making them more efficient. On the flip side, since additional capital enables workers to produce more output, capital can also be seen as replacing labor. But there are limits to the extent that capital can substitute for labor. For example, a farmer using a modern-day combine can harvest wheat much faster than one using an early twentieth century threshing machine. However, one farmer cannot operate two combines at once, limiting the substitution of combines for farmers. In many developed nations, the ability to replace people with capital will have important implications for their economic health and well-being over the coming decades.

Part of the limitation on the substitutability between labor and capital relates to time. In many cases, the capital that workers use to perform their jobs is a fixed entity with certain embedded characteristics. If a manufacturer buys a lathe to make a single part and that lathe requires one full-time operator, then the relationship between labor and capital is relatively fixed in the short term. In a longer-term context, however, the lathe may be automated so it requires only periodic checks, thus freeing the worker to perform other tasks. Or the lathe may make multiple parts, enabling the manufacturer to eliminate unnecessary machines that also require labor for operation.

The substitution of labor for capital happens through natural market adjustments in the relative prices of the two factors of production. As with all goods and service in a market economy, decreasing availability drives up the price. As domestic labor markets tighten in the developed economies, there will be upward pressures on wages. Faced with higher labor costs, business owners will seek other means of expanding their productive capacity. In most cases, this would result in capital investment – substituting machines for the more expensive human capital. But, to the extent that aging populations slow economic growth, less capital investment will be needed since the reduced pace of output growth should also slow the growth of the required capital stock. In other words, the need for capital will decline along with the other factors of production. However, population aging will change the balance between capital and labor. In particular, capital will likely play an increasingly important role in the productive capacity of the developed economies – what economists call capital deepening. A rise in capital intensity would increase labor productivity, which in turn would boost output growth. The boost might not be enough to entirely eliminate output shortfalls, but it would help considerably.

Capital deepening requires an available supply of capital. According to the life cycle hypothesis, aging populations will reduce private savings rates, as a greater share of the population falls into the low-saving/dissaving pensioner population. If savings rates decline, countries may find it increasingly difficult to fund capital investment sufficiently to raise capital intensity. In a worst-case scenario, aging could cause such

Table 9-1. *Distribution of Savings Rates for Various Age Groups across a Number of Countries*

Age	United Kingdom	Canada	Japan	Germany	Italy	United States
25–34	6.22	1.50	11.00	11.00	13.26	8.72
35–44	9.42	4.00	20.15	14.00	15.57	14.21
45–54	12.24	6.50	17.60	16.00	17.65	14.75
55–64	7.62	10.00	19.70	10.00	17.94	10.81
65–74	11.36	6.00	20.20	7.50	16.52	−4.88
75+	19.82	8.00	26.45	10.00	15.70	−6.54

Note: Ages are of the household head/reference person and savings rate in each age group is for all households in their respective samples.

Sources: U.S.: Bureau of Labor Statistics, http://stats.bls.gov/cex/2000/Standard/age.pdf; Japan: Kitamura et al. (2000), Table 3, pp. 5; Italy: Brugiavini et al. (2000), Table 7, pp. 27; UK: Banks et al. (March 2000), pp. 63–64; Germany: Borsch-Supan et al. (2000), Table E1; Burbidge et al. (1994), Figure 1.9, pp. 39–41.

a sharp decline in savings rates that there would not be enough funds available for capital investment despite lower investment demand. However, a more modest decline in savings rates would likely mean an ample supply of available resources.

Comparing cross-sectional survey data across a number of countries in Table 9-1 actually suggests that rather than conforming to the life-cycle model, population aging might lead to increased saving rates. In the United Kingdom and Japan, savings rates seemingly increase steadily with age beginning for the 55-to-64 cohort. In Canada and Germany, savings rates dip from the 55-to-64 age group to the next age category, 65 to 74, but the savings rate picks up again for those 75 years of age and older. In the United States and Italy, the savings rate actually falls from age 55 to 64 onward, but in Italy, the saving rate is still remarkably high. It is only in the United States that savings rates actually turn negative at advanced ages. Overall, the results in Table 9-1 suggest that aging populations might actually result in having more savings available to fuel our capital growth in the future. Recent research studies have generally assumed that aging will cause only modest declines in private savings.[1]

We believe that it is premature to conclude that aging populations will lead to increased savings rates. As you probably recall from the discussion in Chapters 3 and 4, the elderly in most developed countries depend on

---

[1] McMorrow and Roger (2003) at the European Commission assume that private savings will decline at a rate that is consistent with an increase in the capital to labor ratio.

Table 9-2. *Average Annual Growth Rates in Units of Capital per Worker in the Business Sector for Various OECD Countries*

	1960s	1970s	1980s	1990s	1995–2000
Australia	3.24%	2.37%	2.29%	1.55%	1.85%
Austria	7.80	6.24	4.13	3.85	3.51
Belgium	1.97	3.74	2.78	2.16	1.48
Canada[a]	1.80	0.92	1.59	0.69	0.17
Denmark	–	4.54	2.36	3.09	2.83
Finland	–	–	3.19	1.71	−1.78
France[a]	2.33	7.29	4.72	2.82	1.51
Germany	8.40	4.75	1.96	0.62	0.62
Ireland	1.90	2.26	2.62	−0.52	−1.09
Italy	6.46	4.30	2.60	2.88	2.03
Japan[a]	11.45	7.85	4.82	4.18	3.64
Netherlands	–	2.70	1.28	0.81	0.28
Norway[a]	1.75	2.53	2.04	0.52	1.06
Spain[a]	4.82	7.27	2.86	2.85	0.85
Sweden[a]	4.22	4.30	2.43	3.18	1.83
United Kingdom	–	2.77	0.99	2.73	2.40
United States	2.49	1.47	0.94	1.09	1.55

[a] Data series start in 1965; capital is defined as capital stock in the business sector and labor is measured as employment in the business sector.
Source: OECD database for Economic Outlook.

retirement plans for most of their income. In pay-go retirement plans, retiree income is funded by workers' social insurance contributions. These contributions are "consumption loans" made in lieu of workers' "saving" for their own retirement. In funded retirement plans, retiree income comes from the spending down of capital saved and invested during the retiree's working career.

Looking back to Table 7-1, the capital stock in most developed countries has been growing faster than the labor supply. The results are generally confirmed by Table 9-2, where we show decade-by-decade growth rates in the business-sector capital per worker since the 1960s, where available, and for the latter part of the 1990s. In a number of countries, especially France, Germany, Japan, the Netherlands, and Spain, the rate of increase in the capital-labor ratio has been slowing over time. During the 1960s, the countries that were most badly ravaged by World War II registered the biggest increases in their capital to labor ratios. Some of the increase was due to the necessity of rebuilding economies almost from scratch after World War II, and some resulted from public policy initiatives like the U.S. Marshall Plan, which provided investment aid to the countries devastated by the war. In many developed economies, labor force growth during the 1960s was fed by a relatively small number of new workers, as small birth cohorts born during the Great Depression and World War II reached working age. At the same time, aggregated demand in these economies was growing due to the spike in fertility rates after the war. The effects of these factors varied somewhat from country to country.

The baby boom generations born after World War II were much larger in Australia, Canada, and the United States compared to post-war birth cohorts in other developed countries. As these baby boom generations began joining the workforce in the late 1960s, their relative size caused dislocations within labor markets.[2] The influx of a relatively large group of young, low-skilled workers into the labor market in the 1970s created a surplus supply of labor, which was accentuated by higher numbers of women entering the labor force. These developments depressed wage growth for entry-level workers. As labor costs were bid down by the excess supply of workers, the relatively cheaper labor became more appealing to capital owners. The result was a preference for labor over capital, leading to a slowing rate of growth in the capital-to-labor ratio. The three countries with the largest baby-boom populations, the United States, Australia, and Canada, had much slower-growing capital-labor ratios during the 1970s than most of the other countries in Table 9-2.

By the end of the twentieth century, labor force growth had slowed significantly in countries whose postwar baby booms were small and whose fertility rates had fallen significantly below replacement rates relatively early. In several of these countries, the rate of investment in capital was such that the growth in the capital-labor ratio was slowing as well. Part of this slowdown has related to the level of capital deepening already achieved in those economies and the alternative use of resources. However, several countries endured significant macroeconomic shocks over the 1990s that considerably altered the growth in the capital-to-worker ratio. For example, in Finland, unemployment rates spiked from roughly 3 percent in 1990 to above 15 percent by 1995 only to fall back to around 9 percent by the end of the decade. Similarly, unemployment rates in Ireland dropped appreciably over the 1990s, falling from nearly 13 to 4 percent. These fluctuations in employment simultaneously result in large

---

[2] Diane J. Macunovich, *Birth Quake: The Baby Boom and Its After Shocks* (2000), Unpublished Manuscript.

swings in the capital-to-labor ratios, which could alter the long-term trends underlying Table 9-2.

As industrialized nations begin to rely more heavily on capital for the production of goods and services, how well they succeed in meeting the demand pressures in their societies will depend on how efficiently capital is put to use. If each additional unit of capital can continue to be used as effectively as the last, capital deepening could very well substitute for labor, easing the burdens of population aging. Classical economics identifies certain relationships between the factors of production and the level of output. For example, increasing both capital and labor creates a proportionate increase in output. The factors of production can be substituted for each other in producing a given level of output, but as that occurs, the ratio of potential output to the inputs will change. Increasing the level of capital used in production generally diminishes the marginal product of capital. Consistent with standard economic theory, as capital becomes a greater share of productive capacity, the rate of return to capital investment tends to fall. Ultimately, whether rates of return on capital investment decline will depend on rates at which capital is replaced in economies where aging becomes a drag on private savings rates. It will likely also depend on the degree to which capital originating in the developed economies is invested abroad to ameliorate the declining marginal productivity of capital at home. We return to this issue of international capital flows in Chapter 11.

Calculating comparable rates of return on capital across countries and over time is difficult, since the approaches used to estimate many of the underlying variables vary considerably. This is particularly true in estimating capital stock. The OECD has attempted to create consistent estimates of capital stock for inter-country comparisons of capital returns, and publishes estimates for the business sector in the OECD *Economic Outlook*. However, recognizing the difficulties in imputing capital returns that are comparable across nations, the OECD discontinued the series, making 1998 the most current estimates available. A consistent set of estimates for the United States is particularly difficult, since the Bureau of Economic Analysis of the U.S. Department of Commerce ceased publishing a series for gross capital stock. As a result, we use estimates from Poterba (1997) where the underlying source of data is the same as that used by the OECD.[3]

---

[3] James Poterba, "The Rate of Return to Corporate Capital and Factor Shares: New Results Using Revised National Income Accounts and Capital Stock Data" (National Bureau of Economic Research, 1997), Working Paper No. 6263.

Table 9-3. *Comparative Rates of Return on Capital in the Business Sector*

	1971–1981	1982–1985	1986–1990	1991–1995	1996	1997	1998[b]
Australia	10.2	9.3	10.8	11.7	13.5	14.0	14.1
Austria	–	14.9	15.0	14.8	15.6	15.8	15.7
Belgium	12.5	12.0	14.3	13.3	13.8	14.2	14.4
Canada	17.5	17.5	16.7	14.2	14.3	13.6	12.8
Denmark	–	–	7.2	8.7	9.8	9.7	8.9
Finland	8.1	8.6	8.5	7.6	10.3	11.4	12.9
France	13.9	12.1	14.8	15.3	15.7	16.0	16.4
Germany	13.0	11.6	12.9	12.7	13.6	14.3	15.3
Ireland	5.0	6.2	8.9	11.8	15.4	16.0	17.0
Italy	11.8	12.1	14.2	14.4	15.4	15.1	14.6
Japan	15.8	13.2	14.4	13.6	13.6	12.7	11.7
Netherlands	–	–	17.4	17.9	18.6	19.1	18.9
Norway	8.3	6.6	6.4	7.2	7.5	7.4	6.5
Spain	16.6	12.9	18.1	17.8	18.3	18.0	18.2
Sweden	10.3	10.4	10.4	12.1	12.3	12.4	11.8
Switzerland	14.8	13.1	12.4	11.8	12.3	13.1	13.5
United Kingdom	–	–	9.6	10.4	11.6	11.4	11.1
United States[a]	14.3	14.8	16.7	17.9	18.7	–	–

[a] Estimate is from Poterba (1997) since the OECD no longer includes the United States as the U.S. Department of Commerce, Bureau of Economic Analysis has ceased publishing a series for gross capital stock.
[b] This is a preliminary estimate.
Source: OECD Economic Outlook, Annex Table 24, December 1998; Poterba (1997).

Table 9-3 reports estimates for rates of return on capital for a number of OECD countries for various periods over the last three decades. While capital deepening would likely indicate that rates of return should decline, the OECD estimates provide very little indication that returns to capital are in fact falling. To the contrary, rates of return have been rising in several countries, including Germany, France, and Italy. Japan, however, shows a consistent pattern of declines in capital returns throughout the 1990s. The recent experience of rising capital returns in Europe may partly reflect the gains from deregulation and coordination of their economies flowing from the creation of the European Union. It may also reflect the effects of technology.

While we only look at the most recent periods, other research has suggested that demographic aging will generally lead to sharp declines in capital returns in the coming decades. For example, Kieran Mc Morrow and Werner Roger (2003) use a conventional neoclassical, overlapping generations model to assess the impact of aging populations on economic growth and standards of living. In their baseline model, where international capital flows are restricted between the developed and the developing countries and macroeconomic policies are assumed not to change, their simulations indicate that, as a result of changes to savings and investment at the global level, worldwide real interest rates are projected to decline from 5.75 percent in 2000 to roughly 5.0 percent by 2050. This implies that the impact of aging populations will be a greater drag on global investment than on global savings.[4]

When the restrictions on international capital flows are eliminated such that there are much closer global linkages between the developed and developing nations, the opposite occurs. Under this scenario, global real interest rates rise by 0.35 percentage points over the next half century. However, the reliability of a full capital mobility scenario is rather poor as its estimates are "grossly at odds with the observed evolution."[5] In particular, the model clearly does not predict the extent to which foreign capital flowed into the United States over the last 10 to 15 years as the model estimates a net foreign asset (outflow minus inflow) position by 2000. As such, the baseline scenario with restricted capital mobility is likely a more representative forecast of tomorrow.

Axel Borsch-Supan, Alexander Ludwig, and Joachim Winter have analyzed the implications of funding a share of Germany's national pension system. Their analysis suggests that a portion of the added pension funding would represent new savings in Germany, which in turn would add to the capital stock. In the simulations that assume that capital can flow freely across borders, they estimate the capital stock would grow by 110 percent or so over baseline levels by 2030. In simulations that assume a closed-economy scenario, the capital stock would swell to nearly 130 percent of baseline levels. Based on their estimates of the elasticity of substitution between capital and labor in Germany, they estimate that between 2010 and 2026, the return on capital would fall by about 0.7 percentage points as a result of the increased investment in the closed market case. The decrease would only be 0.2 percentage points in the open market simulations.[6] Aaron, Bosworth, and Burtless (1989) reported similar findings when they investigated the impact of a permanent rise in savings by eliminating an annual U.S. government deficit of 1.5 percent of gross

---

[4] See Mc Morrow and Roger, "Economic and Financial Market Consequences of Ageing Populations," European Economy, Economic Papers (2003) No. 182, p. 56.

[5] Ibid, p. 45.

[6] Axel Borsch-Supan, Alexander Ludwig, and Joachim Winter, "Aging and International Capital Flows" (Cambridge, MA: National Bureau of Economic Research, 2001), NBER Working Paper, no. w 8553.

Table 9-4. *Capital Income as a Share of GDP in the Business Sector*

	1971–1981	1982–1985	1986–1990	1991–1995	1996	1997	1998[a]
Australia	32.0	32.5	37.4	38.3	38.0	37.2	37.1
Austria	–	37.4	37.6	38.3	41.7	42.4	43.0
Belgium	32.6	33.6	37.2	35.5	37.3	38.0	38.4
Canada	35.1	35.4	33.7	30.1	31.0	29.5	28.6
Denmark	–	–	32.6	37.0	39.1	38.2	36.1
Finland	29.2	29.6	28.7	28.8	34.2	35.9	37.9
France	34.9	33.9	39.3	40.4	40.7	41.1	41.3
Germany	33.2	33.2	35.7	35.3	37.0	38.6	40.0
Ireland	19.8	22.2	27.1	31.0	35.6	36.5	37.8
Italy	34.4	35.3	38.0	38.6	42.1	41.6	41.9
Japan	32.3	30.4	33.3	33.1	33.2	31.8	30.8
Netherlands	–	–	39.4	39.3	40.0	40.6	40.0
Norway	27.8	27.7	28.7	32.9	33.3	32.4	29.4
Portugal	33.6	36.9	39.2	37.1	39.1	38.7	38.2
Spain	28.9	29.2	37.7	38.2	40.3	39.9	39.9
Sweden	27.7	31.7	30.3	33.2	32.9	32.9	31.3
United Kingdom	–	–	31.9	30.7	32.9	31.9	30.7
United States	32.5	33.2	33.7	33.8	34.7	34.6	33.6

[a] This is a preliminary estimate.
Source: OECD Economic Outlook, Annex Table 24: December 1998.

national product. The increase in savings resulted in a 14.3 percent increase in the capital stock over the baseline between 1990 and 2030, while capital returns were projected to drop more than 0.4 percentage points.

The rate of return on capital can be separated into two components: the capital income share and the efficiency of capital. As described earlier, capital income measures the percentage of output that goes to the owners of capital. The efficiency of capital is determined by the amount of capital it takes to produce a unit of output, which is measured by the ratio of capital to output. So simply dividing the capital income share by the efficiency of capital provides an estimate of the returns to capital investment, which is the ratio of profits to capital. Within this context, in order for a country to increase its returns to capital, either the capital must be used more efficiently, or the share of output going to capital owners in the form of profits must be on the rise. Estimates of how capital income shares have been changing in many of the OECD countries over the last three decades is provided in Table 9-4.

The data show that many of these countries, particularly the European countries, have experienced significant increases in the share of output

Table 9-5. *Ratio of Business Sector Capital Stock to Output for Selected Periods*

	Australia	Austria	Belgium	Canada	Finland	France	Germany	Ireland
1970	–	1.63	2.65	1.66	–	1.58	1.82	4.24
1975	1.39	1.93	2.69	1.64	3.20	1.69	2.15	3.65
1980	1.39	2.17	2.70	1.73	3.32	1.75	2.21	3.46
1985	1.50	2.46	2.90	1.82	3.35	1.89	2.41	3.50
1990	1.56	2.57	2.86	1.83	3.29	1.91	2.35	2.95
1995	1.57	2.86	3.09	1.81	3.47	2.09	2.52	2.55
2000	1.58	3.02	3.10	1.51	2.73	2.05	2.46	1.95
	Italy	Japan	Netherlands	Norway	Spain	Sweden	U.K.	U.S.
1970	2.43	1.31	2.67	1.90	1.36	2.33	3.50	1.45
1975	2.68	1.75	2.64	1.78	1.50	2.52	3.45	1.51
1980	2.57	1.93	2.61	1.79	1.81	2.81	3.36	1.48
1985	2.72	2.20	2.61	1.83	1.95	2.82	3.08	1.47
1990	2.74	2.25	2.48	1.97	1.95	2.83	2.87	1.42
1995	2.92	2.61	2.45	1.83	2.22	2.93	2.89	1.37
2000	3.06	2.84	2.36	1.85	2.22	2.78	2.90	1.32

Source: OECD Economic Outlook, Source OECD.

going to capital. Germany, France, and Italy have all seen a steady rise in capital income shares from their 1970s levels, to a point where roughly 40 percent of output goes to capital owners. Spain has seen the largest increase, raising its capital income share by over 10 percentage points over the last 20 years. However, the United States and the United Kingdom show very little change in the capital share over the last two decades. Canada appears to be an outlier – the only country to show a noticeable drop in its capital share.

The ability of the developed nations to sustain returns to capital in the face of capital deepening will largely depend on the efficiency with which the capital is put to use. Table 9-5 presents estimates of capital efficiency for a number of OECD member countries. Several countries reveal a sustained pattern of rising capital stock relative to output. As a result, over this period many of the industrialized countries have employed a greater amount of capital in order to produce an additional unit of output. For example, in 2000, Germany used roughly 2.5 units of capital to produce one unit of output, up from only 1.82 in 1970. Japan's capital efficiency has declined most significantly. Whereas Japan's capital-to-output ratio was only 1.31 in 1970, by 2000, it had risen to 2.84, more than doubling over the period. While capital efficiency has deteriorated in many countries over recent years, some countries, such as the United States and the United

Table 9-6. *Growing Dependence on Capital and Declining Returns in Japan*

	Index of Real GDP	Ratio of Capital Stock to GDP	Capital Income as Share of GDP	Index of Capital Stock	Index of Capital Income	Rate of Return
(1)	(2)	(3)	(4)	(5)	(6)	(7)
1980	100.0	1.93	0.323	193.0	32.3	0.167
1985	119.3	2.20	0.317	262.5	37.8	0.144
1990	149.7	2.25	0.341	336.7	51.0	0.152
1995	160.7	2.61	0.318	419.4	51.1	0.122
2000	165.4	2.84	0.321	469.7	53.1	0.113

Source: OECD Economic Outlook, Source OECD.

Kingdom, show marginal improvements. Most notable is Ireland, which has more than doubled the productive capabilities of its capital goods. This is likely a major factor behind the run up in capital returns in Ireland in recent years.

The implications of this changing factor combination in producing the outputs in developed countries might best be understood in the context of a brief case study of Japan, which pulls together the messages behind Tables 9-3 through 9-5 as summarized in Table 7-6. The second column in the latter table shows an index of real GDP in Japan in five-year increments from 1980 through 2000. The third column shows the capital stock-to-GDP ratio taken from Table 9-5. The fourth shows the capital share of output in percentage terms. The fifth is an estimate of the capital stock based on the index of GDP in column two multiplied by the capital stock-to-GDP ratio in column three. The sixth column is the capital income stated relative to the GDP and is the product of column two multiplied by column four. The rate of return on business capital in the right-hand column is a rough estimate derived as the quotient of column six to column five. The numbers here closely parallel those from Table 9-3.

The important point in Table 9-6 is that the capital deepening in Japan over the last couple of decades has been paralleled by declining rates of return on capital. In a total macroeconomic context, this story of Japan understates the reality, because it has focused solely on the business sector. Over the past 10 to 15 years, the Japanese government has repeatedly undertaken major structural projects financed with government deficits in order to stimulate demand, in hopes of pumping up the economy. The government debt during this period has gone from one of the lowest in the developed world to one of the highest. The deficits have soaked up much of private household saving. But it has been used on a variety of projects that might provide very negligible returns to the Japanese people over the long term.

Technology has the potential to substitute for labor supply growth and can limit the extent to which returns on capital decline as capital-output ratios increase. However, the Japanese story serves as a cautionary tale. Simply throwing more capital at a stagnant or declining workforce will not necessarily boost productivity indefinitely. The likely results of persistent capital deepening are declining returns on capital investment. Therefore, in order to meet the output growth challenges imposed by aging populations, the industrialized countries will require more than a buildup of capital stock. These economies will need to figure out ways to more effectively align capital with labor in order to leverage the full capabilities of both factors in the production of goods and services.

One likely indicator of how enthusiastically an economy embraces new technologies or new ways of doing things is its level of entrepreneurial activity. Back in the 1930s, Joseph Schumpeter wrote about "creative destruction" being at the center of economic advancement in capitalist economies. He said that we tend to focus on how our economies administer existing structures when the relevant issue is how an economy creates and destroys them. Schumpeter wrote that the process of industrial mutation "incessantly revolutionizes the economic structure from within, incessantly destroying the old one, incessantly creating a new one. This process of Creative Destruction is the essential fact about capitalism. It is what capitalism consists in and what every capitalist concern has got to live in."[7]

In recent years, the London Business School has been developing a "Total Entrepreneurial Activity (TEA) Index" that measures the percent of the labor force in various countries involved in starting new businesses. The higher a country's TEA index score, the more entrepreneurial activity there is. The 2002 survey covered 37 countries including 60 percent of the world population and 92 percent of world GDP. In Figure 9-1 we have plotted the results of their 2002 survey against a measure of aged dependency in the countries in the 2002 survey.

The measure of aged dependency used in developing Figure 9-1 is the ratio of people ages 55 and older to those ages 20 to 54. There appears to be a fairly strong inverse relationship between entrepreneurial activities and

---

[7] Joseph A. Schumpeter as quoted in Richard Foster and Sarah Kaplan, *Creative Destruction* (New York: Doubleday, 2001), p. 30.

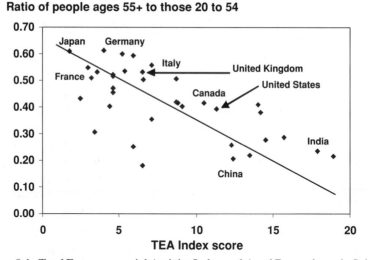

Ratio of people ages 55+ to those 20 to 54

Figure 9-1. Total Entrepreneurial Activity Index and Aged Dependency in Selected Countries. *Source:* Global Enterpreneurship Monitor (GEM) Project at http://www.gemconsortium.org/download/1073483398968/Figure%201.jpg.

aged dependency in these countries. This suggests that aging societies may be less likely to engage in creative destructive activities that accelerate the adoption of technological innovations and can ameliorate the effects of capital deepening on rates of return.

In order to detect any effects that aging might already be having on rates of return on capital, we attempted to quantify the impact of the age structure on value creation in the corporate business sector. A standard way to measure the surplus value of a business is through the ratio of the market value of a company's debt and equity to the replacement cost of its assets. This ratio is often known as Tobin's Q, named after its creator, economist James Tobin. It measures the ability of a firm to earn above average returns on its assets. If countries with aging populations are incurring slowed labor force growth and substituting capital for labor, this should diminish firms' ability to create surplus value. If firms create less surplus value, their rates of return should be lower.

To measure the effect of population aging on rates of return, we estimated the relationship between Tobin's Q for publicly traded firms in the OECD economies and the old-age dependency ratio – the ratio of individuals 55 and older to those ages 20 to 54. A higher dependency ratio suggests a greater reliance on physical capital to meet output needs in the most rapidly aging economies. If the capital deepening in the aging

Table 9-7. *Selected Characteristics of Firms Analyzed to Evaluate Effects of Population Aging on Corporate Returns*

Year	No. Firms	Mean Tobin's Q	Std Dev Tobin's Q	Mean Dependency Ratio	Std Dev Dependency Ratio
1991	3463	1.62	1.86	0.444	0.053
1996	5366	1.78	2.48	0.463	0.066
2001	9000	1.45	1.59	0.544	0.090

Sources: Standards and Poor's Compustat Global Database; UN Population Division, World Population Prospect (2000 Revision).

economies results in lower returns, we expect that where the dependency ratio is high or rising, Tobin's Q will be low or falling. To capture how these relationships have changed over the past decade, we include three separate time periods of 1991, 1996, and 2001 in our analysis. Table 9-7 reports the number of companies and the means and standard deviations for Tobin's Q and the old-age dependency ratios.

Several other factors can have an effect on Tobin's Q, which we controlled for in the multiple regression analysis. For example, the extent to which a firm's market value exceeds the value of its assets on the balance sheet depends on the type of business. We controlled for industry, the number of business lines a firm engages in, and the size – log of total assets – of the firm. A firm's financial characteristics are also likely to affect Tobin's Q. Firms that are more susceptible to cyclical variations display greater variance over the cycle than others. We used the long-term debt leverage of the firm relative to total assets to control for this. Since financial statements do not provide direct measures of labor expense, we used selling, general, and administration expenses and capital intensity as a proxy for labor costs. Additionally, we controlled for asset turnover in our model to account for the ability of organizations to substitute knowledge for working capital. Firms able to better leverage their customer relationships with intellectual capital will be able to turn greater sales relative to their assets. Because of the data limitations, we were unable to control for important factors such as advertising and R&D expense, which increase the value of the firm's non-balance sheet assets. To a certain extent, industry controls account for these influences.

The results from the multiple regression analysis are provided in Table 9-8. A higher dependency ratio in the country in which an organization is incorporated has a significant negative impact on Tobin's Q. This suggests that in countries that have a 0.1 higher dependency ratio, companies, on average, will have an 18 percent lower Tobin's Q. This

Table 9-8. *Multiple Regression of Dependency Ratio in
the OECD Countries on the Financial Performance of
Corporate Firms in Those Countries*

	Estimates	t-Value
Intercept	1.138	7.13
Dep. Ratio	−1.822	−4.81
Dep. Ratio 1996	−0.394	−2.01
Dep. Ratio 2001	−0.464	−2.28
Leverage	−0.200	−9.51
Size	0.000	−0.02
SG& A	0.001	6.78
Capital Intensity	0.014	3.00
Asset Turnover	0.020	4.27
Industry	×	
Country	×	
Year	×	
R-Square	0.1311	
Adj R-Square	0.1289	

Note: The dependent variable is log [(market value of equity plus
debt) divided by total assets]. The dependency ratio is the ratio of
individuals 55 and over to those 20–54.
Source: Watson Wyatt Worldwide.

effect is even stronger for 1996 and 2001. For 1996, a 0.1 higher dependency ratio resulted in a 22 percent lower Tobin's Q, while a similar change
in the dependency ratio in 2001 was associated with a 23 percent lower
Tobin's Q.

Utilizing Existing Human Capital More Efficiently

The aging of populations in the developed world is going to create two
phenomena that will increase the need to utilize workers more effectively
in the future. One of these relates to the prevalence of retirement systems
financed on a pay-go basis. This problem will exist even in countries like
the United States, where the labor force is expected to continue growing.
The other problem relates to the prospect of shrinking labor forces.

In many countries, aged dependency is financed through government
taxing mechanisms imposed on employers and employees. In a free-
market environment, where workers' compensation is equal to their
marginal contribution to the firm, the government's imposition of a payroll tax might simply result in a reduction elsewhere in the compensation

package. But many governments do not allow employers to adjust compensation packages so freely, especially for workers at lower earnings levels. If workers are guaranteed a minimum wage, increasing the payroll tax to support a growing aged population will increase the fixed costs associated with offering low-wage workers a job. If the minimum wage paid to a worker plus the fixed costs associated with offering the job exceed the marginal contribution that worker can provide the employer, the market basis for offering the worker a job disappears. This means that growing aging dependency will potentially create the anomalous situation of marginalizing less productive workers at exactly the same time that labor markets are tightening. The way to offset this phenomenon is to enhance the productivity of these workers.

The shrinking labor supply will arise because of the dynamics of the labor markets, which will evolve outside of the control of individual employers. The labor supply contractions in some of the developed economies will not necessarily be matched by an immediate drop in the demand for workers. If demand does not fall, or does not fall as fast as the supply of labor, these economies may experience significant wage pressures as employers scramble to find the workers they need to keep their operations going. In this case, the variable costs associated with hiring workers will increase. As with the fixed costs of hiring workers, if the variable wage paid to a worker exceeds his or her marginal contribution to the employer, the market basis for the employer offering the worker a job disappears. Those employers who can figure out how to enhance workers' productivity to cover the higher cost of hiring workers in this environment will thrive and those that do not will risk failure.

In the discussion above about the production model used by economists to analyze the operations of national economies, we talked about the factors of production. The overall productivity of a national economy is the cumulative productivity of the enterprises that produce the goods and services in it. In fact, economists have adapted exactly the same production models used to understand the workings of national economies to explain the workings of firms and industries. The same factors of production – capital, labor, and innovation – are as important in understanding the production and productivity within firm and industry analyses as in national analyses.

Separate from the economic literature on productivity, another body of literature has evolved that analyzes organizational effectiveness from the perspective of sociological or behavioral/psychological models. In this context, human resource management is viewed in relation to measures of internal and external environmental factors, such as technology, organizational structure, stage of life cycle, business strategies, and organizational structures. A variety of these models are summarized in S.E. Jackson and R.S. Schuler's review of the literature in this area.[8]

Thomas Stewart, a business writer in the United States, has conceptually combined these two approaches to analyze the operations of an organization under the umbrella of what he calls "intellectual capital."[9] An organization's intellectual capital is comprised of the capital and labor components from the traditional economic model. It also comprises what he calls "customer capital." Customer capital is the value of customer satisfaction, which leads to repeat customers and eliminates the need for direct marketing to land a new customer. It is reflected in the probability of customers continuing to do business with an organization. In Stewart's model of total organizational effectiveness, "intellectual capital" is achieved through the linkage of the various forms of capital the enterprise possesses.

The linkage between the various capital elements in a firm is accomplished through what Stewart calls "structural capital." Structural capital is the set of programs, processes, and practices that enable an organization to leverage its human capital so as to maximize its effectiveness. Employers create structural capital to allow the effective utilization of financial and customer capital assets in combination with human capital. But the structural capital can work as an accelerator on human capital resources, accentuating the organization's ability to create value. The task that employers face is figuring out how to develop and use their structural capital to get the most out of their human capital. Some organizations are clearly better at doing this than others.

As we think about these separate models and what they are attempting to measure, the traditional economic model focuses on the marginal contribution that human and financial capital make to organizational productivity. Beyond attempts to measure the quality of labor, however, the economic model does not explain the other elements of multi-factor productivity, which seem to be very important in understanding variations in productivity from one country or organization to the next. The various approaches summarized by Jackson and Schuler focus on the "structural capital" that Stewart describes organizations using in leveraging human

---

[8] R.S. Schuler and S.E. Jackson, "Linking Competitive Strategies with Human Resource Management Practices," *Academy of Management Executive* (1987), vol. 1, pp. 207–219.

[9] Thomas A. Stewart, *Intellectual Capital* (New York: Doubleday, 1997).

capital for value creation purposes. The first approach is appealing because it allows quantification of the marginal value that human capital contributes to organizational outcomes. It is insufficient for our needs, though, because it does not explain the reasons for the variations in human capital contributions across organizations or countries.

R.S. Schuler and S.E. Jackson have developed a research taxonomy sorting human resource management practices into five basic areas to assess their impact on achieving fundamental business goals. These include planning, staffing, appraising, compensating, and training and development. Each area relates to the acquisition, development, or reward of human capital within an organization. There is a substantial body of research that has analyzed the effectiveness of the model that Schuler and Jackson describe and found that the five elements enhance the productivity of workers to varying degrees.

Luss and Kay have built on earlier research into how human resource management practices affect firm performance in developing the Watson Wyatt *Human Capital Index*^{TM}.[10] Their premise is that managers choose their product, service, financing, and human capital strategies to try to achieve superior firm performance. In the human capital area, Luss and Kay identified specific actions and behaviors that can measurably increase employee satisfaction and productivity and decrease employee turnover. These improvements, in turn, result in higher customer loyalty and satisfaction, creating surplus value within organizations.

Effective human capital management is the key to earning outstanding shareholder returns. Human capital management is a combination of four human resource functions. Recruiting excellence enables the firm to acquire employees who either already possess the general human capital necessary to do their jobs or can be trained in these skills. The next step is to establish a collegial and flexible workplace, so employees work well together. Within this workplace, the firm must promote communications integrity. This involves trusting employees enough to share information with them and encouraging them to communicate outside of hierarchical boundaries. Effective communication is crucial for leveraging human capital into outstanding customer service. Finally, there must be an effective performance management system with clear rewards and accountability, establishing a direct relationship between performance and rewards.

---

[10] Richard Luss and Ira Kay. Creating Superior Returns to Shareholders Through Effective Human Capital Management: The Watson Wyatt Human Capital Index^{TM}. Washington, D.C.: Watson Wyatt Worldwide, 1999.

Luss and Kay's research suggests that human capital management can measurably increase a firm's value. This can only reflect higher levels of productivity within a firm relative to the inputs being used. The research demonstrated that human capital management is related to firm performance, and that their Human Capital Index captures this relation in a single, simple measure. Luss and Kay examined the theory that effective human capital management can increase employee satisfaction, leading to higher customer loyalty and better firm performance. They showed how human capital drivers and specific firm activities are correlated with higher employee satisfaction. They also demonstrated that higher employee satisfaction leads to higher customer loyalty. Finally, they documented the positive relation between high customer loyalty and firm performance.

In the development of a *Human Capital Index* for Europe based on a survey of publicly traded firms there, Luss found lower levels of turnover in Europe than in the United States. This analysis concluded that European companies may provide excessive job security, which can lead to complacency and unmotivated workers. The European study found that providing excessive job security was associated with reduced surplus value levels among the participating firms. The employers with the lowest turnover tended to rely more on tenure-based benefits and recognition programs, and they had more rigid career paths than firms with higher turnover. Firms with low turnover also were more likely to tolerate poor performance and to lack performance-based reward programs.[11]

The results from Watson Wyatt's research in the United States and Europe evaluating the effects of human resource practices on productivity correspond with the recent cross-national economic analysis on productivity growth developed by Gust and Marquez.[12] In the former case, the analysis focused on reported turnover rates at the firm level and found that too little turnover was associated with lower levels of productivity. In the latter case, the analysis focused on regulatory practices at the national level and found that stricter national employment protection regulations impede the adoption of information technologies and productivity growth.

---

[11] Watson Wyatt, "The Human Capital Index®: European Survey Report 2000," Watson Wyatt Worldwide, Washington, D.C., (2000).

[12] Christopher Gust and Jaime Marquez, "International Comparisons of Productivity Growth: The Role of Information Technology and Regulatory Practices," International Finance Discussion Papers, number 727 (Washington, D.C.: Board of Governors of the Federal Reserve System, May 2002).

Thus far, there have been limited attempts to link the human capital and organizational behavior analytical approaches to evaluating human resources within the context of organizational effectiveness. For example, Hansen and Werenfelt separately tested economic and organizational models and then developed an integrated model combining elements of both. They concluded that both models are important and independent, and developed an integrated model that has greater explanatory power than the separate models.[13] Their conclusion about the independence of the two models is important, suggesting that variations in value creation across firms can be more fully explained by looking at an integrated model than by focusing on only one or the other approach. Another interpretation is that not only is the quality of an organization's human capital important to success, but also how that human capital is organized and marshaled for the task at hand.

The implications of these alternative research findings are important for countries that are potentially facing labor shortages in coming years. The findings from the research into national productivity levels clearly indicate that factors other than capital stock and labor supply can increase the GDP in a country over time. Some of the factors identified in this research suggest that public policymakers can adjust the national regulatory environment in a way that makes a country's labor force more productive. And findings from the organizational behavior research clearly indicate that individual employers can adopt specific practices in the management of their human resources that also enhance productivity.

[13] G. S. Hansen and B. Werenfelt. "Determinants of Firm Performance: The Relative Importance of Economic and Organizational Factors," *Strategic Management Journal*, vol. 10 (1989), pp. 399–411.

TEN

Aligning Retirement Policy with Labor Needs

As populations age in the industrialized societies, national governments will face significant challenges in financing their public retirement schemes. Many of the financial pressures will arise from the inherent design of their pay-go pension systems. In Chapter 4, we showed that the financial condition of pay-go pension programs directly relates to the evolution of the old-age dependency ratio and the program's income replacement rate. In the developed nations today, these programs are largely financed through payroll taxes and pay a defined benefit. The demographic transition occurring in nearly all industrialized societies today will significantly inflate the percent of GDP and the tax revenues these programs consume.

On the health care side, the situation is very similar. In many societies, health care costs are rising considerably faster than GDP, and in some cases, will surpass rising public pension costs. Many health programs are also largely financed through payroll taxes and/or other general revenues of the government. However they are financed, the economic reality is that the productivity of current workers must support a rising tide of old age dependents.

In this chapter, we investigate how the structure of public and private pensions, medical and other non-employment programs has affected the industrialized economies. Many of these programs contain imbedded incentives that profoundly affect labor supply and its productivity, the accumulation of capital, and the balance of government budgets. The risks associated with these programs depend on how they are financed. In some cases, however, the actual implications of financing methods are not as clear as they first appear.

The Role of Plan Structure on Retirement and Work Behavior

Public pension programs became popular in the early 1900s, as concern mounted about growing poverty rates among the old due to their declining employability in rapidly industrializing economies. Most policymakers adopted basic means-tested, noncontributory retirement schemes. At that time, these programs were preferred to more broadly based contributory programs, since they were an inexpensive means of eliminating poverty among the elderly. As social insurance schemes became more popular, the contributory plans came to be preferred, mostly because of the disincentives to work and save often embedded in means-tested programs. Although the original intention was usually to establish funded pension programs, most countries moved toward pay-go financing fairly quickly to satisfy policymakers' desire to start paying out benefits without waiting for funding reserves to build.

These early programs provided relatively modest benefits. Table 10-1 provides estimates of gross replacement rates (i.e., before taxes on earned income and benefits) from the late 1930s through the mid-1990s. Estimates for 1939 are based on actual values from Administrative data files,[1] while the years after that are based on synthetic earnings profiles.[2] The latter are earnings profiles that are constructed to reflect actual earnings patterns across typical workers' careers. In 1939, these programs on average replaced roughly 16 percent of retirees' gross earnings – not very generous by today's standards. However, they did serve their original purpose: to provide a bare subsistence and to reduce old age poverty.

By the end of World War II, there was growing interest in enhancing benefits under state pension programs. Noncontributory, means-tested programs were often considered demeaning, since qualifying for these benefits seemed to require an admission of failure. Contributory pensions providing much broader coverage enabled governments to guarantee minimum income support to all older citizens without stigmatizing those who needed it most.

In the aftermath of World War II, many countries were facing crushing financial debts and, in some cases, outright economic chaos. Indeed, the history of funded pensions has often been rocky, because of the turmoil in financial markets during the two world wars and the depression between

---

[1] Gosta Esping-Andersen, *The Three Worlds of Welfare Capitalism* (Cambridge, MA: Polity, 1990).

[2] Sveinbjorn Blondal and Stefano Scarpetta, "The Retirement Decision in OECD Countries," (Paris: OECD, Economics Department Working Papers, 1999), No. 202.

Table 10-1. *Gross Replacement of Earnings Prior to Retirement for Various Years under Old Age Pension Programs*

	Gross Replacement Rates under Pension Program			
	1939	1961	1975	1995
Australia	0.19	0.12	0.20	0.24
Austria		0.80	0.80	0.80
Belgium	0.14	0.60	0.60	0.60
Canada	0.17	0.17	0.38	0.39
Denmark	0.22	0.23	0.27	0.36
Finland		0.24	0.56	0.60
France		0.40	0.50	0.65
Germany	0.19	0.60	0.55	0.54
Ireland		0.23	0.17	0.24
Italy	0.15	0.37	0.62	0.80
Japan		0.22	0.48	0.44
Netherlands	0.13	0.20	0.31	0.30
New Zealand		0.18	0.26	0.39
Norway	0.08	0.16	0.52	0.51
Portugal		0.80	0.70	0.80
Spain			0.50	1.00
Sweden	0.10	0.44	0.67	0.66
Switzerland		0.19	0.37	0.35
United Kingdom	0.13	0.20	0.21	0.39
United States	0.21	0.28	0.35	0.42
Unweighted Average	0.16	0.34	0.45	0.52

Notes: Estimates represent gross replacement rates for a single worker making an average salary. See Sveinbjorn Blondal and Stefano Scarpetta, "The Retirement Decision in OECD Countries," (Paris: OECD, Economics Department Working Papers, 1999), No. 202 for further details on the estimates.

Source: Gosta Esping-Andersen, *The Three Worlds of Welfare Capitalism* (Cambridge, MA: Polity, 1990); Sveinbjorn Blondal and Stefano Scarpetta, "The Retirement Decision in OECD Countries," (Paris: OECD, Economics Department Working Papers, 1999), No. 202; Estelle James, et al., *Averting the Old Age Crisis* (Oxford: Oxford University Press, 1994), p. 104.

them. Funding pensions that would not pay out for some time was hardly acceptable policy where countries were facing reconstruction and the elderly had no other means of sustenance. As a result, many countries abandoned their funding mechanisms for pay-go, payroll tax-financed programs. If nothing else, pay-go financing enabled countries to support those who were already retired and could not wait for years of contributions to build up.

At that time, the conditions for pay-go schemes were ideal. Labor forces and wage rates were both growing rapidly – the two critical foundation blocks of a healthy pay-go pension system.[3] Taking advantage of these favorable conditions, legislators created new social insurance schemes or added a second and larger earnings-related tier to the existing means-tested or flat tier in Switzerland (1949), the Netherlands (1957), Sweden (1960), Norway (1966), and Canada (1966). Japan and the United States implemented major expansions of their existing programs.[4] These enhancements started a clear trend toward higher gross replacement rates over the last half century. As shown in Table 10-1, the unweighted average replacement rate has risen from 16 percent in 1939 to over 52 percent in the mid-1990s. A large part of this growth occurred in the early post-war period, when replacement rates more than doubled in a little over 20 years. However, higher replacement rates have not been universal. Between 1961 and 1995, replacement rates remained relatively stable in societies such as Austria, Belgium, Ireland, and Portugal and fell in Germany. Overall, the rising replacement rates indicate a trend in recent decades toward more generous public pension programs that by their very nature will produce massive lifetime transfers between generations.

While enhancing these programs seemed like a good idea at the time, the long-term implications were often overlooked or underestimated. With the rise in life expectancy and the declines in fertility rates, old-age dependency ratios have already begun to rise and will continue to do so for many years to come, creating a fiscal burden that industrialized societies will be hard-pressed to absorb. As these countries age, the commitments of tax revenues necessary to finance these programs will soon either begin to crowd out other programs backed by government funds or trigger rising budget deficits.

The fallout from high pension costs is already being felt in several countries, such as France and Germany, in the form of strong disincentives to economic growth and job creation and possibly declining interest from foreign investors as well. In 2003, both France and Germany had budget deficits above the 3 percent ceiling set by the European Union's "stability and growth pact," with the prospects for debt containment looking bleak. Ultimately, societies that wish to preserve these systems will need

---

[3] Angus Madisson, "Growth and Slowdown in Advanced Capitalist Economies: Techniques of Quantitative Assessment," *Journal of Economic Literature* (1987), 25:649–98.

[4] Estelle James, et al, *Averting the Old Age Crisis* (Oxford: Oxford University Press, 1994).

Table 10-2. *Payroll Tax Rates for Various Years under Old Age Pension Programs*

	Payroll Tax Rates under Pension Program	
	1967	2000
Australia	0.0	0.0
Austria	16.5	22.8
Belgium	12.5	16.4
Canada	5.9	5.4
Denmark	1.0	1.0
Finland	6.5	17.9
France	8.5	19.8
Germany	14.0	18.6
Ireland	5.2	15.7
Italy	15.8	29.6
Japan	5.5	16.5
Netherlands	10.2	14.5
New Zealand	0.0	0.0
Norway	12.8	22.0
Portugal	13.5	13.9
Spain	16.0	28.3
Sweden	6.4	17.2
Switzerland	4.0	8.4
United Kingdom	6.5	13.9
United States	7.1	12.4

Note: Includes both employer and employee contributions.

Source: Social Security Programs Throughout the World, various issues.

to figure out ways to increase capital inflows into them without imposing unreasonable burdens on their workers.

Since many public pension and health care programs are financed through workers' contributions, one way to increase cash inflows is to raise payroll tax rates. In fact, most societies did just that to finance the increasing generosity of these benefits over recent decades. Table 10-2 shows that the unweighted average payroll taxes for public pension programs has risen from 8.4 percent in 1967 to nearly 15 percent in 2000. In a number of countries with very generous programs, such as Spain, Italy, Austria, and Norway, payroll tax rates now exceed 20 percent. Countries like Germany supplement payroll tax rates with contributions from general revenue financing, which may keep the direct payroll tax cost of their systems below 20 percent when, in fact, the costs are considerably higher. When taxes on medical and unemployment benefits are included, several countries have tax burdens of over 40 percent of gross earnings. New Zealand and Australia are financed through general revenues and therefore have no payroll tax rates on their public pension program.

Despite these increasingly high tax rates, many prognosticators predict massive deficits for most of these programs in coming years, indicating that even these higher contributions cannot keep up with the benefits promised. In Chapter 12, we turn to this point in greater detail and estimate how the generosity of these programs would have to change at current payroll tax rates. But first, what is the impact of a high payroll tax burden on labor market efficiency – and ultimately, on economic growth?

Pension programs financed through payroll taxes were originally designed to be contributory programs, with the payroll tax considered an insurance premium rather than a tax. Ideally, a retiree's benefit would be directly linked to his or her contributions. But most retirement systems today provide defined benefits and are financed on a pay-go basis, thus breaking the link between contributions and benefits. This partly reflects the inherent design of the pension formula. For instance, many countries have purposely designed progressive-based systems as a way to redistribute pension wealth to lower-income groups. In systems that are predominantly funded by payroll taxes, higher-earning workers often receive benefits that are much less than the economic value of their accumulated lifetime contributions.

The implications of this plan structure were masked during the early decades, because the first few generations of beneficiaries all received benefits well in excess of the economic value of their cohorts' contributions.[5] In the future, however, these windfalls cannot persist. Rates of return on contributions are limited to the sum of the rates of growth in the labor force and labor productivity. If labor forces start to shrink, as they will in several countries, labor productivity improvement rates will be too low to provide significant returns on contributions. Income redistribution in combination with negative returns on pension contributions would turn workers' contributions from insurance premiums into taxes. Regardless of how we label the financing, the reality is that the economic deal offered

---

[5] The situation in the United States is documented in Sylvester J. Schieber and John B. Shoven, *The Real Deal: The History and Future of Social Security* (New Haven, CT: Yale University Press, 1999).

by these programs has been changing since their inception. And now, as societies come to grips with rising burdens caused by demographic aging, additional changes have been made or are being phased in that further alter the payouts workers can expect to receive.

When individuals contribute more to a benefit plan than they will receive, this can create distortions in the labor markets. With contributions into social insurance programs now widely viewed as a tax on earnings, governments risk the same unintended consequences as they do from any other tax; namely, that high rates are a drag on economic activity, altering behavior in various ways. Some people might work less, some might choose to work in the informal rather than the formal sector of the economy, and some might even attempt tax evasion. Such maneuvers defeat the purpose of having retirement programs in the first place: to ensure that workers build up savings over their working years so they have a steady income when they retire.

To the extent people choose to work in the informal sector in order to avoid high tax rates, they are likely to have less capital to work with and less on-the-job training, both of which will dampen productivity and thus national output. Having fewer workers formally employed also means less tax revenues for the government. But those individuals will likely still qualify for other government programs or for some portion of the pension program itself, despite contributing very little. This is likely to be a more serious problem in less developed nations, which generally have lax tax enforcement, but even in developed societies, the adverse effects on government budgets and ultimately on economic performance can be quite profound.[6] It may become a more serious problem in the developed countries that increasingly depend on immigrants to stock their labor forces, because immigrants may not have the same traditions and shared experiences that encourage tax compliance.

But the adverse effects of high payroll tax burdens on labor markets are not limited to workers. In many OECD nations, payroll taxes for public pension programs are shared between both employers and employees. So, who bears the costs of these programs becomes important. If a country has high minimum wage rates or other labor market rigidities – like those in a number of the world's developed economies – employers may end up bearing a significant share of the tax burden.

Employers may react to these higher costs in a number of ways. One might be by substituting capital for workers, which creates its own set of economic problems. For example, in a number of EU countries with

---

[6] Estelle James, et al, *Averting the Old Age Crisis* (Oxford: Oxford University Press, 1994).

expensive social programs, the persistently high rates of unemployment largely result from the high fixed costs of hiring workers. But as we discussed in Chapter 7, there are limits to capital deepening. Another possibility is that higher employer taxes on labor may depress real wage growth, thus passing the rising costs of social insurance programs onto workers, which has occurred in several developed economies over the last few decades. Yet another option is for employers to pass along mounting social insurance costs in the form of higher prices. But given the competitiveness of markets and increasing global competition, raising prices may be self-defeating, eventually driving down sales. Finally, some employers will simply choose to move their capital elsewhere, with lower labor costs and higher capital returns. We return to the last point in greater detail in Chapter 11.

Many societies also fund their health care programs on a pay-go basis. As we explored in Chapter 6, the price tag of health care programs has been exploding in a number of countries, because of increasing utilization and escalating health care costs. As populations age, the developed countries are likely to face even steeper costs for health care than for pensions.[7] There will be difficult choices ahead for legislators, who must attempt to finance these programs without creating major impediments to economic prosperity.

Factors Affecting Early Labor Force Withdrawals

High payroll taxes to finance public pension and health care programs have likely already levied substantial efficiency losses on labor markets in the industrialized societies. One of the most striking socioeconomic effects supporting this conclusion is the early withdrawal of older workers from the labor market. During the 1950s and 1960s, it was customary for workers – in particular males – to work well into their 60s. Today, however, this is more the exception than the rule. Table 10-3 shows labor force participation rates for men and women ages 55 to 64 over the last four decades. In nearly every OECD nation, activity rates for older male workers have been on the decline. In France, Austria, and Italy, participation rates have fallen over 40 percent between 1970 and 2000. While in the United Kingdom and Ireland, activity rates for older men were over 90 percent in the 1970s, they had plummeted to nearly 60 percent by 2000.

---

[7] See Thai Than Dang, Pablo Antolin, and Howard Oxley, "Fiscal Implications of Ageing: Projections of Age-Related Spending," (OECD, Economics Department Working Papers, 2001), No. 305.

Table 10-3. *Labor Force Participation Rates for Males and Females Ages 55 to 64 for Various Years*

	Males			Females		
	1970	2000	Change	1970	2000	Change
Australia	82.7	61.5	−21.2	22.8	36.3	13.5
Austria	64.2	42.4	−21.8	24.4	17.6	−6.8
Belgium	73.4	37.7	−35.7	13.8	17.3	3.5
Canada	76.3	61.0	−15.3	32.2	41.6	9.4
Denmark	86.5	64.3	−22.2	33.8	48.5	14.7
Finland	71.2	47.3	−23.9	39.6	44.6	5.0
France	75.6	41.4	−34.2	40.1	32.8	−7.3
Germany	80.1	52.5	−27.6	28.4	33.4	5.0
Hungary	79.9	34.2	−45.7	29.6	13.3	−16.3
Iceland	95.1	94.4	−0.7	34.8	76.3	41.5
Ireland	91.0	64.8	−26.2	21.3	27.9	6.6
Italy	67.9	42.6	−25.3	16.3	16.0	−0.3
Japan	90.3	84.2	−6.1	49.0	49.6	0.6
Korea	78.0	71.1	−6.9	33.6	48.6	15.0
Luxembourg	63.0	35.4	−27.6	15.3	18.3	3.0
Mexico	88.5	81.3	−7.2	14.6	28.8	14.2
Netherlands	80.5	51.3	−29.2	14.9	26.2	11.3
New Zealand	81.5	71.3	−10.2	21.9	47.5	25.6
Norway	83.7	74.5	−9.2	28.4	61.5	33.1
Poland	87.0	40.4	−46.6	59.8	23.7	−36.1
Portugal	83.6	45.0	−38.6	14.6	28.9	14.3
Spain	84.4	60.4	−24.0	22.1	22.6	0.5
Sweden	85.4	72.7	−12.7	44.5	66.0	21.5
Switzerland	91.3	79.3	−12.0	34.7	51.3	16.6
Turkey	85.8	51.5	−34.3	48.9	20.2	−28.7
United Kingdom	91.0	63.4	−27.6	39.5	42.6	3.1
United States	82.9	67.4	−15.5	43.0	51.9	8.9

Source: International Labor Office, Bureau of Statistics, LABORSTA database on labor statistics; OECD Labour Force Statistics.

The decline in male activity rates has been ameliorated somewhat by the trend toward higher female labor force participation. Labor force participation rates for older females have risen in Australia, Canada, Sweden, and the United States. However, activity rates for females at advanced ages have remained relatively flat in Spain, Italy, and the United Kingdom. In fact, in France, older female labor force participation rates have declined nearly 8 percentage points over this period. So far, the trend toward earlier withdrawal from the labor force has not been a burden for many of these societies, largely due to the abundant supply of labor from the baby boom generations. But, as the baby boom generations rapidly approach retirement, the percentage of the population of working age will fall across many of these societies. This will be particularly true where female labor force participation rates have peaked.

There are several reasons why so many older workers have been withdrawing from the labor force early. One explanation is that affluence has enabled higher-income individuals to choose more leisure at older ages. This is especially true for workers who retired during the long introductory phase of these programs and received sizeable windfall transfers. It could also reflect deteriorating labor market conditions due to the huge influx of younger workers as the baby boom generation entered the workforce. Successively younger individuals have acquired more current skills, complementing the technological changes in the OECD nations, which may put older workers at a competitive disadvantage. But the declines in old-age labor force activity rates may also reflect the financial incentives to retire early embedded in public retirement programs. Similar incentives are also offered in occupational pensions and medical schemes and in non-employment based programs, such as unemployment and disability benefits.

A critical component of an individual's decision to retire is when benefits become available or the entitlement age. Individuals are often discouraged from working beyond that age through some form of means testing. In many cases, individuals who keep working while collecting benefits only receive a percentage of their full pension, thus losing benefits. As shown in Table 10-4, the most common retirement age for males is 65, which is the case in over 75 percent of these countries.

Several Nordic countries, such as Denmark, Iceland, and Norway, have set a normal retirement age slightly higher at 67. In a few countries, the standard retirement age for females is younger than for males, but in recent years many countries have eliminated that difference. Several countries have also built an early retirement age into their program, whereby individuals can collect benefits before the normal age of retirement. Benefits are often actuarially reduced to account for the longer pay-out period. However, the amount of the reduction is often not large enough to discourage early retirement – meaning the reduced benefits are more than actuarially fair.[8] Moreover, earnings tests are often stricter for those who access pension benefits before the standard entitlement age, which

---

[8] Sveinbjorn Blondal and Stefano Scarpetta, "The Retirement Decision in OECD Countries" (OECD, Economics Department Working Papers, February 1999), No. 202.

Table 10-4. *Statutory Normal and Early Retirement Ages for Public Pension Programs*

	Statutory Normal Retirement Ages – 2000		Statutory Early Retirement Ages – 2000	
	Males	Females	Males	Females
Australia	65.0	65.0	65.0	62.0
Austria	65.0	61.5	61.5	56.5
Belgium	65.0	60.0	60.0	60.0
Canada	65.0	60.0	60.0	60.0
Denmark	67.0 (2)	50.0	50.0	50.0
Finland	65.0	60.0	60.0	60.0
France	65.0 (1)	60.0	60.0	60.0
Germany	63.0	63.0	63.0	60.0
Greece	65.0	60.0	60.0	60.0
Iceland	67.0	67.0	67.0	67.0
Ireland	65.0	65.0	65.0	65.0
Italy	65.0	65.0	65.0	60.0
Japan	65.0	60.0	60.0	60.0
Luxembourg	65.0	57.0	57.0	57.0
Netherlands	65.0	65.0	65.0	65.0
New Zealand	65.0	65.0	65.0	65.0
Norway	67.0	65.0	65.0	65.0
Portugal	65.0	55.0	55.0	55.0
Spain	65.0	61.0	61.0	61.0
Sweden	67.0	61.0	61.0	61.0
Switzerland	65.0	63.0	63.0	62.0
Turkey	55.0	55.0	55.0	50.0
United Kingdom	65.0	65.0	65.0	60.0
United States	65.0	65.0	62.0	62.0

Notes: (1) Flexible retirement age for both men and women between 60 and 65; (2) It is 65 for those under age 60 on 1 July 1999; it is 67 for everyone else.

Sources: OECD, United Nations, Social Security Administration, and World Bank; Palacios and Pallares-Miralles (2000), and Updates; Watson Wyatt Data Services (2002) Benefits Report.

discourages those who start receiving benefits early from continuing to work. As shown in the last two columns of the table, all individuals, male and female, in the United States, Austria, and Switzerland could collect early retirement benefits in 2000. Italy, Germany, and Australia, however, only allow women to retire early, while early retirement is for men only in France, Finland, and Spain.

In recent years, the growing concern about the effects of population aging and low old-age labor force participation on labor force growth and ultimately on the cost of public retirement programs has prompted a number of countries to increase the normal retirement age. For example, in the United States' public pension program, the normal retirement age will gradually increase from 65 to 67. In fact, as of 2000, over half of the OECD countries had already enacted into law or were scheduled to phase in increases in their statutory normal retirement age.[9] In addition, a number of countries, such as Australia, Belgium, Germany, Portugal, and Switzerland, are somewhere in the process of equalizing the differences in the normal retirement age between men and women. Many countries have also raised the early retirement age limits. In fact, Spain has begun to phase out the early access to pension entitlements altogether.

Another critical component in an individual's decision to retire is whether the benefits available will provide enough income. Table 10-5 provides alternative estimates of the generosity of public pension programs by estimating an individual's pension wealth as a multiple of the average economy-wide earnings for various income groups. Pension wealth estimates represent the cumulative value of the benefits for people who retire at the statutory normal retirement age and live out the average life expectancy. As a result, this estimate combines a number of parameters, including replacement rates, statutory retirement ages, and the average life expectancy, into a single indicator of the richness of the public pension programs in the OECD nations.

Average pension wealth varies quite extensively across the developed societies, reflecting fundamental philosophical differences in pension regimes. Some countries assume more responsibility for providing for the income security of their retiree populations than others. For example, as shown in Table 10-5, the pension schemes in Italy, France, and the Netherlands provide twice the pension wealth to a worker with average earnings at normal retirement age than those in the United States. The countries with the most generous schemes provide all workers with a high proportion of their preretirement earnings. Since the public pension benefits are likely to be a rather sizeable proportion of an individual's total retirement wealth, these national retirement programs are likely to be the primary determinant for many workers' early withdrawal decisions. As a result, public policy changes to peel away the disincentives to work at older ages could be highly effective in increasing retirement ages across these societies.

---

[9] OECD, "OECD Statistical and Analytical Information on Ageing," NBER-Kiel Conference, Coping with the Pension Crisis – Where Does Europe Stand?, Berlin, March 20–21, 2000.

Table 10-5. *Gross Pension Wealth as a Multiple of Economy-Wide Average Earnings for Various Individual Income Groups*

	Gross Pension Wealth as a Multiple of Average Earnings							
	0.3	0.5	0.75	1.0	1.5	2.0	2.5	3.0
Australia	5.2	5.8	6.6	7.3	8.8	11.6	14.5	17.4
Austria	5.0	5.1	7.7	10.3	15.4	20.6	25.7	30.9
Belgium	4.9	4.7	7.0	9.3	11.7	11.7	11.7	11.7
Canada	6.3	6.6	7.0	7.4	7.4	7.4	7.4	7.4
Czech Republic	3.7	5.0	5.6	6.3	6.7	7.2	7.6	8.0
Finland	3.9	4.7	5.8	7.7	11.5	15.4	19.2	23.1
France	5.9	6.9	9.4	12.5	16.8	18.4	20.0	21.6
Germany	2.8	4.9	5.7	7.6	11.3	12.3	12.3	12.3
Hungary	3.8	6.9	10.1	13.2	19.5	25.8	28.2	28.2
Iceland	6.1	6.8	7.7	8.7	11.5	15.3	19.1	22.9
Ireland	4.2	4.2	4.2	4.2	4.2	4.2	4.2	4.2
Italy	3.8	5.8	8.6	11.5	17.3	23.0	28.8	34.6
Japan	4.3	5.3	6.4	7.6	10.0	12.4	12.9	12.9
Korea	7.4	8.6	10.2	11.7	14.8	17.9	21.0	24.1
Luxembourg	7.1	6.6	8.0	10.6	15.9	21.3	26.6	29.3
Mexico	4.9	4.9	4.9	4.9	4.9	4.9	4.9	4.9
Netherlands	5.1	5.2	7.8	10.4	15.6	20.8	26.0	31.2
New Zealand	6.1	6.1	6.1	6.1	6.1	6.1	6.1	6.1
Norway	3.9	3.9	5.0	6.2	8.3	9.1	9.4	9.4
Poland	3.2	4.5	6.7	9.0	13.5	17.9	22.4	22.8
Slovak Republic	2.5	4.1	6.1	8.1	8.1	8.1	8.1	8.1
Spain	4.5	5.8	8.7	11.7	17.5	22.2	22.2	22.2
Sweden	4.9	6.0	7.7	9.8	14.2	18.3	22.4	26.4
Switzerland	3.6	4.4	6.2	7.9	9.0	9.0	9.0	9.0
United Kingdom	4.1	4.1	4.2	4.6	5.7	6.0	6.0	6.0
United States	2.7	3.5	4.5	5.4	7.0	8.0	8.9	9.1

Notes: Includes indexation effects of different components plus pension age effects.
Source: Undisclosed estimates based on Whitehouse (2002).

On the other end of the spectrum, countries like the United States, Canada, Switzerland, and the United Kingdom have less generous public pension schemes. In these countries, the public pension wealth accumulation of high-income individuals is much smaller than those cited above. The focus of the less generous countries is on redistribution, ensuring that all pension income meets a reasonable minimum income level. As a result, workers at higher earnings levels need to supplement their consumption in retirement with other sources of income and savings. Voluntary private pension schemes play a critical insurance role for high-income workers in these societies and thus also affect workers' behavior.

The decision to retire also appears to be sensitive to how pension wealth builds with each additional year of work. In a contributory pension scheme, an individual must contribute some portion of his or her pay in return for future benefits. The tradeoff between working an extra year or not depends on whether the additional contributions paid into the program will be offset by higher benefits paid out in retirement. Blondal and Scarpetta have estimated implicit tax rates that are embedded in old-age pension systems; i.e., the financial losses from working longer.[10] Table 10-6 shows estimates of implicit tax rates for individuals delaying retirement from 55 to 64 and from 55 to 69 for 1967 and 1995, respectively. The estimates are based on a single 55-year-old worker who has worked for 35 years, paying into the system over the entire period or as long as the system existed or was mandatory.

As shown in the table, the loss in pension wealth from postponing retirement can be considerable. This is especially true for societies with very expansive welfare states and thus very high payroll tax rates. In Austria, a worker delaying retirement from age 55 to 64 in 1995 lost 3.4 times average annual earnings. This is equivalent to an average implicit tax rate of 34 percent, over and above other taxes and work-related expenses. A worker who delays retirement until age 69 incurs an even steeper penalty. This is largely the result of the sizeable drop in pension wealth that occurs at the age at which pensions could be accessed. Since many countries have a normal retirement age of 65, this implies that the extra year or more of contributions was not offset by the actuarial increases in pension benefits at retirement.

Since 1967, the losses in pension wealth from delaying retirement have become significantly more extreme. In 1967, the losses in pension wealth from working after age 55 were close to zero in many countries. This again shows a marked movement by old-age pension programs in the industrialized nations toward discouraging work at older ages. In fact, many of the societies with the largest implicit tax rates, such as Austria and Italy, have seen sizable drops in labor force participation over the last few decades.

Effects of Occupational Programs on Labor Markets

Although public retirement programs have played a considerable part in the trend toward early retirement across the industrialized societies, other

---

[10] Sveinbjorn Blondal and Stefano Scarpetta, "The Retirement Decision in OECD Countries" (OECD, Economics Department Working Papers, February 1999), No. 202.

Table 10-6. *Implicit Tax Rates from Postponing Retirement due to Old Age Pension Programs*

	Postponing Retirement from 55–64		Postponing Retirement from 55–69	
	1967	1995	1967	1995
Australia	0.0	0.0	−0.8	−0.9
Austria	−3.1	−3.4	−6.5	−7.0
Belgium	0.2	−2.3	−2.3	−5.0
Canada	1.5	−0.6	−0.1	−1.6
Denmark	0.0	0.0	−0.6	−0.8
Finland	0.0	−2.2	−1.3	−4.9
France	−0.2	−1.4	−1.2	−3.7
Germany	−0.4	−1.4	−2.9	−3.4
Ireland	−0.5	−1.4	−0.6	−2.6
Italy	−3.0	−7.9	−4.5	−11.8
Japan	−1.0	−2.8	−2.1	−3.9
Netherlands	−0.9	−1.3	−2.3	−2.9
New Zealand	0.0	−0.9	−0.5	−2.3
Norway	−0.3	−1.5	−0.3	−3.3
Portugal	−0.5	−0.4	−3.8	−3.7
Spain	–	−1.4	–	−5.9
Sweden	0.9	−1.8	0.0	−3.3
Switzerland	0.2	0.0	−0.7	−1.5
United Kingdom	−0.6	−0.5	−1.4	−1.5
United States	−0.8	−1.2	−1.9	−2.5

Notes: Shows changes in pension wealth measured as a multiple of annual earnings. For example, postponing retirement from age 55 to 64 in the U.S. in 1967 implied that pension wealth decreased by an equivalent of 0.8 times average annual earnings. This is equivalent to an average implicit tax rate of 8 percent, since annual earnings are assumed to be constant and normalized at unity.
Source: Blondal and Scarpetta (1999).

factors affect retirement behavior as well. Secondary employer-based (occupational) programs have had very similar effects. Occupational pension programs vary extensively across the industrialized nations in terms of coverage, type, design, and generosity. As reported by the World Bank in 1994, roughly one in every four old persons and more than one-third of the working population in OECD countries are covered by employer-based pension plans. Employers voluntarily offer occupational programs in the United States, the United Kingdom, and Canada. However, a recent trend has been towards compulsory pension programs to alleviate the burden on the public tier. Employer coverage and employee participation is mandatory in Switzerland, France, and Australia.

These plans are either a defined benefit or a defined contribution scheme. Defined benefit plans generally provide an annuity determined by a specified formula based on years of service and/or the worker's salary, similar to the public retirement programs. In occupational defined benefit plans, however, there is often a qualifying period of employment or vesting period before the worker has a right to the benefits. Individuals can lose their pension rights if they quit or are dismissed before vesting. As a tradeoff, employers bear the investment risk under funded pension programs and bear the longevity risk in annuity-based programs. While private-sector pension programs are generally funded systems in the industrialized nations, several countries, such as France and Germany, maintain pay-go systems. With populations aging so rapidly in these countries, the risk of employer default could become quite significant.

Defined contribution plans, on the other hand, are always fully funded, generally by a combination of employer and employee contributions. As a result, there are fewer vesting restrictions in defined contribution plans, especially with employee contributions. Employees can take their pension with them when they retire or decide to leave the firm, which is often not the case in defined benefit schemes. Many defined contribution plans allow employees to decide how to invest the funds, thus shifting the investment risk to employees. The employees are responsible for accumulating enough capital to ensure their own retirement security.

Occupational pension plans, in particular, defined benefit schemes, affect the efficiency of a country's labor markets similarly to public retirement programs. However, it is important to note that occupational plans are generally voluntary. As such, these programs are set up and designed with very specific intentions, such as to attract and retain top-performing employees and to encourage them to retire on a timely basis.

Since occupational plans may impose vesting requirements and limit the portability of the benefits, they often attract a more stable group of employees, thus creating disincentives for labor mobility. This is likely to be favorable from an employer's standpoint, allowing employers to recoup training costs and increase workforce productivity. Labor mobility is often further discouraged for mid-career workers, because private pension formulas are often based on a worker's last few years of earnings. As a result, pension benefits grow more substantially towards the end of an individual's career – a process known as "backloading."

Although workforce stability is generally considered desirable, it can create inefficiencies if it prevents a healthy rate of employee turnover. This is especially important when markets and industries are rapidly changing, since higher rates of labor immobility could impede the ability of markets to react appropriately to the new environment. If employers are forced to undergo major restructurings to obtain the necessary skill sets, this can be a very costly proposition.

Employer-based plans have also contributed to declines in labor force participation among older workers by creating significant incentives for early retirement. Similar to public retirement plans, employees generally do not acquire any additional increases in pension wealth past the normal retirement age, which is generally around age 60 or 65. Some employer-based plans also have generous early retirement subsidies built into their pension formula. Historically, many employers have used these subsidies as a means of replacing older, supposedly less productive workers with cheaper and younger employees. Additionally, employers may also use temporary early retirement schemes – sometimes referred to as early retirement windows – to substitute for layoffs.

To show the implications of employer-sponsored plan designs, we turn briefly to the United States, where most employer-sponsored defined benefit plans base their benefits on the worker's earnings in the years just before retirement. For workers who terminate employment before becoming eligible to retire, the retirement benefit typically will not be payable until the worker reaches the plan's normal retirement age, which is usually age 65. The benefit is generally determined on the basis of the highest three or five years of pay in the period just before terminating the job. So typically, someone leaving a job at age 40 will not receive a pension for another 25 years, and the benefit will be based on average earnings rates 25 to 30 years earlier.

In the United States, most large employers set up pensions during or shortly after World War II, and most of them set the normal retirement age at 65. During the late 1960s and the 1970s, most large pension plan sponsors introduced early retirement incentives into their plans, to encourage workers to retire before reaching normal retirement age. The early retirement incentives in U.S. employer-sponsored pensions were introduced when the baby boom generation was flooding into the workforce, creating surplus labor. The younger people had a number of highly desirable characteristics. Their average education levels were considerably higher and they were willing to accept much lower wages than older workers.

These various developments led to a benefit structure along the lines depicted in Figure 10-1. The left panel shows the accumulation of a benefit from a plan as originally established. In this case, we assume that the

Accrued benefit as a multiple of annual pay

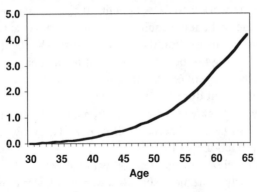

Accrued benefit as a multiple of annual pay

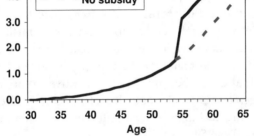

Figure 10-1. Relative Role of the Elimination of Early Retirement Subsidies in the Total Reduction in Benefits in the Shift to a Hybrid Pension in Scenario 2. *Source:* Authors' computation from data provided by Watson Wyatt Worldwide.

worker begins to work at age 30 for an employer that sponsors a typical U.S. plan. By age 50, the worker has earned a benefit that has a value equivalent to one year's pay. If the worker terminates employment at age 50, he or she will not receive this benefit until age 65, when the benefit will be worth the equivalent of the worker's nominal pay at age 50. By age 57, the value of the benefit is up to two year's pay, and by age 61, it reaches three year's pay. Finally at age 65, the present value of the benefit at retirement would be worth about 4.2 times annual pay.

The introduction of the early retirement incentives to this plan is reflected in the bottom panel of the figure. At age 54, the value of the worker's benefit is approximately 1.5 years of pay. Upon attaining age 55, the value of the benefit increases dramatically to 3.1 times pay. This was achieved by two changes to the original pension plan. The first change was allowing the worker to draw benefits at age 55. In most plans, qualifying for the age-55 benefit required at least 10 years of service under the plan, and some sponsors required 20 or 25 years. The second change was actuarially adjusting the benefit to account for its being paid before the normal retirement age of 65. A full actuarial reduction to account for the longer benefit payout duration would range from 6 to 8 percent for each year from age 65 back to the actual retirement date. In many cases, the actual reduction was 2 or 3 percent per year, and in some cases, there was no actuarial reduction at all.

The typical increase in the pension value at age 55, the predominant age at which early retirement subsidies were paid, was equivalent to between one and three year's pay. These early retirement subsidies had a tremendous wealth effect, allowing many of the recipients to maintain their preretirement standards of living, despite having stopped working as early as age 55.

In addition to the early retirement subsidy paid to retirees, another element of the U.S. employer pension plan design further encouraged early retirement. As shown in the bottom panel in Figure 10-1, the early retirement subsidy was maintained for those who worked until age 58 or so, but after that age, it began to decline relative to the normal benefit payable at age 65. The declining value of the early retirement subsidy is reflected by the declining vertical difference between the two lines at each age beyond age 59 or so.

The implication of this design feature can best be understood by example. Suppose that a plan provides a subsidy of 1.5 years of service up through age 62, which is gradually eroded away by the time the worker turns 65. This is the equivalent of a tax of 50 percent per year on the worker's salary. Of course, whatever salary the worker earns would also be taxed at the usual rates. If the statutory taxes on the earnings, including payroll taxes, national government taxes, and local jurisdiction taxes, added another 30 percent – a moderate amount compared to most developed countries – the tax rate on earnings is now up to 80 percent. At some juncture, there is no economic motivation to continue working. For a sample of private plans sponsored by U.S. employers, the implied tax rates embedded in these plans at various ages are shown in Table 10-7. In most cases, these tax rates only apply for three or four years, but in some they may last as long as 10 years.

Until 1961, the social security retirement pension in the United States was not available to male workers until they reached age 65. In 1961, early

Table 10-7. *Annual Implicit Tax Rates from Elimination of Early
Retirement Subsidies as a Percentage of Annual Earnings for a
Long-Service Worker in Pensions*

Implicit Tax Rate	Ages 55 to 60	Ages 60 to 62 (Percent of Plans)	Ages 62 to 65
0.0	48.1%	24.7%	3.9%
0.05 to 4.95	29.9	18.2	7.8
5.0 to 9.95	13.0	19.5	18.2
10.0 to 14.95	0.0	9.1	9.1
15.0 to 19.95	7.8	7.8	9.1
20.0 to 24.95	1.3	3.9	9.1
25.0 to 29.95	0.0	5.2	7.8
30.0 to 34.95	0.0	5.2	9.1
35.0 to 39.95	0.0	5.2	13.0
40.0 to 49.95	0.0	1.3	11.7
50.0 to 54.9	0.0	0.0	1.3

Source: Authors' computations from data provided by Watson Wyatt Worldwide.

retirement benefits were offered to 62-year-old men in the interest of reducing unemployment rates. At about the same time, employers began to allow workers to claim their pensions before age 65. At first, the early retirement incentives were offered to workers who had achieved some target years of service – typically 30 years – under a plan. Ultimately, many employers offered early retirement benefits to workers as young as age 55. Employers introduced the incentives to retire and the disincentives to continue working in the early 1960s, but the practices became significantly more widespread toward the end of the 1960s and throughout the 1970s.

Figure 10-2 shows the labor force participation rates of men in two age groups, 55 to 61 and 62 to 64, from the early 1960s through 2002. In the 20 years after 1961, the labor force participation rates of men ages 55 to 61 fell from 90 to 75 percent. Over the same period, for men ages 62 to 64, they fell from 77 to 47 percent. The early retirement incentives in employer-sponsored pensions help to explain this development. Once the baby boom generation was generally absorbed into the labor market by the mid-1980s, the participation rates of the younger group stabilized, hovering around 75 percent up to the present time. Among the 62- to 64-year-olds, participation rates continued to trend downward until the mid-1990s or so. Since then, they have gone back up slightly.

In the United States, about half the workforce is covered by an employer-sponsored pension. A significant portion of those not covered

Percent of men in the labor force

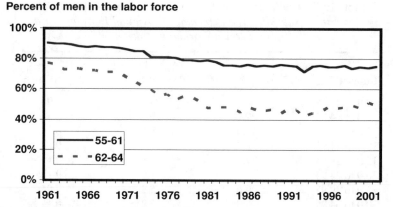

Figure 10-2. Labor Force Participation Rates of Men in the United States Ages 55 to 61 and 62 to 64 for Selected Years. *Source:* Authors' tabulations of the Current Population Survey for various years.

by private plans are in part-time or temporary employment, or are self-employed. But many uncovered workers ultimately will take a job where pension coverage is available, and many others have a spouse covered by a pension plan. As a result, between two-thirds and three-fourths of retirees end up receiving an employer-sponsored pension benefit during retirement.

Canada also has employer-sponsored pension systems that set retirement conditions and incentives that directly affect the state pension system. Canada's statutory normal retirement age under its state pension program is 65 for men and 60 for women. Yet between 1987 and 1990, 29 percent of recent retirees had retired before age 60. By the late 1990s, 43 percent of recent retirees had retired before age 60.[11] Among a sample of 277 larger Canadian private, employer-sponsored pension plans, the median benefit payable at age 60 with 30 years of service was 100 percent of the accrued benefit, and at age 55 with 30 years of service it was 75 percent of the accrued benefit.[12] With relatively full benefits being paid at these ages, it makes sense that many workers take advantage of the opportunity to retire at relatively young ages.

In the United Kingdom, 58.9 percent of males and 56.7 percent of females are currently members of employer pension schemes. Among

[11] Patrick Kieran, "Early Retirement Trends," *Perspectives on Labour and Income* (September 2001), vol. 2, no. 9, p. 5.
[12] Watson Wyatt Worldwide, COMPARISON™ Canada database.

Table 10-8. *Normal Pension Ages for Active Members of Private-Sector Occupational Pension Schemes*

Normal Pension Age	Defined Benefit	Defined Contribution	All Private Sector Schemes
60	30.4%	22.2%	28.6%
Between 61–64	6.5%	0%	5.4%
65	63.0%	77.8%	66.1%
Number of members	4.6 million	0.9 million	5.6 million

Source: Calculations based on "Occupational Pension Schemes 2000 – 11th Survey by the Government Actuary," (London: Office of the Government Actuary), Table 3.12.

all individuals between ages 18 and 59 in the labor force, both in and out of work, some 57.5 percent of males and 48.2 percent of females expect to receive some income from an occupational pension.[13] The statutory retirement age in the United Kingdom's state pension system is 65 for men and 60 for women, the same as Canada's. However, the figures in Table 10-8 show that, in 2002, many occupational plans set normal pension ages below this level. For some 34 percent of those in private-sector occupational plans, and 37 percent of those in defined benefit schemes, the retirement age was younger than 65. Yet, this does not tell the full story. Early retirement is common in the United Kingdom. By 1996, the proportion of men employed at ages 55 to 59 had fallen to less than 70 percent and the proportion employed at ages 60 to 64 fell to around 40 percent. In 2000, just over one-third of 64-year-old men were still in paid employment, approximately one-third reported being retired, and the other third reported having been sick or disabled for an extended period.[14]

Richard Blundell, Costas Meghir, and Sarah Smith examined the influence of incentives within private pension plans on early retirement. They found that employees with a private pension are *more* likely than employees without a private pension to be working in their early 50s. However, by their late 50s, workers with private pensions begin leaving the labor market at a more rapid rate than workers without private pensions. The authors show that the availability of early retirement windows in defined

---

[13] Authors' calculations based upon the British Household Survey (Fall 2001).

[14] See Richard Blundell, Richard Disney, and Carl Emmerson, "Retirement, Pensions and the Adequacy of Saving: A Guide to the Debate," Institute for Fiscal Studies, (October 2002), Briefing Note no. 29.

benefit pension schemes is an important determinant of retirement among plan participants.[15]

The incentives supporting early retirement can be understood more intuitively by examining the terms on which early retirement is available. Among a sample of 361 larger employer pension plans in the United Kingdom, 17.5 percent never allow a worker to retire before the normal pension age, and another 3.9 percent rarely give consent. Some 78.6 percent, however, usually allow early retirement. Of plans that regularly allow early retirement, 15.5 percent offer terms equivalent in value to a deferred pension, and 59.4 percent offer terms equal to the actuarial reserve. Slightly more than one-fourth of plans that usually allow early retirement offer terms that exceed the actuarial reserve.[16] Alternative evidence finds that in 84 percent of plans where the normal retirement age is 65 but the early retirement age is 60, the worker receives 100 percent of the accrued pension. Some 35 percent of private-sector defined benefit schemes in this survey have a normal retirement age of 65 but allow retirement at ages below 60.[17]

In the developed economies where employer-sponsored plans are particularly important, early retirement subsidies were especially popular with some employers throughout the 1970s and well into the 1980s, when many economies had an abundant supply of baby boom workers. Additionally, many employers offered early retirement windows during slack periods in the economy, since the outlook for a plentiful future labor supply appeared favorable. Since it is often difficult for older workers to find employment outside their career jobs, these schemes likely turned into de facto methods for reducing the labor force across the industrialized nations.

Can We Make the Retirement Age More Flexible? The Swiss Debate

By Monica Bütler (HEC)

In 2002, 53 percent of Swiss men and 44 percent of Swiss women retired before the statutory retirement age, although the Swiss first-pillar pension system AVS does not even offer any early retirement options. Most of those who leave the workforce

---

[15] Richard Blundell, Costas Meghir, and Sarah Smith, "Pension Incentives and the Pattern of Early Retirement," *Economic Journal* (March 2002), Vol. 112, No. 478, pp. C153–C170.

[16] Watson Wyatt Worldwide, COMPARISON™ U.K. database, November 2003.

[17] National Association of Pension Funds Annual Survey of Occupational Pension Schemes, 2002.

early benefit from generous packages provided by their occupational pension plan. This route into early retirement, however, suffers from several problems, and may lead to potentially inefficient and inequitable outcomes. Firstly, financial imbalances of many pension providers make it unlikely that these packages will be offered in the future. Secondly, low-income workers do not have access to such plans, as the second pillar is only mandatory for middle and higher-income individuals. As a result, those with the shortest life expectancy work longest, while employees with high levels of human capital can afford to leave the workforce after a relatively short working spell. Indeed, the data show that even for beneficiaries of an occupational pension, richer men (but not women) tend to retire earlier than those with a lower average lifetime income. Not surprisingly, two recent popular initiatives asking for broader access to flexible retirement schemes within the first pillar (along with a general reduction in the retirement age) – though not approved of – enjoyed a large support.

As part of the ongoing reform of the first pillar, the need to accommodate the rising demand for early retirement was undisputed and, therefore, recently discussed by parliament. Due to unfavorable demographic trends and important financial problems of the first pillar, a general reduction in the retirement age did not find a majority – and would hardly be supported at the ballot as recent experience suggests. As part of the proposed reform, however, it will be possible to advance pension benefits by three years, as well as half of the benefits by an additional three years, both at an actuarially fair adjustment rate. It is feared that lower-income individuals might not be able to afford an earlier exit from the labor market, but propositions to reduce the adjustment rate for lower-income groups were abandoned for budgetary reasons. In the end, the combination of early retirement options with several other proposed changes to the first pillar, many of which negatively affect women, led to a somewhat peculiar political compromise in the final version of the reform bill: During a transition period of five years, only women will be granted a reduced adjustment rate if they opt for early retirement. The last word has not been spoken yet. A referendum has been announced, with a high chance to reach the required quorum of signatures. It is then up to the Swiss voters to decide.

The prospect of demographic aging and sizeable labor shortfalls will likely prompt many employers to reconsider their past policies. While worker productivity was once thought to decline at advanced ages due to the years of physical wear and tear on the body, this may no longer hold true as many of the advanced economies have shifted away from vast post-war industrialized sectors toward knowledge-based economies. Employers in many societies have already begun creating new programs such as phased retirement and flexible work schedules to appeal to older workers.

In fact, recent trends throughout the industrialized nations are likely to eliminate some of the incentives for early labor force withdrawals. In most developed societies, there has been a general paradigm shift toward defined contribution programs in lieu of the more traditional defined benefit programs. Since defined benefit plans are designed to encourage people to work until a certain age and then retire, the shift to plans without age-related incentives will likely lead workers to prolong their working careers. By some estimates, workers covered under defined contribution schemes are likely to retire almost two years later than comparable individuals with defined benefit plans.[18]

In the United States, the shift from traditional defined benefit plans to hybrid pension structures – plans that look like defined contribution plans to participants but operate like defined benefit plans for funding purposes – could prolong working careers. Hybrid plans are technically defined benefit plans, but they include various defined contribution features such as portability, lump-sum definition of benefits, and flatter accruals. These plans first started to replace traditional defined benefit plans in the mid-1980s and by the end of 2002, there were 1,200 of them covering 7 million workers. Dan McGill et al. demonstrate that the shift from traditional defined benefit to hybrid pension plans has enabled employers to strip away the early retirement incentives embedded in many of the older programs.[19] While hybrid plans still maintain plan-designated retirement ages, which encourage the timely retirement of older workers, the elimination of the generous subsidies will likely discourage workers from retiring before normal retirement age.

Workforce Incentives Created by Non-Employment Benefits

Older workers often retire before the minimum entitlement age by relying on other types of income support in the interim. In several countries, such as Denmark, Belgium, Luxembourg, and Norway, there are dedicated public schemes for early retirement, which workers can often access through employment or unemployment channels. However, over the last several decades, other countries have transformed long-term unemployment schemes and disability programs into de facto early retirement programs by relaxing the entitlement conditions for older employees. In several OECD countries, nearly one in three males ages 55 to 64 received

---

[18] Leora Friedberg, "Retirement and the Evolution of Pension Structure." (Cambridge, MA: National Bureau of Economic Research, 2003), NBER Working Paper, no. 9999.

[19] Dan M. McGill, Kyle N. Brown, John J. Haley, and Sylvester J. Schieber, *Fundamentals of Private Pensions* (Oxford: Oxford University Press, 2004).

non-employment benefits in 1995, and in Austria, eligibility is over 50 percent.[20]

The generosity of non-employment benefits depends on both the share of earnings they replace and how long individuals are entitled to such benefits. Short-term benefits, no matter how generous, are probably not a significant incentive for early labor force withdrawal. However, if benefits are available for prolonged periods, as is the case in several OECD countries, then even moderate replacement rates create strong incentives for early retirement.

Table 10-9 provides estimates of income replacement rates for disability and unemployment benefits for various years over the last several decades. The estimates assume that an individual starts work at age 20 and works until age 55. Replacement rates are calculated for each year in the 55-to-64 age range and the annual average is derived. The annual replacement rate is entered as zero for all years when benefits are not provided, so countries that do not provide benefits early in the age range have relatively low average replacement rates. It also implies that benefits provided for only a short duration will take on a low value.

Disability programs offer some of the most generous compensation in many of the OECD countries, largely because there are no specific age requirements. The unweighted average income replacement rates have risen from roughly 35 percent of income in 1961 to nearly 48 percent by 1995. Most of the increase took place between 1961 and 1975, with replacement rates remaining fairly flat after that. In a number of societies like Sweden, Germany, Norway, and the United Kingdom, replacement · rates for disability programs have actually declined.

Unemployment benefit programs have become considerably more generous over the last several decades. In fact, the unweighted average replacement rates have more than doubled from nearly 15 to over 33 percent over the indicated periods and have risen at a much steadier pace than disability replacement rates. Many of the Nordic countries have tended to provide quite substantive benefits and thus early retirement incentives through their unemployment benefit programs, while the United States, Japan, and the United Kingdom have far less generous schemes.

Disability programs have long faced the administratively challenging task of providing benefits to those unable to work due to sickness or

---

[20] Sveinbjorn Blondal and Stefano Scarpetta, "Early Retirement in OECD Countries: The Role of Social Security Systems," OECD Economic Studies (Paris: OECD, 1997), No. 29.

Table 10-9. *Synthetic Replacement Rates for Disability and Unemployment Schemes for Various Years*

	Disability Schemes			Unemployment Schemes		
	1961	1975	1995	1961	1975	1995
Australia	0.127	0.219	0.275	0.175	0.219	0.269
Austria	0.537	0.645	0.681	0.287	0.462	0.489
Belgium	0.479	0.507	0.583	0.425	0.446	0.389
Canada	0.139	0.239	0.331	0.154	0.167	0.179
Denmark	0.240	0.327	0.388	0.179	0.350	0.715
Finland	0.219	0.530	0.600	0.016	0.383	0.641
France	0.500	0.500	0.250	0.167	0.439	0.230
Germany	0.482	0.490	0.441	0.412	0.409	0.394
Ireland	0.281	0.254	0.322	0.014	0.165	0.240
Italy	0.222	0.555	0.600	0.137	0.286	0.500
Japan	0.058	0.194	0.251	0.035	0.040	0.030
Netherlands	0.656	0.800	0.700	0.028	0.390	0.525
Norway	0.219	0.605	0.570	0.020	0.038	0.172
New Zealand	0.214	0.287	0.252	0.424	0.284	0.240
Portugal	0.700	0.747	0.717	0.000	0.016	0.616
Spain		0.550	0.715		0.422	0.371
Sweden	0.632	0.771	0.744	0.025	0.140	0.144
Switzerland	0.247	0.462	0.434	0.018	0.020	0.107
United Kingdom	0.308	0.332	0.275	0.219	0.181	0.169
United States	0.313	0.393	0.448	0.021	0.076	0.064
Unweighted Average	0.346	0.470	0.479	0.145	0.247	0.324

Notes: Replacement rates are calculated for each year in the 55-to-64-year age range and the annual average is derived. This implies that schemes that become available relatively later take a low value as the annual replacement rate is zero for all early years. It also implies that benefits provided for only a short duration, such as unemployment benefits in some countries, will take on a low value.

Source: Blondal and Scarpetta (1999).

impairment while preventing those able to work from collecting benefits. The criterion for whether a person is able to work or not can be highly subjective, making disability schemes vulnerable to misuse or errors of judgment. That this has become a problem is evidenced by increasing disability rates across many developed societies despite the vast improvements in medical technology, life expectancies, and general health over the same period.

However, the increasing disability rates are not only the result of program misuse. Many countries have eased the eligibility criteria for disability benefits in recent decades. This is most notable in the countries that enacted explicit labor market criterion for granting disability pensions, mostly in the 1970s.[21] Countries like the Netherlands allowed individuals to move from partial to total disability if it was determined that the person could not find suitable work in the local labor market. Similarly Finland's labor market criteria was based on the claimant's being unable to return to his or her most recent line of work, rather than being unable to find any suitable employment. Many societies such as Sweden also linked program eligibility to individuals' having exhausted unemployment benefits. Even in the United States and the United Kingdom, where benefits depend on rather rigid medical standards, medical criterion appears to have become more lenient without changes to the legal requirements for program eligibility.

Entitlement conditions were also relaxed over a similar time period for unemployment benefits, especially for older workers. In fact, Blondal and Scarpetta report that, in 1995, it was possible to draw unemployment-related benefits from the age of 55 to 64 in over half the OECD nations on the basis of age.[22] A common change was to exempt unemployed workers over a certain age from job-seeking requirements or what is commonly referred to as a work test. As a result, older individuals – generally 55 and older – could collect benefits for a specified period of time under the ordinary unemployment insurance system. In some societies, such as the United Kingdom, Australia, Belgium, and New Zealand, these benefits were relatively open ended in the late 1990s, making it possible to collect benefits for extended periods of time. However, in others, if duration specifications were exhausted, more formalized programs known as unemployment pensions were established for the old age unemployed.[23] This is the case in Finland, with its "pipeline to unemployment pension" scheme for those ages 55 to 59. Under this program, unemployed individuals ages 57 through 60 can qualify for an extended unemployment benefit period. After exhausting these benefits, the individuals become eligible for an unemployment pension from age 60 to the standard retirement age. Denmark has a similar program.

Over recent decades, several countries have also developed specific early retirement programs that are separate from the disability and unemployment programs. A dedicated early retirement plan is one where

[21] Sveinbjorn Blondal and Stefano Scarpetta, "The Retirement Decision in OECD Countries" (OECD, Economics Department Working Papers, February 1999), No. 202.

[22] Ibid., p. 28.

[23] Aino Salomaki, "Remain in or Withdraw from the Labour Market? A Comparative Study on Incentives," European Commission Economic Papers, (October 2003), No. 193.

the worker's decision to retire early is voluntary, where an agreement with the employer is not required, and where there are no labor market restrictions. These programs are not widespread and are being curtailed, but Denmark, Finland, Italy, and Sweden provide early retirement programs that are close to being dedicated. Workers can take advantage of these programs whether they are employed or not at the time they apply. But, these schemes are often based on rather long contribution periods and whether the retiring worker is replaced by a young entrant to the labor force or an unemployed person, although most countries have lifted these latter restrictions in recent years. Generally, the benefits are considerably more generous than unemployment benefits. Italy has one of the most generous early retirement schemes, which is now restricted for certain younger cohorts, allowing eligible beneficiaries to collect benefits for quite a long period – 10 to 12 years – before payouts begin in the old age pension program.

While many of these early retirement schemes served a useful effective purpose during the 1970s and 1980s, as the baby boom generations grow older and become eligible for many of these generous benefits, the costs of these programs will be prohibitive. Many countries have either dissolved the schemes altogether or are peeling away certain underlying eligibility requirements. For example, Italy significantly tightened its dedicated public early retirement scheme in the 1990s and has not authorized any additional recipients since 1998. France has adopted similar provisions, while Norway has actually eased the access to early retirement benefits by lowering the eligibility age. Similarly, countries have also made changes in their other non-employment benefits. Finland will gradually phase out its "pipeline" unemployment benefit between 2009 and 2014. The Netherlands and Sweden have abolished the explicit labor market criterion in granting disability pensions.

Many non-employment benefit schemes have effectively been turned into early retirement programs where older workers can collect supplemental income until they become eligible for a pension. Easing many of the eligibility requirements for these programs over the last few decades has created considerable incentives for older workers to withdraw from the labor force. While every country faces its own set of unique challenges to the demographic puzzle, legislators may want to reexamine these generous non-employment benefit programs and other retirement-related schemes as a cohesive package. Raising the normal retirement age without also modifying access to non-employment benefit schemes would likely be ineffective. Many more people would qualify for disability, unemployment, or early retirement benefits, essentially transferring costs from the standard pension program to these non-employment schemes. Countries able to tighten disability eligibility or to curtail their dedicated early retirement schemes and boost work test requirements for older workers – similar to the pension and non-employment benefit environment in countries like the United States, Japan, Iceland, and Switzerland – could better rein in the burgeoning costs created by demographic aging.

ELEVEN

Funding Pensions and Securing Retiree Claims

Chapters 4 and 5 explored the relative operations of funded versus pay-go retirement programs under a range of alternative demographic and economic scenarios. The economic and demographic conditions leading up to the 1960s and 1970s allowed public policymakers to rationalize the operation of national retirement systems on a pay-go basis. By the early 1990s, however, financial market operations and changing demographic outlooks significantly altered the terrain of pension financing. In its 1994 study that set off much of the world discussion about pensions, the World Bank advocated basing national retirement structures on three "pillars" of income security. The first pillar should be a pay-go, publicly managed defined benefit system. The second pillar should be a funded defined contribution system, in which the assets are privately managed. The third pillar should be private savings.[1] By the end of the 1990s, the model envisaged by the World Bank was up and running in several countries.

Case Studies of Nations Shifting to Funded Pensions

The approach that probably has received the most attention and has been emulated most widely is that of Chile.[2] Chile's May 1981 reform of its

---

[1] Estelle James, et al, *Averting the Old Age Crisis: Policies to Protect the Old and Promote Growth* (New York: Oxford University Press, 1994).

[2] See, for example, Peter Diamond and Salvador Valdes-Preito, "Social Security Reforms," in Barry P. Bosworth, Rudiger Dornbusch, Raul Laban, *The Chilean Economy: Policy Lessons and Challenges* (Washington, D.C.: The Brookings Institution, 1995, and Vittas, Dimitri, "Strengths and Weaknesses of the Chilean Pension Reform," mimeo of the Financial Sector of the Development Department of the World Bank, May 1995.

pay-go retirement plans was truly radical. The Chileans basically transformed their system into private individual retirement accounts, which are mandatory, fully funded, fully vested, and portable. Workers must contribute 10 percent of earnings to their retirement accounts. Workers choose where to invest their retirement savings from funds offered by highly regulated, specialized, private fund management companies. Workers also must purchase term life insurance and disability insurance offered by the same pension managers. The combined contributions covering retirement, life and disability insurance, and administrative expenses are about 13 percent of payroll. Upon retirement, Chileans can choose between a phased withdrawal of their account balances or an inflation-indexed annuity sold by insurance companies.

Has Pension Privatisation in Latin America Worked?

By Juan Yermo, OECD

The last two decades have been a period of tumultuous economic and social changes in Latin America. The privatisation of the pension system, pioneered by Chile in 1981, has been amongst the most important of these changes. Since then, 10 Latin American countries have introduced mandatory, privately managed individual accounts. The new system is dominant in countries such as Chile, El Salvador, and Mexico where the state's role as provider is limited to guaranteeing a basic pension that is set in relation to the minimum wage. At the opposite end of the reform spectrum, Costa Rica has maintained a relatively generous earnings-related pillar managed by the social security institute on a pay-as-you-go basis.

While it is too early to judge the long-term benefits of the reforms, they can already be praised for meritorious achievements.* The new defined contribution formula has eliminated some gross inequities of the previous system. It also automatically adjusts benefits to increases in life expectancy. In principle, it may have been possible to get similar results by introducing such a formula in the old pay-as-you-go schemes. However, the past mismanagement and abuse of social security in Latin America called for an overhaul of existing paradigms. The reforms have also contributed to a much-needed modernisation of the financial system and a reduction in public pension liabilities.

Unfortunately, these improvements have not been without costs. Contributors have to pay the bill of establishing and operating a brand new pension fund industry where competition is increasingly absent. In addition, the diversion of mandatory contributions towards individual accounts has accentuated short-term budgetary pressures. Regulators have responded by veering pension fund portfolios towards domestic government securities. Real returns have been high as a result, but largely thanks to the risk premium on government debt. Such premiums can materialise into significant capital losses that discredit the new systems. Argentina has had a firsthand experience with this danger. A few other Latin American governments are also battling through fiscal fragility, probably the biggest threat to the future of their funded systems.

Ultimately, the mandatory savings scheme popularised by Chile will be judged on the extent to which workers find it worth participating. The key policy challenge is how to replicate as far as possible the low administrative costs of a centralised system while encouraging competition, individual choice, and diversification of pension fund portfolios.

These schemes also need to be supported by solid poverty-prevention pillars. In most Latin American countries, this role is performed by the minimum pension guarantee, which tops up the savings in the individual account of poorer workers who comply with contribution requirements. Policymakers, however, have not paid much attention to those who have not made sufficient contributions (some countries do not even have social assistance pensions) or to the potential conflict between the individual's need for portfolio choice in the savings pillar and efficient risk management of the guarantee. In countries such as Chile that have already introduced portfolio choice, poorer workers face unwarranted incentives for risk-taking. It may be time to reconsider the virtues of a basic poverty-prevention pillar that is financed and managed separately from the savings pillar.

* See *Keeping the Promise of Old Age Income Security in Latin America*, Indermit Gill, Truman Packard and Juan Yermo, The World Bank, 2004, *http://wbln0018.worldbank.org/LAC/ LAC.nsf/ECADocbyUnid/146EBBA3371508E785256CBB005C29B4?Opendocument.*

A number of special features of the Chilean reform deserve mention. First, in 1981, the demographics of Chile were sharply different from those in any of the developed countries today. There were more than nine people of working age for each retiree, which made the transition from their old pay-go system to a funded system much easier. Second, the Chilean government was running a large fiscal surplus when it made the transition, so it could fund the transition costs out of general government revenues. Needless to say, the same fiscal conditions do not exist in most developed countries today. Third, the Chilean plan guaranteed participants a minimum rate of return and a minimum pension, but the guarantees are less than meets the eye. Basically, the Chilean taxpayers put a floor under the outcomes experienced by the Chilean pension participants. Of course, in Chile, as in most countries, there is a very large overlap between the tax-paying population and the pension participant population. Presumably the risk inherent in the investments in the pension funds is still present in the economy, regardless of who backs up the "guarantees." Fourth, the very favorable returns on financial assets that were realized over the system's early years and the huge cash flows into the pension funds may relate to the relatively low level of economic development at the time the system got underway and to the relatively youthful population. There are concerns about how this scheme will fare when it is mature or when it faces the kind of aging population, and perhaps net withdrawals, which the developed economies will face between 2020 and 2040. Finally, the Chilean system was relatively expensive to administer. Despite these qualifications, the Chilean pension reforms were hailed as a big success by the World Bank and others, and similar reforms were undertaken across several Latin American countries. Indeed, the three-tier retirement security model that the World Bank advocated in its 1994 study was essentially the one that Chile had adopted in 1981.

Roughly a decade after Chile adopted its pension changes, Australia embarked on an equally radical but quite different program of retirement income provision. The basic Australian government pension system, or age pension as it is called, is financed out of general government revenues and is subject to both an earnings test and an assets test. The means tests in the Australian system are a strong disincentive to accumulate wealth beyond the exempt levels, and the sizeable number of qualifying participants signified trouble ahead, prompting policymakers to mandate a pension savings program. After July 1, 1992, employers were required to provide minimum pension benefits for all employees. The initial mandated contribution was 3 percent for "small" employers and 4 percent for "large" employers, and it was scheduled to gradually rise to a mandatory contribution rate of 9 percent for all employers on July 1, 2002.

Before the adoption of the new mandated savings program, many Australian employers sponsored pensions for their workers. These plans tended to be defined benefit plans organized more along the lines of those in the United Kingdom, with joint trusteeship by worker organizations and management, than those in the United States, where most plans are trusts established and managed by the employer. With the adoption of the new mandated savings programs, many employer-sponsored plans in Australia have been terminated or converted to defined contribution plans and serve as the accumulator of workers' mandated contributions, which then flow into the investment markets on a pooled basis. This latter feature is thought to have made the investment of pension savings somewhat more administratively efficient than it is in the Chilean or similar systems. Australian policymakers, however, decided to allow workers to set up individual accounts separate from the pooled schemes and so some of the efficiency of pooled investment is being lost.

The conditions leading up to reform and the reforms themselves in Chile and Australia proved to be somewhat unique, however, and perhaps not a realistic model for other countries hoping to shift their large pay-go systems toward a more substantially funded status. In Chile, the combination of a youthful population and budget surpluses allowed the government to continue paying out the previously accrued pensions without having to tap current workers' contributions, which were deposited in their individual accounts under the new regime. In Australia, the basic pension was means-tested, about 25 percent of average wages, and was financed out of general tax revenues. Over the short term, the new mandated pension would not encroach on either the funding or benefits of the existing system. Over the long term, it had the potential to significantly reduce the financial drain on the basic pension.

In the initial years after the release of its 1994 report, the World Bank staff advocated pension reforms along the lines of the model they had laid out with almost religious zeal. Over the years, however, they have significantly tempered that zeal because of the difficult real-world situations they have encountered in many countries, both developed and developing, where pension reform has been considered. Today, they are much more sensitive to the "initial conditions" that many countries confront as they consider modifying systems that already have sizeable pension obligations and will soon be hit by massive shifts in aged dependency, all in the face of significant budget constraints. The World Bank has also come to believe that a basic pillar, something they now characterize as the zero pillar, along the lines of the basic pensions sponsored in Australia, Canada, and the United Kingdom, is important. They still advocate a first pillar of a publicly managed defined benefit plan with benefits being tied to earnings. They still believe in a mandated, funded second pillar against which pension design and reform should be evaluated. But the World Bank now acknowledges that systems might operate successfully without this element. The last element of individual savings is still part of the overall model, but there is a growing recognition by many analysts that this pillar will not provide significant retirement security to the most vulnerable workers, who will face income shortfalls if the other pillars are not robust.[3]

Despite the maturing of their own views on pension reforms and their recognition of the importance of flexibility in dealing with varying situations in different countries, the World Bank staff members, who have

---

[3] Robert Holzmann, Indermit Gill, Richard Hinz, Gregorio Impavido, Alberto R. Musalem, Michal Rutkowski, and Anita Schwarz, "Old Age Income Support in the 21st Century: The World Bank's Perspective on Pension Systems and Reform" (Washington, D.C.: The World Bank, forthcoming).

been more directly involved in pension reform around the world than any other group, still advocate the merits of pension funding. They know that the underlying interactions of economic and demographic variables that we explored in Chapter 4 cannot be ignored. In 1994, the World Bank advocated funding in their recommended second tier of defined contribution accounts. Today, however, they believe that funding is desirable in all the elements of what they now perceive to be a four-pillar system. Regardless of perceptions about the relative importance of the respective roles of each of the four pillars now espoused by the World Bank, most pension analysts today support substantial funding of pension obligations. The World Bank has done substantial research into how the various pillars of an assortment of countries' systems have been funded and the effectiveness of that funding.

Asset Management and Utilization in Funded Pension Systems

Table 11-1 shows the fund organization and the funding level as a percentage of the mandated retirement systems in a number of countries that we have touched upon throughout this discussion. These are taken from a World Bank study published in 2000, but the data on funding levels were gathered from the late 1980s through the 1990s.[4] In many cases, the level of funding would be considerably higher today than they are in the table. The important point is more about the range of approaches being taken by various countries to fund their future pension obligations, and then to use that as a basis for analyzing the potential effectiveness of that funding.

There are three different classifications of fund organization among the plans listed in Table 11-1. The partially funded defined benefit plans are the traditional systems, many of which went through a period of paygo financing, but which are now accumulating some assets in the centrally managed government fund. The centrally managed defined contribution plans are the provident funds that have been popular in parts of Asia and Africa. The privately managed defined contribution funds are from mandated plans, but the management requirements vary somewhat from system to system. In some cases, such as Australia and the United Kingdom, workers have some control over where their assets are invested, although they are often required to use pooled arrangements provided

---

[4] Augusto Iglesias and Robert J. Palacios, "Managing Public Pension Reserves Part I: Evidence from the International Experience," World Bank Social Protection Discussion Paper Series (Washington, D.C.: The World Bank, January 2000), p. 5.

Table 11-1. *Publicly Mandated Pension Fund Reserves and Fund Management in Selected Countries*

Country	Fund Organization	Fund Size as Percent of GDP
Argentina	Privately managed D.C.	3.0
Australia	Privately managed D.C.	61.0
Canada	Partially funded DB	11.0
Chile	Privately managed D.C.	45.0
Egypt	Partially funded DB	33.1
Hungary	Privately managed D.C.	0.4
India	Centrally managed D.C.	4.5
Japan	Partially funded DB	25.0
Malaysia	Centrally managed D.C.	55.7
Mexico	Privately managed D.C.	0.5
Netherlands	Privately managed D.C.	87.3
Poland	Privately managed D.C.	1.1
Sweden	Partially funded DB	33.1
Switzerland	Privately managed D.C.	117.0
United Kingdom	Privately managed D.C.	74.7
United States	Partially funded DB	5.0

Note: Under its reformed retirement system, Sweden also has privately managed defined contribution accounts but its defined benefit system is still the largest of the funds.
Source: Augusto Iglesias and Robert J. Palacios, "Managing Public Pension Reserves Part I: Evidence from the International Experience," World Bank Social Protection Discussion Paper Series (Washington, D.C.: The World Bank, January 2000), p. 6.

by the occupational pensions to which they belong. In the Scandinavian countries, the assets tend to be pooled at the national level and then parceled out to investment managers, but under the direction of a central, nongovernmental authority.

While getting to the point of funding mandated pension savings is an important step, what is done with the funding as it grows matters just as much, in terms of both reducing long-term pension costs and ensuring that benefits are secure. For example, assume that a worker begins a career at age 21 and participates in a funded pension plan over her career. The worker realizes annual real salary increases of 1.5 percent until retiring at age 65. Assuming that this worker lives out a typical life expectancy in the developed economies today, she will need to accumulate around seven to eight times her final salary by age 65 to maintain her pre-retirement standard of living. The amount may be higher or lower depending on actual life expectancy, the taxation of pre- and post-retirement income, and the interest rate at which the assets can be invested during retirement.

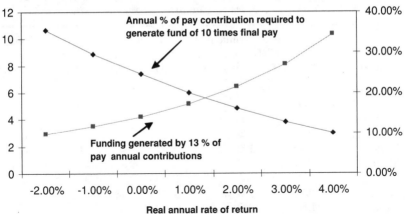

Figure 11-1. Accumulated Assets at Retirement Based on a 13 Percent Per Annum Pension Contribution and Alternative Contribution Rates Required to Accumulate a Pension Balance of 10 Times Pay at Retirement at Alternative Real Rates of Return on Assets. *Source:* Developed by the authors.

Figure 11-1 illustrates how alternative rates of return affect pension cost and at least one element of benefit security. The upward sloping line in the figure shows the accumulated benefit at retirement as a multiple of pay. If this worker's annual savings are invested at a negative 2 percent real return per year, at age 65, she will have an accumulated fund between 2.5 and 3.0 times final annual earnings. This will be about one-half of what she would need to live approximately as well after retirement as before it. At a positive 4 percent real return, the benefit will accumulate to 10 times final annual earnings. This might be somewhat more than the worker needs to maintain pre-retirement living standards, but the reader should keep in mind that we are using a rough rule of thumb retirement income goal in this case. The downward sloping line in Figure 11-1 shows the annual contributions required to generate an accumulated balance of eight times final pay by age 65. At a minus 2 percent real rate of return, the worker would have to contribute about 36 percent of annual pay. At a 4 percent positive real rate of return, her required contribution would drop to about 10 percent of pay.

Table 11-2 shows how the assets in several mandatory national pension systems were invested during the 1990s. India and Malaysia had provident fund systems, while all the other countries had traditional defined benefit systems. The allocation of assets in virtually all of these plans raises

Table 11-2. *Investment of Assets in Publicly Managed Pension Fund*
Portfolios in Selected Countries during the 1990s

Country	Year	Government Bonds or Fixed Deposits	Loans, Mortgages or Housing Bonds	Equity Shares	Real Estate or Other
Canada	1991	100%	0%	0%	0%
Egypt	1995	100	0	0	0
Switzerland	1997	100	0	0	0
United States	1995	100	0	0	0
India	1995	100	0	0	0
Korea	1997	89	3	3	6
Japan	1995	63	17	19	0
Malaysia	1996	63	21	15	1
Sweden	1996	42	40	0	18

Source: Augusto Iglesias and Robert J. Palacios, "Managing Public Pension Reserves Part I: Evidence from the International Experience," World Bank Social Protection Discussion Paper Series (Washington, D.C.: The World Bank, January 2000), p. 22.

fundamental questions about the utilization of assets backing pension promises for future generations.

Investing Pension Funds in Government Bonds
In Chapter 5, we questioned whether a state pension system's assets being invested in the state's own bonds constituted true funding. While there is not widespread evidence on the implications of pension surplus buildup being invested in government bonds or other government expenditures, an analysis by John Cogan at Stanford University found that this sort of pension funding may simply add to other government spending.[5] In Chapter 5, we cited a number of other studies that came to the same conclusion regarding state pension accumulations in the United States and across a number of other OECD countries. If that is the case, then this type of pension buildup is not a form of national saving at all. A recent article in the *New York Times* analyzing the financing of the U.S. government's rising deficits in this decade argues that the federal government has been using Social Security funding assets to mask the true size of the operating deficit in other government operations.[6]

---

[5] John F. Cogan, "The Congressional Response to Social Security Surpluses, 1935–1994" (Paolo Alto, California: Hoover Institution, Stanford University, 1998).
[6] Daniel Gross, "How to Make the Deficit Look Smaller than It Is," New York Times (November 23, 2003).

Beyond the issue of whether a national pension system investing in government bonds is real funding, there is a further question about the potential rates of return from such a conservative investment. In reasonably organized economies with stable governments, one would expect that central government debt financing would be among the most risk-free assets available, and thus would pay relatively low returns. This is a problem because the government bond return probably will lag the general return on productive assets in the overall economy. Thus, a more diversified investment strategy would earn higher average returns than investing in government bonds.

Even where publicly managed pension assets are not invested in government bonds, they tend to be invested in other assets with relatively low rates of return. The prevalence of pension assets being invested in housing loans reflected in Table 11-2 suggests that pension assets are being used to support public policies that have nothing to do with retirement benefits. In its seminal study on the problems of aging and public pensions around the world, the World Bank noted, "as government gets privileged access to large pension reserves, it may be induced to spend and borrow more. Borrowing from the pension fund is less transparent than that from the open capital market."[7]

At the end of June 1998, Malaysia opened a new top-of-the-line airport in Kuala Lumpur. It was largely financed by a $373 million loan from the Employees Provident Fund (EPF) at less than market interest rates.[8] If that were all the Malaysian authorities had been up to, workers might not have been so concerned. In the fall of 1997, they announced the use of the EPF assets to reverse their stock market declines. When their support program for the market began in September 1997, the Kuala Lumpur Stock Exchange index was at around 780. By mid-December it was under 560.[9]

The World Bank reported that the National Investment Bank of Egypt credits its pension system with negative real interest rates. In Ecuador, mortgage and personal loans to members of the elite accounted for

---

[7] World Bank, *Averting the Old Age Crisis* (Oxford: Oxford University Press, 1994), p. 94.

[8] Anil Netto, "Malaysia: Workers Unhappy Over Management of Pension Fund," Inter Press Service, June 24, 1998.

[9] Mukul G. Asher, "Investment Policies and Performance of Provident Funds in Southeast Asia," a paper prepared for the Economic Development Institute of the World Bank workshop on Pension System Reform, Governance, and Fund Management, Yangzou City, Jiangsu Province, China, January 13–15, 1998.

19 percent of the loan portfolio. Mexico and Venezuela channeled pension funds to housing subsidies realizing below market returns.[10]

Augusto Iglesias and Robert Palacios analyzed the difference between annual compounded real returns on publicly held pension assets and bank deposits or short-term government debt across 20 countries and found that most of them realized returns on the pension assets well below these short-term rates. In all but three countries, the real returns on pension assets were considerably below the rates of growth in real incomes per capita. In their analysis of private pension investment in 20 countries, on the other hand, they found that real returns on pension assets exceeded per capita real income growth in all but one case and averaged nearly 4 percent per year across all the countries. The two sets of countries where they developed the return comparisons did not have much overlap but in the four countries where they did overlap – Canada, Japan, Sweden, and the United States – the difference in private asset real returns over income was 4 percent per year greater than for public plan returns. Figure 11-1 shows that these sorts of differences can have very large effects on pension costs and the share of benefits that actually are funded over the long term.[11]

Constrained Asset Allocations for Government Pensions:
The Canadian Case

By Professor Moshe A. Milevsky, York University and The IFID Centre, Toronto, Ontario, Canada

Amongst a growing demographic concern for the viability of the Canadian Pension Plan (CPP) – which was enacted in 1966 – in early 1998 the government announced a series of measures to improve the solvency of the plan. Foremost in the revamped strategy was the creation of a Board with a mandate to achieve a maximum rate of return without undue risk of loss. But, a number of asset allocation restrictions imposed by The Act governing the fund might actually hamper the performance of the plan in the long run.

First, some background. Canada is amongst the handful of countries with pay-go (first pillar) state-run pension plans that have introduced steady state financing, which is a balance between fully funded and completely unfunded pay-go plans. Technically this was implemented by creating a Crown corporation called the CPP Investment Board which manages the assets that have been transferred to it from the CPP.

---

[10] James et al, *Averting the Old Age Crisis*, p. 127.

[11] Augusto Iglesias and Robert J. Palacios, "Managing Public Pension Reserves Part I: Evidence from the International Experience," World Bank Social Protection Discussion Paper Series (Washington, D.C.: The World Bank, January 2000).

Like many other public (unfunded) pay-go systems, Canada's CPP is currently incurring larger contributions – at 9.9 percent of payroll – than they are paying out in benefits. However, this would be expected to reverse itself by the year 2020, which is when the fund would start paying benefits. This gives the Board a very long horizon vis a vis the duration of their liabilities, and one that is suitable for a substantial exposure to equity and other growth investments.

The Board has an investment target of 4.25 percent on a real (after-inflation) basis and uses strict index benchmarks to monitor and control risk as well as investment performance.

As of September 2003, the consolidated assets available to the Canadian Pension Plan consisted of $64.4 billion (CAD) of which 62 percent was allocated to fixed income bonds and 38 percent was allocated to equities and real estate. This asset mix is relatively conservative – even by Canadian standards – especially when compared against other public pension plans of the same size that average no more than 30 percent to fixed income. And in fact, the 62 percent weighting to fixed income is only part of the story. Approximately $37 billion is allocated to long-term non-traded bonds that are effectively loans by the Federal government to the 11 provinces and territories at below market rates.

These legacy bonds provide the provinces and territories the additional option to roll over the maturing bonds at market rates for a period not to exceed 20 years. Since these bonds (i.e., loans) contain some unique options and do not trade in the open market, it is impossible to mark them to market and the Board uses hypothetical market valuations to determine the worth of close to $37 billion of their portfolio.

In addition to the above-mentioned legacy bonds that place serious constraints on the risk and return opportunity set faced by the fund, the Investment Board operates under a 30 percent restriction on foreign investments – limiting 70 percent of the CPP fund assets to Canada. While this 30 percent restriction is the law of the land for all private as well as public pension plans, many private-sector pension funds use derivative instruments to synthetically replicate exposure to foreign equity and bond markets. The Investment Statement governing the activities of the Board strictly prohibits the use of derivatives to exceed the foreign property restrictions. And yet, the Board has made an innovative commitment to have 10 percent of its assets in private equity, and has already placed $5.5 billion with 41 limited partnerships.

It is worthy of note that with the benefit of hindsight, the decision to refrain from an over-allocation to international equities and bonds has proven prophetic during the year 2003, given the more than 20 percent appreciation of the Canadian dollar against the U.S. dollar and other major currencies. Indeed, one could argue that these politically motivated and patriotic portfolio restrictions actually saved money. But, it is hard to make a case for this continuing given the fact that U.S. and international equity markets have outperformed Canadian markets by an average 2 percent compounded during the last 30 years. The reasons for this underperformance are hotly debated.

In sum, it will be very interesting to see how the Canadian Pension Plan's Investment Board and its ever-increasing fund size will go about generating the mandated maximum rate of return that is in the best interests of the contributors and beneficiaries with ongoing asset class and allocation restrictions.

In a follow-up to the paper that he did with Iglesias, Palacios subsequently looked at five case studies of countries that have modified the management of their public pension funds to deal with some of the concerns raised earlier. The countries were Canada, Ireland, Japan, New Zealand, and Sweden. Palacios identified a number of specific practices that he found encouraging, including:

- Setting explicit funding targets and mechanisms to achieve them
- Utilizing commercial investment policies aimed at maximizing risk-adjusted returns
- Using professional boards that operate at arms length from government sponsors of plans
- Prohibiting economically targeted investments
- Using external managers to actually invest pension assets
- Avoiding portfolio limits of specific classes of investment-grade assets
- Establishing high standards of reporting and disclosure[12]

Motivations for Individual Account Systems and Their Operation
Despite the fact that some countries seem to be moving toward more appropriate centralized investment of pooled assets, reservations remain about central government intrusion into investment markets and the potential conflicts of interest. Some analysts have suggested that one way around the problem of centralized pension asset management of mandated retirement savings is to set up a system of defined contribution accounts and give workers some autonomy over investment decisions. Countries that have adopted this approach have done so through a variety of mechanisms.

As part of its 1981 pension reform, Chile created a set of independent investment entities, Asociacion de Fondos de Pension (AFP), to manage the funds of workers participating in their individual account pension system. The AFPs were highly regulated institutions, with limits on how much an AFP could earn on assets relative to other AFPs, how it could invest the assets, and how much it could charge in terms of fees. Plan participants could only invest their assets through one AFP at a time. At least during its early years of implementation, the AFPs generated relatively high rates of return and the Chilean reform became the poster

[12] Robert Palacios, "Managing Public Pension Reserves Part II: Lessons from Five Recent OECD Initiatives," World Bank Social Protection Discussion Paper Series (Washington, D.C.: The World Bank, July 2002).

child for reforms of this sort.[13] The one criticism of the system was the relatively high level of administrative costs associated with the AFPs.[14]

Sweden adopted an individual account pension reform measure in the mid-1990s with implementation of the new system beginning in November 2001. The largest part of the system is still a pay-go financed system, although contributions are notionally accumulated, in a bookkeeping sense, and the notional account is credited with an annual rate of interest equal to the rate of growth of personal income. In the context of funded individual accounts, Sweden also established a system whereby mandatory contributions of 2.5 percent of pay are invested through its administrative arm, the Premium Pension Authority (PPM). Under this system, workers have a wide range of investment options for their 2.5 percent contributions. The PPM is a centralized bookkeeper and clearinghouse for the system. Working plan participants deal directly with the PPM in making investment choices and designations and can change their selections on any working day at no cost. The PPM collects all the daily transactions from participants, aggregates them across all participants, and then makes net daily trades with individual investment managers as needed. The net fund transactions are much smaller than the aggregate of all individual fund transactions, thus holding net costs down.[15] Some students of national pension systems and the move toward individual account reforms believe that such reforms should follow the Swedish rather than the Chilean model.

The Swedish Premium Pension System

By Stefan Engström and Anna Westerberg

Introduced in 1999, the new Swedish pension system comprises two parts: a notional defined contribution pay-as-you-go scheme and an advance-funded defined contribution scheme. The former defined benefit system is gradually being phased out. The new system is based on a fixed contribution rate of 18.5 percent on earnings, 2.5 percent of which goes to the defined contribution premium pension system. The premium pension system is based on a state-run clearinghouse model in

---

[13] Olivia S. Mitchell and Flavio Ataliba Barreto, "After Chile What? Second-Round Pension Reforms in Latin America" (Cambridge, MA: National Bureau of Economic Research, 1997), NBER Working Paper, no. 6316.

[14] Peter Diamond, "Administrative Costs and Equilibrium Charges with Individual Accounts," (Cambridge, MA: National Bureau of Economic Research, 1999), NBER Working Paper, no. 7050.

[15] Joakim Palme, "The 'Great' Swedish Pension Reform," found at the web site: http://www.sweden.se/templates/Article____5524.asp.

which more than 600 mutual funds are available to invest in. individuals can split their pension assets between one and five funds in the scheme. The premium pension system is mandatory for the entire workforce and hence provides us with a unique opportunity to deepen our knowledge of individuals' financial decision-making.

Overall active participation in the premium pension system is high. When the system was launched in 2000, 67 percent of the population (4.4 million) made an active investment decision. This high participation rate is likely the result of the massive information campaign by the government and extensive marketing by mutual fund companies. Engström and Westerberg (2003a) study why some individuals make active investment decisions and show that individuals' previous experience of financial markets is positively related to an active investment decision. For instance, individuals who work in the financial sector or who have a high income or financial wealth, more education, or private pension savings are more likely to participate actively in the system. Interestingly, some findings in Engström and Westerberg (2003a) contradict previous studies by showing that women are more active than men and that younger individuals are more active than older individuals.

Another related finding in Engström and Westerberg (2003b) suggests that information asymmetry significantly affects individuals' choice of mutual funds. Specifically, individuals prefer funds that are more familiar to them. For instance, if the performance of a Sweden-based fund is similar to that of a foreign-based fund, the Sweden-based fund will attract significantly more investors. Similarly, funds that belong to one of the four main banks in Sweden receive higher inflows of capital. This study also confirms previous documented preferences for low-fee funds but also suggests that past returns are a less important decision variable.

Overall, the above evidence suggests that familiarity breeds investments. Individuals who possess previous savings experience make more active investment decisions and invest in funds that they are familiar with. This highlights the importance of financial education especially when the public pension system relies on individuals making investment decisions. Hence, prior to the launch of such systems, the government must take measures to improve the public's knowledge of private savings.

References

Engström, Stefan and Anna Westerberg. 2003a. *Which Individuals Make Active Investment Decisions in the New Swedish Pension System? Journal of Pension Economics and Finance, 2(3), November.*

Engström, Stefan and Anna Westerberg. 2003b. *Information Costs and Mutual Fund Flows, Working Paper, Stockholm School of Economic.*

The regulatory restrictions imposed on the Chilean individual account system suggest that the mere establishment of individual accounts does not necessarily eliminate problems with centrally managed pension funding. Argentina implemented a modified pension system in 1994 along the lines of the three-pillar system then being advocated by the World Bank. The first pillar of this system was a national defined benefit plan structured to pay a flat benefit whose value was 27.5 percent of the national covered wage. For the second pillar, workers could choose between an ongoing publicly funded pay-go system, the Additional Pension for Permanence (PAP) plan, or a defined contribution system managed by private Pension Fund Administrators (AFJPs). All options in the second tier cost employees 11 percent of covered earnings.[16] As Argentina descended into its financial crisis in 2000 and beyond and could not raise cash in world economic markets, the government looked to the pension savings of workers to help bail it out of its crisis. In December 2000, the AFJPs committed to loan the government U.S. $3 billion. In March 2001, the government leaned on banks and pension funds to come up with another $3.5 billion. In November 2001, the AFJPs were forced into accepting lower interest loans instead of high-interest, dollar-denominated bonds. This was followed by virtual seizure of pension fund assets, by forcing the funds to transfer $2.3 billion in fixed-term deposits to the state-owned bank in trade for more government bonds. Finally, in an effort to stimulate the economy, the government cut the contribution rate from 11 percent of covered pay to 5 percent. By the time the government financing totally collapsed, 70 percent of the AFJP investments were in government bonds.[17]

Foreign Investment as a Means to Achieving Fair Returns

The shift toward funding public pension programs would create additional savings, which would promote investment and thus higher rates of growth. As Axel Borsch-Supan contends, funded systems also promote a more efficient capital market and thus lead to higher rates of productivity growth.[18] In part, however, this will be achieved by an inevitable decline in asset returns caused by capital deepening in the industrialized societies. Many argue that the shift toward funding will fuel economic growth over the coming decades, making the transfer

---

[16] Olivia S. Mitchell and Flavio Ataliba Barreto, "After Chile What? Second-Round Pension Reforms in Latin America" (Cambridge, MA: National Bureau of Economic Research, 1997), NBER Working Paper, no. 6316, p. 11.

[17] Thomas Catan, "Argentina's Pension System Vision in Tatters," *Financial Times* (April 28, 2002), found at the web site: http://specials.ft.com/ftfm/FT396A6FI0D.

[18] Axel Borsch-Supan, "Population Ageing, Savings Behaviour and Capital Markets," 2001.

of resources to vast numbers of senior citizens far less painful than it would be through pay-go financed systems, which encumber economic prosperity.[19]

While a shift from a pay-go to a funded system could have tremendous merit for the free flow of capital throughout the world, societies should be careful not to move too quickly. Countries that go into funding in a big way over the next few decades could risk creating a situation where national savings rise too quickly to keep pace with efficient investments. This could drive capital returns to even lower levels than would be implied by aging populations.

In some regards, the problems that have mounted in Japan over the 1990s can be attributed to a decline in capital efficiency. Andrew Smithers argues that Japan's rate of capital investment to GDP was significantly greater than other developed nations during the 1990s.[20] What made this over-investment possible was Japan's exceptionally high savings rates, which resulted, in part, from its advanced aging. With a baby boom generation about 10 years older than that in the United States, a very high percentage of Japan's population was already in age cohorts that historically save the most. And Japan has maintained a high national and private rate of savings in recent decades, suggesting a cultural difference. While many economists view high savings as promoting more business investment and thus propping up economic growth, this did not happen in Japan. Instead, during the 1990s Japan suffered through one of the longest periods of slow to no growth in the modern era.

Robert Dugger concludes that Japan's problems arose from its continuing to invest in old-line, low economic return industries rather than promoting the growth of new higher-return sectors. In Japan, older-sector companies make up the largest portion of GDP and employ the most workers. Older voters are often closely tied to these older industries, either because they still work in them or because they receive retirement income from them. Politicians, who depend on older voters for their reelection, have responded to these public preferences by propping up these old-line companies through a variety of public expenditure programs. This was not an economically sensible strategy, and Japan fell into what has been described as a structural trap, whereby low rates of return

[19] Dieter Brauninger, Bernhard Graf, Karin Gruber, Marco Neuhaus and Stefan Schneider. (2002) "The Demographic Challenge," Deutsche Bank Research, September.

[20] Andrew Smithers "Japan's Structural Savings Surplus," Smithers & Co. Ltd., April 1999, Report No. 132.

on assets weakened the overall economy.[21] The scenario seemed to be almost the opposite of the creative destruction that Joseph Schumpeter suggested is necessary for economic stimulation and renewal, as discussed in Chapter 9, and the Japanese economy suffered accordingly.

With most developed societies likely to mature into a demographic pattern similar to Japan's in the coming decades, does Japan's experience foreshadow their future? The answer will depend on what other societies have learned from Japan's troubled last decade. Countries that shift rapidly toward funded systems over the next few decades – before most individuals retire and draw down their savings – are likely to have abundant capital to invest in their economies or in other societies to support their aging populations. Whether the higher savings will translate into greater prosperity down the line will depend on the efficiency with which the capital is invested. Countries able to adapt to the changing economic climate – supporting growth industries while channeling excess capital away from declining ones – may very well avoid some of the pitfalls that beset Japan over the 1990s. But there are also tremendous opportunities for countries that look outside their own borders to earn higher rates of return. As we will see in the rest of this discussion, many societies have already made considerable strides in this regard.

Most of the discussion thus far has focused on how developed countries can deal with aging populations and stable or declining workforces within the confines of their own boundaries. However, there is another option for developed economies. If they cannot find adequate labor within their own borders to effectively use capital, they can export capital to other parts of the world where there are ample and growing supplies of workers. Countries with ample labor and tremendous potential to utilize additional capital surround most of the developed economies. The movement of capital to higher growth areas is much easier to achieve under a funded public pension system, since pay-go based systems largely depend on the fundamentals of the domestic economy.

The highly developed industrial countries of the world are somewhat clustered in three areas. Four of the G-7 are in Western Europe and are surrounded by a number of smaller countries at similar stages of development. In the South Pacific, Japan has been the dominant economy for the past several decades. In North America, Canada and the United States fill

---

[21] Robert H. Dugger "Why is Japan Trapped?" *The Globalist*, May 2003.

Table 11-3. *Working-Age Populations in Various Sections of the World in 2000 and as Estimated by the United Nations for Selected Future Years*

	2000	2010	2020	2030	Change from 2000–2030
European Union	229,312	231,239	224,121	205,250	−24,062
Eastern Europe[a]	185,665	191,725	177,748	157,947	−27,718
Northern Africa[a]	85,730	113,316	137,611	157,713	71,982
Western Asia including Middle East[b]	92,431	120,024	149,407	178,509	86,078
Region North of Arabian Sea and Persian Gulf and around Caspian Sea[c]	132,886	178,300	226,419	275,691	142,806
Japan	79,074	75,904	68,993	65,070	−14,004
Australia/New Zealand	13,709	15,258	15,979	16,108	2,399
China	770,108	877,195	914,719	900,254	130,146
India	519,958	645,151	765,617	854,728	334,770
Southeast Asia[a]	275,172	341,031	398,645	433,773	158,601
Canada	18,943	20,911	21,517	20,985	2,043
United States	167,105	186,967	197,288	198,257	31,152
Mexico	51,316	63,492	74,047	80,586	29,269
Central America less Mexico[a]	16,497	22,262	28,745	34,984	18,487
South America[a]	186,693	227,782	259,997	281,967	95,274

[a] These areas are grouped in accordance with the United Nations Population Division's classification system.

[b] The largest populations in this part of the world reside in Iraq, Saudi Arabia, Syria, Turkey, and Yemen.

[c] The countries included here include Afghanistan, Iran, Kazakhstan, Kyrgyzstan, Pakistan, Tajikistan, Turkmenistan, and Uzbekistan.

Source: United Nations Population Division, *World Population Prospects* (The 2000 Revision).

out the G-7 list. Table 11-3 shows the working-age populations in each of these countries or sections of the world in 2000 and in 10-year intervals out to 2030. It also shows the similarly aged populations in a number of other countries or regions nearby the various major developed countries. The areas of the world included here were intentionally chosen because they allow us to explore some of the challenges the developed countries will face in using foreign investment. For purposes of putting together this table, we considered the working-age population to be everyone from ages 20 to 64.

Focusing first on the European Union countries, the working-age population is expected to shrink by about 10 percent over the next 30 years or so, with Germany, Italy, and Spain being somewhat worse off than the other countries. There has been some talk of Eastern Europe's becoming a source of immigrants who could be easily integrated into the existing societies in Western Europe. But Eastern Europe is expected to have an even more significant contraction in its working-age population over the next 30 years than Western Europe. To the extent that Western Europe might offer workers better jobs with higher pay than Eastern Europe, there could still be considerable migration from east to west. But several of the Eastern European countries have been reorganizing since their shift away from communism, and some have shown a willingness to curtail their welfare state programs to a greater extent than their Western European counterparts. Eastern Europe could become a more worker-friendly environment as the decade evolves than the Western European countries that are facing the most severe contractions in their workforces.

Much of the cross-border migration that is causing the angst about immigration in Europe is from the other three sets of countries in the first group of nations in Table 11-3. Every one of these regional collections of nations has major countries with tremendous development potential today and with the further prospect of adding far more workers over the coming decades than the potential worker loss in the developed countries of Europe.

Moving around the world to the Australia-Asian segment of the table, the projected contraction of the working-age population in Japan is significant, but it is miniscule in comparison to the anticipated growth in the working-age populations of the major population centers in that part of the world. Once again, China, India, and most of the countries in Southeast Asia have tremendous development potential today, with the prospect of adding far more workers over the coming decades than will be lost in Japan.

Moving further on around to the Americas, Canada and the United States are unique among the G-7 countries in that their working-age populations should continue growing in coming decades, although Canada's growth rate is expected to peak between 2020 and 2030. And growth rates in the United States will be much lower than those over the past half century or more. But Mexico falls within the North America Free Trade Area (NAFTA) and could potentially add nearly as many workers as the United States could add between now and 2030, even starting from a base that is only one-third that of the United States today. The rest of Central and South America also has tremendous development potential today, offering the prospect of more than enough workers over the coming decades to make up for any shortfalls in Canada and the United States due to slower-growing labor forces.

Capital-labor ratios will likely continue to rise in countries where the rate of growth in the labor pool is slowing. The ratios could rise relatively rapidly when working populations actually start falling in the developed economies. Further increases in the capital-labor ratios in some developed economies today almost certainly imply that relative rates of return will be lower in those economies than in others where capital could be used more efficiently because of more ample labor supplies. If the capital owners in the developed economies of the world are concerned about the efficient use of their capital and find rates of return declining in their domestic markets because labor pools are shrinking, they need to reposition their capital to available labor. If restrictions on immigration stand in the way of importing labor to domestic markets, they can take the capital to the workers in other parts of the world.

With an abundant supply of labor and a lower stock of capital, developing nations have the potential of generating higher rates of return to capital investment than countries with high capital-labor ratios. Industrialized economies can take advantage of more favorable economic opportunities by shifting capital abroad and the production capacity that goes along with it. In the context of using this potential to meet the consumer demands that will likely persist in aging societies as labor supplies start to contract, capital owners will be able to repatriate returns on capital investments abroad in the form of goods and services. Thus, capital flows have the potential to ease the rising demand pressures for goods and services that are likely to ensue with the aging of the developed societies.[22]

This is not simply a one-sided opportunity for the developed nations of the world to take advantage of their less-developed neighbors. The shifting of capital has tremendous potential to dramatically increase the productivity rates in the underdeveloped economies over the coming decades. Raising productivity in poorer nations should have exactly the same effects on the workers there as it did in the developed countries of the world in the decades after World War II. The tremendous increases in the standards of living that occurred in those countries after the war were largely attributable to the rapid increases in the productivity of workers in them.

Capital flows are generally classified into two major categories: portfolio investment and direct investment. Both types of investments are components of a country's capital account in the balance of payments.

---

[22] Axel Borsch-Supan, Alexander Ludwig, and Joachim Winter, "Aging and International Capital Flows," (National Bureau of Economic Research, October 2001), working paper 8553.

While both investment types infuse foreign capital to finance investment and stimulate economic growth in the receiving country, there are some major differences between the two. In a nutshell, the key factor distinguishing the two types is control. Portfolio investments represent the flow of funds abroad for the purchase of financial assets of a firm or government in order to receive interest, dividends, or capital gains in return. The flows of funds for portfolio purposes are investments in which the lender gains no operating control over the borrower. With direct investment, however, the investor does gain control. Typically this refers to the purchase of land or the acquisition of ownership shares in an attempt to control a foreign business operation. However, the line between what is considered control is often nebulous. For example, if a U.S. corporation purchases shares in a Mexican firm, it may or may not gain operating control, depending on how many shares it buys. Official U.S. government statistics and statistics from the OECD assume that ownership of 10 percent or more of the ordinary shares or voting rights of an enterprise wields some influence over its management and constitutes direct control. This is consistent with the International Monetary Fund classification, but does not necessarily represent the definition used by all countries.

Potential International Demand for Pension Fund Savings

As the developed nations of the world grapple with the effects of population aging and capital deepening in their domestic economies, it is likely that they will induce international capital flows in the form of foreign direct investment and portfolio flows. Empirical evidence indicates that this mechanism may already be at work with the surge of capital flows in recent years. To gain a sense of how foreign capital flows have become more important in the world economy in recent years, Table 11-4 shows the inflows of net private capital and its components to various emerging regions of the world. Between the 1970s and 1990s, the emerging market economies have seen roughly an eight-fold surge in net private capital investment. Nearly all regions of the world have benefited from these inflows, with Africa being somewhat an exception.

There was a slowdown in net private capital flows at the end of the 1990s, largely a result of the financial crises experienced in Asia and Russia that severely damaged investors' confidence abroad. In fact, capital flows to many of the Asian economies over the late 1990s completely dried up. While the slowdown is evident in portfolio flows and bank loans extended to the developing world, the long-term expectations remain strong.

Table 11-4. *Net Private Capital Flows to Emerging Markets (in Billions of U.S. dollars)*

Net Private Capital Flows	1971–1975	1976–1980	1981–1985	1986–1990	1991–1995	1996–2000
Total emerging market economies	67.0	85.4	69.4	104.3	717.3	481.7
Africa	27.5	54.9	32.5	13.0	30.9	45.6
Developing Asia, crisis countries	10.4	36.2	49.2	15.2	182.7	−1.8
Other Asian emerging markets	8.2	12.7	17.4	28.1	90.3	71.2
Middle East	−20.2	−115.9	−46.2	14.3	156.1	19.0
Western Hemisphere	39.4	111.8	48.5	18.0	194.2	286.1
Net Private Direct Investment						
Total emerging market economies	14.3	25.7	52.0	77.8	304.9	722.1
Africa	4.7	3.4	5.4	10.7	14.5	36.1
Developing Asia, crisis countries	2.9	5.1	7.9	17.4	35.4	47.3
Other Asian emerging markets	2.1	4.6	12.2	16.3	120.8	228.5
Middle East	−3.1	−4.3	3.7	2.1	18.4	30.4
Western Hemisphere	10.2	19.3	25.0	31.3	84.9	284.0
Net Private Portfolio Investment						
Total emerging market economies	1.1	3.1	30.1	19.5	320.9	167.1
Africa	0.9	−0.7	0.7	−4.6	9.2	20.4
Developing Asia, crisis countries	0.3	0.9	8.7	1.2	68.9	47.4
Other Asian emerging markets	0.1	0.2	0.9	−2.1	13.5	−5.5
Middle East	0.0	0.0	13.2	27.4	40.2	−26.4
Western Hemisphere	−0.2	3.0	6.4	−2.2	148.8	98.7
Bank Loans and Other						
Total emerging market economies	51.5	56.5	−12.7	7.0	91.4	−407.5
Africa	21.7	52.2	26.4	6.8	7.2	−10.9
Developing Asia, crisis countries	7.0	30.1	32.7	−3.4	78.5	−96.8
Other Asian emerging markets	6.1	7.9	4.2	13.9	−44.1	−151.8
Middle East	−17.0	−111.6	−63.3	−15.3	97.6	15.1
Western Hemisphere	29.7	89.7	17.0	−11.0	−39.5	−96.6

Source: International Monetary Fund, *The World Economic Outlook (WEO) Database,* October 2001.

Foreign direct investment has continued to show remarkable growth, more than doubling for all emerging economies from what it was as recently as the early 1990s. The upsurge in foreign direct investment has been far-reaching across the developing world with the Latin American countries showing the greatest boost. The sharp slowdowns in portfolio flows between 1996 and 2000 reflects their oftentimes short-term nature and the ease with which these funds can "round-trip" or be withdrawn with little more than the flick of a computer key. The fact that foreign direct investment constitutes control by the investor has made it common to view it as a more stable commitment, reflecting the confidence of investors about the long-term prospects of an economy.

In that sense, Table 11-5 provides an indication of how expectations and confidence of many foreign investors has grown over time in the developing world. By examining the directional flow from various OECD countries to the rest of the world, we gain some sense of which countries are expanding their borders in search of greater efficiencies and higher rates of return. Foreign direct investment outflows as a percentage of GDP moving to the developing world have shown widespread growth over the last 20 years. Nearly all countries have shown sizable jumps in outflows of foreign direct investment, with the biggest surge in the last half of the 1990s. In fact, Spain, Sweden, and the Netherlands reveal the greatest propensity for shifting capital abroad, while Italy and Australia show only small increases relative to GDP.

The increasing flow of direct investment from rich to poor nations is quite apparent. The trend in the flows in the other direction have been somewhat mixed but are generally of much smaller magnitude. Only Belgium-Luxembourg had more foreign direct investment flowing into them from non-OECD countries between 1996 and 2000 than flowing in the other direction.

The pattern of foreign direct investment increasingly flowing from the developed to less developed countries with much less growth of flows in the other direction makes eminent sense in the context of the capital deepening that has been occurring in the developed economies. Calvo et al. argue that a major impetus for rising foreign capital flows throughout the early 1990s was the sustained decline in world interest rates.[23] One of the potential explanations for the low interest rates in the developed nations

---

[23] Guillermo A. Calvo, Leonardo Leiderman, and Carmen M. Reinhart, "Inflows of Capital to Developing Countries in the 1990s," *Journal of Economic Perspectives* (1996) vol. 10, No. 2, pp. 123–139.

Table 11-5. *Foreign Direct Investment Inflows and Outflows to and from Non-OECD Economies*

	Outflows of DI to Non-OECD Countries (Percentage of GDP)				Inflows of DI from Non-OECD Countries (Percentage of GDP)			
	1981–1985	1986–1990	1991–1995	1996–2000	1981–1985	1986–1990	1991–1995	1996–2000
Australia	0.131%	0.213%	0.001%	0.190%	0.039%	0.414%	0.566%	0.413%
Austria	0.036	0.031	0.085	0.395	0.045	0.030	0.049	−0.076
Belgium-Luxembourg	0.083	0.503	0.093	0.746	0.103	−0.004	−0.021	1.637
Canada	0.503	0.167	0.404	0.781	0.053	0.052	0.088	0.135
Denmark	0.055	0.061	0.063	0.428	0.006	0.000	0.056	0.279
Finland	0.060	0.240	0.127	0.272	0.007	−0.007	0.009	0.041
France	0.057	0.354	0.603	0.472	0.044	0.234	0.263	0.040
Germany	0.111	0.035	0.130	0.328	0.019	0.023	0.019	0.081
Ireland	–	–	–	–	0.071	0.015	0.028	0.002
Italy	0.174	0.096	0.143	0.160	0.067	−0.026	0.036	0.014
Japan	–	–	–	0.327	–	–	–	0.039
Netherlands	0.077	0.446	0.637	1.346	0.174	0.276	0.188	0.526
Norway	–	0.328	0.092	0.930	–	0.011	0.004	0.366
Spain	0.095	0.088	0.225	2.257	0.195	0.531	0.160	0.048
Sweden	0.580	1.089	0.802	3.613	0.191	0.246	0.518	1.410
Switzerland	–	0.671	0.538	2.120	0.817	0.049	0.027	0.153
United Kingdom	0.454	0.394	0.455	0.837	0.092	0.121	0.082	0.097
United States	0.088	0.161	0.311	0.335	0.068	0.059	0.031	0.094

Source: OECD, Source OECD, International Direct Investment.

was the demographic effect on national savings rates. Large segments of the populations in the developed economies were in the middle of their careers during the 1990s, at earnings level peaks that filled tax coffers, drove down public deficits, and increased savings rates. Lower interest rates in the developed nations attracted capital owners to the higher-yielding investment prospects of the developing economies. The 1997 World Bank Policy Research Report suggests the trend also reflects the growing integration of world capital markets and the globalization of investments.[24]

---

[24] World Bank, *Private Capital Flows to Developing Countries: The Road to Financial Integration* (New York: Oxford University Press, 1997).

TWELVE

Macroeconomic Policies for Improved Living Standards

Throughout much of this discussion, we have emphasized the need to consider the implications of population aging within the broader context of the macroeconomic burden that aging dependency will pose across all segments of societies. Discussions of population aging often devolve into debates over how to reduce pension costs or the more general costs of government operations. An alternative approach is to explore policies and institutional changes that would promote economic growth. Economic growth both supports rising standards of living and fills the public coffers that finance public pension programs.

In this section, we look at several scenarios in which countries can pursue enhanced economic growth. Namely, we estimate how the growth in standards of living would change if policies were adopted to: 1) increase workforce activity rates and 2) enhance labor efficiency. In addition, we sort through how increasing economic growth can raise standards of living for both the elderly and non-elderly segments of the population.

No one disputes the prediction that population aging will increase the future costs of public pension and health care programs. In recent decades, rising age-related spending has been exacerbated by the trends toward earlier retirement and longer life expectancy. The combination of these two trends has reduced tax contributions and increased retirement expenditures because more pensioners are collecting their retirement benefits for longer periods of time.

Pursuing Higher Labor Force Participation Levels

One way countries can dampen the effects of population aging on pension costs is to reverse early retirement trends, thus increasing labor supply.

Increasing the labor supply is more than just an early retirement issue, however, as many societies also have other segments of the population – namely women and younger workers – with relatively low labor force participation rates. Countries able to entice greater numbers of women and younger workers into the labor force and to encourage older workers to delay retirement will push up rates of economic activity, which would certainly ameliorate some of the cost burdens anticipated from their aging populations. As Table 12-1 shows, labor force participation rates vary widely for males and females across the developed societies. Given the variations in labor market activity of the working-age populations across the world's developed societies, the ability of countries to stimulate their own economic growth through labor market mechanisms will vary widely as well.

Some analyses of aging issues manipulate retirement ages to reduce dependency ratios or calculate benefit reductions in order to control pension costs in the future. While this may help to convey the scope of the problems various countries face, it is probably not realistic. For example, it seems unlikely that Austria or Italy will drive up their average retirement ages from around age 60 today to 75 by 2020.

We have taken a somewhat different approach in assessing what countries might do in response to the increasing aging dependency that demographic patterns now suggest. Across some important labor market variables, we have considered what would happen if various countries were able to match behavior already being achieved by a number of other countries. For example, older males in Austria, Finland, France, and Germany would have to work quite a bit more to match workforce participation rates in many other countries. In fact, males ages 55 to 64 in Austria and France would need to more than double their workforce participation to catch up to their counterparts in Japan and Iceland. Female labor force participation rates in Ireland, Italy, Korea, and Spain lag far behind those in many other countries. In many of the Nordic countries, labor force participation rates for women are 20 to 25 percent higher than those in other developed societies. Iceland has some of the highest workforce participation rates in the world for older people and women.

To give a sense of how much room for improvement there is across the developed societies, we start with estimates of the median of the Top-5 labor force participation rates for males and females for various age groups across the range of countries covered in Table 12-1. The Top-5 countries in each category have labor market policies and institutional frameworks that promote economically healthy rates of workforce participation for

Table 12-1. *Labor Force Participation Rates for Males and Females at Various Ages*

	Male LFPRs – 2000				Female LFPRs – 2000			
	15–24	25–54	55–64	65+	15–24	25–54	55–64	65+
Australia	69.7	90.3	61.5	9.9	68.1	70.7	36.3	2.9
Austria	61.8	93.3	42.7	3.8	51.1	75.6	17.4	1.7
Belgium	38.8	92.1	36.5	2.2	32.6	73.1	15.9	1.1
Canada	65.8	91.1	61.0	9.5	62.8	78.6	41.6	3.3
Czech Republic	51.3	94.9	54.5	6.8	40.6	81.8	23.6	2.4
Denmark	75.4	91.5	64.3	3.9	68.6	84.4	48.4	1.6
Finland	50.6	90.8	48.8	4.1	50.7	85.0	45.4	1.1
France	33.2	94.1	41.5	1.9	26.2	78.4	32.7	0.9
Germany	57.6	95.9	53.6	4.6	48.0	77.0	32.9	1.7
Greece	43.5	94.5	58.5	8.4	36.1	62.2	25.7	2.7
Hungary	43.8	84.5	34.1	2.5	32.9	70.3	13.3	1.1
Iceland	70.2	96.1	94.7	29.0	73.3	88.1	76.8	12.0
Ireland	56.7	92.0	64.9	14.7	47.1	64.9	27.9	2.9
Italy	44.6	90.6	42.6	5.8	34.1	57.9	15.9	1.6
Japan	47.4	97.1	84.1	34.1	46.6	66.5	49.7	14.4
Luxembourg	37.7	94.1	38.3	2.3	30.5	64.5	16.8	1.2
Mexico	69.8	96.3	81.3	50.1	36.4	45.7	28.8	14.5
Netherlands	71.0	93.4	48.5	5.4	70.6	71.4	23.9	1.3
New Zealand	65.9	91.3	72.3	11.8	59.8	73.8	48.1	4.4
Norway	66.0	91.4	74.5	7.7	60.8	83.5	61.5	3.8
Poland	40.0	88.5	40.4	12.4	33.1	76.6	23.7	5.2
Portugal	51.6	92.7	65.0	25.4	42.1	77.2	42.3	13.5
Korea	31.9	91.9	71.0	39.8	37.1	57.5	48.2	22.5
Slovak Republic	51.7	93.9	40.8	2.0	42.6	82.8	10.7	0.6
Spain	51.5	92.9	60.2	2.5	41.1	63.1	22.7	0.9
Sweden	51.1	90.6	72.8	7.9	49.8	85.6	66.0	2.8
Switzerland	70.5	96.7	79.3	14.3	66.0	78.0	62.4	8.2
Turkey	58.7	89.4	53.1	32.0	27.2	28.0	19.9	10.4
United Kingdom	72.6	91.8	63.2	7.9	65.1	76.1	42.8	3.4
United States	67.3	91.6	67.3	17.5	62.0	76.8	51.8	9.4
Top 5 LFPRs	**71.0**	**96.3**	**81.3**	**34.1**	**68.6**	**85.0**	**62.4**	**14.4**

Source: The OECD Labour Market Statistics Database found at: http://www1.oecd.org/scripts/
cde/members/LFSDATAAuthenticate.asp.

those age/gender groups. In some sense, the countries in the Top-5 can
be seen as having the "best practice" levels of labor force participation.
Of course, policies that succeed in one society may be less successful in
another, as each country faces its own unique set of challenges. However,
what has been achieved in one developed country can often be replicated
in others if the right environmental factors and incentives are put in place.

For countries whose current workforce participation rates are relatively low, we explore what would happen to their GDP if they matched the workforce levels achieved by the Top-5 countries. In the initial analysis, we assume that 1990s rates of improvement in labor productivity would persist into the future. The baseline scenario assumes that age and gender workforce patterns of the late 1990s persist into the next decade, and projects that demographic aging will be a significant drag on GDP. Table 12-2 shows estimates of the boost to standards of living that could be attained by achieving workforce participation rates commensurate with the Top-5 countries in each age and gender group by 2030.

Absent improvements in workforce participation, countries such as the United States, Spain, New Zealand, and Portugal could witness declines in the average annual rates of growth in GDP per capita of between 0.8 and 1.0 percentage points over the coming decades.[1] But if these countries could achieve the Top-5 labor force activity rates, most of them would enjoy significant increases in per capita GDP growth between 2000 and 2030. This would go a long way toward ameliorating the burdens of aging populations and would enable several countries to maintain their 1990s rates of GDP growth. In many cases, however, workforce behaviors would have to change radically over the next three decades to achieve the best-practice labor force activity rates. And there are limits to the extent that economic growth can be increased through higher labor force participation rates.

Potentially one of the most important messages from Table 12-2 is that the evolving demographic forecast, which is often considered primarily a retirement problem, may be addressed more effectively from the broader perspective of general dependency and the potential economic productivity of the entire working-age population. In addition to focusing on retirement ages and incentives to encourage workers to delay retirement, policymakers should apply equal scrutiny to educational systems that delay the entry of young people into the workforce and to environmental factors that discourage prime working-age women from doing so as well.

Pursuing Higher Rates of Productivity Growth

Another way to stimulate growth in standards of living is to improve labor efficiency. As described throughout this analysis, stimulating productivity

---

[1] Similar estimates by the European Policy Committee show that the annual average rate of growth in GDP per capita, relative to the baseline of no demographic aging, is expected to decline by around 0.4 of a percentage point in the EU and Japan, and by 0.25 of a percentage point in the United States (EPC, October 2003).

Table 12-2. *Growth in Standards of Living under Alternative Labor Force Scenarios*

| | Growth in GDP per Capita | | | Growth in GDP per Capita at 1990s Productivity Growth | |
	1970s	1980s	1990s	Base LFPR 2000–2030	Top-5 LFPR 2000–2030
Australia	1.34	1.69	2.24	1.79	2.51
Austria	3.50	2.16	1.81	1.36	2.61
Belgium	3.16	1.92	1.87	1.16	2.61
Canada	2.83	1.52	1.76	1.14	1.83
Denmark	1.84	1.90	1.93	1.67	2.29
Finland	3.09	2.67	1.81	2.54	3.47
France	2.66	1.84	1.50	0.84	2.05
Germany	2.61	2.02	1.27	1.03	2.02
Greece	3.64	0.23	1.83	1.51	2.74
Iceland	5.18	1.61	1.46	0.21	0.19
Ireland	3.26	3.32	6.43	3.17	4.05
Italy	3.09	2.21	1.38	1.03	2.69
Japan	3.28	3.53	1.17	0.85	1.37
Luxembourg	1.85	4.42	3.96	1.62	2.91
Mexico	3.26	−0.33	1.66	1.07	1.80
Netherlands	2.08	1.62	2.25	0.73	1.72
New Zealand	0.46	1.86	1.70	0.70	1.32
Norway	4.21	2.02	2.80	1.99	2.49
Portugal	3.44	3.19	2.67	1.71	2.27
Korea	5.80	7.61	5.18	4.44	5.11
Spain	2.47	2.58	2.38	0.91	2.23
Sweden	1.60	1.87	1.40	2.25	2.91
Switzerland	1.19	1.54	0.18	0.22	0.70
Turkey	1.78	2.77	1.70	2.93	4.47
United Kingdom	1.81	2.46	1.94	1.61	2.32
United States	2.12	2.23	2.21	1.29	1.78

Sources: OECD Economic Outlook – Source OECD Database; United Nations Population Division, *World Population Prospects: The 2000 Revision*; OECD Labour Market Statistics Database at http://www1.oecd.org/scripts/cde/members/LFSDATAAuthenticate.asp.

growth can occur through many channels. Countries that enact policies that improve the efficiency of their workforces could realize modest improvements in standards of living over the next few decades. Under the productivity improvement scenario, we assume that each country is able to increase its average annual rate of productivity growth between 2000 and 2030 by one-third its 1990s rate.

Table 12-3. *Growth in Standards of Living under Alternative Labor Force and Productivity Scenarios*

| | Growth in GDP per Capita | | | One-Third Increase in 1990s Productivity Growth | |
| | | | | Base LFPR | Top-5 LFPR |
	1970s	1980s	1990s	2000–2030	2000–2030
Australia	1.34	1.69	2.24	2.56	3.18
Austria	3.50	2.16	1.81	2.07	3.27
Belgium	3.16	1.92	1.87	1.94	3.15
Canada	2.83	1.52	1.76	1.71	2.33
Denmark	1.84	1.90	1.93	2.29	2.97
Finland	3.09	2.67	1.81	3.35	4.47
France	2.66	1.84	1.50	1.24	2.46
Germany	2.61	2.02	1.27	1.60	2.52
Greece	3.64	0.23	1.83	2.41	3.32
Iceland	5.18	1.61	1.46	0.38	0.28
Ireland	3.26	3.32	6.43	4.75	5.14
Italy	3.09	2.21	1.38	1.60	3.21
Japan	3.28	3.53	1.17	1.32	1.74
Luxembourg	1.85	4.42	3.96	2.59	3.51
Mexico	3.26	−0.33	1.66	1.58	2.03
Netherlands	2.08	1.62	2.25	1.47	2.14
New Zealand	0.46	1.86	1.70	1.14	1.62
Norway	4.21	2.02	2.80	2.84	3.23
Portugal	3.44	3.19	2.67	2.47	2.88
Korea	5.80	7.61	5.18	6.09	6.62
Spain	2.47	2.58	2.38	1.82	2.67
Sweden	1.60	1.87	1.40	2.85	3.74
Switzerland	1.19	1.54	0.18	0.55	0.92
Turkey	1.78	2.77	1.70	3.67	5.38
United Kingdom	1.81	2.46	1.94	2.31	2.97
United States	2.12	2.23	2.21	1.85	2.27

Sources: OECD Economic Outlook – Source OECD Database; United Nations Population Division, *World Population Prospects: The 2000 Revision*; OECD Labour Market Statistics Database at http://www1.oecd.org/scripts/cde/members/LFSDATAAuthenticate.asp.

Table 12-3 shows the results of this simulation, which indicate that, in many countries, productivity advancements would increase GDP per capita to about the same extent achieved by better labor utilization. For example, in the United States, increasing productivity growth from roughly 1.5 to 2.0 percent per year over the coming three decades would raise the average annual growth in standards of living to 1.85 percent per annum, from our baseline estimate of 1.36 percent per year. This is

Table 12-4. *Annual Growth in per Capita Consumption Apportioned between the Elderly and Non-Elderly Population with the Non-Elderly Receiving the Residual*

	Total Consumption per Capita	Active Workers and Dependents per Capita	Elderly Population per Capita	Total Consumption per Capita	Active Workers and Dependents per Capita	Elderly Population per Capita
	Base Labor Force and Productivity			Alternative Labor Force and Base Productivity		
	2000–2030	2000–2030	2000–2030	2000–2030	2000–2030	2000–2030
Australia	1.79	1.77	2.05	2.51	2.69	2.05
Austria	1.36	1.17	1.99	2.61	3.01	1.99
Belgium	1.16	1.06	1.62	2.61	3.03	1.62
Canada	1.14	1.11	1.50	1.83	2.01	1.50
Czech Republic	2.22	2.21	2.50	3.08	3.37	2.50
Denmark	1.67	1.62	2.07	2.29	2.45	2.07
Finland	2.54	2.45	3.00	3.47	3.75	3.00
France	0.84	0.78	1.23	2.05	2.36	1.23
Germany	1.03	0.91	1.49	2.02	2.35	1.49
Greece	1.51	1.49	1.76	2.74	3.14	1.76
Hungary	3.88	3.86	4.16	5.40	5.84	4.16
Iceland	0.21	0.27	0.27	0.19	0.23	0.27
Ireland	3.17	3.18	3.30	4.05	4.24	3.30
Italy	1.03	0.89	1.54	2.69	3.24	1.54
Japan	0.85	0.84	1.12	1.37	1.60	1.12
Luxembourg	1.62	1.59	1.84	2.91	3.18	1.84
Mexico	1.07	1.16	0.69	1.80	1.99	0.69
Netherlands	0.73	0.62	1.27	1.72	1.99	1.27
New Zealand	0.70	0.72	0.89	1.32	1.51	0.89
Norway	1.99	1.99	2.24	2.49	2.66	2.24
Poland	5.20	5.23	5.38	6.31	6.66	5.38
Portugal	1.71	1.73	1.82	2.27	2.48	1.82
South Korea	4.44	4.50	4.55	5.11	5.37	4.55
Spain	0.91	0.84	1.31	2.23	2.67	1.31
Sweden	2.25	2.27	2.49	2.91	3.18	2.49
Switzerland	0.22	0.16	0.65	0.70	0.88	0.65
Turkey	2.93	2.98	2.78	4.47	4.72	2.78
United Kingdom	1.61	1.58	1.93	2.32	2.54	1.93
United States	1.29	1.30	1.48	1.78	1.93	1.48

Note: The growth in total consumption is based on the feasible rates of GDP growth. This assumes historical productivity growth rates under our (1) baseline and (2) alternative, "best practice" projections of labor force growth. Per capita consumption for the elderly population (ages 60+) is assumed to grow at the 1990s productivity growth rate. Consumption of the non-elderly (ages 0–59) is treated as the residual.
Sources: OECD Economic Outlook – Source OECD Database; United Nations Population Division, *World Population Prospects: The 2000 Revision*; OECD Labour Market Statistics Database at http://www1.oecd.org/scripts/cde/members/LFSDATAAuthenticate.asp.

very similar to the 1.78 percent per year estimates from improvements in labor market utilization (Table 12-4). However, countries with relatively low labor force participation rates for various age and gender groups, such as Spain, Italy, and France, have considerable room for quickening the pace of GDP per capita through employment policies. Combining the two scenarios in the last column of Table 12-5 indicates that most countries could match or even elevate their rates of improvement in standards of living over the next three decades compared to those achieved in the last decades of the twentieth century. This is true even in some of the most rapidly aging societies, such as Japan, Germany, Italy, and Spain.

Enhancing standards of living through higher productivity would certainly provide policymakers with more room to maneuver as they modify their public pension programs over the coming decades, thereby alleviating some of the cost pressures caused by aging populations. However, rising productivity by itself may not alleviate the fiscal burdens of old-age retirement programs, which depend on the linkage between productivity, wages, and retirement benefits.

In many public retirement programs, including those in Germany, Austria, Denmark, Portugal, and the Netherlands, retirement benefits are indexed to earnings. As such, if higher productivity drives up wages, pension benefits will likely rise in lockstep with productivity. So, in countries where retirement benefits are directly linked to productivity growth, rising productivity may not alleviate the future burdens of aging on public retirement programs. In countries that do not link pension benefits to earnings, however, such as Finland, France, Spain, and the United Kingdom, increasing productivity could be a successful strategy for managing rising pension costs.

Spreading the Benefits of Added Economic Growth

Increasing labor force activity and enhancing productivity are positive achievements in their own right, boosting economic growth and thus standards of living. But, how would this greater prosperity be divided among various groups in the society? If public pension benefits grow along with productivity, the elderly would likely be protected from a slowdown in growth. This would shift a large portion of the aging burden onto workers and their dependents, likely slowing growth in workers' standards of living. However, if societies choose to protect workers' claim on their own productivity by reducing benefits, retirees might have to live with slower-growing standards of living over the coming decades.

Table 12-5. *Annual Growth in per Capita Consumption Apportioned between the Elderly and Non-Elderly Population with the Non-Elderly Treated as a Residual*

	Total Consumption per Capita	Active Workers and Dependents per Capita	Elderly Population per Capita	Total Consumption per Capita	Active Workers and Dependents per Capita	Elderly Population per Capita
	Base Labor Force and Productivity			Alternative Labor Force and Productivity		
	2000–2030	2000–2030	2000–2030	2000–2030	2000–2030	2000–2030
Australia	1.79	1.77	2.05	3.18	3.37	2.73
Austria	1.36	1.17	1.99	3.27	3.68	2.65
Belgium	1.16	1.06	1.62	3.15	3.57	2.16
Canada	1.14	1.11	1.50	2.33	2.51	2.00
Czech Republic	2.22	2.21	2.50	3.91	4.20	3.33
Denmark	1.67	1.62	2.07	2.97	3.14	2.75
Finland	2.54	2.45	3.00	4.47	4.75	4.00
France	0.84	0.78	1.23	2.46	2.77	1.65
Germany	1.03	0.91	1.49	2.52	2.85	1.99
Greece	1.51	1.49	1.76	3.32	3.73	2.34
Hungary	3.88	3.86	4.16	6.79	7.24	5.54
Iceland	0.21	0.27	0.27	0.28	0.33	0.37
Ireland	3.17	3.18	3.30	5.14	5.33	4.40
Italy	1.03	0.89	1.54	3.21	3.76	2.06
Japan	0.85	0.84	1.12	1.74	1.97	1.49
Luxembourg	1.62	1.59	1.84	3.51	3.78	2.45
Mexico	1.07	1.16	0.69	2.03	2.22	0.92
Netherlands	0.73	0.62	1.27	2.14	2.42	1.69
New Zealand	0.70	0.72	0.89	1.62	1.80	1.19
Norway	1.99	1.99	2.24	3.23	3.40	2.98
Poland	5.20	5.23	5.38	8.10	8.46	7.17
Portugal	1.71	1.73	1.82	2.88	3.08	2.43
South Korea	4.44	4.50	4.55	6.62	6.88	6.06
Spain	0.91	0.84	1.31	2.67	3.11	1.75
Sweden	2.25	2.27	2.49	3.74	4.01	3.32
Switzerland	0.22	0.16	0.65	0.92	1.10	0.87
Turkey	2.93	2.98	2.78	5.38	5.64	3.70
United Kingdom	1.61	1.58	1.93	2.97	3.18	2.57
United States	1.29	1.30	1.48	2.27	2.41	1.98

Note: The growth in total consumption is based on the feasible rates of GDP growth. This assumes historical productivity growth rates under our (1) baseline and (2) alternative productivity growth rates (one-third increase in 1990's rate) under our "best practice" projections of labor force growth. Per capita consumption for the elderly population (ages 60+) is assumed to grow at the 1990s productivity growth rate. Consumption of the non-elderly (ages 0–59) is treated as the residual.

Sources: OECD Economic Outlook – Source OECD Database; United Nations Population Division, *World Population Prospects: The 2000 Revision*; OECD Labour Market Statistics Database at http://www1.oecd.org/scripts/cde/members/LFSDATAAuthenticate.asp.

We looked at two scenarios. In one scenario, workers shoulder the burden of population aging; in the other, retirees feel the pinch of rising costs in the form of reduced incomes. We built upon the previous scenarios by estimating how economic growth would be shared between the elderly (ages 60+) and non-elderly (ages 0 to 59) when countries are able to boost both workforce participation and productivity. This required us to re-estimate the growth in total consumption expenditures between 2000 and 2030 under the improved workforce participation and higher productivity scenario compared to our baseline scenarios. In dividing total consumption between the elderly and non-elderly, we again used an indexed profile of consumption expenditures by age and assume that each group's average propensity to consume remains constant over the estimation period.

In Table 12-4, we estimate the rates of per capita consumption growth for workers and their dependents and for retirees, assuming that workers bear the costs of aging populations. This scenario assumes that retirees' standards of living will continue improving at the rate of worker productivity over the next three decades. Workers and their dependents will get whatever is left. In this table and the next, we provide our baseline estimates from Table 7-12, which assume current workforce patterns and 1990s productivity growth. To see how changes in economic growth affect the distribution of output between the elderly and non-elderly, we look at two sets of estimates to compare the sensitivity of the distributional effects to varied sources of economic growth. In Table 12-4, we estimate how growth in per capita consumption is affected by higher rates of labor force activity.

As retirees become a greater share of the population, per capita consumption growth for retirees will outpace that of workers and their dependents between 2000 and 2030. This is evident in the second and third columns of Table 12-4, in the way per capita consumption growth for workers and their dependents trails the elderly population in many of the developed societies. If countries are able to adopt policies to entice higher rates of employment across all ages and both genders, higher rates of economic growth will enable workers and their dependents to experience marked increases in standards of living compared to the baseline scenario. In France, Italy, the Netherlands, and Spain, per capita consumption growth for the non-elderly population would be more than three times that of our baseline scenario, while the pace in Germany and Austria would more than double between 2000 and 2030.

Table 12-5 shows our results when we consider changes in both rates of labor utilization and advancements from 1990s productivity growth rates. Combining advancements in productivity with higher labor force activity rates would further raise the levels of affluence for both retirees and workers. As shown in the last column in Table 12-5, this scenario assumes that retirees' per capita consumption increases at one-third the 1990s productivity growth rates. While this certainly adds to retirees' income in retirement, workers and their dependents also show discernible improvements in their standards of living – such that a rising tide lifts all boats. Comparing the estimates between the two scenarios in Table 12-4 and Table 12-5, the non-elderly population stands to see considerable spillover benefits from the increases in economic activity, despite retiree benefits maintaining their share of workers' productivity.

Tables 12-6 is a counterpart to Table 12-4. Here we shift the burden from aging populations back onto retirees. Under this scenario, we assume that the non-elderly population's improvement in standards of living fully reflects their improving productivity and their increasing labor supply. The retiree population receives what is left.

Table 12-6 provides alternative estimates from our baseline scenario whereby total consumption expenditures grow at the combined Top-5 labor utilization rates and 1990s productivity growth. Under the baseline case, retirees in developed nations would have to endure a significant slowdown in standards of living growth. Retirees in roughly half of the nations in the table would actually face declines in per capita consumption between 2000 and 2030. However, adopting policies that entice higher labor force activity rates could partially offset the deterioration in retirees' standards of living. While active workers and dependents will certainly gain from higher rates of labor force growth, some of the benefits of higher growth would also pass to the elderly population. In fact, retirees in countries with relatively lower labor force utilization rates could see their standards of living grow over a full percentage point per annum from the baseline scenario.

Retirees could see even greater improvements in their standards of living, if higher workforce participation rates are matched by advanced rates of productivity growth. As shown in Table 12-7, most retirees would see advances in their standards of living as a result of the advanced economic growth. However, the pace of per capita consumption growth in many societies would still fall short of their most recent increases in worker productivity.

Table 12-6. *Annual Growth in per Capita Consumption Apportioned between the Elderly and Non-Elderly Population with the Elderly Population Treated as a Residual*

	Total Consumption per Capita	Active Workers and Dependents per Capita	Elderly Population per Capita	Total Consumption per Capita	Active Workers and Dependents per Capita	Elderly Population per Capita
	Base Labor Force and Productivity			Alternative Labor Force and Productivity		
	2000–2030	2000–2030	2000–2030	2000–2030	2000–2030	2000–2030
Australia	1.79	2.18	0.26	2.51	2.91	0.95
Austria	1.36	2.11	−0.48	2.61	3.36	0.81
Belgium	1.16	1.67	−0.16	2.61	3.11	1.30
Canada	1.14	1.64	−0.60	1.83	2.33	0.07
Czech Republic	2.22	2.75	0.59	3.08	3.62	1.47
Denmark	1.67	2.15	0.27	2.29	2.76	0.89
Finland	2.54	3.11	0.97	3.47	4.04	1.92
France	0.84	1.26	−0.40	2.05	2.47	0.80
Germany	1.03	1.64	−0.39	2.02	2.62	0.62
Greece	1.51	1.94	0.44	2.74	3.16	1.68
Hungary	3.88	4.33	2.60	5.40	5.84	4.16
Iceland	0.21	0.67	−1.59	0.19	0.65	−1.61
Ireland	3.17	3.45	1.88	4.05	4.34	2.72
Italy	1.03	1.64	−0.33	2.69	3.29	1.37
Japan	0.85	1.50	−0.65	1.37	2.01	−0.12
Luxembourg	1.62	1.85	0.76	2.91	3.15	1.99
Mexico	1.07	1.42	−1.82	1.80	2.16	−1.17
Netherlands	0.73	1.35	−1.13	1.72	2.35	−0.13
New Zealand	0.70	1.14	−1.00	1.32	1.76	−0.39
Norway	1.99	2.44	0.61	2.49	2.94	1.11
Poland	5.20	5.73	3.47	6.31	6.83	4.60
Portugal	1.71	2.07	0.63	2.27	2.64	1.20
South Korea	4.44	5.18	1.35	5.11	5.84	2.02
Spain	0.91	1.50	−0.56	2.23	2.81	0.79
Sweden	2.25	2.79	0.92	2.91	3.45	1.58
Switzerland	0.22	0.99	−1.60	0.70	1.46	−1.11
Turkey	2.93	3.26	0.45	4.47	4.81	1.83
United Kingdom	1.61	2.07	0.31	2.32	2.78	1.02
United States	1.29	1.68	−0.23	1.78	2.17	0.24

Notes: The growth in total consumption is based on the feasible rates of output growth. This assumes historical productivity growth rates under our (1) baseline and (2) alternative "best practice" projections of labor force growth. Consumption for the non-elderly population (ages 0–59) is assumed to grow at the rate of productivity growth plus the growth in the labor force. Consumption for the elderly (ages 60+) is treated as the residual.

Sources: OECD Economic Outlook – Source OECD Database; United Nations Population Division, *World Population Prospects: The 2000 Revision*; OECD Labour Market Statistics Database at http://www1.oecd.org/scripts/cde/members/LFSDATAAuthenticate.asp.

Table 12-7. *Annual Growth in per Capita Consumption Apportioned between the Elderly and Non-Elderly Population with the Elderly Population Treated as a Residual*

	Total Consumption per Capita	Active Workers and Dependents per Capita	Elderly Population per Capita	Total Consumption per Capita	Active Workers and Dependents per Capita	Elderly Population per Capita
	Base Labor Force and Productivity			Alternative Labor Force and Base Productivity		
	2000–2030	2000–2030	2000–2030	2000–2030	2000–2030	2000–2030
Australia	1.79	2.18	0.26	3.18	3.59	1.60
Austria	1.36	2.11	−0.48	3.27	4.02	1.49
Belgium	1.16	1.67	−0.16	3.15	3.65	1.84
Canada	1.14	1.64	−0.60	2.33	2.83	0.55
Czech Republic	2.22	2.75	0.59	3.91	4.45	2.32
Denmark	1.67	2.15	0.27	2.97	3.45	1.58
Finland	2.54	3.11	0.97	4.47	5.04	2.93
France	0.84	1.26	−0.40	2.46	2.88	1.21
Germany	1.03	1.64	−0.39	2.52	3.12	1.12
Greece	1.51	1.94	0.44	3.32	3.75	· 2.27
Hungary	3.88	4.33	2.60	6.79	7.23	5.59
Iceland	0.21	0.67	−1.59	0.28	0.74	−1.52
Ireland	3.17	3.45	1.88	5.14	5.44	3.75
Italy	1.03	1.64	−0.33	3.21	3.80	1.90
Japan	0.85	1.50	−0.65	1.74	2.39	0.26
Luxembourg	1.62	1.85	0.76	3.51	3.76	2.56
Mexico	1.07	1.42	−1.82	2.03	2.39	−0.98
Netherlands	0.73	1.35	−1.13	2.14	2.77	0.30
New Zealand	0.70	1.14	−1.00	1.62	2.06	−0.10
Norway	1.99	2.44	0.61	3.23	3.69	1.84
Poland	5.20	5.73	3.47	8.10	8.63	6.43
Portugal	1.71	2.07	0.63	2.88	3.24	1.81
South Korea	4.44	5.18	1.35	6.62	7.35	3.52
Spain	0.91	1.50	−0.56	2.67	3.24	1.24
Sweden	2.25	2.79	0.92	3.74	4.27	2.42
Switzerland	0.22	0.99	−1.60	0.92	1.68	−0.89
Turkey	2.93	3.26	0.45	5.38	5.73	2.64
United Kingdom	1.61	2.07	0.31	2.97	3.42	1.66
United States	1.29	1.68	−0.23	2.27	2.67	0.71

Notes: The growth in total consumption is based on the feasible rates of output growth. This assumes two scenarios (1) historical productivity growth rates under our baseline projections of labor force growth and (2) alternative productivity growth rates under our "best practice" projections of labor force growth. Consumption for the non-elderly population (ages 0–59) is assumed to grow at the rate of productivity growth plus the growth in the labor force. Consumption of the elderly (ages 60+) is treated as the residual.

Sources: OECD Economic Outlook – Source OECD Database; United Nations Population Division, *World Population Prospects: The 2000 Revision*; OECD Labour Market Statistics Database at http://www1.oecd.org/scripts/cde/members/LFSDATAAuthenticate.asp.

The scenarios show that if countries can entice higher rates of labor force participation and/or promote higher rates of productivity growth, the financial prospects would be a lot brighter for both workers and retirees over the coming decades. While higher rates of economic activity would likely reduce the burden of their aging populations, it may not have enough horsepower to completely insulate public pension programs from the mounting deficits on the horizon. As we have discussed, most national retirement systems throughout the developed world operate on a pay-go basis. In Chapter 4, we showed that two very important ratios determine the cost of the program. The tax rate or cost of these systems, t, is the product of the ratios of beneficiaries under the program to the number of workers contributing to it (Nb/Nw) times the ratio of average benefits to average wages (B/W).

We can use this model to consider how aging populations will affect the ability of countries to meet their benefit obligations under a strict pay-go financing scheme. To estimate the total value of benefits that an individual will receive throughout retirement, we use a simple adjustment to the model described above. Many of the study countries would like to preserve these programs without further increasing the payroll tax rate. So our estimates assume that the payroll tax stays the same. Assuming that the payroll tax rate remains constant, the average benefit, B, would be calculated as follows:

$$B = t \cdot W \cdot (Nw/Nb).$$

The implication of this assumption is that we allowed the average benefit and ultimately the replacement rate to vary over time. The ratio of workers to beneficiaries is declining in every country over the coming decades. So in order for these programs to remain in balance, the income replacement ratios across these countries will fall, unless major changes are made or these countries take on rising levels of debt. As shown in Table 12-8, the average replacement rate would fall over 40 percent across the developed nations over the next three decades. This result closely corresponds with the declines in per capita consumption of the elderly under our baseline scenario, where workers and their dependents are insulated from the burdens of their aging populations. While a number of countries are considering significant changes to their programs, we have not incorporated any of them into this analysis.

How much could increases in economic activity due to higher labor force utilization reduce the growing fiscal pressures of these countries' public pension programs? Achieving the Top-5 workforce participation rates for all ages and both genders would soften the fall of income

Table 12-8. *Changes in Gross Replacement Rates Necessary to Stabilize Pay-Go Funded Pension Programs Assuming Fixed Contribution Rates at 2000 Levels*

		Gross Replacement Rates		Total Growth Rates	
	2000	Base LFPRs 2030	Alt. LFPRs 2030	Base LFPRs 2000–2030	Alt. LFPRs 2000–2030
Australia	52.0	32.0	38.8	−38.5	−25.4
Austria	80.0	37.7	53.9	−52.9	−32.6
Belgium	60.0	37.4	53.7	−37.6	−10.6
Canada	56.4	30.8	37.2	−45.3	−34.0
Czech Republic	44.5	24.6	31.6	−44.6	−28.9
Denmark	22.0	12.5	15.3	−43.4	−30.4
Finland	60.0	30.2	42.3	−49.7	−29.5
France	71.2	43.3	62.4	−39.1	−12.3
Germany	46.3	26.6	35.0	−42.6	−24.5
Greece	46.0	33.6	44.1	−26.9	−4.1
Hungary	84.5	48.3	79.4	−42.9	−6.0
Iceland	73.4	42.8	41.5	−41.7	−43.4
Ireland	30.2	23.8	27.1	−21.1	−10.2
Italy	65.9	37.5	60.5	−43.1	−8.1
Japan	53.1	31.7	35.9	−40.3	−32.4
Luxembourg	71.2	59.0	78.3	−17.1	10.0
Mexico	39.7	21.2	24.4	−46.5	−38.5
Netherlands	70.0	37.1	45.4	−47.0	−35.2
New Zealand	38.0	22.5	26.1	−40.7	−31.3
Norway	52.6	33.3	37.6	−36.7	−28.6
Poland	70.2	37.4	52.7	−46.7	−25.0
Portugal	77.0	56.0	63.3	−27.3	−17.8
Korea	71.0	28.0	33.0	−60.6	−53.5
Slovak Republic	64.7	34.7	45.6	−46.4	−29.5
Spain	88.0	56.9	73.0	−35.4	−17.0
Sweden	76.0	43.4	56.6	−42.9	−25.6
Switzerland	58.2	30.1	33.6	−48.3	−42.3
United Kingdom	36.8	22.9	27.9	−37.8	−24.1
United States	44.8	27.9	31.7	−37.8	−29.2
Unweighted Average	58.7	34.6	44.4	−40.7	−24.8

Sources: OECD Economic Outlook – Source OECD Database; United Nations Population Division, *World Population Prospects: The 2000 Revision*; the OECD Labour Market Statistics Database at http://www1.oecd.org/scripts/cde/members/LFSDATAAuthenticate.asp; Unpublished series from Whitehouse (2002).

replacement rates considerably. Current average replacement rates of 58.7 percent would decline to 44.4 percent under the advanced growth scenario, which is a considerable improvement from the baseline 34.6 percent decline. This would amount to a 30 percent improvement in income replacement rates as a result of expanded labor force utilization.

To the extent higher rates of GDP growth boost both standards of living and government tax coffers, it will indeed open a window of opportunity for industrialized nations faced with the task of overhauling their public pension programs while reducing the burdens on their populations at large. But, these partial estimates do not recognize the extent to which higher per capita output feeds back into public pension expenditures. This ultimately depends on the programs' institutional framework as well as on the mechanism by which output is increased. There may be additional pressures for spending on public pensions if economic activity receives a boost. These estimates also do not account for the higher taxes and payroll contributions that are likely with increases in output. To fully understand the impact of enhancements of economic growth on public pension expenditures would require a general equilibrium approach. So, while higher economic growth should certainly ease the fiscal pressures of declining aging populations, it would not justify complacency about future pension obligations. Even countries that have made progress should stay the course, pursuing avenues to promote adequacy, financial sustainability, and modernization of the pension systems.

Investing in Developing Economies

The discussion so far has been about the potential implications of changing labor force participation rates or productivity growth rates within the domestic economies of aging nations. But as we saw earlier, increases in pension funding that create additional savings can promote economic growth through added capital investment. However, as we also noted in earlier chapters, countries will need to look beyond their own borders for investment opportunities, as higher rates of capital deepening would likely be a drag on capital returns across the developed economies.

While certain benefits may be realized from capital owners in the developed economies investing abroad, this option has its own risks. The shocking realities of the risks faced by capital owners investing in developing nations are often played out through high financial market instability – the worst of which end up as crises. This was made readily apparent with the 1995 Tequila crisis in Mexico, the Asian crisis of 1997–98, and the Russian and Latin American crises in 1998–2000.

In most cases, crises are the result of massive financial inflows – especially portfolio flows – not being channeled to the most productive investment opportunities, leading to a progressive deterioration in the balance sheets of the domestic financial sector. Without adequate capital controls to limit the flight of capital, these countries are subject to sudden reversals, which could decimate domestic financial markets. This high volatility reflects the limited depth of financial markets in many developing countries, as well as the maturity mismatch in trying to finance long-term projects with short-term money.[2] These risks, which have come to rattle the emerging markets in recent years, have certainly undermined investor confidence and hampered the returns to global financial integration. The degree of financial volatility, crises, and contagion has made the current state of affairs socially costly and politically disappointing in emerging economies.[3]

To avoid the hardships of capital reversals while continuing to liberalize the financial markets will require developing countries to pursue policies that maximize the benefits from global capital flows and avoid the associated dangers. The World Bank policy research report suggests that developing nations must pursue a sound macroeconomic policy framework, a sound domestic banking system with a supervisory and regulatory framework, and a well-functioning market infrastructure and regulatory framework for capital markets.[4] Many countries have made significant changes to their regulatory structures to open their financial markets. But the 1997 World Bank Report contends that many of the countries "lack the prerequisites for a smooth journey, and some may be so ill prepared that they lose more than they gain from financial integration."[5] While the path toward financial liberalization is inevitable with advancements in communication and new developments in finance, the developing countries may decide at what pace they wish to travel to avoid the potential pitfalls of opening their financial markets.

Getting the economic infrastructure in place in the world's developing countries is only part of the challenge that both the developed and developing segments of the world face. The countries in the groups

---

[2] Eduardo Fernandez-Arias and Ricardo Hausmann, "Is FDI a Safer Form of Financing," *Inter-American Development Bank*, (2000a), Working Paper #416.

[3] Eduardo Fernandez-Arias and Ricardo Hausmann, "What's Wrong with International Financial Markets," *Inter-American Development Bank*, (2000b), Working Paper #429.

[4] World Bank, *Private Capital Flows to Developing Countries: The Road to Financial Integration* (New York: Oxford University Press, 1997).

[5] Ibid, p. 1.

Table 12-9. *Starting-a-Business Indicators: Procedural, Cost and Capital Requirements to Formally Start a Business in Various Developing Countries*

	Number of Procedures	Duration (Days)	Cost (% of Income per Capita)	Min. Capital (% of Income per Capita)
East Asia & Pacific	8	66	57	647
Europe & Central Asia	10	47	22	114
Latin America & Caribbean	12	74	70	86
Middle East & North Africa	11	50	55	1104
OECD: High income	7	30	10	61
South Asia	8	44	76	86
Sub-Saharan Africa	11	71	255	278
Argentina	15	68	8	0
Brazil	15	152	12	0
China	11	46	14	3856
India	10	88	50	430
Indonesia	11	168	15	303
Malaysia	8	31	27	0
Mexico	7	51	19	88
Philippines	11	59	24	10
Russian Federation	12	29	9	30
Singapore	7	8	1	0
Thailand	9	42	7	0
Turkey	13	38	37	13
Venezuela	14	119	19	0

Source: World Bank (2004), "Doing Business in 2004: Understanding Regulation," http://rru.worldbank.org/DoingBusiness/default.aspx.

listed in Table 12-9 in the general geographic proximity of Europe have predominantly Islamic populations. The two countries with the largest populations in the Southeast Asian segment, in the geographic proximity of Japan, are the Philippines and Indonesia – again countries with sizeable Islamic populations. At the beginning of the twenty-first century, many of the nations with predominantly Islamic populations seem to be at political odds with many of the nations in the developed world in one way or another. These tensions will have to be resolved in some mutually agreeable fashion, if anyone expects to see significant investment flows from the developed countries to these less developed ones.

There are other potential barriers to significant investment by foreign capital owners in some parts of the developing world. Capital owners cannot invest in opportunities without a reasonable legal framework of regulatory and civil law that is enforced on an evenhanded basis. The legal registration and disclosure requirements imposed on entities based in the developed economies of the world require that business dealings be aboveboard and open to review. There also has to be a statute- and case-based legal system that allows disputants in business deals to resolve differences that might arise on a timely basis.

Other major impediments to higher rates of foreign investment are the complications companies face in formally starting up business operations in another country. Cumbersome entry procedures not only limit foreign investment but can have many other undesirable effects such as less competitive prices, higher corruption, and the escape of entrepreneurs to the informal sector of the economy. These sorts of problems create inefficiencies and limit economic growth and returns on capital.

A recent report by the World Bank evaluates and classifies the sorts of entry regulations and hurdles faced by an entrepreneur trying to legally establish and operate a business in various countries. To make the businesses comparable across countries, the study is restricted to limited liability companies that operate in the most populous city and are wholly owed domestic operations. In addition, the report considers only those procedures that are required in all but exceptional cases or businesses.

The World Bank study divides the process of starting a business into distinct procedures for the purpose of estimating the costs and time necessary to accomplish each requirement. Table 12-9 provides estimates for each of the indicators of time, cost, and minimum capital requirements for various countries. The time measurement captures the average amount of time it takes an entrepreneur to complete each of the procedures and assumes that the entrepreneur completes the process in the fastest means possible, independent of cost. Cost estimates represent those from the official legal fee schedules. If no official schedule is available for a particular procedure, a government officer's estimates or estimates of incorporation lawyers are used as the source. In addition to the regulatory costs associated with setting up a business, the minimum amount of capital required to establish the business varies considerably from country to country. The minimum amount of capital reflects the amount that the business needs to deposit in a bank account to obtain a business registration number. The minimum deposit is typically specified by the Commercial Code or the Company Law.

As Table 12-9 indicates, on average, the OECD nations have the fewest number of procedures and thus require the least time commitment to set up a new business operation. While it takes approximately 30 days to create a limited liability entity in the developed nations, it requires over twice that amount of time in many of the East Asian and Latin American countries. In fact, it takes over five times as long in both Brazil and Indonesia. Not surprisingly, the cost of establishing a business is highly related to how long the process takes. Establishing a business is rather inexpensive across the OECD nations, roughly 10 percent of an average citizen's income. Costs in Asia and Latin America are quite a bit higher. For example, an entrepreneur in India must spend roughly half the average person's income to meet all of the procedural requirements of starting a business. But it can be quite inexpensive to start a business in Singapore, Thailand, and Russia. China is also relatively inexpensive, costing on average 14 percent of per capita income. But while its procedural costs are relatively low, China requires very high minimum capital investment to start a company. In fact, it requires over 60 times more capital as a percentage of average income to create a company in China as it does in the average OECD nation. India and Indonesia also have very high minimum capital requirements. However, many of the Latin American countries such as Argentina and Brazil require none at all.

Concerns about the financial markets and the political and legal infrastructures in many parts of the developing world have left investors wary about investing in developing markets. Instead, many foreign investors, in particular pension funds, maintain a "home bias" and invest the greatest portion of their assets domestically. Robert Holzmann reports that in 1995, the earliest data that was available, OECD countries invested nearly 89 percent of their pension assets in their own domestic markets.[6] This is not particular to the developed economies, as 99.3 percent of non-OECD pension assets were invested within each country's domestic borders. The tendency for pension funds to stay in their home country results partly from the lack of investor confidence, but largely from the restrictions many countries impose on the investment of pension assets in foreign securities. As long as such barriers exist, both the developed and the developing countries will miss out on the potential benefits from greater integration of the developed and developing economies.

---

[6] Robert Holzmann, "Can Investments in Emerging Markets Help to Solve the Aging Problem?" (The World Bank: Social Protection Discussion Paper, May 19, 2000), No. 00010.

A recent analysis of foreign direct investment (FDI) in China by the International Monetary Fund identifies some of the benefits and pitfalls a developing country faces as foreign investors make inroads into their economies. The report quotes China's Statistical Yearbook as showing that FDI inflows into China have increased from $2.3 billion per year in the late 1980s to $40.6 billion during the late 1990s. While these estimates might be slightly exaggerated, the IMF concludes that FDI in 1996 was at least $38 billion. In 1999, 28 percent of the FDI came from the European Union, United States, and Japan. Sixty percent of the investment was directed toward manufacturing and 24 percent to real estate. For regulatory reasons, investments have been concentrated largely in the coastal provinces in eastern China.[7]

The IMF study concludes that low labor costs appear to have played a significant role in attracting FDI to China. Within China, the provinces with more developed infrastructure have attracted more of the foreign investment funds. There is evidence of signaling effects such that once a province reaches a critical mass of FDI, it becomes easier to attract more. One of the critical factors in increasing FDI has been the deliberate effort undertaken by the Chinese government to create a legal framework where foreign investors feel comfortable.

One of the hurdles that China has had to contend with in attracting foreign investment is the perception that its legal system is ambiguous, and that disputes are settled through personal contacts rather than controlled by formal contracts and court enforcement. China scores poorly relative to the developed countries on corruption and governance indicators. The IMF notes that this has inhibited investment more from the United States and Europe than from Hong Kong.

While there have been some hurdles to overcome in expanding foreign investment in China, the results suggest the potential that developing countries can realize by addressing the issues that inhibit the inflow of capital. The added capital flowing into the Chinese economy added 0.4 percentage points to its GDP growth rate during the 1990s. Empirical estimates suggest that foreign investment has added an additional 2.5 percentage points of growth in GDP per year in the 1990s because it raised total factor productivity. Output from foreign-funded enterprises (FFEs) grew at four times the rate of the domestic industrial enterprises during the 1994 to 1997 period, and labor productivity was twice that of publicly

---

[7] Wanda Tseng and Harm Zebregs, "Foreign Direct Investment in China: Some Lessons for Other Countries," International Monetary Fund, February 2002, IMF Policy Discussion Paper.

owned enterprises. Employment at FFEs between 1991 and 1999 grew from 1.5 million to 6 million workers.

In the late 1970s, when China began opening its economy, its GDP per capita was $225 in U.S. dollars, very close to India's at $197. By 2000, India, which was still largely a closed economy, had doubled its GDP per capita while China had quadrupled its. In 1978, India's and China's exports were 4.6 and 5.1 percent of GDP, respectively. By 2000, they were 9.2 and 19.1 percent of GDP, respectively. Net inward FDI flows had increased from nothing in the two countries at the beginning of the period to 3.6 percent of GDP in China compared to 0.4 percent in India in 2000. FDI represented 9.8 percent of total investment in China in 2000 compared to 1.9 percent in India. The IMF report concludes, "FDI will continue to be an important source of growth and will help offset potential output losses and create employment opportunities for workers that have become redundant in state enterprise and banking reforms. It is significant that the Chinese authorities have invited foreign participation in restructuring of state-owned enterprises and the resolution of the nonperforming loan problems in the banking sector."[8]

In parts of the developed world today, there is a growing sense of angst about the movement of capital and jobs from the local economies to the developing ones. There is a concern that wealthy capital owners are simply moving their assets to areas where cheap labor is available and where greater profitability will make the already wealthy capitalists even wealthier yet. For example, a recent editorial in the *Washington Post* argued: "Outsourcing has turned the phrase "investment-led growth" into the grimmest of oxymorons. It means that Bush's tax policy subsidizes job growth in India and China rather than the United States. And in failing to create more employment here at home, the tax cuts have also helped depress wages." The editorial concludes that the burden of proof is on policymakers "to demonstrate how private investment in a global economy creates jobs here at home. And why the hell our tax policy should boost income in Bangalore, not Baltimore."[9]

The phenomenon of jobs moving from the United States to less developed countries has gotten so much attention lately that it now has a name: offshoring. The issue that will become increasingly critical for public policymakers in the United States and other developed countries is how to structure public policies to best utilize their national savings.

---

[8] Ibid., p. 22.
[9] Harold Meyerson, "Good for Investors, Bad for the Rest," *Washington Post* (January 14, 2004), p. A-19.

As with many public policy issues, there will be both short- and long-term perspectives and these may often conflict. Japan is a case study. With its economy in the doldrums over much of the past decade, the government has run repeated stimulus programs in an effort to jump-start economic growth. These efforts have cost some ¥136 trillion, of which about 45 percent has been spent on public works projects, a short-term boon to construction companies and their workers but probably not a long-term "investment" warranted by economic considerations. An example of the sorts of projects that have been included is the "airport in the ocean" built in Osaka Bay.

This airport was conceived back in the 1970s. It required the building of a 500-hectare or 1,300-acre island in water an average of 18 meters or 60 feet deep, and the construction of elevated expressways and rail lines to the island doubled the cost. Building the airport required 30 meters of fill bringing the surface four meters above sea level to guarantee that the airport would not be swamped by the high tides associated with the typhoons that hit the coast every September. The extra seven to 10 meters over the 18-meter depth of the water and four-meter height of the island was to compensate for settlement of the fill. But abnormal settlement during construction required an added three meters of fill. Cost overruns were significant.[10]

The airport opened in September 1994. From the outset, it has been beset by problems. A recent article in *Japan, Inc.* describes it as:

one of the most appealing structures of its kind – not just in Japan, but anywhere in the world. Designed by Italian architect Renzo Piano, the four-story structure is a 1.7 kilometer-long aluminum and glass frame topped off with a roof which arcs in the shape of an undulating wing. Over the past few years, using the airport has become an increasing pleasure – if you enjoy the misfortune of others. Fewer and fewer airlines are landing at or taking off from KIX, due to a steep decline in passenger demand. Peak travel times aside, the place often feels virtually deserted. Indeed, when catching a recent red-eye to Bangkok, I felt like the only traveler in the whole airport. Designed to offer a liberating sense of space and freedom, the terminal's strength becomes its weakness when deprived of its lifeblood–the myriad passengers who should be scurrying to and fro, forming the background hubbub and endless shuffle of any truly international airport.[11]

---

[10] Richard deNeufville, Department of Civil Engineering at the Massachusetts Institute of Technology, "Airport Development in Japan," found at: http://ardent.mit.edu/airports/ASP_papers/airport%20development%20in%20Japan.PDF.

[11] Dominic Al-Badri, "Kansai Airport: A Beautiful Loser: Kansai International Is Stunning – But Sinking into Debt and Desolation. Care for a Date?," *Japan, Inc.* (September 200d3), found at: http://www.findarticles.com/cf_dls/m0NTN/47/108722609/p1/article.jhtml?term=.

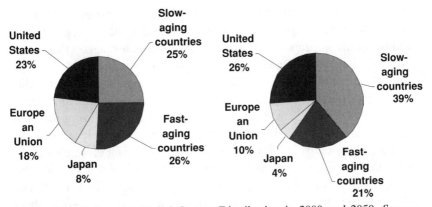

Figure 12-1. Estimated Global Output Distribution in 2000 and 2050. *Source:* European Commission, Office of Economic and Financial Analysis, March 2003.

Since its opening, the airport has continued to be plagued by a variety of problems. In 2000, it was reported that the man-made island it was built upon was sinking into the ocean more rapidly than anticipated. Domestic travelers find the location of the new airport inconvenient and continue to use the old airport instead. Landing fees are the highest in the world. As a result of low utilization and high operating costs, many airlines have cut back on using the airport, so traffic loads are much lighter than expected. In October 2003, All Nippon Airways gave up office space on which it was paying ¥400 million a year.[12] There are many other similar examples where public works projects in Japan have not worked out according to plan.

The point here is not to single out Japan but to show how aging countries run the risk of squandering their savings on "investments" that have little potential of providing long-term returns of any significant value. From 1983 through 2003, Japan's gross public debt rose from 68.4 percent of GDP in 1992 to 147.3 percent; its net financial liabilities as a percentage of GDP rose from 14.5 to 71.8 percent.[13] Much of this went to finance the sort of public works projects just described.

The European Commission has developed a general equilibrium model to analyze the implications of the demographic evolution of the world's economies over the half century beginning in 2000. The summary results of their analysis are represented in Figure 12-1, which shows the estimated distribution of global output in 2000 and 2050. The population shifts that

[12] Ibid.
[13] Ibid.

are now underway imply that a far smaller share of the world's output will be produced in the rapidly aging societies, including the European Union and Japan, in the future than it is now. The EC estimates suggest that unless current policies are changed, GDP per capita will grow in the future at 1.25 percent per year in the European Union and Japan, and could possibly dip below 1 percent per year.[14] These results are consistent with ours.

Our analysis suggests that changing labor force behavior, some capital deepening, and utilizing human capital more effectively all have the potential to avoid some of the economic dangers lying in wait for aging societies. But even if the most rapidly aging economies do all of these things right, they may still meet with slowing economic growth by the end of this decade or during the next one. The only way that we see for these countries to get economic production where it needs to be in order to keep living standards on the rise is by tapping the increasing economic capacity of other societies. The only legitimate path to this outcome that we can see is through an investment process – whereby the rich countries invest in the developing countries, thereby increasing labor productivity in the latter. Years down the road, as developed societies' ability to produce enough output to satisfy their needs becomes limited by labor force realities, the returns on the foreign investment could augment domestic production, helping to satisfy consumer demands that otherwise may go unmet.

It is a mistake to conclude that the capital that is flowing across national borders today is simply the booty of the rich seeking high returns through utilization by low-cost labor. At the end of 2002, private employer-sponsored defined benefit and defined contribution plans in the United States held $3.5 trillion in assets between them. Privately held individual retirement accounts had another $2.3 trillion. These assets may be somewhat more concentrated among higher earners than lower earners, but they are broadly distributed across some two-thirds of the U.S. workforce and retiree populations. Many of these trillions of dollars are either invested directly in other economies through pooled international funds offered by investment companies or indirectly through holding of equities in U.S. domestic companies with significant foreign direct investment holdings outside the United States. This and similar mechanisms elsewhere in the developed economies offer tremendous potential to diversify the flow of capital to the developing markets of the world and to spread the potential long-term rewards broadly across the future retiree populations in the rich but aging societies.

[14] Ibid.

THIRTEEN

Risks Associated with Alternative Public Policies

The industrialized nations face considerable economic challenges in the years ahead. In a macroeconomic context, they must try to keep standards of living on an upward trajectory and to allocate these improvements equitably across their populations. In earlier chapters, we noted that retirement systems are fundamental to this allocation process, serving to transfer economic resources from workers to retirees. In the future, pension and health care programs will become the crucial linkage between the macroeconomic prosperity of aging societies and the relative welfare of all segments within them.

The European Commission (EC), the OECD, the World Bank, and various other entities have projected much higher costs for the pension systems in nearly all developed nations under their current policies. The evidence so far indicates that most of these countries have yet to take measures to reduce costs in ways that do not jeopardize income adequacy for retirees of the future.[1]

The EC has identified a number of objectives that encompass three main economic goals: income adequacy for dependent populations; financial sustainability, not only of pension systems but of the entities that support them; and modernization of pension systems. Countries with high debt ratios need to adopt measures for budgetary consolidation. Enacting policies that promote longer working careers and higher workforce

---

[1] European Commission. (2003) "Joint Report by the Commission and the Council on Adequate and Sustainable Pensions," Communication from the Commission to the Council, the European Parliament, the European Economic and Social Committee, and the Committee of the Regions, March.

activity rates are an important strategy in making pensions sustainable. And the EC suggests that adapting public pension programs as well as secondary pillar schemes to serve today's more flexible employment and career patterns could play an important part in providing diversified forms of pension income in retirement. But the EC also strongly emphasizes that the key to successful pension reforms is for policies to encompass all the objectives, achieving a balance between social and financial concerns. Effective reforms necessitate a holistic response.

In the following discussion, we attempt to sort out the risks related to alternative policy choices by examining the tradeoffs each society will face as its population ages. Protecting the income security of the elderly should remain a primary goal in devising strategies to deal with aging populations, according to the EC and others. The retirement systems we have today evolved because of the widely embraced public obligation to ensure that people who are too old to work would continue to receive an adequate income. Over the years, many of these systems have expanded to cover other contingencies, such as disability. In addition, perceptions about when these various contingencies legitimately limit individuals' ability to meet their own economic needs have changed over time.

Retirement systems are generally designed to insure against a range of risks associated with being unable to continue earning a living. System adequacy is measured by how well it protects against the various risks. In this regard, it is important to distinguish between the period over which the rights to benefits are accumulated – the accumulation period – and the period over which the benefits are paid out – the decumulation period.

During the accumulation period, at least five types of risks must be considered. First is the risk of dying prematurely and leaving behind juvenile dependents with unmet needs. Second is the risk of becoming disabled and unable to work. Third is the risk of bad labor market experiences during the working career resulting in low lifetime earnings from which it would be impossible to save enough to provide for retirement needs. Fourth is the risk that individuals will suffer from myopia, not realizing until too late what they have to do to provide for their own retirement security. Fifth is the risk associated with the accumulation devices used to actually secure retirement income.

On the decumulation side, one big risk is of outliving one's resources. A slight variant on this one is the risk of not having sufficient resources to live comfortably during retirement. A third is the risk of unexpected circumstances, such as a catastrophic illness or the death of a spouse, dealing a blow to one's assets or source of income. A fourth risk is that inflation will erode one's benefits. The final risk is of changes to the retirement or health care system that occur after retirement, in response to demographic imbalances in the society.

Insuring Against Economic Risks during the Working Period

Most social security programs provide some survivor protection for juvenile dependents of working adults who die before they retire. Most of these programs operate as a form of term insurance. When people insure themselves against misfortune, they generally want to get a good actuarial value, and so weigh the cost of the protection against their probability of catastrophe. Social security covers this contingency because policymakers deemed it necessary and because private markets were not providing protection at levels and rates deemed prudent. If the social security system did not insure against the premature death of workers with young dependents, most of these workers would likely purchase their own insurance. For example, even given Social Security's survivor provisions, U.S. citizens purchased nearly $2.9 trillion of life insurance in 2002. Of this, 80 percent was term insurance purchased by individuals or through group-life insurance arrangements.[2] While some workers might not buy any life insurance unless such coverage was mandated, concerns about free riders would likely result in mandates for alternative equivalent coverage if social security coverage did not exist.

In some regards, providing disability benefits through a national social insurance system is similar to the early survivor benefits provided on a similar basis. The risk of a working-age individual not being able to earn an income due to disability is relatively moderate. In many developed countries, however, the problem is that their national disability programs have become early retirement vehicles for workers who become unemployed late in their careers. Unless the rules for qualification are tightened up and enforced more stringently, this situation will increasingly strain already stretched resources as populations age.

There are essentially two separate retirement security accumulation "hazards" that are typically insured against through the social insurance systems. One of these is the risk that all workers face of having an unsuccessful career experience in the labor market. The other is the risk of myopia in regard to saving adequately to meet retirement needs during

---

[2] American Council of Life Insurance, *Life Insurance Fact Book 2003* (Washington, D.C.: American Council of Life Insurance, 2003), pp. 95–96.

the working career. The provision of insurance to cover these two risks raises widely different implications about the organization of national retirement programs and is delivered through a variety of mechanisms from country to country.

Although some people do not plan ahead carefully enough, even the best-laid plans can go awry. Some people simply never do well in the labor market because they lack the human capital that warrants a wage that can support sufficient levels of savings to finance adequate retirement security. Others may be successful for a portion of their career but face circumstances at some point that derail their ability to accumulate retirement security on their own. These dislocations can occur because of illness or other personal problems, structural reorganizations of the economy, business decisions by one's career employer, and a host of other forces beyond the worker's control.

Some countries, such as Australia, Canada, and the United Kingdom, provide protection from prolonged adverse labor market experience through their basic pension pillars. The United States, on the other hand, has built redistribution directly into its national pension formula, which ties benefits to lifetime earnings but weights low earnings more heavily than higher ones in determining retirement benefit levels for retirees. In many countries, the pension formula provides benefits that are relatively proportional to earnings but limits the amount of earnings covered under the system, thus inherently favoring lower-level earners.

Table 13-1 shows estimated gross replacement of preretirement earnings by the mandatory retirement programs in a range of OECD countries at different earnings levels. In most countries, benefits tilt in favor of workers at the lower end of the earnings spectrum. For example, in Ireland, workers whose preretirement earnings are 30 percent or less of the national average receive a gross benefit that is 100 percent of earnings. At an earnings level three times the average salary, the gross benefit is only 10 percent of earnings. New Zealand has a similar tilt, and Canada is close behind. At the other end of the spectrum, Italy's gross benefit as a percentage of preretirement earnings is very similar for low- and high-level earners.

The risk that workers will be myopic about the need to save for their retirement security until too late in their career to adequately provide for their own needs is distinctly different from the risk of bad labor market outcomes. A funded retirement system requires a long period of contributions to accumulate sufficient assets to support a preretirement standard of living after retirement. If workers delay saving for retirement until

Table 13-1. *Gross Replacement of Preretirement Earnings by Mandated Retirement Programs in Selected OECD Countries in 2003*

	Preretirement earnings level as a multiple of average earnings							
	0.30	0.50	0.75	1.00	1.50	2.00	2.50	3.00
	(Retirement benefit as a percentage of preretirement earnings)							
Australia	114.0	78.6	60.9	52.0	43.2	42.5	42.5	42.5
Austria	122.9	80.0	80.0	80.0	80.0	80.0	80.0	80.0
Belgium	100.9	60.6	60.0	60.0	50.5	37.9	30.3	25.3
Canada	159.0	100.4	71.1	56.4	37.7	28.3	22.6	18.9
Czech Republic	88.4	70.6	53.4	44.5	31.8	25.4	21.6	19.0
Finland	102.6	73.6	60.0	60.0	60.0	60.0	60.0	60.0
France	118.8	79.8	71.2	71.2	64.2	53.5	47.0	42.7
Germany	69.4	59.6	46.3	46.3	46.3	37.6	30.1	25.1
Hungary	84.5	84.5	84.5	84.5	84.5	84.5	75.8	63.1
Iceland	159.0	109.9	85.3	73.4	65.8	65.8	65.8	65.8
Ireland	100.8	60.5	40.3	30.2	20.2	15.1	12.1	10.1
Italy	73.2	65.9	65.9	65.9	65.9	65.9	65.9	65.9
Japan	98.3	72.5	59.6	53.1	46.7	43.4	36.3	30.3
Korea	141.0	101.0	81.0	71.0	61.0	56.0	53.0	51.0
Luxembourg	141.3	84.8	71.2	71.2	71.2	71.2	71.2	65.4
Mexico	76.7	46.1	41.8	39.7	37.5	36.4	35.8	35.4
Netherlands	113.2	70.0	70.0	70.0	70.0	70.0	70.0	70.0
New Zealand	126.8	76.1	50.7	38.0	25.4	19.0	15.2	12.7
Norway	109.0	65.4	56.1	52.6	46.6	38.4	31.8	26.5
Poland	83.7	70.2	70.2	70.2	70.2	70.2	70.2	59.6
Slovak Republic	65.0	65.0	65.0	64.7	43.1	32.3	25.9	21.6
Spain	110.1	88.0	88.0	88.0	88.0	83.8	67.1	55.9
Sweden	129.0	94.2	79.6	76.0	73.7	71.6	70.2	69.4
Switzerland	87.6	64.3	60.2	58.2	44.1	33.1	26.5	22.1
United Kingdom	108.9	65.3	45.5	36.8	30.7	24.2	19.4	16.2
United States	74.7	57.6	49.1	44.8	38.6	32.7	29.2	25.0

Source: Edward Whitehouse and Axia Economics estimates developed for this study.

late into the career, they may be as likely to end up in poverty as in the other case. The way to avert this situation, either through a funded system or through a "consumption loan" system as Paul Samuelson characterized pay-go pensions, is to require workers to contribute to the pension program over most of their careers.

In one fashion or another, most retirement systems cover both sorts of retirement accumulation risks. The effects of widespread pension reform on these two sorts of risks will vary from country to country, depending on the nature of the reforms. The key principles stressed by oversight groups like the EC and World Bank is that national retirement systems should provide "basic income security" and "poverty alleviation."[3] Policymakers must be careful not to adopt reforms that would eliminate or diminish the insurance feature that today protects people with low earnings histories from poverty in old age.

Benefit reductions can take two general forms: targeted benefit reductions or across-the-board reductions. Across-the-board reductions simply have a proportional effect on all the elderly. Targeted reductions are aimed at subsets of the older population. For example, reductions could be disproportionately targeted to people with high preretirement earnings, sparing those who earned less during their careers. Some benefit reductions that appear to be targeted can end up being across-the-board reductions. For example, several countries have a younger retirement age for women than for men, and some of these countries are now equalizing the ages. To the extent that older women live in households with preretirement earnings spread across the range of earnings levels, raising women's retirement ages will reduce social security pensions across the board. Because women make up a disproportionate share of the retiree population and their pay levels lag behind men's, the benefit reductions may disproportionately hit the more economically vulnerable of the elderly. This potential problem notwithstanding, eliminating the disparity in retirement ages by gender may be a good idea, because earlier retirement ages for women encourage potentially productive workers to withdraw from the workforce too early.

Gender Issues in Social Security Reforms

By Dr. Estelle James (Urban Institute)

Most old people are women, most of the very old are female, and pockets of poverty among the old are concentrated among very old women in many countries. Therefore, in designing a pension system it is essential to take account of the gender impact. Pension reforms may have different impacts on men and women because of their differing employment histories and demographics. Recent empirical research indicates that women gained more than men from the pension reforms in Latin America, but this may not be true in the transition economies, because of detailed design differences (James, Edwards, and Wong 2003a, 2003b). The major gender differences:

---

[3] Robert Holzmann, Indermitt Gill, Richard Hinz, Gregorio Impavido, Alberto R. Musalem, Michal Rutkowski, Anita Schwarz, *Old Age Income Support in the 21st Century: The World Bank's Perspective on Pension Systems and Reform* (Washington, D.C.: The World Bank, 2003).

Less formal labor market work, lower wages. Even though the labor force participation rate of women has been rising, it is still only 75 to 80 percent that of men and much of that work is part-time in countries such as the United States, the United Kingdom, Canada and Australia, and convergence has slowed down recently. The average hourly wage rate of women is also 15 to 30 percent below that of men in these countries (Ginn et al., 2001; U.S. General Accounting Office, 1997). These factors lead to lower pension for women in defined benefit systems and lower retirement saving accumulations in defined contribution systems.

Greater longevity. Since women live two to four years longer than men, on average, in most countries, any given retirement accumulation yields lower annual annuities for women, if gender-specific mortality tables are used for annuitization. Some analysts have recommended that unisex tables should be used to avoid this outcome – but this poses complex efficiency, equity, and political considerations.

Widowhood. Since they have greater life expectancy and are typically younger than their husbands, women are much more likely to become widows than men are to become widowers. In the United States, 34 percent of women aged 65 to 69 are widows, compared with 7 percent of men, and these proportions rise to 72 percent and 27 percent, respectively, by age 80 to 84. In the 85+ age group, 48 percent of men but only 9 percent of women are living with their spouse (Posner, 1995). Due to household economies of scale, it costs one person about two-thirds as much to live as two. Yet, without widows' benefits, household income is likely to fall to one-third of its previous level when the higher-earning spouse, the husband, dies. Families often do not save and insure enough on a voluntary basis to eliminate this gap (Bernheim et al. 2003). The end result is that very old women are relatively poor in many countries. This underscores the importance of survivors' benefits to women.

Given these basic economic and demographic facts, which features of old age security programs are of particular importance to women and how should pension systems, particularly multi-pillar systems, be designed to be "gender-friendly"?

A redistributive social safety net. Because women are low earners, they benefit disproportionately from a system that redistributes to those with low retirement income. In a multi-pillar system, this could be accomplished through a non-contributory "pillar 0" (such as Australia's broad-based means- and asset-tested benefit or the flat benefit in the Netherlands), and/or a first pillar that is part of the contributory system (e.g., Chile's minimum pension guarantee, the basic pension in the United Kingdom, or Switzerland's progressive defined benefit). Simulations for Chile, Argentina, and Mexico show that women are the major net beneficiaries of these redistributive arrangements (James et al. 2003a, 2003b).

Eligibility conditions that do not exclude most women. In some systems, the years required for eligibility for the public benefit are set at a level that most men, but few women, achieve. For example, the full flat benefit in Argentina requires 30 years of contributions, a requirement that makes most women ineligible. (Most women are eligible for a reduced flat benefit.) An advantage of defined contribution plans is that women are eligible for some benefits, corresponding to their contributions plus investment earnings, regardless of how many years they have been in the system.

Equal retirement ages for men and women. Given their periods of withdrawal from the labor market and greater longevity, the retirement age should be at least as high for women as for men. Yet, many countries permit women to retire five years earlier. Simulations for Chile and Argentina show that women's annuities from the funded pillar would rise by 50 percent if retirement ages were equalized (even if they didn't work more) – simply because interest would accumulate for five extra years and payouts would be made for five fewer years (James et al. 2003a, 2003b).

Annuitization or gradual withdrawal requirements. Annuitization, which provides a guaranteed income for life, is especially important for women in view of their greater longevity and the likelihood that voluntary family savings will be used up before they die. This requirement – at least up to the poverty line – could be built into mandatory individual account systems (as it is, for example, in the United Kingdom).

Indexation of the public and private benefits. Inflation insurance is especially important to women – otherwise the purchasing power of their pensions will fall substantially as they age and they age longer than men. In many developing countries, benefits are not price-indexed. In industrial countries, the public benefit is usually indexed. Indexation of annuities from the private pillar is also important but more difficult and expensive to achieve, given the paucity of indexed financial instruments in which insurance companies can invest. In Chile, annuities are price-indexed; this is feasible because many public and private securities are also issued in an indexed currency. To facilitate indexation of annuities, governments should issue long-term indexed bonds; this is already done in the United States and United Kingdom. Weighing the desirability of indexation against the higher price (lower money's worth ratio) of indexed annuities, policymakers might require partial inflation indexation or indexation up to a cap in the mandatory system (as in the United Kingdom).

Joint pensions. As discussed above, survivors' insurance is particularly important to women. Yet, these provisions have not always been well structured – for example, in some cases they have transferred overly generous amounts to middle class spouses at the expense of low-earning and single taxpayers. Some countries (e.g., those in the transition economies) have been cutting back on these benefits in their public pillars to help achieve fiscal balance. This places the living standards of many older women in jeopardy. In multi-pillar systems, these problems can be avoided by requiring that spouses purchase survivors' insurance while working and joint annuities or other joint pensions when they retire – as is required in Chile, Mexico, and Argentina. In effect, this formalizes the informal family contract that led wives to work and earn less in the first place. It protects older women without placing a burden on the public treasury. An added bonus is that joint annuities reduce the impact on payouts of gender-specific versus unisex mortality tables, hence they defuse the contentious unisex issue.

Avoid the crowd-out of own-pension by widow's pension. In many countries, working women must choose between their own benefit and the widow's benefit – they can't get both. Thus, women who work in the market for much of their lives pay substantial taxes with no incremental benefit. This is done to avoid a double burden on the treasury. In the case of a joint annuity, however, there is no such reason to make women choose between the two. In the reformed systems in Chile, Mexico, and Argentina, the widow keeps her own annuity as well as the joint annuity. Her participation in the formal labor market is thus encouraged, rather than being penalized. And the combination of the two compensates for household economies of scale, enabling her to maintain her prior standard of living. Simulations show that this provision has improved gender ratios of lifetime benefits substantially and has led women to be the main gainers from the pension reforms (James et al 2003a, 2003b).

Legal protection in case of divorce or cohabitation. Since divorce and cohabitation without formal marriage are becoming more common, legal protections regarding retirement accumulations and payouts are obviously needed in these cases. These might include, for example, joint pension requirements for legally recognized partners and sharing of pension assets acquired during the marriage in case of divorce.

Investor education. Some evidence from the United States and elsewhere indicates that women may choose more risk-averse portfolios with lower expected rates of return than men, in which case their retirement accumulations and annuities would end up lower. While this is undoubtedly due in part to women's lower incomes, it is also likely related to their lesser experience investing savings (U.S. GAO 1997). Investor education is important to both genders, but it is especially important for women, in multi-pillar pension reforms.

References

Bernheim, B. Douglas, Lorenzo Formi, Jagadeesh Gokhale, and Laurence Kotlikoff. 2002. "The Mismatch Between Life Insurance Holdings and Financial Vulnerabilities: Evidence from the HRS." *American Economic Review*, 93:1.

Ginn, Jay, Debra Street, and Sara Arber. 2001. *Women, Work and Pensions*. Buckingham, UK: Open University Press.

James, Estelle, Alejandra Cox Edwards, and Rebeca Wong. 2003a. "The Gender Impact of Social Security Reform." *Journal of Pension Economics and Finance*.

James, Estelle, Alejandra Cox Edwards, and Rebeca Wong. 2003b. The Gender Impact of Social Security Reform: A Cross-Country Analysis. Policy Research Working Paper 3074, Washington D.C.: World Bank.

Posner, Richard A. 1995. *Aging and Old Age*. Chicago: University of Chicago Press.

U.S. General Accounting Office. (1997). *Social Security Reform: Implications for Women's Retirement Income*. GAO/HEHS-98-42.

One can argue that raising the retirement eligibility age is not a reduction in benefits. After all, one reason that aged dependency is rising is

Monthly benefit level in dollars

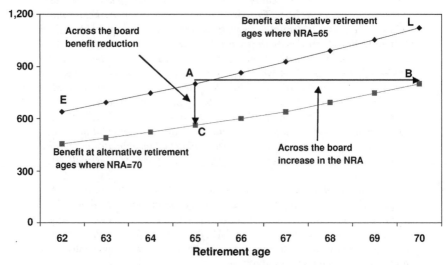

Figure 13-1. Equivalence of Advancing the Social Security Normal Retirement Age and Reducing Benefits. *Sources:* Benefit levels were calculated by the authors based on actuarial adjustment factors from the Office of the Actuary, Social Security Administration.

that life expectancies are increasing. If retirement ages and benefit levels remain constant while people live longer, then lifetime benefits increase along with life expectancies. Indexing the retirement age so it rises along with life expectancy might be the most reasonable way to stabilize average lifetime benefits.

To examine the equivalence of increasing retirement ages versus simply reducing benefits across the board, we consider the case of the U.S. social security retiree pension program. Before 2003, age 65 was the normal retirement age at which full benefits were paid. People could retire as early as age 62, but their benefits were actuarially reduced five-ninths of 1 percent for each month before age 65 that they retired. The actuarial reduction is supposed to equalize lifetime benefits taken anytime between ages 62 and 65. Workers who continued working beyond age 65 received actuarial increases to their benefits to account for the delayed retirement and the shorter life expectancy over which benefits would be paid.

Figure 13-1 shows how raising the normal retirement age from 65 to 70 affects a worker. The upper line shows the monthly benefit amounts at various retirement ages for someone whose full age-65 benefit is $800 per month, shown at point A. This person could retire at age 62 and receive $640 per month (shown as point E), or he could opt for any point on the line segment defined by points E and L. For instance, if the worker delays retirement until age 70, his beginning benefit would be $1,120 per month (shown as point L).

Now consider what happens if the normal retirement age rises from age 65 to 70. Assuming the basic benefit formula remains the same, the person must wait until age 70 to receive the full $800 per month. Before the increase, someone who waited until age 70 to retire would have received 140 percent of his or her age-65 benefit, using the two-thirds of 1 percent a month rule that will apply to those born in 1942 or later. The change from 140 to 100 percent of the basic benefit (that is the movement from point L to point B) is a dramatic decrease in benefits – about a 28.5 percent decrease to be precise. Benefits are not just lower at age 70 – they are lower at every retirement age. The new choice set is the lower sloping line in Figure 13-1.

So far, we moved to this new choice set by raising the normal retirement age from age 65 to 70. However, we could have ended up with the same reduction by leaving the normal retirement age at 65 and simply reducing benefits by about 28.5 percent. That is, we could have lowered the basic benefit formula so that this person would have received about $570 at age 65 (point C) rather than the $800 (point A) before the cut. This may seem like an austere benefit reduction, but it would achieve exactly the same effect as raising the normal retirement age by five years. Either option cuts monthly benefits for any retirement age. The bottom line is that the difference between cutting benefits and raising the retirement ages is mostly about presentation.

The United States Congress modified the U.S. system in 1983 to gradually increase the normal retirement age. The transition from age 65 to 67 began in 2000. When this is fully implemented, a worker retiring at age 62 will receive a benefit that is 13.33 percent less than it would have been under the previous normal retirement age of 65. The incentive is clear – workers will have to work a bit longer to achieve the same standard of retirement income available to retirees born a few years earlier.

Germany has recently adopted changes to its retirement system that have a very similar practical effect to those being implemented in the Unites States. Germany has implemented benefit reductions by basing benefits on after-tax wages rather than on gross earnings, and by reducing the target replacement rates slightly. Sweden has adopted even more sweeping reforms, which will base benefits for future generations of re-tirees on life expectancy at the cusp of retirement eligibility. The new process will utilize an automatic demographic adjustment factor to keep benefit obligations aligned with contribution levels. Many other countries are adopting or considering changes along this same spectrum of options.

In practical terms, one goal of these modifications is to encourage peo-ple to work longer. Someone facing the prospect of a reduced pension – whatever the precise nature of the reduction – needs to work longer to achieve the same standard of living once available to those who retired earlier. The problem is that the modifications in Germany, Sweden, and the United States do not actually require people to work longer before qualifying for their initial benefits. German workers become eligible for the state pension at age 65, but many workers qualify for a disability benefit before then, which is simply an early retirement benefit disguised as something else. When Sweden's modifications are fully implemented, workers will still be able to retire at age 61 and receive a reduced benefit. The United States is raising its normal retirement age and reducing the share of the full benefit payable at age 62, but the age-62 benefit is still available.

In the United States, the fact that the age-62 benefit remains avail-able even after the normal retirement age goes up has been the sub-ject of a number of empirical analyses. The general conclusion is that to change early retirement behavior patterns, the system must also raise the age of early retirement eligibility. In a particularly insightful work, Alan Gustman and Thomas Steinmeier model the clustering behavior actually reflected in U.S. retirement patterns. In the United States, more people begin taking their social security pension at age 62 than at any other age. In their latest work, Gustman and Steinmeier hypothesize that people have relatively strong preferences either for leisure or for material goods and services. Many people whose preferences are for leisure over material goods are constrained financially until they qualify for some social secu-rity pension, but at that point, they are willing to settle for the reduced benefit. Those whose preference for material things outweighs their taste for leisure will wait until they qualify for a full benefit before quitting work. Gustman and Steinmeier's simulations lead them to conclude that early eligibility ages will have to be raised to curtail the early retirement phenomenon.[4]

---

[4] Alan L. Gustman and Thomas L. Steinmeier, "The Social Security Early Retirement Entitlement Age in a Structural Model of Retirement and Wealth" (Cambridge, MA: National Bureau of Economic Research, 2002), NBER Working Paper, no. w9183.

Table 13-2. *Distribution of Wealth among the Near Elderly in the United States*

Position in the Wealth Holding Distribution	Retirement Purchasing Power from:			
	Personal Financial Wealth (Percent)	Social Security Wealth (Percent)	Pension Wealth (Percent)	Total Wealth (Percent)
Bottom 10th	3.4	93.6	3.0	100.0
1/3 from bottom	18.1	63.4	18.5	100.0
2/3 from bottom	29.9	35.7	34.4	100.0
Top 10th	65.2	10.2	24.6	100.0

Source: James F. Moore and Olivia S. Mitchell, "Projected Retirement Wealth and Savings Adequacy," in Olivia S. Mitchell, P. Brett Hammond, and Anna M. Rappaport, eds., *Forecasting Retirement Needs and Retirement Wealth* (Philadelphia: University of Pennsylvania Press, 2000), p. 72.

We took up this consideration of reducing benefits in the context of a discussion about retirement systems insuring against bad labor market outcomes, which have the potential to leave retirees with inadequate incomes. Having shown how benefits can be reduced across the board through a variety of mechanisms, we now focus on the implications of benefit reductions for this particular form of insurance, currently offered by many retirement systems. Increasing normal retirement ages or otherwise cutting benefits across the board has widely different implications for workers at different points on the lifetime earnings spectrum. This point is best explained by adapting an analysis developed by Olivia Mitchell and James Moore in a study they did at The Wharton School at the University of Pennsylvania Their analysis uses the *Health and Retirement Study* (HRS) sponsored by the U.S. National Institute on Aging.[5] The original HRS conducts interviews every two years with a representative sample of the general U.S. population from the ages of 51 to 61 in 1992.

Mitchell and Moore have used this data set to estimate the participating households' wealth levels. Their calculations include four classes of wealth: 1) net financial wealth, including savings, investments, business assets, and non-residential real estate less outstanding debt not related

[5] James F. Moore and Olivia S. Mitchell, "Projected Retirement Wealth and Savings Adequacy," in Olivia S. Mitchell, P. Brett Hammond, and Anna M. Rappaport, eds., *Forecasting Retirement Needs and Retirement Wealth* (Philadelphia: University of Pennsylvania Press, 2000), pp. 68–94.

to housing; 2) net housing wealth, or the current market value of the residential housing less outstanding mortgage debt; 3) pension wealth, or the present value of employer-sponsored retirement benefits; and 4) the present value of Social Security benefits.

Table 13-2 has been derived from Mitchell and Moore's analysis. The derivation does not include housing wealth in the calculation of the wealth distributions because most homeowners do not sell their homes at retirement, or if they do, they tend to buy another one. Our definition of wealth includes personal financial assets, business assets, non-residential properties, and pension wealth. We are interested in looking at assets in these folks' portfolios that will generate a stream of income that they can use to buy groceries, go to the movies, and so forth, during their retirement. The results are instructive.

The people at the bottom end of the wealth distribution hold almost all of their wealth in the form of the social security pension. Those people one-third of the way up the distribution still hold nearly two-thirds of their wealth in the same form. Those two-thirds of the way up the distribution have a rough parity between their social security pension, an employer-sponsored pension, and other financial wealth. Those at the top of the wealth distribution depend very little on the social security pension. The retirement security risks associated with potential reductions in social security pensions are clearly not randomly distributed across the wealth distribution.

The implications of this distribution of relative wealth to support retirement consumption can best be understood in the context of the increase in the normal retirement age now underway in the U.S. Social Security program. For people in the bottom 10 percent of the wealth distribution represented in the table, a 12.5 percent reduction in their Social Security benefits would amount to roughly an 11.7 percent reduction in their retirement income resources, because nearly 94 percent of all their retirement wealth, other than their homes, is tied up in Social Security. In the top 10 percent, on the other hand, the 12.5 percent Social Security benefit reduction would represent a 1.3 percent reduction in retirement resources.

Across-the-board reductions in state pensions will disproportionately hurt those toward the bottom of the earnings distribution in countries where those in the middle- to upper-earnings ranges expect to receive a substantial portion of their retirement income elsewhere. This suggests that countries should seriously consider enhancing the "zero pillar" of their retirement security systems, to use the World Bank's term, or should consider skewing any benefit reductions toward those who can better afford the hit.

The costs of insuring against career failure can be minimized and the target efficiency of benefit delivery maximized by implementing a means test for benefit qualification. The general reluctance to implement means tests for these programs suggests that means testing is difficult to achieve politically, at least within a defined benefit structure. Some policy analysts prefer a redistributive defined benefit structure, because it partially masks the true extent of redistribution. Assuming that countries do not want to implement a means test but do wish to retain a defined benefit approach, a flatter benefit structure would reduce the costs of this element of the program. Recasting this element in a defined contribution environment akin to what Sweden or Italy has done could achieve redistribution by supplementing the contributions of low-wage workers during their careers. These supplements would have to be financed either out of general tax revenues or by added marginal contributions from higher-wage workers.

After considerable study, the World Bank has concluded that all elements of the retirement infrastructures can benefit from some funding,[6] and we do not quarrel with that conclusion. Fully funding the "zero tier" benefits, however, would be the equivalent of declaring that each generation of citizens is responsible for assuring the basic welfare of their own age class across their respective lifetimes. Given the other cross-generational transfers that take place in most societies, this seems to be a relatively narrow perspective on supporting the general welfare over time. Some funding may be economically efficient for these benefits, but financing some part of them on a pay-go basis – as long as costs are kept to manageable levels – may be a better way to spread the costs.

Insuring against workers' myopia about their own need to save for retirement is completely different from insuring against the prospect of an unprofitable career or unforeseen circumstances. The fundamental purpose of mandated retirement benefits is to encourage workers to spread their consumption such that their lifetime earnings will support a relatively consistent standard of living over their entire lives. In the heyday of pay-go funded national pension systems, we could achieve this by leveraging the combined benevolent effects of workforce and

---

[6] Robert Holzmann, Indermit Gill, Richard Hinz, Gregorio Impavido, Alberto R. Musalem, Michal Rutkowski, and Anita Schwarz, "*Old Age Income Support in the 21st Century: The World Bank's Perspective on Pension Systems and Reform*," (Washington, D.C.; The World Bank, forthcoming).

productivity growth. With the slowdown in anticipated workforce growth now anticipated for much of the developed world, this function is more achievable via funded pensions than with pay-go systems. The intergenerational transfer characteristics of the latter probably cannot sustain the costs that anticipated elderly burden rates imply these systems will face.

The conclusion that inter-temporal retirement transfers ought to be funded does not answer the questions of how this might best be achieved. As we noted in Chapter 10, a number of countries seem to be moving toward funding through centrally managed mechanisms that have been immunized against undue political influence and manipulation and that are not disruptive to the private capital markets. In countries like the United States, on the other hand, there is considerable skepticism about whether the current fund buildup in its social security pension system is true funding. There is also a great deal of reluctance to grant a central authority discretion to invest these funds in private capital markets. Quite a number of countries have moved toward individual account, defined contribution plans to preclude the buildup and political manipulation of a large pool of pension assets. For many countries, this may be the most promising way to go, but the experiences in Argentina and Mexico described earlier suggest that this approach poses its own set of risks.

Insuring against Economic Risks during the Retirement Period

Mandated retirement programs are generally structured to protect against a number of potential risks to retirees. These risks derive partly from evolving demographics, especially in the developed economies, and the threat they pose to the sustainability of retirement systems on which workers have come to depend. They also derive from the changing structure of retirement programs over the last decade in many parts of the world. Finally, they derive in part from the normal economic vagaries that all economies face over time.

The evolving demographics portend higher costs of aged dependency in the future in most developed economies no matter how their retirement systems are organized. In Chapter 7, we concluded that the demographic composition of some developed societies might slow economic growth to the point that some segments of the population may experience stagnating incomes and some may actually see their income fall. This is not far-fetched when one considers that in the United Kingdom, the basic pension will grow at rates below expected wage growth rates. This means that the standard of living provided to retirees through the U.K. basic pension will gradually decline compared to the standard of living achieved by workers. A number of other countries either have adopted similar measures to limit future pension growth or are considering them.

Across much of the world in recent years, there has been a distinct shift away from defined benefit plans toward defined contribution plans. In Chapter 10, we discussed the Chilean style reforms that have swept across much of Latin America. But even in the more developed world, Australia, Sweden, and Italy are all moving toward significant dependency on defined contribution benefits. In the United Kingdom, introducing an option to contract out of the state pension has effectively transformed much of that country's system to operate like a defined contribution pension. In the United States, where there is substantial dependence on employer-based pensions that are less integrated with the state pension than in the United Kingdom, the shift of employer-sponsored plans toward defined contribution structures is moving the combined system in the direction of a defined contribution environment.

The risks posed by defined contribution plans vary from country to country. In a traditional defined benefit plan, the specified formula promises an annuity for life. If the full annuity is payable at 65, it makes little difference to a single retiree if a new cohort of retirees has a life expectancy as a beneficiary of 15 or 20 years. If longevity is increasing and the age at which full benefits are paid is not, the workers financing the benefit are the ones taking on the risks posed by longevity. In the new Swedish system, annuity rates are calculated when a cohort of workers actually reaches retirement age. This links life expectancies and the commensurate annuity to known conditions much more closely than is possible in a traditional pension system, where life expectancy after retirement is estimated many years before a worker retires. So Sweden has transferred the longevity risk to the individual beneficiary and away from the taxpayer.

The Annuitization Problem

By Professor Olivia S. Mitchell, The Wharton School (mitchelo@wharton. upenn.edu)

Retirement analysts are interested in the question of how to manage one's assets during the retirement period. This question is difficult because people do not know exactly how long they will live, so they face the risk of exhausting their assets prior to death. The risk can be reduced by consuming less per year, but then one faces a greater chance of dying with "too much" wealth left over. A natural way to offset such longevity risk is to purchase a lifelong annuity paying a benefit as long as the retiree survives.

Despite the logical appeal of annuities, however, people seem surprisingly reluctant to purchase such products. Several explanations for low annuitization rates have been advanced. One is that retirees are misinformed about survival probabilities. While one survey found that expected survival patterns track actuarial tables quite closely among pre-retirees, another reported that only one-third of respondents realized that people face a substantial chance of living beyond their life expectancy. Another reason retirees do not annuitize is that they wish to keep liquid assets to cover bequest motives or to finance long-term care costs. But such goals could be met by buying life insurance and long-term care coverage, and annuitizing the rest of wealth. A third explanation for why people appear to under-consume annuities is that substantial portions of their wealth may already be de facto annuitized – either through Social Security, company pensions, or housing wealth. A fourth rationale is that people may have unusually high discount rates, which lead them to prefer lump sums. Finally, some believe that insured products are uncompetitive with pure investment vehicles due to loads levied by insurers. But recent research finds that money's worth ratios are quite decent in many countries. It is fair to say that low levels of annuitization during retirement continue to puzzle retirement analysts.

References

This discussion is drawn from Olivia S. Mitchell and Steven Utkus, Eds. Pension Design and Structure: New Lessons from Behavioral Finance. Oxford University Press, forthcoming.

Sweden has embedded another risk in its system. Benefit adjustments in the future will take into account the demographic composition of the population at the time a cohort of workers retires. If an increasing aged dependency ratio will create future financing problems, the system will adjust benefits as needed to bring the system back into financing balance. This risk exists in all retirement systems to some degree, but in most systems, the benefit adjustments require legislative action. In Sweden, the empowering legislation is already in place so rebalancing will be a mechanical administrative function.

In Sweden's case, at least, retirees still receive their benefits in the form of annuities. In a number of countries that have been shifting toward defined contribution pensions, retires may choose between an annuity and a lump-sum payment. In many cases, retirees opt for the lump sum – posing even greater risks for the individual retiree.

Policymakers and analysts often talk about life expectancy in retirement, which is calculated based on the average retirement age and the

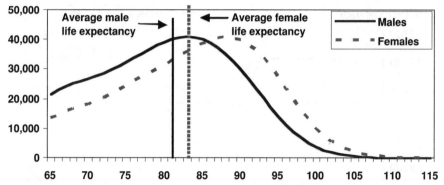

Figure 13-2. Distribution of Expected Deaths of 1 Million U.S. Men and 1 Million U.S. Women Aged 65 in 2000 Based on Cohort Mortality Rates. *Source:* Social Security Administration, Office of the Actuary, cohort mortality rates used in preparing the 2000 Social Security Trustees Report.

mortality patterns for a given group. In designing retirement plans, the goal is to accumulate sufficient assets during the working life to finance consumption needs in retirement. While the concept of a specific life expectancy has meaning for a broad population, it cannot predict how long an individual will live. A major challenge for retiring workers who take their accumulated pension benefits in a lump sum is not knowing how long their money needs to last.

The risk is reflected in Figure 13-2, which shows expected death rates for the U.S. 1935 birth cohort reaching age 65 in 2000, for men and women separately. Actual mortality rates by age in that year are adjusted to account for expected improvements in life expectancy. The solid vertical line shows the average life expectancy of these men at age 65, 15.7 years, and the dashed line shows the average life expectancy of these women at age 65, 18.9 years. Focusing on the men for the moment, the problem for the retiree with a lump-sum retirement benefit who chooses not to buy an annuity is determining how much he can spend each year.

Suppose the worker in this case has accumulated $100,000 and retires at age 65. Assume that this money can be invested at 7 percent annually. The retiree has a number of options for managing that money over his retirement period. One approach might be to look out over his remaining life expectancy and take a set of equal payments over that period. This is labeled the "Draw on LE @ 65" in Figure 13-3. The retiree can withdraw $10,275 per year, thus exhausting the fund at the end of his life expectancy.

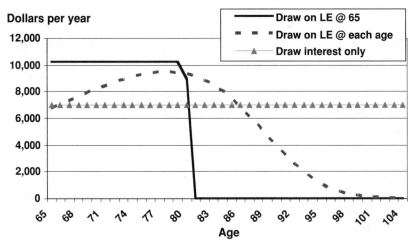

Figure 13-3. Alternative Benefit Paths for a 65-Year-Old Male Retiree Self-Annuitizing $100,000 at Retirement. *Source:* Calculated by the authors.

The problem with this option is that there is a 50 percent probability that the retiree will outlive his life expectancy. Even if he withdraws only $8,500 per year, he would have more than a 20 percent probability of outliving his assets.

Another option in Figure 13-3 is labeled "Draw on LE @ each age," and in this case, the retiree would estimate his remaining life expectancy at each birthday and withdraw a pro rata share of the remainder of the fund over that year. The initial annual benefit would be just under $7,000 and would grow during the initial years as life expectancy drops off. Ultimately, the annual draw would peak at just under $9,500 and then begin to decline. If the man lived to age 90, his annual withdrawal would be less than half its peak level.

The final option depicted in Figure 13-3 is for the retiree to withdraw interest only, preserving the principal. At 7 percent interest, the accumulated capital would generate $7,000 per year in retirement income. This option would enable the retiree to leave behind his retirement fund as an inheritance. While the probabilities of leaving behind a substantial portion of unused retirement savings in the earlier two examples are much less, they are significant. The problem with this outcome is that the retiree is forced to consume less than he would like in order to protect against the risk of outliving his resources.

The risks associated with self-annuitizing go beyond those outlined in the discussion around Figure 13-3. Other risks made headlines during the worldwide financial market and economic downturns that began during 2000. Many investors lost considerable amounts of money during the turmoil that persisted at least through 2002. Losing assets intended to provide basic retirement income security means a reduced standard of living in old age. In recent years, falling asset values have resulted from financial market downturns. In other periods, assets have lost value when inflation has outpaced increases in asset values. There are a variety of circumstances that can threaten retirement assets.

Another risk is that financial management will become more difficult in old age, as mental faculties may decline. Living in a defined contribution world poses significant challenges for the unclear of mind. The risks of losing assets due to fraud, abuse, or even above-board errors multiply significantly for people at very advanced ages.

The bottom line is that reducing the financial risks aging populations impose on national retirement systems is often a matter of shifting the risks away from taxpayers to the individual worker. This is not all bad. Responsibility can be a very effective motivator, and shifting risks to individuals is likely to prompt behaviors more in line with the reality of evolving conditions, such as delaying retirement and saving more, than would occur under traditional defined benefit systems.

The United States has witnessed a substantial shift among employer-sponsored pensions toward defined contribution plans, or defined benefit plans with very similar characteristics to Sweden's notional defined contribution plans. These modified defined benefit plans are called cash balance plans and tend to pay benefits as lump sums. As asset prices fell during the 2000 to 2002 turmoil in the U.S. financial markets, many retirees saw the cash value of their retirement savings plummet. At the same time, there was a perceptible increase in workforce participation rates among people in their late 50s and early 60s. Empirical evidence suggests a direct linkage between the two phenomena.[7] In this case, it was the decline in potential retirement income due to falling asset prices that encouraged workers to delay retirement. By the same token, other factors that would reduce retirement income, such as extended longevity or demographic imbalances, might convince more workers to work a little longer. These may be exactly the incentives we need to avert a crisis in the coming years. At the same time, we need to be very careful not to cast the

---

[7] Alan L. Gustman and Thomas L. Steinmeier, "Retirement and the Stock Market Bubble" (Cambridge, MA: National Bureau of Economic Research, 2002), Working Paper 9404.

physically infirm or economically vulnerable adrift. The challenge will be to encourage able-bodied, productive workers to continue making an economic contribution while still holding out support to those who cannot do without it.

Pensioner Poverty

By Professor Timothy M. Smeeding,
Maxwell School, Syracuse University,
and Director, Luxembourg Income Study

Great strides have been made in reducing poverty amongst the elderly in most rich countries over the past 40 years. But pensioner poverty has not been eradicated, especially in the Anglo-speaking nations. In fact, pensioner poverty may rise again in the coming decades. Poverty amongst younger pensioners is no longer a major policy problem. Rather poverty in old age is almost exclusively an older women's problem. Poverty rates amongst older women rise with both age and changes in living arrangements. Three quarters of the poor elders, age 75 or older, in each rich nation are women; almost 60 percent of all poor age 75 and over in each nation are women living alone (Table 1, page 180).

Countries that do best in the fight against elder poverty are those with high minimum "first tier" traditional (defined benefit type) social retirement plans for all elderly (e.g., as in Germany, France, Italy, Sweden and Finland). But population aging in coming decades will put pressure on these governments to reduce exactly these benefits and to turn their systems more toward defined contribution-type pension plans. Targeted income-tested benefit strategies as in Canada are also successful in reducing elderly female poverty at a much lower overall cost. Such schemes as these should be considered, even if national pension systems are becoming of a defined contribution variety.

Poverty rates amongst older women are highest amongst the divorced, widowed, and never married. And these are groups whose prevalence within the elder population will rise significantly over the next decades. For instance, in the United States, divorced and never-married women, who were 10 percent of all older women in the 1990s, will be over 25 percent of all aged in the 2020s. And these groups have poverty rates more than double the overall elder population poverty rates, despite the high labor force participation rates and increasingly higher pension benefits of women in their cohorts.

The challenge will be to design systems of retirement benefits that guarantee minimum standards of living for very elderly women, especially those who are survivors, divorcees, or who have never been married.

References

Smeeding, Timothy M. 1999. "Social Security Reform: Improving Benefit Adequacy and Economic Security for Women." Center for Policy Research Policy Brief Series No. 16, The Maxwell School. Syracuse, NY: Syracuse University.
Smeeding, Timothy M. 2003. "Income Maintenance in Old Age: Current Status and Future Prospects for Rich Countries." Genus LIX(1) (April–June): 51–83.

Table 1. *Poverty[1] Rates and Composition Among the Aged [2]: Percent of Population with Incomes Less than Given Percent of Adjusted National Median Disposable Income and Fraction of the Elderly Poor Who Are Women*

I. Country	Year	40% Median	50% Median
A. All Elderly			
United States	2000	15.0	24.7
United Kingdom	1999	10.2	20.9
Germany	2000	5.2	11.6
Canada	1998	1.7	7.8
Sweden	2000	2.1	7.7
Italy	2000	5.6	13.7
Finland	2000	1.1	8.5
Average		5.8	13.6
B. Elderly Women (65+)			
United States	2000	17.7	28.6
United Kingdom	1999	14.4	26.2
Germany	2000	5.6	13.9
Canada	1998	1.5	9.6
Sweden	2000	2.5	10.3
Italy	2000	6.8	16.2
Finland	2000	1.8	11.8
Average		7.2	16.7
C. Elderly Women (75+) Living Alone			
United States	2000	30.4	48.3
United Kingdom	1999	26.7	41.3
Germany	2000	8.7	18.4
Canada	1998	0.8	19.8
Sweden	2000	4.3	19.6
Italy	2000	10.5	28.3
Finland	2000	4.2	26.4
Average		12.2	28.9

II. Average Composition of Poverty in Same Nations	
All Persons 75 and Over Who Are Female	62%
All Poor Persons 75 and Over Who Are Female	73–74%[3]
All Poor Persons 75 and Over Who Are Single Females Living Alone	58–60%[3]

Notes: [1]Poverty is defined as percentage of elderly living in households with adjusted disposable income less than given percent of median adjusted disposable income for all persons. Incomes are adjusted by E = .05 where adjusted DPI = actual DPI divided by household size (S) to the power E: Adjusted DPI = DPI/sE.

[2] Aged are all persons at least aged 65 and older. Person level and household level files were matched and income data weighted by the person sample weight from the person level file.

[3] Using first the 40 and then 50 percent Poverty Line.

Source: Luxembourg Income Study, http://www.lisproject.org, October 2003; Smeeding.

While annuitization of retirement savings will provide insurance against longevity risks, other risks also must be considered in designing the annuity. Inflation protection is important to preserve the purchasing power of retirement income. Most governments running national retirement programs provide such protections today. To the extent that the shift to defined contribution plans eliminates or minimizes the government's role, it should be possible for commercial markets to provide annuities by securing the liabilities associated with an indexed annuity with inflation-indexed bonds that many governments now issue. Some policy analysts advocate providing even more protection for the oldest in our societies, such as special benefit increments at advanced ages, to ward off the higher incidence of poverty that is common among that segment of the population. Since much of this poverty is concentrated among older widows, another alternative is to make sure that survivor annuities make up for the economies of scale that are lost when a spouse dies.

The Political Economy Risks in Aging Societies

It is impossible to conclude a discussion about the risks associated with alternative public policies related to the aging phenomenon that does not at least touch on our systems of political economy. The concept of political economy means different things for different people. In this context, we mean the stipulation of a set of economic policies that might be considered within the framework of a set of principles, such as those laid out by the World Bank or the EC.

In the case of population aging, societies may need to guard against two particular political economy risks as they consider their options. The first of these is denial that a problem exists. The second is the natural tendency to delay dealing with disturbing realities that may demand potentially politically unpopular solutions. The particular concern here is that delaying treatment is likely to necessitate stronger cures and portend a more dismal prognosis. These risks may be exacerbated by the prevalent political structures across the developed economies of the world.

The Risks of Denial of a Problem

EU members are subject to the Stability and Growth Pact, which requires that they run their government budgets "close to balance or in surplus." The expectation that each member of the EU will abide by this agreement gives this set of developed economies, all with aging populations, a unique cross-national interest in addressing the problem of rising aging obligations. It is no coincidence that the EC and the OECD have made the major contribution in identifying the costs of aging across the developed economies. Both the EC and the OECD are based in the heart of the EU, and its members constitute the EC and make up a significant portion of the OECD.

The views held by the EC and OECD about the appropriate responses to aging are undoubtedly affected by countervailing pressures from their members. On the one hand, each country has a vested interest in making sure that the others do not pursue policies that would adversely affect them, while at the same time pursuing policies in their own home countries that meet the needs and desires of their local populations. In this regard, it is unacceptable that a member of the EU simply ignore the claims future aged dependency will impose on its economy under the assumption that deficit financing can cover the rising costs. Such an approach would impose a drain on savings, diverting them from productive investment that would contribute to economic growth and would drive up interest rates. Both would have adverse effects on other member countries. The alternative of simply driving up contribution rates is also unacceptable because of its implications on labor costs and the adverse incentives on labor supply.

At the same time there are pressures across the membership of the EU to control programs supporting the elderly, there is also a counteracting long history of social democratic institutions and sense of social solidarity within the societies. The historical goals of adequacy of benefits, social redistribution, and access to health care are fundamental principles in these countries.

The cross-national concerns about increasing costs from aging dependency have prompted the EU to tackle the issue head-on. A recent report by the Director General for Economic and Financial Affairs noted:

There is a growing recognition that there are benefits to addressing issues related to ageing populations at the EU level, with the result that the issue has featured prominently on the agendas of several recent European Council's (Stockholm of March 2001, Nice of December 2000 and Lisbon of March 2000). A comprehensive approach has been taken drawing upon the report *Maintaining Prosperity in an Ageing Society* (OECD, 1998), which proposed policies through which societies can transfer resources to a rapidly growing number of retired persons without creating major economic and social strains. Such an approach recognizes that budgetary sustainability in light of ageing populations must be accompanied with sustainability.[8]

---

[8] European Commission, Directorate-General for Economic and Financial Affairs, *Public Finances in the EMU* (Brussels: European Commission, 2001), No. 3.

The European Council has established a Committee on Social Protection to develop policies to address both the budgetary and social concerns associated with aging in the member countries. The treaty establishing the EU relegates the development of pension and health policy within member countries to those countries themselves under its "subsidiarity" principle. This policy notwithstanding, the European Council has agreed to extend the "open method of co-ordination" to pensions. It also released a report in December 2001 addressing the quality and sustainability of the pension systems, which was discussed at the European Commission meeting held in Barcelona in March 2002.

In the December 2001 report, the authors conclude:

Member States have already launched a wide range of reforms with the aim of tackling the ageing problem which they collectively face. Notwithstanding the reforms undertaken up until the end of the 1990s, the latest estimates of the effect on growth and on public expenditure on pensions confirm that the impact of ageing will be so significant and widespread that additional reforms will still be needed in order to address the associated growth loss and to put the public finances on a sounder footing. In this regard, the design and structure of public pension systems play a crucial role in determining the scale of the budgetary growth impact of ageing and consequently a discussion on the relative merits of individual pension systems is of the utmost importance.[9]

The EC's earlier report, quoted above, reviewed the budget plans of the EU members for conformity with the standards in the Stability and Growth Pact from both a short-term and intermediate-term perspective. In virtually every case, their country reviews included comments on the sustainability of the national pension system under current law. In a number of cases, they also commented on the health costs associated with aging populations. In 10 of the 15 country reviews, the EC recommended that the country further adjust its pension system to comply with the Stability and Growth Pact over the longer term. This recommendation was based on the EC's modeling of the pension systems and assumed that other non-age-related functions of the various governments would continue to play roughly the same size role in the overall national economy as they do now.

Many countries outside the original EU members have undertaken various pension reforms or at least have them on the agenda. Several Eastern European countries are undertaking so many reforms as they

---

[9] European Commission, Directorate-General for Economic and Financial Affairs, *European Economy* (Brussels: European Commission, 2001), No. 73, p. 213.

transition to market-based economies that it is difficult to assess the long-term viability of their government-sponsored retirement systems. Many of these countries have adopted far more significant pension reforms than most of the developed countries. Australia's fundamental reform of its retirement income system should reduce its costs significantly. New Zealand has not been able to craft politically sustainable reform of its pension system thus far and faces essentially the same challenges as a number of Western European countries, albeit with a slightly less severe aging problem. Korea has a much younger population than most, so its pension financing problems are still decades away. Japan is already in the throes of rapid aging and has shown a remarkable willingness to adjust its retirement system to make it more affordable. Still, there are a host of structural social and economic issues that raise concerns over the long-term viability of the Japanese system.

In North America, Canada has accelerated payroll tax increases and reduced some benefits, thus putting its pension commitments on a much sounder footing than it was just a few years ago. But there are still doubts over whether Canada's reforms have gone far enough. In the United States, a higher normal retirement age is being phased in, but there is still nearly universal agreement that the pension system will come up short when the baby boomers retire. Moreover, recent legislation has added a drug benefit to the medical insurance program covering the elderly, but no apparent means of paying for it. There is not a glimmer of consensus on how to rescue the U.S. system from its current underfunding.

The shaky footing of pension systems across the developed economies suggests that most countries have yet to directly confront the challenges of aging populations. The picture drawn by the EC relative to the EU countries is clear. Ignazio Visco, who has directed the project at the OECD in developing the projections on aging costs in the developed economies, reaches the same conclusion. He observes that "the need to continue responding as early as possible to the economic and fiscal pressures associated with ageing populations is, therefore, not reduced when the most recent reforms introduced in OECD countries are taken into account."[10]

When national retirement programs operate in a deficit situation, or are expecting one shortly, bringing them back into balance presents public policymakers with an unpopular choice: either raising someone's taxes or

[10] Ignazio Visco, "Paying for Pensions: How Important is Economic Growth," *BNL Quarterly Review* (March, 2001), no. 216, p. 99.

cutting someone's benefits. Given that the really dire conditions are projected a comfortable distance into the future, there may be some pressure to cast a positive slant on the prospects of future cost increases. A little reading between the lines of the EC's and OECD's analyses of long-term retirement costs could lead one to believe they have been under some pressure from member states to tone down the prognosis.

We have analyzed the underlying assumptions that form the basis of recent aging-related cost projections for the developed countries around the world. We looked closely at the demographic, behavioral, structural, and economic assumptions underlying the OECD projections. This analysis finds that the EC and the OECD have reasonably concluded that support systems for the aged in the developed economies need to be significantly reformed and the sooner the better. However, the analysis also suggests that the EC and the OECD may have underestimated the magnitude of cost increases many of the developed economies will face.[11]

A variant of the risk of denying the economic risks imposed by an aging population is suggesting that solutions are at hand, when, in fact, they do not yet exist or are too weak to effect a cure. Many countries have enacted reforms in response to the aging phenomenon. The problem with fixing things now for the future is that the actual resources that we will have to live on down the road do not yet exist. We are simply attempting to put in place mechanisms to generate sufficient resources to meet our needs and desires in the future, and to allocate those resources in a way that will satisfy future populations.

At various points in the discussion, we have spent considerable time analyzing alternative options for allocating future resources in the developed societies in comparison to our current baseline distributions. In practical terms, the way that retirement systems have traditionally shared improvements in living standards with retirees is through indexing of retirement benefits to worker productivity or wage growth. A number of countries have recently moved away from this linkage between worker productivity improvement and retirement benefits toward mechanisms that will tie future benefits to price increases.

A number of countries, including Italy, Germany and Sweden, have introduced automatic demographic triggers that will adjust benefits in reverse proportion to increases in the aged dependency ratios in their

---

[11] Steven A. Nyce and Sylvester J. Schieber, "Our Assumptions about Aging and What We Are Doing About It," paper presented at the American Economic Association Meetings, Atlanta, Georgia, January 6, 2002.

systems. It appears that many people in these societies do not fully appreciate what will happen when aged dependency ratios – currently in the 0.4 to 0.6 range – soar to 1.0 and even higher over the next couple of decades. We are concerned that as these triggers start to automatically reduce benefits, political realities will force retrenchment and prove the promise of current policy to be false.

The implication of the various policies being put in place is that, over time, retiree pension benefits will shrink relative to wage levels. If workers fail to grasp the long-term implications of current policies and so fail to save more while they are working or retire too early, then the relative welfare of retirees compared to working-age people will decline steadily over time. Such a phenomenon will raise fundamental equity questions that future societies may not be able to escape. Indeed, in some cases the full ramifications of the policies now on the books may not be supportable in the spirit of solidarity that now underpins the social cohesion in many developed societies.

Does Britain Have a Pension Crisis?

By David Willetts, MP, U.K. Shadow Secretary of State for Social Security

There is a widespread belief that Britain has avoided a pension crisis by taking tough decisions to hold down the value of its social security pension. As a result many forecasts show British public spending on pensions running at about 5 percent of GDP for evermore, whereas across the rest of Europe it is in the 9 to 16 percent range. But this is much too optimistic for the following three reasons:

- *Funded pensions, which Britain relies on heavily to provide even a modest income for retirees, are in financial crisis. We have expensive pension promises borne not by the state but by companies; making them good would have a significant impact on long-term corporate profitability.*
- *The British system has more means-tested welfare payments than most other countries. This expenditure is excluded from many international comparisons. If pensioners' incomes from funded sources underperform, then expenditure on means-tested welfare will be even greater.*
- *Most international comparisons include public-sector pensions for other countries but these are excluded from the UK data.*

What Britain needs is a new settlement for its pension system based on three principles:

1. *Gradually restore the position where the state social security pension is worth more than means-tested welfare.*
2. *Cutting back the obligations on company pensions so that companies can afford to keep them going.*
3. *Providing new incentives to save.*

Britain doesn't have the same problems as many other countries when it comes to pensions. But we have a distinctive set of problems of our own and they do need to be tackled.

During the late 1960s in the United States, President Lyndon Johnson declared a war on poverty. Among other results of this effort, his administration, policymakers, and the general public became much more aware of the hardships that poverty entails. One of the people who took up this issue in public discussion was a revered newscaster, Walter Cronkite, who had a daily national news program on one of the three major national television systems in the United States at the time. He would periodically run a segment on his news hour about the economic plight of the elderly. One particularly distressing segment was about low-income old people being reduced to eating cat and dog food because they could not afford anything better. At the time, the official poverty rate among the elderly in the United States was three times that of the general population, a situation that the public and policymakers came to deplore. This consensus led to legislation in the late 1960s and early 1970s to provide better social security benefits to the elderly, raising their income levels and cutting their poverty rates to levels equal to or below that of the rest of the population.

In the future, we will continue to confront questions of fairness about how we allocate the goods and services our societies produce, and it will likely not be any more tolerable down the line to see our elderly living in poverty than it was in the past. Part of the issue we will face is deciding what is substandard. In analytical terms, it may seem completely reasonable to make sure that future generations of retirees are as economically well off as current retirees – and this is what price-indexed retirement systems attempt to achieve. By the time we get to the future, however, such standards may have changed.

The concept of minimal economic needs goes back at least two centuries to Adam Smith who classified consumer goods as "either necessaries or luxuries." He classified necessaries as "not only the commodities which are indispensably necessary for the support of life, but whatever the custom of the country renders it indecent for creditable people, even of the lowest order, to be without."[12] While this concept of minimal need is absolute, it is not universal. For example, Smith explained that in late eighteenth century England, leather shoes had become an absolute necessity and no creditable person would be seen in public without them.

---

[12] Adam Smith, The *Wealth of Nations* (first published in 1776, quotation from New York: Random House, Modern Library Edition, 1994), pp. 938–939.

Yet in Scotland, custom had rendered them a necessity for men but not for women. Thus, women could still walk about barefooted without embarrassment. And in France, they were a necessity to neither men nor women. So Smith's concept includes not only the minimum level of goods needed to survive, "but those things which the established rules of decency have rendered necessary to the lowest rank of people."[13] This sense of what is decent rises and falls along with general standards of living. Policies that will have the practical effect of freezing future retirees' standards of living at today's levels may not withstand the test of social acceptability in the future. If that is the case, the perception that the aging phenomenon has been dealt with will prove false. This scenario brings to mind Macbeth's lament: "We have scotched the snake, not killed it: She'll close and be herself again while our poor malice remains in danger of her former tooth."

Political Risks from Delay in Addressing Aging Issues

If our public institutions are underestimating the magnitude of the aging phenomenon, it might simply be a manifestation of the political risks the developed economies face in operating their national retirement systems. These risks are likely to intensify as populations age.

Policymakers face a set of conflicting goals that they will ultimately have to balance. On the one hand, they cannot ignore the social democratic principles that led them to set up their social insurance programs in the first place. On the other, they cannot ignore projections of retirement costs that have the potential to stifle long histories of economic growth and improving standards of living. Balancing these goals is complicated by the time spans over which retirement benefits are earned and delivered.

Policymakers are being encouraged to adopt changes to their retirement systems and to phase them in gradually, to give workers plenty of time to adapt. But many voting citizens, especially those already retired or near retirement age, look at these programs from a cash-flow perspective and see that current benefits are being sustained by taxpayers' willingness to pay the fare now needed to cover operating costs. This perception of program costs puts pressures on policymakers to defer program changes until the public sees a clear-cut need to adopt them.

Human nature being what it is, there is a tendency to put off tasks that are perceived as adverse or burdensome as long as possible. It becomes even more tempting if, by putting things off, one can shift the burden to someone else. This temptation is accentuated in democratic

---

[13] Ibid., p. 939.

political situations where policymakers have to periodically stand for re-election. If voters favor public programs that provide them benefits and resist programs that cost them money, programs that cost them money in one election period but provide them benefits in another offer policymakers opportunities for political arbitrage.

James M. Buchanan, who won a Nobel Prize in economics for his theories on public choice, that is, economic and political decision making, based his theory on the assumption that the "average" or "representative" individual is motivated by self-interest in expressing preferences concerning collective choices. He said he was influenced by Knut Wicksell, a late nineteenth and early twentieth century Swedish economist, who believed that if you wanted to improve politics you could not do it by improving politicians because they would act according to their own self-interests.[14]

Buchanan concedes that his public choice model is foreign to the "idealist theory-philosophy of political order," that people pursue policies to promote the common good or some other higher purpose. Buchanan argues these other perspectives belong in the area of moral philosophy and that we should not look to them as guidelines for structuring our political institutions but as guidelines for an individual ethic. Sorting out which of these two models is the correct one in explaining the organization of democratic states is an empirical task.

Buchanan and Gordon Tullock develop an example in their analysis that is quite relevant to the issue at hand. The example focuses on the variability of income across a worker's lifetime. A worker expecting that he will have some good years of income and some bad might be willing to buy insurance in the good years to augment his income in the bad years, in the interest of maximizing his utility across time. At the outset of his working life, however, the worker cannot afford to buy adequate insurance to maximize his utility over his lifetime. Private insurance providers cannot enforce contracts to implement an adequate income insurance program in such a world.[15]

In such a setting, the individual may see a solution in collectivizing the redistribution of income to accomplish the result that private insurance fails to provide. The mere collectivization does not change the fact that the

---

[14] James M. Buchanan, "Marginal Notes on Reading Political Philosophy," in James M. Buchanan and Gordon Tullock, *The Calculus of Consent* (Ann Arbor: The University of Michigan, 1962), pp. 307–322.

[15] James M. Buchanan and Gordon Tullock, *The Calculus of Consent* (Ann Arbor: The University of Michigan, 1962), pp. 192–197.

contingency was not insurable in a private market, and thus participants in the program have to accept the costs of being included. As the plan is being devised, the individual has to make sure the rules are going to be equitably and universally applied across all workers in the society.

Once a system of this sort is underway, one potential problem is that a coalition of participants in it could vote to impose net taxes on other participants in order to enhance their own benefit. This creates the potential for the system to become too large – that is, the cost of participation would be higher than its potential value to the participant. Buchanan and Tullock conclude that, "The amount of redistribution that unrestrained majority voting will generate will tend to be greater than that which the whole group of individuals could conceptually agree on as 'desirable' at the time of constitutional choice."[16]

It is the change in the future outlook relative to what Paul Samuleson expected when he was analyzing his "consumption loan" model that has raised concerns about the pay-go approach for national retirement system financing. Samuelson's analysis still applies, but it portends very different benefits for current participants in the national retirement systems than those he predicted. Instead of each generation receiving relatively positive returns on lifetime contributions, younger generations are now facing marginally positive returns or even the possibility of negative returns. National retirement systems whose costs seemed reasonable a decade or two ago may now be too expensive from the perspective of workers who have to support them. But following Buchanan's public choice model, the self-interested voting behavior of participants may make these systems impervious to change.

Individuals in democratic societies do not vote their respective interests at consistent rates across a variety of personal characteristics. But when it comes to political support for governmental retirement programs, the voting habits of people at various ages might be particularly important in understanding the positions that policymakers take on these programs.

Table 13-3 includes a set of estimated voting rates in a number of European countries compiled on the basis of national elections held during the early 1990s, with the exception of the Netherlands where the data pertain to a parliamentary election in September 1989. These data were collected by survey, and, in most of these countries, self-reported voting rates exceed official voting rates. The authors of the book surmise that, in surveys, people who do not vote often report that they have because

---

[16] Ibid., p. 194.

Table 13-3. *Voting Rates by Age in Selected European Countries*

	18–29	30–39	40–49	50–59	60–69	70+
Belgium	96.7%	97.9%	97.6%	97.9%	95.6%	93.5%
Denmark	86.0	93.8	92.0	93.7	91.7	89.2
Finland	68.6	84.4	92.9	93.6	96.1	90.1
France	63.2	79.8	83.9	86.4	91.9	93.6
Germany	84.8	90.5	92.1	93.6	93.0	93.4
Great Britain	81.0	88.4	89.4	88.7	90.0	89.4
Greece	88.5	98.9	98.0	100.0	98.1	97.4
Ireland	64.1	89.2	92.2	96.1	96.9	90.5
Italy	95.4	97.0	97.8	98.7	96.7	89.3
The Netherlands	86.2	93.5	96.0	96.1	94.8	92.5
Norway	75.9	85.4	89.4	89.1	93.5	93.0
Portugal	63.7	84.6	93.2	89.3	93.5	90.0
Spain	80.6	85.1	89.9	88.8	90.5	84.3
Sweden	89.3	93.3	95.6	96.8	94.6	94.5
Switzerland	50.2	62.6	66.8	72.6	75.0	62.3
Average	78.3	88.3	91.1	92.1	92.8	89.5

Source: International Institute for Democratic and Electoral Assistance, *Youth Voter Participation* (Stockholm, Sweden: International IDEA, 1999), p. 26.

of the potential negative stigma they might feel from admitting the truth. We adjusted the data in Table 13-3 on a pro rata basis to reduce overall reported voting rates so they agree with the official voting rates reported in the respective countries.

The important point in Table 13-3 is that the younger population is less likely to vote than the older one. We have similar data for Canada, the United Kingdom, and the United States, although the age categories are slightly different in each case, but the voting patterns in these countries are very similar. In the context of preferences for publicly financed pensions, this may have significant implications. Even if a pension system pays very low rates of return overall, some people will get a better deal than others will. The outlook is very different for a 20-year-old than for a 55-year-old. At any point in time, an individual's perception about the public pension program largely depends on a basic economic question – how much more do I need to put into the program versus how much will I get out at retirement?

We took the adjusted voting rates that we derived from Table 13-3 plus those from Canada, the United Kingdom, and the United States and applied them to the projected age structures of the respective societies at various points in the future to show how population aging could affect

Table 13-4. *Estimated Share of Voters over Ages 50 and 60 for Selected Years*

	Share of Voters 50 and Over				Share of Voters 60 and Over			
	2000	2010	2030	2050	2000	2010	2030	2050
Belgium	42.41	47.00	54.95	57.96	27.33	29.33	38.98	42.06
Canada	39.66	46.51	54.27	56.33	23.27	26.82	37.98	39.97
Denmark	43.64	47.57	54.88	56.28	25.22	30.05	38.18	38.74
Finland	46.60	52.51	58.15	61.25	27.30	33.05	42.41	44.15
France	46.17	50.95	57.80	59.66	30.24	32.92	41.79	44.84
Germany	44.76	49.02	58.34	61.37	29.34	31.38	43.22	45.68
Greece	44.42	47.98	59.63	63.45	29.31	31.39	40.30	48.62
Ireland	39.53	42.38	50.37	52.96	23.03	24.81	30.92	38.00
Italy	44.00	47.98	60.76	63.22	28.23	31.33	41.96	47.68
Netherlands	40.46	45.86	54.90	56.93	23.50	27.62	38.73	40.07
Norway	43.95	48.06	55.91	58.83	27.38	30.56	40.15	42.39
Portugal	44.32	47.08	58.37	61.30	28.82	30.33	38.02	45.69
Spain	41.46	45.35	61.08	65.47	27.13	29.18	40.44	51.10
Sweden	47.00	49.50	57.36	62.49	28.74	32.88	41.29	45.52
Switzerland	47.48	53.84	62.30	65.33	28.14	33.60	46.47	47.17
United Kingdom	43.52	46.36	54.84	58.41	27.34	29.92	39.59	42.28
United States	45.13	50.35	56.20	58.03	27.43	29.74	39.06	40.32

Source: Estimated by Watson Wyatt Worldwide.

voting ages. Our results are presented in Table 13-4. In every country but France, more than 55 percent of all voters were under age 50 in 2000. By 2030, more than half the voters in all of the countries will be 50 years of age or older. Whereas in 2000, between 25 and 30 percent of the voters in all of the countries were age 60 or above, by 2030, around 40 percent will be this age in most countries.

It is naïve to assume that everyone in a democratic society votes purely their individual interests when they elect their policymakers. And most people do not base their voting decisions on a single issue, such as pension reform. Finally, it is cynical to assume that policymakers, once elected, consistently vote in accordance with the desires of the majority of their electorate. However, it is safe to assume that self-interest does affect voting behavior and candidate preferences, and that these have some influence on policymakers' decisions to support particular policies.

To put this into the context of national retirement programs, one needs to think about the relative perspective people at different ages might have about an underfunded pension system. If they truly believe it is underfunded and that money does not grow on trees, they will realize that bringing the program back into balance will require reductions in benefits, increases in revenues, or some combination of the two. It is likely that the preferences for one approach or the other will vary according to age.

Older people – those retired or very close to it – generally prefer the idea of maintaining benefits rather than cutting them. While holding benefits constant almost certainly means that taxes will have to rise, for those retired or close to it, the added taxes will be relatively minimal or non-existent. In fact, older people often perceive benefit cuts as losing money they have already contributed to the system, making the cuts a bad bargain for them. For younger people the situation is just the opposite. If they perceive that their current contributions are worth more than their future benefits, they would likely prefer to have benefits cut rather than taxes raised.

Undoubtedly, there is some intergenerational concern in all societies – children do not want to see their parents face hardships. And parents do not want to see taxes so high that their children cannot afford to buy a house, marry and start a family, and otherwise provide adequately for their own needs. But there are limits to the extent that one generation is willing to forego its own interests to support the other. The aging of the populations reflected in Table 13-4 shows that, in the future, the voters who are likely to favor retaining current benefits are likely to outnumber those who might prefer reducing benefits. This suggests that delays in addressing future pension problems will simply make it harder for policymakers to navigate the politics involved in their search for reasonable and equitable solutions.

FOURTEEN

Roadmap to the Future

One of the most interesting aspects of the population aging phenomena is the remarkable diversity of the situations that countries are facing. This is partly due to the diversity of the populations themselves – we have seen that several different patterns of aging are evolving, and that, even within a particular pattern, there are multiple variations. In some societies, populations are homogeneous, and the shared sense of heritage and values enhances the possibility of reform by consensus. Others are extremely heterogeneous, weaving together immigrant populations from the far corners of the world. In these societies, consensus is often more difficult to attain. But in their diversity also lies a strength, when you consider immigration as part of the solution to the demographic challenges the developed countries face.

Variations from country to country also arise from the wide range of policy choices that were made decades ago and that cannot be easily undone this late in the game. Countries that have traditionally relied on pay-go pension systems face a much different challenge than those with more integrated public and private tiers in their retirement systems, especially where the private systems have been funded and the assets invested in broadly diversified holdings. But even countries that have established significant funding for their retirement systems will not completely escape the need to make adjustments as their populations age.

We have seen that population aging is more than a pension problem, although pensions play an important role in the story. For example, pension problems in the United States appear relatively minor compared to those in other developed nations. But the looming deficits in the U.S. health care system may turn out to be the far more serious issue. While

351

the U.S. health care problem may be unique in its magnitude, health care and long-term care financing may double the relative claims – an added 5 to 8 percent of GDP – on several of the aging societies over the next 25 to 50 years.

Given the broad diversity of situations across the world's developed economies, it is impossible to spell out specific policy proposals that would be appropriate in every case. It is possible, however, to stipulate a set of principles that policymakers should consider as they consider their options. We believe that the set of principles that we outline in this last chapter have relatively universal application.

Principles for Reforming National Pensions

In Chapter 13, we described a variety of risks that workers face as they accumulate their retirement assets during their working lives and as they spend them during their retirement years. Any policies aimed at helping developed countries deal with the aging challenges should be mindful of these risks and should attempt to minimize them to the extent possible.

Maintain Disability and Early Survivors Programs as Social Insurance
Much of the discussion here has focused on the burden that increasing life expectancies and population aging will place on our social insurance systems. Generally speaking, people are living longer and healthier lives than ever before. But we have not yet been able to eliminate premature deaths or disability. People still die at all ages, sometimes leaving behind juvenile dependents. Accidents and illnesses sometimes cause disability, leaving people unable to provide for themselves, long before reaching retirement age.

In virtually all developed societies, social insurance provides protection against these misfortunes. To avoid the possibility that those most vulnerable to these circumstances do not voluntarily purchase insurance against them, it is in the general public interest to mandate participation in these insurance programs. Since the administrative and other loading costs on broadly universal social insurance coverage are so minuscule relative to those of private insurance companies, operating these programs through collective public entities is usually economically efficient. Providing these benefits through a government institution eliminates the commercial costs associated with private market alternatives.

Despite believing that countries should continue to provide disability insurance to their citizens, we recommend undertaking a careful review of existing programs. As we have documented, many of the systems currently operate as de facto early retirement systems for people who are too young to qualify for a retirement pension. Allowing people to self-select into such plans when they are still capable of working imposes just as much of an economic burden on society as allowing them to retire under an age-related pension and raises fundamental equity questions as well.

Continue to Provide Extra Protection to the Economically Vulnerable
One of the great accomplishments of retirement systems during the twentieth century was significantly reducing general poverty among the elderly. Lacking social insurance, people who fared badly in the labor market during their working career would be left to their own devices in old age, often spending their final years in poverty and want. Bad labor market outcomes can result from poor health, a poor economy, or just lousy luck. In any event, to the extent that workers are unable to save enough for their retirement needs, often due to circumstances beyond their control, a redistributive social insurance program can ameliorate the situation. Forcing people who have spent a working life at the margins of poverty to spend their retirement years in even further reduced circumstances is simply not acceptable in the richest societies in the world.

The extent to which any system tends to pay higher relative benefits to workers with lower lifetime earnings is an indication of the insurance that system provides against prolonged adverse labor market experience. Our own preference for providing this sort of protection is through a basic pension, which is prevalent in many existing social insurance systems. Of course, it is possible to integrate income redistribution into a basic pension formula that bases benefits on lifetime earnings, with few people being the wiser. The United States has taken this approach. We believe that this indirect approach to income redistribution often leads to misunderstandings by program participants about what their contributions support and what they themselves receive.

The Citizen's Pension

By Larry Willmore

The citizen's pension is a universal flat pension which covers all the elderly. Benefits are the same for everyone, regardless of income, assets, or work history. A means-tested pension provides reduced benefits or none at all for those with other income or assets. A minimum pension or top-up does nothing for unpaid caregivers or those employed in the informal sector.

The citizen's pension has advantages over means-tested, contribution-tested, and retirement-tested schemes. It is simple to administer, does not stigmatize recipients, avoids disincentives to work and to save, and can ensure that no elderly person lives in poverty.

Nonetheless, in the OECD, only one country – New Zealand – provides a universal and meaningful pension to its aged population. New Zealand is also unique in that its government has never mandated contributions to earnings-related pension plans. A proposal to replace the citizen's pension in New Zealand with a mandatory, defined contribution scheme was defeated 12 to 1 in a 1997 referendum that attracted a record 80 percent of registered voters.

The cost of public pensions in New Zealand is relatively low because they are set at a modest flat rate, equal to about 42 percent of per capita GDP. The 11.7 percent of the population older than 65 years, who qualify for the citizen's pension, should cost taxpayers (0.42)*(0.117) or 4.9 percent of GDP. Actual costs net of taxes are lower (4.1 percent of GDP), largely because benefits are taxable as income, but also because pensions are reduced for beneficiaries who are married or share accommodations.

Citizens ought to be attracted to the idea of a citizen's pension, for it provides peace of mind regarding one's own fate, or the fate of a parent, grandparent, aunt, spouse, friend, or neighbour, in old age. Provided the pension is not set at too high a level or given at too young an age, this peace of mind comes at an affordable price. Nonetheless, the citizen's pension is surprisingly rare even though governments do not hesitate to force workers to contribute to earnings-related schemes.

In light of problems with contributory pension arrangements in developing countries, the World Bank has taken notice of the citizen's pension and indeed it features as part of a "zero pillar" introduced in its new position paper.

Saving Through Retirement Savings Programs Increases Flexibility

We have seen in the discussion throughout the analysis here that the major challenge facing pay-as-you-go retirement systems is the rising aged dependency ratios that are driving pension costs above the level that several advanced societies are willing to endure. Adding a tier of savings in the social insurance system can relieve some of the cost pressures due to population aging. Within the domestic economy this is achieved because funded systems require more rapid adjustments in the face of changing demographics if they are to remain funded than are generally brought to bear in the case of pay-as-you-go systems. In a larger global context, pension funding builds capital reservoirs that allow the sort of cross national investment that may be part of the economic solution to changing demographics in the most rapidly aging societies as we discussed in Chapter 12.

There are many different ways of setting up savings systems. We see virtues in individual account mechanisms, because they potentially provide more benefit security than plans where assets are held by the government. Sometimes centrally held funds are diverted by policymakers for purposes other than providing retirement security. While there may be virtues in individual account programs, such programs can be expensive to administer, as we documented in the case of Mexico. In addition, such funds are not immune from diversion for other social causes, as has been the case for some of the Asian provident funds. Finally, we acknowledge that when governments are facing general financial turmoil, as has been the case in Argentina in recent years, funded pensions are politically tempting sources of funds in a crisis. No system is immune from problems.

Providing for retirement should be the most important motive for saving on the part of the majority of citizens in the developed economies of the world. Saving for retirement will create more wealth for future workers, as well as stimulating higher productivity and higher real wages. Taking a look at countries that have adopted savings policies tied to their retirement systems in recent years, Sweden provides an excellent example of a sound approach. Its system is not perfect, but the individual retirement savings accounts in which workers can direct the investment of their funds through approved investment managers imparts a sense of ownership to workers that is impossible in a traditional pay-go pension system. The organization of the Swedish system is more administratively efficient than many other individual account systems implemented elsewhere.

Not all societies are willing to go as far as Sweden has. Canada's approach – building up a central fund to be invested in real assets – is an alternative. As long as the funds are segregated and managed by an independent board, this funding approach can be even more administratively efficient than the Swedish approach. The lack of individual ownership of funds, however, could potentially make the accumulating assets a tempting target for political purposes. We believe pension funds should be invested solely in the interest of plan participants, with no other social or political encumbrances attached.

Despite our concerns about Canada's approach, it is far superior to investing pension trust funds solely in the government bonds of the sponsoring country. The evidence cited in Chapter 5 suggests to us that much of the supposed "pension saving" being done in this fashion is being diverted to other government purposes. Our analysis there leads us to conclude that real saving invested in real assets is the best way to secure the retirement consumption needs of future generations.

Pension Reform should Provide Equitable Treatment
between Participants

In Chapter 3, we discussed the underlying issues of the day during the period when the national pension systems were introduced or modernized during the twentieth century. In many cases, early generations of participants received tremendous economic windfalls as their programs got off the ground. As we look forward, the days of excess benefits are long gone. But in reforming our systems, we should strive to ensure that young workers are not unduly disadvantaged by joining the system this late in the game. By the same token, we need to be mindful that current retirees played by the rules during their working lives and should not be unduly penalized by changing the rules when it is too late for them to change their behavior accordingly. But many of the problems we now face have been known to us for some time, so the full burden of our delayed response should not fall on the backs of workers, many of whom were not even born when existing retirement systems were crafted.

In countries where spousal dependent benefits are subsidized or other such subsidies are paid, the pension systems create inequities. In the United States, for example, a worker whose spouse does not work for pay outside the home is paid a benefit that is 1.5 times that paid to a single worker at the same income level. There is no reason why a single-earner couple should receive such a subsidy. If the retirement system is structured to provide benefits that are 70 percent of career earnings, because that is what the society considers to be adequate, it is not clear why subsidies should be paid to a couple who managed on a single income during their working years.

Pension Funding Transition Costs should be Spread Across
Generations

To the extent that countries decide to shift toward greater funding of their retirement systems, the transition from pay-go arrangements has the potential to create cross-generation equity problems that can be ameliorated by spreading the costs over several generations. The liabilities that have already accumulated in the existing systems cannot be ignored; many people are counting on these benefits for their sustenance in old age. For some period of time, those obligations will still have to be met under the old pay-go model. If societies are simultaneously moving toward a funded program, doing so rapidly would hit one or two generations of workers with a double bill – paying off the consumer loans to their parents' generation while also funding their own retirement benefits. Such an outcome would be unfair.

Pension Accounting should be done on an Accrual Basis
Much of the pension accounting today is done on a pay-go basis. As we saw back in Chapter 5, this approach to tracking pension flows can lead to misconceptions about pension saving. To the extent that accruing obligations are outstripping contributions, short-term cash surpluses may imply that considerable savings are being accumulated, even as a plan is careening toward unsustainability. Accrual accounting also will help sort out the true economic costs associated with a shift from a pay-as-you-go system toward one that is partially funded for societies that choose to go this route.

The Pension System should be Structured to Encourage Economic Efficiency
In many countries, there has been a longstanding debate about whether social security contributions are essentially taxes or deferred compensation – i.e., pension contributions. In many existing systems, the link between marginal contributions and marginal benefits is weak, so most people view the pension scheme as a tax/transfer system rather than a deferred compensation system. For people whose covered work histories are either short or very long, there is no return on making additional marginal contributions. Since spousal benefits accrue to non-working spouses who make no contributions at all, the connection between contributions and benefits may be minimal or nil for secondary earners in two-earner households.

If many people view payroll taxes, which can range up to 20 to 30 percent, as a marginal tax with little or no offsetting marginal benefits, then the distortionary costs of the overall tax system are greatly increased. Imposing an expensive payroll tax on top of an income tax can result in an excessive tax burden across the earnings spectrum. The efficiency costs of the tax system, which goes up with the square of the marginal tax rate, can easily triple or quadruple due to the payroll tax. A closer link between marginal contributions and benefits can lower the effective marginal tax rate, thereby enhancing economic efficiency.

A very important aspect of improved economic efficiency is eliminating existing incentives that encourage still productive workers to retire. In order to minimize these disincentives, workers who delay retirement should be rewarded accordingly. At normal retirement age or another specified age, the pension system should either suspend payroll tax contributions, or increase benefits to reflect the additional contributions from working later in life and the shortened retirement period.

Assure that Risks Borne by Individuals are Diversified and at Tolerable Levels

All retirement plans carry a certain amount of risk. Some analysts are particularly concerned that the type of retirement systems adopted by Chile or Australia leave workers too vulnerable to financial market risks. On the other hand, many people have long considered large national defined benefit plans to be relatively risk-free. Citizens of Germany and Japan have recently learned otherwise. One of the first principles for dealing with risk in financial markets is diversification. While we may not think about our national social security systems as being part of the financial markets, they represent a substantial portion of the savings portfolio for many people. In that regard, a well-crafted, two-tier system might significantly reduce the risks associated with existing national pension plans. The first tier would serve as a safe harbor against catastrophic financial market outcomes. The financial assets in the second tier would help to ameliorate the burden on the centralized pension and reduce the political risks that benefit levels promised by current systems will not be sustainable.

Keep Administrative Costs Low

In our earlier discussion about funding, we pointed out that some countries manage pension plan asset accumulations more efficiently than others. The difference in a half-percentage or even 1 percent return per year has tremendous implications for the economic horsepower of savings over a worker's career. Back in Chapter 3, we used an example of a worker saving over her career to fund her retirement needs. We assumed she would realize an annual rate of return of 5 percent per year on her pension savings. Increasing that assumption to 5.5 percent per year would increase her pension accumulation at retirement by 10 percent. At a 6 percent return, it would be 23 percent higher. In the case of the individual account systems established in Mexico and Sweden, Mexico's annual administrative fees probably cost at least 1.5 percentage points of assets per year more than Sweden's. The long-term implications on benefit levels are immense.

Some Portion of Retirement Savings should be Annuitized at Retirement

In Chapter 13, we explored the risks associated with self-annuitization of retirement assets and the unfortunate consequences when people underestimate or overestimate how long they will live. If retirees cannot achieve at least a minimally secure standard of living on their own, they tend to depend on the state to make up the difference. In order to minimize this prospect, it is in the public interest to ensure that everyone has an acceptable level of income during retirement. This can be achieved most successfully by requiring retirees to take some portion of their retirement savings in the form of a life annuity. In most developed societies, the literature on utilization of voluntary annuities suggests that only a small minority of people buy them. One reason may be that existing pension systems are so generous that most people do not think they need further insurance against outliving their assets.

We do not know exactly how people might react under a revamped pension regime, but it is in the state's interest to require that total pension annuities at least meet the minimal standard of living test set by public policy. The annuitization of pension savings should take into account any level of first-tier benefits the pension system might provide. We believe that beyond this level of annuitization, retirees should have complete control over their remaining assets. If someone wants to live more cheaply in retirement to preserve their assets for heirs, that is for them to decide, not the government.

Annuitization should be on a Joint and Survivor Basis for Couples

Even in the developed world, poverty is disproportionately concentrated among older women. Overall, women do not work as many years as their male counterparts, and they tend to earn less over their careers than men do, even when they work full-time. Because of these differences, women often end up with smaller pensions than men. Another reason that older women are more likely to be poor than men is that women live longer, on average, than men. In a typical couple, the husband, who is often slightly older than his wife, dies first. Under many pension systems, the husband's death reduces the total pension income paid to the surviving wife. We believe that it would make more sense to finance full joint and survivor benefits, with a slight reduction in the benefit paid to both husband and wife while they are alive. The annuity cost is relatively moderate and the potential reductions in old-age poverty could be significant.

Reforms should Assure Long-Term Solvency of the Pension System

Historically, many countries have not done long-term projections on their pension systems. Even projections of 25 or 50 years may not allow enough time to plan for the implications of changing demographics. Fifty-year projections may seem too far off for present-day policymakers to worry about, but most of the people who will receive a pension 50 years from now are already here. On the demographic side, at least, we have a fairly good idea of how population changes will affect these systems. We should strive to organize systems that will be sustainable, given what we now know about pension plan operations and our evolving populations. If we do not make a sincere and determined effort to create stable pension institutions for our citizens, the people will lose faith in our democratic forms of government.

Pension Reforms should be Explicit and Transparent

If nothing else, we hope that this story has convinced readers that we must act now to prepare for aging populations across virtually all the developed world. Most of the options for reform being discussed today involve policies our policymakers would prefer to ignore. Failing that, they may try to promote policies that will achieve the necessary ends, but downplay – or even disguise – the implications for those who will be affected by the reforms, essentially everyone. In Chapter 13, we talked about changes that Italy and Sweden have made to their pension systems. We are not convinced that the public in these countries fully understands the long-term implications of their pension reforms on benefit levels. We fear that as the true implications begin to unveil themselves, there will be tremendous public pressure to reverse course on difficult decisions already taken. To avoid unhappy surprises among pensioners and workers, changes to pension systems should be presented to the public in the clear light of what we know and expect.

Another tack that policymakers sometimes pursue is to tap "free" sources of income to achieve their policy goals. For example, in the latter years of Bill Clinton's presidency in the United States, policymakers advocated using the federal budget surpluses to shore up financing for the U.S. Social Security system, so when the baby boomers began to retire, the system would be ready for them. One issue they failed to address, however, was that virtually all of the surpluses in the unified budget were attributable to cash-flow surpluses in the trust fund programs – programs like Social Security and Medicare. Outside of the trust funds, U.S. government operations have run only four surpluses from the Great Depression through the end of 2000. And the trust fund accounts themselves were scheduled to go into deficit early in the twenty-first century.

Our assessment of the pensions systems across many countries is that they are underfunded, and future generations of retirees may not be able to retire in the manner they have come to expect. If we wish to sustain our basic retirement patterns, we will have to save more, take smaller benefits in retirement, or convince taxpayers to ante up more of their earnings. The magnitude of the problem is far too enormous for resolution by sleight-of-hand or magic bunnies pulled from a hat.

Benefits in Reformed Pension Systems should be Transparent
Some countries, such as Germany, have historically tied benefits to life-time earnings and contributions to the pension system. Others, like the U.S. system, have commingled the adequacy and equity elements of their program in a way that people cannot decipher. We believe people will not support these systems unless they understand how and why the rules for accruing a pension work the way they do.

Pension Reforms should be Undertaken as soon as Possible
One of the authors had a philosophy professor at university who observed that our happiness depends on the extent to which our realizations matched our aspirations. Throughout much of this discussion, we have used a variety of examples and models to calculate how pension benefits and standards of living might change under a range of alternative scenarios. The fact of the matter is that most people do not use the sorts of models we have been using here to plan their future retirement. We believe that most people use a somewhat simpler model – what we might call a "looking-around" model. Most people grow up in their communities, go to school, then to work and rub elbows daily with the people around them. They watch their parents' generation go through life, working, raising children, and so forth, and then reaching retirement. They also watch older siblings, cousins or fellow workers do the same thing. Over time, they develop certain expectations and aspirations about how their own life will play out. They come to assume that if they behave in certain ways, they can expect certain outcomes. This is all fine and works well in a stable environment. But the looking-around model is prone to breaking down in an unstable environment like the one many developed countries are rapidly approaching.

In Chapter 3, we described the pension financing process and discussed alternative approaches in delivering benefits during start-up phases of alternative systems. The problem we are likely facing as we move forward with pay-go plans is that their desirable characteristic – delivering relatively instant benefits during start-up – will likely look a lot less desirable when it inverts, and the plan delivers relatively instant benefit cuts in response to the new demographic realities. Policymakers are trying to encourage private savings vehicles to compensate for pay-go system cutbacks. But as we also saw in Chapter 3, it takes a funded plan a long time to accumulate the assets it needs to deliver an appropriate level of benefits. The longer we delay adjusting pay-go systems, the larger the cuts that are likely to be required. The longer we delay getting people into savings vehicles, the smaller their cash reserves will be when the real financing crunch hits. In short, the longer we delay taking action, the steeper the fall will be from the pension aspirations most people acquired from watching their parents' generation in retirement.

The Developing World: A Short Window to Address Global Ageing Issues

By Todd Petersen, Help Age International

In an increasingly globalised world, many issues once seen as exclusive either to "developed" or "developing" countries, are becoming the shared experience of both. The challenge posed by population ageing is one such issue which has emerged onto the policy agenda even in many developing and middle-income countries. Awareness that the numbers of older people in developing countries, which are already home to two-thirds of the global population over 65, will grow substantially in the coming decades has focused thinking on this brief window of opportunity to implement policies to meet the growing challenge. A central focus of policy thinking has been on welfare issues, with pension reform at the core of the discussion.

A strong challenge to public welfare provision has been mounted in recent years, led by the World Bank with its publication of Averting the Old Age Crisis in 1994. The World Bank report questioned the sustainability of unfunded, pay-as-you-go state pension systems in the face of growing numbers of older people worldwide and declining formal workforces. It proposed mandatory savings by individuals in privately managed accounts, based on the model introduced in Chile during the Pinochet regime. Since the mid-1990s, the World Bank has become a leading adviser on pension reform along these lines to governments in Africa, Asia, Latin America, and East and Central Europe.

However, this approach has not gone unchallenged. Critics of systemic pension reform agendas have aimed to reconceptualise the problem of pension reform as a longstanding public-private partnership issue rather than as a new challenge stemming from existing or anticipated state failures. Questions exist both for public and private provision in the developing world. One is the development of a secure and transparent framework for insurance-based contributory pensions provided to the small but growing numbers of retirees from formal public and private-sector jobs. Another is the place of a welfare-based system reaching the very large numbers of those growing old in poverty in developing countries. There has, for example, been a call for the provision of "[small but regular] cash incomes ... universally to all the elderly, including, especially, the hard to reach, elderly poor" (Charlton and McKinnon). This view counters prevailing approaches to pension system reform, with their strong orientation towards economic growth and their de-emphasis of pensions as welfare instruments for protection of vulnerable and increasingly large segments of populations.

While fostering economic growth is the only way to reduce poverty in the long term, the potential of growth and equality may also be a viable dual goal. Indeed, at a local level, pension transfers to older people can have not only a "welfare" impact, but also significant redistributive effects, stimulating local economies, as research has shown for example in South Africa. These debates are likely to grow in volume in the coming years, as the brief window of opportunity – provided by the recognition of a challenge which is not yet a crisis – begins to close.

References

World Bank: Averting the Old Age Crisis, 1994. New York, Oxford University Press.

R. Charlton and R. McKinnon, Pensions in Development. 2002. U.K., Ashgate Press.

Principles for Reforming Employer-Based Pensions

A number of countries have sizeable employer-based pension systems. In a number of cases, these systems seem to be under considerable stress themselves. Some of this pressure results from regulatory burdens imposed on the systems. We believe a larger part relates to some of the same funding issues that plague public pensions. It is impossible for us to take up the full scale of issues around employer-sponsored pensions in the context of this discussion – one text on the U.S. employer-based pension regulatory and operating environment alone runs to more than 800 pages[1] – but one issue is so importance that we must address it.

In some cases, employers have been allowed to set up and operate their pensions on a book reserve or even pay-go basis. In the case of the book reserve funding, the assets of the sponsoring organizations back the pension. In pay-go funding, the ongoing successful operation of the organization backs it. In today's dynamic world, where entire industries can vanish from our national landscapes in relatively short periods of time,

---

[1] Dan M. McGill, Kyle N. Brown, John J. Haley, and Sylvester J. Schieber, *Fundamentals of Private Pensions* (Oxford: Oxford University Press, 2004).

no private organization can be certain that it will exist in its current form 10 or 20 years down the road. Workers in these organizations are in the same boat as the workers in our national economies. They work for 30 or 40 years and then retire for another 20 years or so. Their involvement with their pensions can easily last for 60 years, and it would not be uncommon for it to last up to 80 or more years, including both the work and retirement periods. If these workers depend extensively on the benefits provided by the employer-sponsored plans, the benefits have to be secured. The only way that benefits can be secured in this situation is to actually fund them as they are earned and to require that the savings be invested in a relatively diversified portfolio of financial assets.

Bringing Health Care under Control

In Chapter 6, we explored the growth in health costs across the developed economies of the world. We concluded that the evolution of technology was one major reason that our health systems are growing faster than almost every economy in the developed world. We are not the only analysts to come to this conclusion. In a recent OECD report based on their three-year health project, Elizabeth Docteur concluded that: "Given the role of health-related technology as the primary factor contributing to health cost growth, better management of technology has been recognized by policy makers as an important frontier for efficiency improvements."[2]

If new technology is the major cost driver of health expenditures and health costs have to be brought under control, it is time to step back and review how we are spending our R&D money and how we finance the beneficial products and services that evolve from it. Burton Weisbrod and Craig LaMay call for a rethinking of R&D incentives. There are at least a couple of ways that policymakers could help in this regard. One is to put the financing of certain technologies outside the realm of financing through health insurance plans. The other is to sponsor more structured research on efficient delivery regimens and best practices in health service delivery.[3]

When a new drug broke onto the market several years ago that restored sexual potency for men, many insurance programs moved fairly quickly to cover prescriptions. While there is little doubt that this drug enhanced the

---

[2] Elizabeth Docteur, *Toward High-Performing Health Systems* (Paris: OECD, 2004), p. 105.

[3] Burton A. Weisbrod and Craig L. LaMay, "Mixed Signals: Public Policy and the Future of Health Care R&D," *Health Affairs* (March/April 1999), vol. 18, no. 2, pp. 112–125.

quality of life of many people, it is hard to make a case that the problem it treated was life threatening or even inhibited a relatively normal life. Yet there is little doubt that the coverage of this drug under health insurance programs significantly increased the demand for the product and total health costs covered under third-party payment arrangements.

The coverage of questionable medical procedures or products is complicated by a legal and regulatory environment in some countries that encourages coverage of new technologies as they come on line. Judgments about necessary and appropriate care should be made in the context of good information about the outcomes of treatment alternatives. But there are huge variations in physician practice patterns that "appear to be determined largely by local medical opinion concerning the value of surgery or its alternatives."[4]

That assessment was aimed at the U.S. health delivery system, but cross national studies evaluating the rate of adoption and patterns of health-related technologies show similar results. One study compared the levels of intensity of care and medications given to heart attack patients in 17 countries over the past decade. They grouped countries into three classes: early adopters, fast growth; late start, fast growth; and late start, slow growth. The United States, Japan, and possibly France fell into the first group. Australia, Belgium, and the Canadian provinces, except Ontario, fell into the second. The United Kingdom, the Scandinavian countries, and Ontario fell into the third. The researchers found similar patterns of diffusion for new high-cost drugs but no similar pattern for low-cost, easy-to-use medications.[5]

While the United States may be a major power center in developing new health care technology, it is not always the leader in its applications. In the area of imaging technology, in 2001, the United States had 12.8 computed tomography (CT) scanners in operation per million people in the population. Docteur claims the U.S. estimates significantly understate reality, because they report the numbers of hospitals with units and do not capture the extent that these hospitals have multiple units.[6] By comparison to the U.S. number, though, the United Kingdom had only 4.8 units, France 9.0 units, and Canada had 9.7 units per million people. But Austria had 26.7 units, Korea 27.3 units, and Japan somewhere

---

[4] John E. Wennberg, Elliott S. Fisher, and Jonathan S. Skinner, "Geography and the Debate over Medicare Reform," *Health Affairs*, 13, February 2002, pp. 96–114.

[5] Elizabeth Docteur, *Toward High-Performing Health Systems*, p. 64.

[6] Ibid., p. 64.

around 90 units per million people. The prevalence of multiple reso-
nance imaging (MRI) scanners was somewhat narrower. In this case, the
United States had 8.2 units per million compared to the United Kingdom's
4.5 units, Canada's 4.2 units, and France's 2.4 units per million. Austria
had 11.7 MRIs, Finland 11.0, and Switzerland 12.9 units per million people.[7] One study that compared the usage of these devices in the United
States and Canada found that even where hospitals had similar access to
the machines, U.S. patients received many more CT and MRI exams than
Canadians. The result was largely the result of more intensive use of the
equipment for the elderly in the United States than in Canada.[8]

Just because a country is a reluctant adopter of one sort of health
procedure or technology does not mean they are not significant users
in other areas and vice versa. For example, in the United States during
2001, doctors performed 106.5 coronary bypass operations per 100,000
people in the population. Canada, by comparison, had 133.2 of such operations. The United Kingdom, with one of the most controlled systems in
the developed world, had 46.8 operations per 100,000 people, Italy 47.2,
France 41.2, and Austria 54.4.[9]

As the OECD health project has unfolded over the past three years,
there has been a growing effort to systematically track the net results of
alternative practice patterns. For example, among 12 countries reporting
30-day, in-hospital mortality rates for people suffering from acute my-
ocardial infarctions, the mortality rates ranged from nine to 14 percent
across the countries, but from 17 to 28 percent among patients between
the ages of 75 and 89. In tracking deaths attributed to asthma in people
ages five to 39 across 16 OECD countries, there were 0.1 to 0.9 deaths per
100,000 people. There was some concern about variations in the quality of
data across countries in coding cause of death. Still, New Zealand, which
had a much higher mortality rate than other countries in this case, tracked
the result back to treatment practices – the use of high-dose fenoterol, a
beta-antagonist linked to asthma deaths. Following changes to their practice, the mortality rates dropped significantly over the past decade and
now are comparable to those in other developed countries.[10]

Whether primary responsibility for controlling the utilization rests with
consumers, physicians and delivery systems, or the insurance institutions

---

[7] OECD, *OECD Health Data 2004* (Paris, 2004).
[8] S.J. Katz, L.F. McMahon, and W.G. Manning, "Comparing the Use of Diagnostic Tests in
Canadian and U.S. Hospitals," *Medical Care* (1996), vol. 34, no. 2, pp. 117–125.
[9] OECD, *OECD Health Data 2004* (Paris, 2004).
[10] Elizabeth Docteur, *Toward High-Performing Health Systems*, p. 36.

themselves, we need far better information about the patient outcomes associated with various treatment alternatives. Recently, a number of countries have begun health technology assessment programs to encourage and facilitate health service delivery on the basis of scientific evidence. Part of the challenge in bringing better information to bear on what works in the health sector and what does not is the development of cross-national data systems, so procedures and practice patterns can be measured and compared, and study results can be passed back to practicing medical staff on a systematic basis. Practices that do not provide measurable, medically proven value should neither be delivered nor funded by the health care system. More sophisticated data systems to track treatment and prescription regimens for individual patients could enhance their health while reducing the delivery of unnecessary services.

There is fairly broad agreement, even among analysts who believe that continued investment in health technology is worthwhile, that much of the health care delivered today does little to improve health or the quality of life. Given the size of the bill that will be coming due over future decades, as an increasing percentage of our populations ages into the peak health demand years, this area cries out for policy attention. Health care is a cross-national issue to a much greater extent than pensions, at least within the narrow context of costs associated directly with aging populations.

Public policymakers need to redirect some of the money currently spent on R&D into efforts to identify effective treatment procedures and protocols. Weisbrod and LaMay point to efforts in other areas that demonstrate the potential of rearranging the incentives. In 1993, the Whirlpool Corporation won a $30 million dollar prize offered by a consortium of 25 electric utility companies to whoever could develop an energy-efficient refrigerator that would run on 25 percent less electricity than current models, without using chlorofluorocarbons. Reaching further back in history, they point to a prize awarded in 1714 by the British Royal Academy. It seemed that British shipping companies were losing cargo because of the inability of mariners to measure longitude. The Academy offered a prize to anyone who could solve this problem, which had eluded Galileo and Isaac Newton. John Harrison set to work, solved the problem and won a cash prize that would be equivalent to $24 million today.[11] Mankind has repeatedly shown tremendous ingenuity in solving life's problems when an attractive reward is in the offing.

---

[11] Burton A. Weisbrod and Craig L. LaMay, "Mixed Signals: Public Policy and the Future of Health Care R&D," *Health Affairs* (March/April 1999), vol. 18, no. 2, p. 124.

Facilitating Cross-National Capital Flows

In Chapter 11, we discussed the promise of cross-national investing as a means of relief from the economic pressures that aging populations will bring about in the developed economies of the world. To clear the way for significant cross-national investing, several important changes must be made in many areas of the developed world.

One reason the developed economies have been able to thrive as they have over most of the twentieth century is the relatively free flow of capital into economic activities that investors perceive as good investments. While there has been significant investment in a number of the developing countries in recent years, some evidence indicates that much of that investment has performed at sub-par levels. For example, in China, much of the industrial investment that has flowed into the country has been channeled into joint ventures, as the Chinese government forced companies from the developed economies to link up with former state-owned enterprises as the price of admission to play in the economy. Joe Studwell, a contributing writer to *The Economist* and editor-in-chief of the *China Economic Quarterly*, suggests that much of that investment has gone down the drain, because the local entities could not or would not play the capitalist game in ways that have succeeded elsewhere. For example, he draws a distinction between Taiwan and mainland China:

Through the 1980s and 1990s Taiwan reinvented itself, ditching the low value-added manufacturing of toys and clothing to become one of the world's leading centres of high-tech production. The island is the dominant global player in note-book computers, the world's third largest manufacturer of semi-conductor wafers and a regional force in petrochemicals. This modernization was not achieved through central planning and government largesse. Taiwanese companies prospered through their own endeavours; they have the lowest debt-to-equity ratios in Asia while Taiwanese banks boast the lowest bad debt ratios. The degree of openness of the Taiwanese economy, compared with that of the mainland is shown by the remarkable fact that through the 1990s Taiwan imported more goods from the United States that did the whole of mainland China. An island of 22 million people was a bigger U.S. export market than a continent-size country of 1.3 billion people.[12]

Studwell's story about China is full of examples like that of Manang Steel, which went public on the Hong Kong stock exchange in 1993, raising $795 million in its public offering. Within a year of going public, it had committed most of the capital it had raised to expanding product

---

[12] Joe Studwell, *The China Dream* (New York: Atlantic Monthly Press, 2002), p. 268.

lines for which there was little market demand. The company propped up sales by extending credit to buyers – $240 million in the first year. The holding company that "owned" 62 percent of the operating company had no say in appointing senior management, who were chosen by the Ministry of Metallurgical Industry of Beijing and the local provincial Party committee. After the company's first year, its managers decided to pay a dividend but refused to pay the share owed to the holding company. The company also refused to pay for services and iron ore it had received from the holding company. It did "book" a profit and paid taxes to the central and local governments. A year after the listing, the holding company was insolvent.[13]

A number of preconditions must be met before capital can flow freely from the developed economies and become a major factor in helping the developing countries advance, while providing some relief to the aging nations. First, capital markets must be structured to allow for the efficient allocation of capital. Second, established legal frameworks must require proper disclosure of all financial transactions. Third, legal mechanisms for resolving disputes in accordance with a codified system of laws must be created. This code of laws should protect the property rights of owners over their capital and its utilization. Fourth, capital owners must be able to repatriate the returns on their investments. If the scenario we have painted of developed nations investing in developed nations plays out, the repatriation of investment returns will likely be mostly in the form of goods and services flowing back to the aged developed nations – helping to ameliorate the pressures on their own productive capacities as aging populations and aged dependency ratios swell. Fifth, labor laws and practices must be put in place to encourage the efficient use of capital in a work environment that is just and humane.

Most of the less developed countries of the world have a way to go to meet all these conditions. We believe that it is in the collective interest of the developed economies act now to encourage the evolution of these preconditions across as broad a range of countries as possible. Organizations such as the World Bank and World Trade Organization are best suited to provide this assistance. Without successful reforms to provide an environment that can sustain successful cross-national capital flows, we believe the standards of living in both the developed and developing countries will not be where they could be.

---

[13] Ibid, p. 242.

Conclusion

It was the ample supplies of labor and their efficient utilization that gave birth to the tremendous improvements in standards of living in the developed world over the past century. Indeed, there was surplus labor capacity in many of the developed economies over much of that period. This long history of ever-rising standards of living has engendered expectations that the future will unfold in the same vein. But the outlook for the future, at least on the labor front, is starkly different from what it was in the past.

As the full implications of population aging become evident, policymakers will have to respond. But there will be tremendous resistance to proposals for change. One only has to look at the anti-immigration fever sweeping many developed nations today to get a glimpse of the challenges ahead. And the challenges go well beyond immigration policy.

The Berlusconi government in Italy has encountered tremendous resistance and labor strife as it has attempted to restructure the regulatory environment to improve the efficiency of its labor markets. The labor movement in France began to resist even before the government proposed changes to address pension policy in coming years. Fist fights have broken out on the floor of the Japanese diet as it has debated legislation to bring its pension programs into balance. Public officials are likely to face tremendous political pressure to put off changes as long as conceivably possible. Even in Sweden and Italy, which have already adopted significant reforms, the effects of these reforms will not hit pensioners in their pocketbooks for several decades.

Employers will be affected by the aging phenomenon and its implications, but they are not in the hot seat in the same way that public policymakers are. Public policymakers must worry about the implications of population aging on overall levels of economic activity. They need to adopt policies that encourage labor force participation and enhance worker productivity. National retirement systems can have significant effects on each. Policymakers also have to worry about the structure of retirement systems and the way they affect the distribution of economic output. The latter is not so much the worry of employers, although it may affect their ability to attract needed workers into the workplace.

Increasing labor productivity will help employers deal with the labor shortfalls ahead, but it may be of less use to policymakers. If the benefits from increasing worker productivity are taxed away to the welfare state, workers may not be nearly as willing to make the effort to increase productivity in the first place.

The biggest potential benefit policymakers can realize from changing retirement systems is higher rates of labor force participation. The mathematical reality of population aging in the world's developed economies likely dictates that the citizens of these countries will have to work much longer than their forebears had to, or else resign themselves to reduced standards of living in retirement. Giving up the political achievements of the past, however, will not be easy medicine to swallow. It looks like modifications now on the books or merely in the planning stages may not be quick enough to change labor force behavior in the immediate future. Because of the slowdown in the growth of their labor forces, employers in several developed economies may be facing substantial shortfalls in the number of workers required to produce desired levels of output by the end of this decade. If labor productivity continues to grow at the rate it did during the 1990s, Belgium, France, Germany, Italy, and Spain could all fall short of the labor they need to sustain their past rates of growth in GDP per capita. In the final analysis, it will be the employers in all of these countries that have to deal with the new labor realities of the twenty-first century. Tight labor markets will undoubtedly mean that employers will have to compete more aggressively for employees, which will drive up wages. Although employers may succeed in bidding new workers into the workplace and/or retaining their current staff, the current analysis indicates that the erosion of labor supplies over the coming decade may be too severe for employers to overcome through attraction and retention policies. Subsequently, in order for employers to meet their production needs in the future, they will have to reconsider the structure of their workplace arrangements. More specifically, employers may need to create a workforce environment that leverages their human capital to entice more production out of their existing employees.

The tightening labor markets will not give employers any free passes on managing the capital that is in their keeping. The growth in funded pensions in the world's developed economies will likely mean an increasing role for institutional investors, who are prone to demand that capital be managed for maximum efficiency. Once again, it is likely that the firms that manage their workforces most effectively, despite tight labor markets, will be the most successful at dealing with the realities of an aging world.

Ultimately, the success of nations, workers, and capital owners in responding to the challenges of aging populations will depend in some significant part on the evolution of the global economy. Many of the same forces that resist political responses to population aging will also resist the utilization of the global economy in responding to the aging phenomenon and all that goes with it. Once again, the mathematical realities of the situation will dictate the outcomes.

As employers meet the realities of tightening labor markets in the coming decade, they will have limited options for responding to them. To the extent they stay in the developed economies with tight restricted labor supplies, they are going to have to adopt policies that maximize the efficiency of their labor. To the extent they cannot realize adequate returns on capital in the developed economies, they will likely seek out alternative labor in the global economy where they can operate on a sustainable basis.

This concluding discussion may hold out some hope for workers in the developed economies that they are going to be a premium element in the ultimate solution to the challenges we face. We hope that is the case and that workers will flourish as the generations before them have in the countries that have been our primary focus. In order for this to happen, policymakers will need to consider a whole range of changes to facilitate this process. These range from modifying policies that discourage employers from hiring available workers, to policies that encourage workers to stop working at an age when they could still make a major economic contribution to themselves and their societies.

We opened the discussion here by referring to Shakespeare's seven ages of life and noted that when he wrote the play, "As You Like It," life expectancy at birth was 25 to 30 years of age. Jumping forward to more modern times, at the beginning of the 1900s, before most pension systems were operating, life expectancy was still decades shorter than it is today. Yet across most of what is now the developed world, people who lived well into their 60s in the early 1900s mostly supported themselves by continuing to work. There may be some disappointment if we have to retrench on some of the early retirement achievements our parents or grandparents were able to enjoy, but we should consider that it beats the alternative. All the investments we have made in health care, improved living and working conditions, and the like have paid us a tremendous dividend in the form of extended healthy lives. We have considerably pushed back Shakespeare's seventh stage of life when we live in oblivion, our senses largely gone. If we can accept a somewhat shorter push back in our retirement dates, then our future realizations may not be far out of line with our aspirations for a better life for future generations.

Index